THE OTHER SIDE OF JOY

THE OTHER SIDE OF JOY

Religious Melancholy among the Bruderhof

Julius H. Rubin

New York   Oxford

Oxford University Press

2000

Oxford University Press

Oxford   New York
Athens   Auckland   Bangkok   Bogotá   Buenos Aires   Calcutta
Cape Town   Chennai   Dar es Salaam   Delhi   Florence   Hong Kong   Istanbul
Karachi   Kuala Lumpur   Madrid   Melbourne   Mexico City   Mumbai
Nairobi   Paris   São Paulo   Singapore   Taipei   Tokyo   Toronto   Warsaw

and associated companies in
Berlin   Ibadan

Published by Oxford University Press
198 Madison Avenue, New York, New York 10016

Library of Congress Cataloging-in-Publication Data
Rubin, Julius H.
The other side of joy : religious melancholy among the Bruderhof /
Julius H. Rubin.
p.   cm.
Includes bibliographical references and index.
ISBN 0-19-511943-6
1. Hutterian Brethren—Membership. 2. Depression, Mental—
Religious aspects—Christianity—History of doctrines.
3. Depression, Mental—Epidemiology.   I. Title.
BX8129.B65R83   1998
289.7′3—dc21   97-24740

1 3 5 7 9 8 6 4 2

Printed in the United States of America
on acid-free paper

I dedicate this book to my father, Irwin S. Rubin, who has lived his life in the midst of Anabaptist and German Pietist church-communities in southeastern Pennsylvania.

PREFACE

AS SOCIOLOGIST Robert K. Merton has noted, serendipity shapes much of sociological inquiry. During the spring of 1991, after finishing the first draft of *Religious Melancholy and Protestant Experience in America*, I was searching for a contemporary Pietist group whose adherents might suffer from this spiritual malady. While working as a consulting faculty examiner at Charter Oak State College, an external degree program, and reviewing graduation essays, I happened upon the life history of an ex-Bruderhof woman. She agreed to an interview and put me in touch with Ramón Sender, the originator of KIT (Keep In Touch), the Bruderhof apostate newsletter and support group. From this fortunate accident, I became acquainted with this small, minority religion, the Bruderhof, and have spent the last five years following the evidence wherever it has taken me.

Ramón Sender has graciously assisted my research, making this book possible. In all participant-observation research, the investigator requires a key informant who will vouch for the stranger, educate the newcomer, and assist the outsider in gaining a foothold within the existing group or social network. Ramón served in this capacity. He invited me to attend annual KIT reunions, welcomed and introduced me to the group, opened KIT archives, encouraged other apostates to cooperate in my research, and asked me to assist in the preparation of KIT autobiographies for publication. Scores of apostates have generously and courageously shared their stories with me by granting research interviews, in public testimonials at KIT reunions in America and Europe, and in their articles in the newsletter. I wish to offer special acknowledgment to several people for their important assistance: Elizabeth Bohlken-Zumpe, Jere Bruner, Joel Clement, Miriam Arnold Holmes, Barnabas Johnson, Hannah Goodwin Johnson, Timothy Johnson, Charles Lamar, Joy Johnson MacDonald, Belinda Manley, Nadine Moonje Pleil, Blair Purcell, and Margot Purcell.

After the publication of my first letter in *KIT* in May, 1991, several Bruderhof members invited me to visit their hofs in New York and Connecticut in order that I might experience life in a Christian commune, or open my heart as a person seeking an authentic Christian life of discipleship. Possibly, a visit might dispel the criticism directed against the Bruderhof by KIT correspondents. I declined these invitations, requesting instead that the leadership grant permission to study their historical and medical archives, interview Bruderhof patients suffering from spiritual affliction and depression, and interview their physicians. The Bruderhof Servants of the Word and spokespersons have steadfastly rejected my repeated requests (made in 1991 and 1995) to conduct systematic, on-site research. This study relies upon apostate life histories and the many books published by the Bruderhof press, the *Plough*, that represent their authorized history and orthodoxy.

This study presents findings drawn largely from a limited number of persons who were expelled or who left during the charismatic leadership of Heini Arnold (1951–1982). We recount the spiritual problems and crises of conversion suffered by many persons in a generation past and during a historical phase of the Bruderhof Movement. With limited empirical and medical evidence, we do not know whether these cases are representative or typical of the experiences of the Bruderhof faithful. We cannot attempt a quantitative presentation of rates of depressive illness among the Bruderhof in past times or today. We cannot compare Bruderhof rates of depression associated with spiritual issues with other evangelical Protestant groups or with the American population in general. We do, however, present compelling accounts of the lives of Bruderhof apostates that foundered over the issues of faith, and we relate these crises to the central tenets of Bruderhof theology, spirituality, and communal life.

Benjamin Zablocki published *The Joyful Community* in 1971—the only critical sociological monograph devoted to the Bruderhof. My work, *The Other Side of Joy,* researched a generation later, builds upon Zablocki's insights. In our many conversations he has contributed much to my understanding of the Bruderhof.

John A. Hostetler has translated and given me German source material on Hutterite prayers for those afflicted with *Anfechtung*. He has read early versions of the manuscript and made helpful suggestions guiding the direction of my research. I have been instructed and inspired by the probing social criticism written about the Paraguayan Bruderhof in the 1950s by my mentor at the New School for Social Research, the late Benjamin Nelson.

At Saint Joseph College, Janet Demo has kept me continuously supplied with newspaper clippings about the Connecticut Bruderhof community. Catherine Posteraro has assisted with countless online searches and bibliographic research. Kathy Kelley has graciously and promptly supplied my many interlibrary loan requests.

Saint Joseph College has supported my research by a travel grant to England in 1992, through faculty development funds, and a sabbatical. I have been fortunate to enjoy Yale University library privileges throughout my research and a Yale Visiting Faculty Fellowship in 1995–1996.

Cynthia A. Read, Executive Editor at Oxford University Press, provided invaluable advice when I was writing this book. Her careful editing of the manuscript has helped me write a more focused and integrated work.

I wish to thank my wife, Loretta, for her abiding love and support, and my children, Elise and Joshua, for understanding why their father has needed to spend so many holidays and weekends sequestered in his study.

Bethany, Connecticut   J. H. R.
January 1998

CONTENTS

THE OTHER SIDE OF JOY

INTRODUCTION

"The Best Argument for Christianity?"

> The best argument for Christianity is Christians: their joy, their certainty, their completeness. But the strongest argument AGAINST Christianity is also Christians— when they are somber and joyless, when they are self-righteous and smug in complacent consecration, when they are narrow and repressive, then Christianity dies a thousand deaths.
>
> —Sheldon Vanauken,
> *A Severe Mercy*

Sheldon Vanauken recorded these observations in a spiritual journal during his graduate studies at Oxford University in the 1950s before he became a Christian. In Vanauken's terms, the Bruderhof (also known at different times in their history as the Society of Brothers and the Eastern Brotherhood of the Hutterian Brethren) appear to exemplify the best argument for Christian faith and a life of radical discipleship. Founded in Germany in the 1920s by Eberhard Arnold, they established an exclusive, redemptive church-community set apart from the sin-ridden secular world. Today this new religious movement is centered in America with more than two thousand members living in seven communities or "hofs" in New York, Pennsylvania, and England. They have achieved economic self-sufficiency, indeed wealth, earning $20 million in 1995 through the manufacture and sale of high-quality children's toys, under the trade name Community Playthings, and devices for the physically disabled, through their Rifton Enterprises corporation.

The Bruderhof emulate the Apostolic Church by devoting themselves to the fulfillment of the Sermon on the Mount. They espouse the principles of pacifism and nonresistance to evil. The Brotherhood holds all things in common, rejecting the divisiveness caused by private property and the pursuit of worldly privilege and power. The faithful are

3

bound together in unanimity of thought and belief and espouse an ethic of brotherly love. In strict conformity to the teachings of Jesus in the Sermon on the Mount, the community enforces purity of conduct, thought, and intentionality in the hearts and minds of believers. The church community keeps close watch to ensure that members hold to their religious ethos, directed by the leadings of the Holy Spirit. They practice forms of fraternal correction and brotherly watch to purify themselves from sin. Their ethos strictly regulates all forms of conduct, belief, appearance, dress, and demeanor, with particular emphasis upon the repression of premarital and extramarital sexual expression. Brothers and sisters in the life are prohibited from gossip and idle chatter. Should differences or conflicts arise between members, they must go directly to the person or persons in question and strive to bring a peaceful and loving resolution of these differences, or "unpeace." Church discipline requires public confession and repentance of sin, and exclusion of the errant sinner into the world. Only by fostering absolute unity and faith, the Bruderhof maintain, can they collectively form a vessel to capture the Holy Spirit in childlike joy, humility, and surrender to Jesus.

Visitors to the Bruderhof encounter a peculiar combination of a medieval village community and late twentieth-century technological sophistication that includes ultramodern telecommunications, Japanese manufacturing techniques, a community-owned Gulf Stream jet, and extensive computerization. Bruderhof families live simple, ascetic lives. Violent crime, illicit drug abuse, and economic and material concerns are largely absent from their lives. Premarital sex is prohibited, and single-parent families are largely unknown. Divorce is not permitted; thus, Bruderhof families are not disrupted by the family patterns that characterize the wider society.

The Bruderhof offer a remarkable case study of a successful and enduring religious intentional community. They have resolved the central questions and prerequisites of community continuance, which include: (1) creation of a stable and adequate economic foundation; (2) recruitment of new members and the retention of children born into the community; (3) routinization of the charisma of the founder into a stable power structure and division of labor; and (4) formulation of a religiously grounded worldview and structure of conversion that produces fervent devotees who make a lifetime commitment to their commune and religious movement.[1]

A sociological investigation of a religious group like the Bruderhof must avoid adopting a theoretical perspective or concepts that will be perceived by religionists and others to be derogatory or make negative evaluations about the authenticity of the group. The sociologist must also eschew uncritical, apologetic stances that produce exegetical summaries of a religious creed, articulate a polemical defense of the faith, or, in the guise of social science, write a sanitized portrayal of only the laudable aspects of life in a religious community. We must avoid either polemical attack or apologetic defense.

Instead, this study explores how the vicissitudes of Bruderhof theology, communal organization, ritual practice, child rearing, and church discipline have combined to create a distinctive "Bruderhof ethos." The Bruderhof ethos places premiums upon certain types of ethical conduct, enjoins believers to achieve a heightened inner spirituality in relationship to Jesus and the church-community, and fosters a special religiously grounded personality and life-order.

We will examine the origin and subsequent vicissitudes of the Bruderhof "theological imagination,"[2] which articulates a comprehensive worldview that provides adherents with emotionally satisfying answers to the ultimate questions of human existence: the relationship of humanity to God, theodicy and the problem of evil in the world, and the sublime promise of this-worldly and otherworldly salvation for the in-gathered faithful. The Bruderhof ethos and communal ritual life bind believers to one another through the commemoration of Christian holy days, seasonal calendrical rituals, and Love Feasts marking rites of passage—birth, baptism, marriage, and death.

Much of the Bruderhof's lived experience is joyous and salubrious. From their own accounts, however, Bruderhof devotees pay a dear price for unity. In an often cited and reprinted article that represents Bruderhof "orthodoxy," published in 1985 by Barbara Thompson in *The Christian Century*, members speak of the demands placed upon them, the "costs" paid by God's revolutionaries. Thompson inquires: "Have you experienced God's kingdom in your life together?" She receives this reply from representatives of the Bruderhof:

> This is a deep matter, and we tremble to speak of it. . . . Yet, we believe, and have experienced that God's kingdom has to do with the unity of hearts and the love with which Christ loved his disciples. To experience something of this unity and love, we must in repentance go very, very low, because the Holy Spirit seeks the lowest place. . . . When in repentance we seek God's kingdom, then Christ himself is present and our life together becomes an atmosphere where a deeply wounded soul can find rebirth.[3]

As a voluntary sectarian group, they restrict church membership and baptism to religiously qualified adults. Bruderhof piety and identity have ever foundered on the antimonies of religious individualism and Pietist devotionalism, which require the faithful to cultivate an inner religious fervor and assurance of grace. Yet, through repentance and the pious practice of self-examination for evidence of indwelling sin, the community also requires each believer to accept total surrender to Jesus. Not infrequently, true believers succumb to times of spiritual desolation or religious melancholy as they embrace the travails of Pietism.

Bruderhof evangelical Pietist theology, which we shall term *Innerland piety*, after the work of their founder Eberhard Arnold, enjoins devotees to embrace the inner, contemplative dimension of devotional piety, which necessitates the methodical exercise of repentance or evangelical humiliation for individual and collective sin. Only the repentant, humiliated sinner who repeatedly attempts self-abnegation will find release from guilt and sin in ecstatic surrender to Jesus and to the elders of the church-community. As I attempted to demonstrate in my 1994 study of evangelical Pietism, *Religious Melancholy and Protestant Experience in America*, Protestants who dedicate their lives to the fulfillment of this form of religiously grounded selfhood, and who seek the highest spiritual ideals of evangelical Pietist conversion, enjoy ecstatic selflessness that alternates with seasons of religious despondency. In past times, theologians and psychiatrists referred to this experience as "religious melancholy." This study investigates how Bruderhof social structure, evangelical child rearing, gender relations, and religiously grounded selfhood engender the religious experiences of joy and melancholy.

This study employs an explanatory model of mental health and illness that goes back to Robert Burton's conceptualization of religious melancholy in *The Anatomy of Melancholy* (1621). Burton first identified and defined a new type of religious madness that afflicted members of evangelical and Pietistic sects. They succumbed to conversion crises, declaring themselves to be forsaken by God's love. "As a form of madness, religious melancholy entailed extreme guilt about sin—obsession with having committed unpardonable sins through blasphemy against the Holy Spirit. With clear and terrifying evidence of their damnation, of having grieved the Holy Spirit and sinned away the day of grace, the mad could find no solace in this world and only the haunting specter of eternal punishment in the next."[4] In this study, we employ a religiously grounded and archaic diagnostic category, eschewing modern social scientific or psychiatric concepts that fail to account for religious experience and expression on their own terms.

For example, functionalist theory in sociology and psychology assumes that religious behavior and experience, termed "religiosity," can both contribute to and impede mental health defined as individual well-being and social-psychological adjustment. Religion creates a symbolic system of meanings and ultimate values that offers comprehensive answers to the vexing questions of human existence: the meaning of life, the relationship of men and women to God, the problem of evil and suffering in the world, the nature of ethical conduct, and the promise of salvation or one's fate after death. Religious affiliation affords membership into integrated groups, collective identifications that support individual identity, and participation in emotionally satisfying cathartic rituals. Thus, the positive functions or contributions of religion to well-being include reduction of existential anxiety, a sense of hope, a coherent ethos to guide conduct, social support in times of adversity, avoidance of self-destructive behavior, and a feeling of agency for believers assured of their relationship with a transcendental Other. Dysfunctional or detrimental consequences of religiosity involve low self-esteem, immobilizing guilt, repressed anger, sexual repression and maladjustment, anxiety over salvation, and impediments to personal agency and self-determination.[5]

Empirical studies of "religion" and "mental health" assume that a researcher can conceptualize religion and mental health/illness as discrete variables and then proceed to demonstrate a statistical correlation or causality between these factors. However, the formulation of abstract, general constructs of religiosity and standardized measurement instruments tends to overgeneralize, oversimplify, and distort the very conduct and experience that social scientists want to understand and measure. They employ "religion" as a variable that is divorced from the social-cultural milieu and dynamics of actual religious collectivities. The formulation of the general variable "religion" does not promote an adequate explanatory understanding when applied to the complexities and nuances of conduct and belief among devotees of the untold hundreds of denominational, sectarian, and new religious groups in America. Is religiosity the same behavior, belief, and lived experience, for example, for members of Pentecostal healing churches, among adherents to a new religious sect, the Church of Unlimited Devotion, or Spinners, who proclaim the prophecy of the late Jerry Garcia of the rock group "The Grateful Dead," and for social elites who worship in urban Episcopal churches? Can we state with any confidence, in the most general terms, that religion causes mental health or illness? Not surprisingly, research findings prove contradictory or inconclusive.[6]

Sociology, psychology, and psychiatry have created their own explanatory models of religiosity, mental health, and illness that are divorced from theological perspectives, experiences, and life-worlds of the individuals and collectivities that they would investigate. The *Diagnostic and Statistical Manual* (*DSM-IV*) of the American Psychiatric Association provides a nosology of mental disorders that presupposes that mental illnesses are objective disease entities, found in varying frequencies and proportions across cultures, societies, and groups—contemporarily and in past times. Richard N. Williams and James E. Faulconer argue that, from this modernist perspective of the social sciences, "religious explanations of mental disturbance are primitive—impoverished and imperfect attempts to account for something, the true nature of which has become clear to us in the modern era. In other words, the contemporary psychological assumption is that modernism has a privileged understanding of mental health phenomena."[7] From the vantage point of modernist thought, a person afflicted with an objective, clinical pathology, identifiable in the *DSM-IV*, may use religious language or vocabulary to express the underlying illness. Religious experience and expression become epiphenomenal to a functional, somatic, and clinical pathology.

Here, social science and psychiatry provide a reductionistic and deterministic account of the religious tension, conflict, or symptomatology experienced by believers in psychological distress. It is assumed that a person suffers from an affective disorder and searches for a religious vocabulary of motive to express what psychiatrists view as an underlying functional or somatic illness. When the patient exclaims, "Because of my sin, God has forsaken me!" the secular alienist interprets this as symptomatic of a clinical disease and ignores the religious significance of this statement. Samuel Pfeifer terms this "ecclesiomorphic" when a patient shapes his or her pathology using religious terminology. He writes, "It is not personal faith or a dysfunctional church that causes pathology, but it is the psychological disorder that tends to affect, among other areas of life, the religious perceptions, emotions and religious social life."[8]

Revisions in the *DSM-IV* have attempted to correct the long-standing antipathy between psychiatry and religion. To this end, a new diagnostic category, "Religious or Spiritual Problem," was introduced. "This category can be used when the focus of clinical attention is a religious or spiritual problem. Examples include distressing experiences that involve loss or questioning of faith, problems associated with conversion to a new faith, or questioning of spiritual values that may not necessarily be related to an organized church or religious institution."[9]

The revised *DSM-IV* would avoid reductionism that relegated culture to a function of biological-organic primacy, and thus accord culture the status of an independent variable and sui generis reality. Nevertheless, the exacting logic of the medical model of mental disease, and the overwhelming inertia of one hundred years of biological primacy, have prevented psychiatry from readily employing cultural and religious explanations, voiced by their patients, to understand their distress and spiritual crisis.

Psychoanalytic studies have also shown an inability to understand and explain religion on its own terms. Antoine Vergote's *Guilt and Desire* reduces the varieties of religious psychopathology (e.g., obsessive guilt, ritual impurity, possession, trance, ecstasy, and mysticism) to a psychic causality produced by early childhood trauma or neurosis. He discounts religious explanations or meanings and explains that "experience has shown that [religious] pathologies are indeed *psycho*-pathologies, that the mode of causality operative in them is a psychic one, and that any treatment of them must depend on therapeutic techniques that operate on the structures and representations underlying these religious aberrations."[10]

In this study, we have grounded our concepts and explanations within a cultural and historical sociology of a distinctive religious group, the Bruderhof. We have pursued a structural phenomenology of religious experience by investigating the Bruderhof on their own terms. We wish to avoid the pitfalls of psychological reductionism or modernist explanatory models that neglect the lived experiences of believers.

In the spirit of Max Weber, we investigate the origins and vicissitudes of the Bruderhof religious community that constitutes a rationalized life-order. Believers imposed upon themselves and their children the unending burdens of forging a religious vocation through the systematic formulation of a religiously grounded personality. They endeavored to unify and pattern their lives through the fulfillment of ultimate values, asceticism, a social ethic of brotherhood, and a death of the "natural man" in rebirth through Christ. Religionists must foster an "Ethic of Inwardness," or *Gesinnungsethik,* "which requires that people consistently and systematically regulate their conduct on the basis of conscience, without concern for reward, over the course of their lives."[11] The Bruderhof faithful embraced the challenges of discipleship that demanded yieldedness to the will of God and the mandate of the United Brotherhood known in their theology as *Gelassenheit.* They accepted the continuing struggle with pride, the flesh, and temptation to sin. Their inward spiritual pilgrimages, consistent with a Pietist theology of conversion, entailed times of doubt and desolation punctuated by times of repentance, renewed faith, and assurance of God's love. Not infrequently, excessively scrupulous adolescents and youth proclaim that they have committed the unpardonable sin, blasphemed against the Holy Spirit, and can never enjoy God's pardon requisite to rebirth. Bruderhof youth have foundered in this religious failure. We shall reconstruct their spiritual crises.

Richard K. Fenn's *The Persistence of Purgatory* provides important insights into the paradox of how a religious community devoted to creating a place of joy, a heavenly church-community in this world, could become a purgatory. According to Fenn, the idea of purgatory, which emerged in the thirteenth century, burdened each soul with new and heightened expectations of piety, purity, and repentance that began in this life and extended into the next. Heaven-bound souls needed to achieve enhanced spiritual attainments. As Fenn explains: "Purgatory was a collective belief-system, as important to the people who embraced it as it was to the institutions, like the monasteries and churches, that used it for the regulation of duty and obligation. . . . Indeed, purgatory was a collective spiritual drama, infused with magical thinking, in which the soul was endangered and eventually redeemed."[12]

Purgatory envisioned seemingly limitless spiritual possibilities through the unfolding of time where the souls of faithful, themselves the locus of more demanding obligations of religious personhood and heightened moral responsibility, continually struggled with purity, sinfulness, and renunciation of the prideful self.[13] Each soul needed to identify with the souls of departed saints and ancestors while arduously struggling to break free of the burdens of guilt and past hatred and affection.

Fenn identifies a "Purgatorial Complex," which involves a capacity for ceaseless self-examination and self-torment. He explains, "There is a masochistic element in the modern self that has internalized the oversight of authoritative and controlling presences and made that its own. Subordination to scrutiny thus becomes a way of life."[14]

The Bruderhof's doctrine of the church-community envisioned a conventicle of reborn and baptized believers, bound together in unity and purity, who would form a vessel to capture the Holy Spirit. In the assurance of their individual and collective religious vocations, the commune enjoyed the promise of a joyful, brotherly, heavenly life in this world, and the assurance of eternal salvation for each individual professor of the faith. However, assurance was fragile as the Brotherhood repeatedly succumbed to crisis. Individual members fell into sin, disunity, and church discipline. During periods of collective crisis in the commune, and periodically in the lives of individual members, Fenn's Purgatorial Complex was operative, and not agape, or heavenly joy.

Innerland piety and the morphology of conversion in Bruderhof evangelical Pietism provide the commune with dedicated, godly men and women who ardently surrender their lives to Jesus, who make a lifetime commitment to the Bruderhof, and who endure prodigious suffering, self-sacrifice, and self-renunciation to build their vision of the Kingdom of God. We will investigate the religious experience and lifeworld of Innerland piety: joyful fusion within the church-community alternating with religious melancholy and depressive disorders among the faithful. We will explore the special burdens that women face in submission to a patriarchal church-community, the consequences of the use of church discipline and disfellowship, the traumatic disruptions of families, and the injuries inflicted by the severity of evangelical child rearing. We will explore a peculiar irony: How does a new religious group that strives to build the Kingdom of God in this world—to create a heavenly community of love, joy, and brotherhood—become, for many fervent believers, a purgatory of penance, pain, and religious despondency?

Bruderhof Primitivism and Pietism within the Tradition of American Religious Pluralism

In the 1920s, the Bruderhof, guided by Eberhard Arnold, withdrew from the modern world to create a community of goods in fulfillment of the Sermon on the Mount, using the Apostolic Church as a timeless, archetypal model of authentic Christianity. The early Bruderhof expressed the fervent hope that they would recreate the time of origins, the first times, a Bruderhof *primordium*[15] as the restoration of the primitive church. Their "new Jerusalem," in radical separation from the world, living in purity and simplicity, envisioned a salvation community that would redeem the faithful from the tragedy of history and escape the tribulations of a dying age.[16]

Bruderhof primitivism resonates with a significant theme in American religious history—the appeal to biblical primitivism. Theodore Dwight Bozeman's *To Live Ancient Lives* explores this long-neglected aspect of the Puritan errand in the wilderness—to establish a Puritan *primordium* in conformity with unspoiled Christian origins. "To move forward was to strive without rest for reconnection with the paradigmatic events and utterances of ancient and unspoiled times."[17] Seventeenth-century Puritans founded their lives and church-communities upon the principles of purity and simplicity, and looked to the Bible as a record of historical events that would serve as archetypes to guide and inspire their lives. The narratives, letters, poems and laws of Scripture served as "a living word, a recapturable mythic drama, an avenue of return to a sacred past."[18] The institution of visible sainthood, the doctrine and church polity found in the Cambridge Platform of 1648, and the shaping of civil government constituted a mimesis or dramatic reenactment of timeless truths and ageless orders found in the Bible.

Throughout the colonial period, Anabaptist groups including Mennonites, Church of the Brethren, Moravians, and numerous small sects migrated to America to restore their respective visions of biblical primitivism. In the nineteenth century, the call to restore the primordium proved central to the experience of Shakers, Baptists, Disciples of Christ, Mormons, Methodists, Hutterites, and many utopian and perfectionist communities like Oneida and Hopedale.[19] When the Bruderhof migrated to America with their model of the primitive Apostolic Church, they became yet another illustration of primitivism in American religion.

Richard T. Hughes and C. Leonard Allen, in their work *Illusions of Innocence*, expand upon Bozeman's discussion, arguing that primitivist groups frequently begin their pilgrimage in America by an appeal to religious freedom, empowering believers to forsake the historical errors of established churches to restore a primordial, apostolic purity. Ironically, many denominations like the Disciples of Christ or the Landmark Baptists evolved, over the course of several generations, into coercive, controlling and intolerant sects, foundering over issues of diversity, freedom of conscience, and religious pluralism. Hughes and Allen state that "in the face of a bewildering array of Christian denominations, sectarians found that the appeal to pure beginnings was the surest way to cut through the confusion of religious pluralism. To proclaim one's own sect a reproduction of the ancient, apostolic order was to anoint one's sect the one, true church while others were merely historic, tradition laden, and therefore false."[20]

The primitivist ideal reflects this dual tendency in our culture by legitimating the call for the exercise of unlimited liberty of conscience (championed by Roger Williams and other dissenting groups) and, alternatively, by legitimating authoritarianism—submission to religious authority represented by New England's covenanted village communities.[21] Primitivism has provided the basis for enlarging or restricting human and religious freedom, for iconoclastic breaks with repressive traditions and the formulation of new absolutisms. Hughes and Allen maintain that "time and again, zealots of one faith or another would particularize and even absolutize the primordium, elevating one's conception of the primordium to standard and authoritative status. On these terms, liberty was possible only for those who conformed themselves to the particularized and absolutized norms."[22]

The Puritan primordium institutionalized in "A Modell of Church and Civill Power" (1634), John Cotton's *Keys of the Kingdom of Heaven* (1644), or Thomas Hooker's *Survey of the Summe of Church Discipline* (1648) led to a theocracy in which civil authority enforced orthodoxy, suppressed heresy, and punished Antinomians such as Anne Hutchinson, expelled and executed Quakers, and banished dissenters like Roger Williams.[23] Puritan village communities in the colonial period implemented Calvinistic models of social order. Civil authority acted in concert with ecclesiastical authority as cooperating agents of repression to control both the elect and the unregenerate. According to Calvinist political ideology, after the Fall, men and women existed in depraved and sinful estrangement from God. Obedience to the laws and regulations of a Christian commonwealth was essential to curtail human concupiscence. Michael Walzer explains, "like the secular state, the Christian commonwealth would be coercive; unlike the secular state, it would be founded upon the consent of conscientious men."[24] In this manner, saints voluntarily submitted themselves "to communally mediated (and potentially coercive) obedience to true ethical standards derived from a divinely ordered cosmos."[25]

Barry Alan Shain has argued persuasively in *The Myth of American Individualism* that in the post–Revolutionary War era, 95 percent of all Americans lived in agrarian villages, in geographic isolation, and committed to traditional local communalism characterized by ethnic, ethical, and religious homogeneity and intolerance of dissent or social deviance. "Morally intrusive and coercively communalistic"[26] village-communities until the middle of the eighteenth century practiced community surveillance and brotherly admonition, and they attempted to enforce godly living. Absent a modern notion of privacy and private life, community controls required church attendance and keeping the sabbath. They punished tippling, gambling, fornication, and other violations of public morality.[27] Shain maintains that life in these ethically intrusive organic communities resembled totalitarian forms of social control.[28] Citizens and congregants devoted themselves to the public good and understood that their liberty depended upon voluntary submission to the orders of divine or natural law. Neither republican political ideology nor the liberalism of "possessive individualism"[29] defined America after the Revolution. In Shain's estimation, "the vast majority of Americans lived voluntarily in morally demanding agricultural communities shaped by reformed-Protestant social and moral norms. These communities were defined by overlapping circles of family—and community-assisted self-regulation and even self-denial, rather than by individual autonomy and self-defining political activity."[30]

In the nineteenth century, the American enthusiasm for restoring religiously grounded primordia found expression in the efflorescence of utopian intentional communities. The Oneida community was located within the "burned-over" district in upstate New York, the site of evangelical religion during the Second Great Awakening. Mormons, Shakers, Harmony, and Zoar, to name just a few of the scores of communities founded, enjoyed the freedom to build their kingdoms in niches in sparsely settled areas of New England and New York, and on the ever-changing western frontier—the Connecticut Reserve in Ohio and the midwest in the early decades of the nineteenth century. These utopian religious communities, in separation from the world, implemented communistic associations at the periphery of a society aggressively committed to the individual accumulation of property.

Carol Weisbrod's study of utopian religious communities, *The Boundaries of Utopia*, identifies the tendency to institutionalize coercive, even tyrannical, control in these primitivist communes. She explains that "communities were sometimes hierarchial, if not tyrannical, in their internal governments, stressing order, obedience, and renunciation of self-interest in a society dedicated . . . to the legitimacy of the pursuit of individual interests by free men."[31]

However coercive or harsh the bargain, religious utopians exercised their fundamental rights as free citizens to enter, voluntarily, into what Weisbrod terms a "utopian contract." Members gave over all their property to the community and renounced the opportunity to accumulate private property, wages, and any expectation that the community would return their property or compensate them should they leave. In return, communities promised to provide support for each member in their collective pursuit of the primordium.[32] The utopian contract expressed a moral obligation and served as a constitutional document of a voluntary association, a church covenant, and a binding legal contract.[33]

Today, we view nineteenth-century utopias as high-minded experiments in pursuit of noble ends. In their own time, however, these communities engendered controversy and criticism, not unlike contemporary religious debates surrounding new religious movements in which critics disparage them as cults engaging in mind control of their members.[34] Utopian primitivism manifested a dark side when seceders, apostates, and backsliders expelled from Oneida, Harmony, Shaker, and other communities brought suit, enlisting the state to remedy what ex-members considered to be fundamentally unsound contracts that violated the common good and public policy, involved fraud, abrogated individual religious liberty, or enslaved persons. Weisbrod uncovers legal case histories which reveal that the courts consistently upheld the validity of utopian contracts. An apostate always had the opportunity to leave the community and return to secular society, but usually at considerable cost—the loss of a life's work and without claim to property or wages from the community.[35]

During the late eighteenth century and the early republic, the alternative tradition of religious freedom achieved increasing salience through the constitutional principles of the separation of church and state and the charter myth that American citizens were individuals, endowed by God, with inalienable rights to life, liberty, property, and religious freedom. During the first half of the nineteenth century, the term "individualism" entered the English language and came into American usage to refer to the liberation of the person from restrictive social, familial, religious, or political controls.[36] Independent of social moorings, and not mediated by communalistic institutions, individuals could pursue their own self-interest through the exercise of the rights, initiatives, and agency of legal personhood, religious personhood, and possessive individualism. Individuals were free to choose from among the many competing options found within secular civil society, a market economy, and a voluntary system of coequal denominations, and religious, charitable, and reform associations.

The evangelical tradition of the Great Awakenings, from the eighteenth through the twentieth centuries, envisioned the conversion of men and women who, upon entering the covenant of grace, would voluntarily join churches, choosing from among the array of competing sects and denominations. Jonathan Edwards and New Light theology conceived of the newly regenerate soul beginning a lifelong pilgrimage of progressive sanctification, growing in grace through godly conduct. Gracious souls were motivated by love to God and humanity, by self-denial and disinterested benevolence. These attributes served as the mark of assurance of spiritual maturity as a child of God.[37] The newly regenerate, motivated by disinterested benevolence, would labor unceasingly to promote religion, moral order, and the public good. Joseph A. Conforti argues that Edwardsian social ethics and the doctrine of disinterested benevolence "were rooted in a traditional moral economy of restraint and self-denial that was under assault from an emergent capitalist commercial order."[38] Edwards's writings served as evangelical classics handed down across the generations to guide individuals in the transition from a traditional rural village economy to a modern urban market economy.

The Bruderhof's migration to America needs to be understood as one case study from among the patchwork of small sects characteristic of American religious pluralism. Increasingly, scholars have turned their attention to researching the neglected significance of diverse religious groups in the American experience.[39] I have written that

The history of American Protestantism unfolds as the story of separatists from England and Holland, in the early seventeenth century, who undertook an errand in the wilderness. Bound to God through a covenant of grace and to one another through the *communitas* of the church covenant, these immigrants forged a distinctly American idea of self and nation. The founding ideal of a holy commonwealth gave way to the nineteenth-century Republican civil religion of America as God's chosen nation and the millennial expectations of building God's Kingdom. The religious awakenings in the 1740s and the era of grand revivals from 1790–1860 were understood as visitations of the Holy Spirit reanimating the covenants of grace, of church communities, and the national covenant of America as a chosen people. God would bless America, her manifest destiny as a redeemer nation—a people brought *en masse* to salvation rededicating their lives to Christian activism, reform, and missionary endeavor within the constitutional framework of a secular civil society.[40]

In every era, "religious outsiders"[41] have emerged as a counterpoint to "mainstream" American churches or denominations, offering innovative responses to the challenges posed by the American covenants. "Small sects" organized according to Adventist, perfectionist, Pentecostal, and communal and other themes dot the religious landscape.[42] Varieties of folk religion, popular religion, magic, occultism, and apocalyptic and millennial thought ever characterize the American scene.[43] During times of religious efflorescence and national spiritual awakenings, such as the Second Great Awakening, or the post–World War II revival and counterculture, America becomes a "spiritual hothouse."[44]

Perfectionist intentional communities like the Shakers, Hopewell, Oneida, New Harmony, and the Christian Commonwealth[45] found fertile ground in nineteenth-century America. Throughout our history, new prophets and charismatic leaders have come forth professing radical visions, extraordinary gifts of grace, and special revelations of divine will. Charismatic leaders have unfailingly attracted disciples and formed new religious communities as exemplified by the short-lived Kingdom of Matthias during the 1830s. As Paul E. Johnson and Sean Wilentz write in *The Kingdom of Matthias*:

> While revivals shaped the landscape of mainstream American Protestant-ism, smaller groups went beyond evangelical orthodoxy into direct and often heretical experience of the supernatural. Young women conversed with the dead; male and female perfectionists wielded the spiritual power of the Apostles, farmers and factory hands spoke directly to God; and the heavens opened up to reveal new cosmologies to poor and uneducated Americans like Matthias and Joseph Smith. Building on more than two centuries of occultism and Anglo-American millennarian speculation, the seers of the new republic set the pattern for later prophetic movements down to our time and gave birth to enduring religious institutions, including Smith's Church of Jesus of Latter-day Saints.[46]

Heterodoxy, pluralism, and innovation characterize long-settled or new immigrant religions in America. As R. Laurence Moore suggests, " 'mainline' has too often been misleadingly used to label what is 'normal' in American religious life and 'outsider' to characterize what is aberrational or not-yet-American. In fact the American religious system may be said to be 'working' only when it is creating cracks within denominations, when it is producing novelty, even when it is fueling antagonisms."[47] Religious outsiders, minority religions, or alternative religions represent authentic responses to the enduring tasks that confront each generation of Americans as they embrace the covenants of grace, church, and nationhood.

For nearly three hundred years, Anabaptist and Pietist groups including Mennonites, Amish, Church of the Brethren, Schwenkfelder, Hutterite, and Moravian conventicles have established their exclusive ethnic-religious enclaves in America. When the Bruderhof Anabaptist community of goods, under the charismatic leadership of Heini Arnold, opened the first American hof, Woodcrest, in Rifton, New York, in 1954, they continued a long-standing American pattern as religious outsiders—sectarians, seekers of the kingdom, founders of true Christian community, and evangelicals who would build a "city upon a hill" for the world to behold.

The Bruderhof came to an America energized by the Fourth Great Awakening, a revival of popular religion unprecedented in the twentieth century. The Billy Graham Crusades swept through American cities filling sports stadiums with masses drawn from many denominations who came forward to "make a decision for Christ." In addition to the neo-evangelical revivals, neo-Pentecostal groups conducted healing revivals and neo-Fundamentalism entered the mainstream. Americans joined churches in record numbers, fueling an explosion of church building. Polls found a nearly universal belief in God and increased weekly church attendance. Americans responded to the publicized appeal and efficacy of personal prayer including "Dial-a-Prayer" telephone services, eagerly consuming the proliferation of new religious magazines, paperback books, and radio and television programs. These developments compelled Americans immodestly to proclaim that they were the most religious people on the face of the earth.[48]

The resurgence of popular religion was not without its critics among sociologists of religion, like Peter Berger, and theologians Paul Tillich and Reinhold Neibuhr. As James Hudnut-Beumler explains in *Looking for God in the Suburbs*, secular and religious criticism produced a new variety of the American Jeremiad.

> In their eyes it was not real religion that was successful; it was something less than the religion of the God of Abraham, Isaac and Jacob. In the language of the Bible, the critics believed that people had "gone off after idols and false gods." By the end of the decade they would call the

nation's true faith "the American Way of Life," compare the suburbani-zation of the middle-class churches to the captivity in Babylon, and even suggest that God did not appreciate the sounds filtering up to him from America's solemn assemblies.[49]

The Bruderhof leadership in America echoed these criticisms and embraced the neo-orthodoxy of Karl Barth and Dietrich Bonhoeffer. The appeal to an authentic Christian vocation, a total commitment to the fulfillment of the dictates of the Sermon on the Mount and for a radical discipleship, meant a rejection of the "cheap grace" proffered by populist religion. The many American converts to the early Bruderhof in the 1950s, drawn from Society of Friends, Church of the Brethren, and other Protestant denominations and from intentional communities, spurned the suburban ideal that had become synonymous with the American dream. They embraced a variant of Anabaptist, Pietist, and Fundamentalist religion that rejected modernity, Mammonism, and mass society. They welcomed a life in community that they believed offered the fulfillment of Christian eschatology, that gave men and women understandable models for family life with clearly defined, subservient roles for women and children.[50]

The Bruderhof have enjoyed forty years of religious toleration and public acceptance in America. They have built up their holy common-wealths with traditional, patriarchal families and have prospered as an outsider religion. They urge others to join them and continue to prose-lytize this alternative theological imagination with its distinctive forms of religiously grounded identity, work and family life, salvation, and the building of the Kingdom of God in America. And the Bruderhof mes-sage continues to attract converts who, like so many Americans through-out our history, have struggled with questions of owning the covenant with God, paradoxically embracing the freedom of religious toleration to participate in high-demand sectarian communities while abridging these liberties within their Spirit-led *Gemeinde* (congregational church-community).

Arnold's primordium, transplanted to America, constituted a utopian rejection of individualism and the rationalization of modern society, and harkened to a return to the traditional, covenanted village-community. The Bruderhof rejected the kingdom of the world to build the Kingdom of God in their *Gemeinde*. Ever obsessed with purity, simplicity, and unanimity of thought and action by the United Brotherhood, the Bru-derhof required nothing less than the surrender of the prideful self in radical discipleship to Jesus.

The Bruderhof faithful, in their search for salvation and godly living, adopted the practice of piety—the examination by each believer of his or her subjective state, and an abiding concern with inwardness. Boze-man's analysis of seventeenth-century Puritan Pietism holds true for the twentieth-century Bruderhof. He states that Pietism demonstrated a preoccupation with "preparation for conversion; conversion; the great warfare with flesh, world, and devil; the watch upon behavior; a marked degree of religious insecurity coupled with a quest for the assurance of salvation; introspection; a close attention to psychological dynamics that amounted virtually to a Puritan psychoanalysis; cases of conscience; disciplines of prayer and meditation. . . ."[51]

Eberhard Arnold envisioned a true, authentic church made up of the ingathered faithful in possession of the outpouring of the Holy Spirit and bound together in love to God and brotherly love. "Unless we are completely surrendered to the Spirit of Life and His Unity, we cause divisions, for we are emotional and divided people."[52] Community life was possible, according to Arnold, only by intercession of this consuming Spirit where the united church-community formed a vessel to capture it. However, to achieve unity and to capture this Spirit, individual pride, sin, and self-will needed to be vanquished. He writes in *Why We Live in Community*: "Community life is like martyrdom by fire: it means the daily sacrifice of all our strength and all our rights, all the claims we commonly make on life. . . . In the symbol of the fire, the individual logs burn away so that, united, its glowing flames send out warmth and light. . . ."[53]

As we shall see, however, Bruderhof primitivism became increasingly authoritarian, developing extensive external controls to contain human freedom and regulate acceptable conduct. Life in this community required ceaseless repression, through the imposition of unity and conformity in public, private, and intrapsychic spheres. Bruderhof Pietism, correspondingly, fostered a spiritual discipline and a religious personality that embraced repression, self-regulation, and internal controls.

Like many American sects, the Bruderhof have committed themselves to the fulfillment of the highest ideals of Christianity—the restoration of the Apostolic Church. They have labored steadfastly and enthusiastically to build a primitivist and Pietist religious brotherhood—a community of goods where all things are held in common. They are a people united by faith, having surrendered their lives in discipleship to Jesus and to this salvation community. They yearn for a life of joyous, childlike simplicity and humility in the pursuit of their religious vocation.

However, there is another side of joy. Throughout Bruderhof history, Pietist spirituality and conversion have informed their ethos and practical divinity encouraging experiences of joyous fusion within the Brotherhood punctuated by times when many feel forsaken by God. We will question why Bruderhof true believers fervently desire the renunciation of self and the primacy of the collective over the rights of the individual, and why the faithful experience their spiritual travail as expressions of love (*agape* and *philos*).

Arnold's words that "community life is like martyrdom by fire" have proved prophetic. As we will see, individual freedom of conscience and religious liberty have had to "burn away" in the fires of community

unity. This primitivist sect has needed to impose authoritarian measures as they have struggled to institutionalize Eberhard Arnold's vision of the authentic church. Religious brotherhoods like the Bruderhof have concentrated spiritual and temporal power in the hands of church leadership, making possible the exercise of power by an ecclesiastical elite or "inner circle" of leadership.

Here we will relate a twice-told tale about the routinization of the founder's charismatic theology and the fate of the ideas of "primitivist church" and "utopian community of goods" that would redeem believers from the ills of modernity. This is a story of how a new religious movement needed to accommodate to the practical exigencies of the "world" to ensure its survival, of the internecine struggles for power waged by the sons of the founder, the peregrinations of the movement from Europe to South America and America, and the burden that each succeeding generation confronted about how best to reform and revitalize the commune. Finally, this is a story about the interplay of several enduring themes in American cultural and religious history-primitivism, Pietism, and utopian communitarianism—as religious outsiders have sought salvation at the periphery of mass society.

One

THE LENGTHENED SHADOW
OF ONE MAN

*Innerland Piety: The Contradictions of
Bruderhof Religious Identity*

Ralph Waldo Emerson's essay "Self-Reliance" offers a paean to American individualism and heroic genius.

> Every true man is a cause, a country, and an age; requires infinite spaces and numbers and time fully to accomplish his design; and posterity seem to follow his steps as a train of clients. . . . An institution is the lengthened shadow of one man; as Monachism of the Hermit Anthony; the Reformation, of Luther, Quakerism of Fox; Methodism of Wesley.[1]

Author, theologian, publisher, visionary, charismatic leader, and founder of the Bruderhof, a utopian Christian socialist community that continues to this day, Eberhard Arnold (1883–1935) exemplified Emerson's characterization of an extraordinary personality. Today, more than two thousand of his followers live in seven communities in the United States and Britain "and seem to follow his steps as a train of clients."

Indeed, the Bruderhof resembles the lengthened shadow of one man. The strengths and weaknesses of this movement reflect the many questions and concerns that motivated Arnold in his search for answers to the crises of modernity. He wrestled with the question of how best to serve God and live in the imitation of Christ in a secularized society. How could modern Christians fulfill the spirit of the Sermon on the Mount and achieve authentic individual piety and a collective ethos of brotherly love? He agonized over issues of war and peace, social justice, and the immiseration of the urban, industrial working classes. Arnold was influenced by, and entered into a dialogue with, the major thinkers and social movements of his time, including the emerging German sociological school of Ernst Troeltsch and Max Weber; Jewish utopian and socialist thinkers (Gustave Laudaner and Martin Buber); the German

21

Christian Youth Movement and the resurgent evangelical groups in postwar Germany; the Swiss religious-socialists (Hermann Kutter and Leonhard Ragaz); German Protestant evangelical Pietist and mystic thinkers (Sebastian Francke and Johann Blumhardt); Karl Barth and the shattering challenge to religious vocation of Barth's 1918 *Epistle to the Romans*; the Schlüchtern Socialist Movement in Hesse, publishers of the *New Work*; and the Anabaptist Movement represented by the North American Hutterite communities of goods.

Fifty years after Arnold's death, the contemporary Bruderhof communities continue to proclaim his message. Most utopian communities quickly pass out of existence, failing because of a variety of problems: inadequate economic and material resources, difficulties recruiting new members, the declining fervor of succeeding generations, or the absence of organizational structures, a coherent division of labor, and a normative code.[2] How remarkable, then, that Eberhard Arnold's utopian experiment in Christian socialism endures after sixty-five years.

Bruderhof devotees consider Eberhard Arnold's writings to be enduring truths derived from Scripture and the biblical literalism of the early Christian Church. Arnold's primitivism offers "timeless" verities that delineate authentic Christian discipleship and community for humanity in past times, in the present age, and for future generations. For the faithful, these ideas stand outside of time. Sociologists and historians of religion, however, need to situate theological ideas within their specific social, cultural, political, and economic milieux. Religious groups put ideas into practice within the exigencies of a historical context infused with a zeitgeist, or spirit of the times.

Eberhard Arnold was a product of his time, responding to the crises of his age and, most importantly, to the religious revivalism of the Third Great Awakening that spread from the United States to Europe in the 1880s. His teachings alternate between the millennial hopes and the apocalyptic fears that haunted moderns after the First World War. Arnold wrote between 1913 and 1935, relying upon sources and movements of the period. Bruderhof devotees, from the 1920s until today, have embraced Arnold's teachings, his worldview, and the ardors of his conversionist theology—a theology that demands surrender to Jesus and renunciation of the self to the power of the United Brotherhood. They believed, then and now, that the church-community forms a vessel to capture the Holy Spirit. Believers in the contemporary Bruderhof speak with the religious vocabulary from the past and are committed to the realization of these ideas of a past age. They organize their identities and experiences as religiously grounded selves in a manner strikingly reminiscent of late nineteenth-century Protestants. They are anachronisms, people out-of-time. It should not surprise us that these believers routinely encounter the crises of conversion and the trials of faith—the religious melancholy, *psychomachia*, or war against the self, that so afflicted evangelical Pietists in the past.[3]

Eberhard Arnold's theology and the Bruderhof communities that continue as his legacy deserve careful study. They represent both a model of an enduring Christian utopian community and a case study of the psychological costs and burdens of living in a primitivist and Pietist movement that has moved beyond moral absolutism into authoritarianism. The Bruderhof has always promised each devotee a joyful surrender to Jesus, the realization of acosmic love in a united brotherhood and church-community, and the certitude of this-worldly and otherworldly salvation.

Max Weber defined acosmic love associated with the new congregational salvation communities of the Apostolic Church. Here the ethic of religious brotherliness assumed new forms as believers were enjoined to form a "communism of loving brethren" that transcended the natural and social divisions of family, ethnicity, social class, or gender. Weber writes about believers thus:

> They rose to the attitude of *caritas*, love for the sufferer per se, for one's neighbor, for man, and finally for the enemy. . . . Above all, the peculiar euphoria of all types of religious ecstasy operated psychologically in the same general direction. From being "moved" and edified to feeling direct communion with God, ecstasies have always inclined men towards the flowing out into an objectless acosmism of love. In religions of salvation, the profound and quiet bliss of all heroes of acosmic benevolence have always been fused with a charitable realization of the natural imperfections of all human doings, including one's own.[4]

This study examines the fate of acosmic love in Arnold's theology and utopian experiment. We shall explore the unresolved contradictions of this sectarian rejection of the world—the alternation between collective crisis and euphoria, the propensity of true believers to suffer times of spiritual desolation, and the paradox that obsession with absolute unity leads to schism, disunity, and expulsion of apostates. If the Bruderhof continues as the lengthened shadow of Eberhard Arnold, we should first look to his life and theology to illuminate the dialectics of this variant of Protestant identity and church-community.

Eberhard Arnold was born in Königsberg, Germany, on July 26, 1883. His American-born father, Carl Franklin Arnold, assumed a position as professor of church history at Breslau and directed his son toward academic study in theology. Eberhard Arnold studied theology, philosophy, and pedagogy at the universities of Breslau, Halle, and Erlangen, and received his doctorate in 1908 after completing a thesis, "Christian and Anti-Christian Influences in the Work of Friedreich Nietzsche."[5]

Arnold met Emmy von Hollander in 1907, and the couple married in 1909. During the years before the war, he supported his wife and growing family with lecture fees for speeches he delivered to the German Student Christian Movement and other evangelical youth groups. Emmy Arnold remembers:

During the first years of our marriage, Eberhard was much sought after as a lecturer. He spoke in various German cities, such as Halle, Leipzig, Berlin, Dresden and Hamburg about the critical problems of the time. Some of his subjects were "Early Christianity in the Present Day," "Social Distress," "Freedom for Every Man," "The Distress and Enslavement of the Masses," "Present-Day Religious Struggles," "Jesus As He Really Was," and "Nietzsche's Criticism of Christianity."[6]

Arnold contracted a serious pulmonary illness in 1913 and convalesced with his family in the southern Tyrol near Bozen. He began writing his most significant work of practical theology, *Innerland*, during this time. Drafted into the army at the onset of World War I in 1914, he served a brief stint as a driver in the Service Corps in eastern Germany before receiving a discharge for ill health in 1915.

From 1915 to 1920, Arnold worked as an editor for the Furrow Publishing House in Berlin. During this period he became increasingly engaged by pacifism, the Apostolic Church as a model for modernity, and the possibility of creating an alternative community of goods in radical separation from secular society. He participated in conferences with representatives of the religious socialist movement and began an association with the New Work Movement and Schlüchtern socialists in Hesse. Arnold became convinced that authentic Christian discipleship required an absolute break with the world and a total commitment to the fulfillment of the dictates of the Sermon on the Mount within an alternative Christian community. His ideas crystallized during the Whitsun Conference in Marburg in October 1919. Erwin Wissman, correspondent for "The Furrow" wrote:

> The focus of all that was said and thought was Jesus' Sermon on the Mount. Eberhard Arnold burned it into our hearts with passionate spirituality, hammered it into our wills with prophetic power and the tremendous mobile force of his whole personality. . . . Whoever wants to belong to this kingdom, must give himself wholly and go through with it to the last! To be a Christian means to live the life of Christ.[7]

Arnold's genius permitted him to reconcile the tensions from among sources from which he drew his inspiration, syncreticly blending evangelical Pietism, Lutheran mysticism, Manicheanism, Anabaptism, and a radical emulation of the primitive Apostolic Christian Church. He died suddenly and unexpectedly of complications from surgery to repair a broken leg on November 22, 1935, leaving his theology incomplete. As one biographer put it: "Confident expectation of the coming of the kingdom of God, which would reveal itself in repentance and a radical change in beginning a new life of love and justice in fraternal communion and a sincere responsibility for public life, was the fundamental recognition and act of this life."[8]

Innerland: A Guide into the Heart and Soul of the Bible is Arnold's most important theological thesis, articulating the spiritual foundations of his experiment in Christian socialism. Begun in 1913, the treatise would evolve through five published editions and was completed only days before Arnold's unexpected death in 1935. Anyone who seeks to understand the theology of Eberhard Arnold and the mandate for the Bruderhof communities, past and present, must begin with an exegesis of this work.

In the tradition of evangelical German Pietism, *Innerland* eschews dogmatic or systematic theology and does not advance, in linear fashion, a series of theses, disputations, and proofs. As the title suggests, this work was intended as a guide to conversion and to daily, devotional piety—prayer, scripture reading, self-examination and repentance of sin, meditation, and contemplation of God. The object of the practice of piety was cultivation of the inner life turned toward God at the core of identity, thought, and agency, unifying each believer's heart, soul, and will in God's glorification. This five-hundred page work reiterates, in every chapter, how each person—a new creation reborn in God's grace, love, and Spirit—needs to come forward to laud, extol, praise, and proclaim the majesty of God the Father, Jesus the Son, and the rapturous Holy Spirit.[9] Innerland piety constituted the vital, experiential core set forth as a guide of the soul's progress toward conversion and the making of a life in absolute dedication to the fulfillment of God's mandate.

Chapter 1, "The Inner Life," calls upon each person to withdraw from the distractions and frenzy of modern life to pursue inward clarity, an integrated, unified life grounded in the pursuit of religious values, and an inner-worldly mystical unity with God. Arnold demands that each believer embrace what Weber would term an ethic of conviction—radically restructuring personality (*Gesamthabitus*) in the heroic struggle to accomplish ultimate religious values. Believers needed to forge an ethic of inwardness (*Gesinnungsethik*) that provided the existential core for believers who would stand in dynamic tension to the life-orders of the world. Arnold urged upon his followers a constitution of personality and rationalization of self consistent with Weber's four fundamental conditions of personality. As Harvey Goldman explains:

> First, there must be the creation or existence of a transcendental-like ultimate goal or value that gives leverage over the world through the tension it creates between the believer and the world. Second, there must be a "witness" to action that is not social, seeing the "outer" person transcendent, regarding the "inner." Third, there must be the possibility of salvation or redemption from death or from the meaninglessness of the world and the attainment of a sense of certainty about it. And fourth, there must be no ritual, magical, or external means for relieving one's burden, guilt, or despair.[10]

For Arnold, authentic Christian existence begins with an outward rejection of the political economy and mass movements of modernity, including (1) Mammonism—the incentives of a modern capitalist market economy and (2) a Nietzchean will to power and the intoxications of mass political movements. The Christian ethic of inwardness—the religiously grounded personality—turns inward for illumination by the Spirit and looks outward in "true resistance born of the Spirit."[11] In light of the economic, political, and social dislocations that transformed Germany from Bismarck through the First World War and the Weimar Republic, Arnold called for a religious rejection of the world of National Socialism, totalitarianism, class warfare, ethnic and racial strife, and the secular-ideological appeals to this-worldly salvation emanating from the Third Reich, Marxist-Leninism, and Freudian psychoanalysis. He writes that Christians, grounded in the Spirit, can resist the unholy fanaticism of mass political movements that then enthralled European societies.

> Should our blood be gripped and swept along by the excitement in all those around us, we often fall prey to it entirely because we are not able to put up a true resistance born of the Spirit. The distress of our own class or our own nation has a particularly strong effect on us. Mass suggestion used by great national movements appeals to our blood ties and class solidarities.[12]

Healing could only proceed by religious conversion, by traversing the *ordo salutis* (spiritual itinerary) beginning with the natural man condemned to sin and death and ending with the regenerate "New Adam" as a child of God. The sinner finds healing through the inner-worldly mystical infusion of pneuma irradiating each believer's heart in rapturous joy. Citing Meister Eckhart, Arnold urges a spiritual pilgrimage of detachment from the world so that the inner life can flourish. Stripped of self-will, repentant of sins, plunged into abject despair at the utter inability to find salvation through one's own effort, the circumcised heart awaits the bridegroom.

> We must first become quite empty, before God in Christ can enter into us through the Holy Spirit. Stripped of all comfort and all pride, we must lie prostrate at God's feet before God can lead us, the dead and the slain to resurrection. An utter agony of despair must knock at the doors of our hearts—only then are we allowed to hear about faith.[13]

Arnold combines the idea of mystic illumination and joy with a Christocentric conception of Luther's Theology of the Cross. Luther suffered from a lifelong and at times overpowering awareness of his own sinfulness. His inner battles of *Anfechtung*—feelings of sinful alienation from God—plunged him into recurrent episodes of spiritual desolation that the sacramental grace of the Catholic Church could not dispel.

Luther's answer to the crisis *Anfechtung* (scrupulosity) was the imitation of Christ's suffering on the cross. The suffering and sacrifice made by Jesus allowed all humanity to find remission of their sins.[14] Crushed before the prospect of God's justice, tormented by inexpressible spiritual despondency, Luther fell prostrate.[15]

He bridged this infinite gulf between God and humanity with the concept of justification by faith alone (*sola fide*) offered to believers through the redeeming sacrifice of the crucified Jesus. Christ served as an intermediary between each believer and God. Arnold emphasizes not justification by faith alone but Luther's "new relationship of mutual exchange,"[16] with Christ as a model of inner-worldly mystical surrender. Arnold calls for the imitation of Christ—the crucified savior who remained steadfast in love.[17] "New in this experience is having Christ in us"[18]—the ingrafting of the Holy Spirit in the heart of each believer.

Like Luther before him, Arnold used his own conversion experience as a model for Innerland piety, universally applicable to all who would forge authentic Christian lives. Arnold had begun the inward pilgrimage toward God in 1899, during a summer visit with his uncle Ernst Ferdinand Klein at Lichtenrade, outside of Berlin. As a sixteen-year-old-boy, he battled the temptations of intense sexual impulses and interest in girls and felt an awakening concern for spiritual matters. He avoided the drinking and dueling clubs common among his peers. His uncle introduced him to the practice of daily devotional piety, the aggressively conversionist stance of the Salvation Army that sought to win souls and the world to Christ, and a social gospel appeal to justice for poor and laboring classes.[19]

Eberhard returned home resolved to quench his prideful ambitions and sinful lust through the practice of piety. He exclaimed from his devotions in early fall 1899: "O God, O Christ, I will not leave this room before you have accepted me and given me the strength of the new birth through steadfast assurance."[20] Like Luther, Arnold surrendered to God and found forgiveness of sin and rebirth. The intercession of Jesus, evidenced in the pneumatics of the Holy Spirit, produced a psychological union with God. The moment of his conversion is retold in one Bruderhof biography: "So there came over Eberhard, who was still the same foolish half-grown youth, the stream of love of God. It flowed over his heart as unspeakable joy. The finger of the Holy Spirit touched him. The voice of Jesus spoke to him, 'I will accept you, I come to you. Your sins are forgiven you. Go and witness to my truth.' "[21]

Arnold embraced the mystical themes of Eckhard and Luther's Christocentrism, but he steadfastly rejected Eckhard's solitary withdrawal from the world, known as the "detached heart," or any tendency toward quietism. He exhorted his followers that "we must never withdraw from the rushing stream of present-day life into a selfishness of soul."[22] The social ethic of the new creation, required of each brother and sister in faith, pushed them outward into the fulfillment of God's will through life in community together, bound to a church covenant. Membership in the church-community involved an unswerving commitment to individual and collective religious vocation—the founding of a new people and a radical church. Around the church "the Hof of communal dwelling arises once more. Around the radiant fire of the Holy Spirit, the spiritual Temple is built as a tangible House of God: the City on the Hill. . . ."[23]

Eberhard Arnold owes a large debt to German evangelical Pietism. *Innerland* reverberates with themes from this eighteenth-century religious movement that also found a prominent place in the late nineteenth-century Revival Movement (*Erweckungsbswegung*).[24] The work of August Hermann Francke inspired Arnold. During 1690–1691 at Erfurt, Francke searched, in the spirit of Luther's Christocentrism, for certainty of grace. Out of the depths of despair, from the yoke of sin, the enslavement of the flesh and the servant of the devil, Francke was suddenly transformed. Arnold quotes Francke's testimony of conversion at length.

> For in the twinkling of an eye, all my doubts were gone; I was assured in my heart of the grace of God in Christ Jesus. . . . At once all the sadness and unrest in my heart was taken away; I was suddenly overwhelmed by such a flood of joy that I praised God with my full heart for showing me such great grace . . . I had bent my knees in great distress and doubt, but I got up in great certainty and unspeakable joy.[25]

F. Ernest Stoeffler calls this the foundation stone of Francke's theology of assurance—the necessity of an intense, emotionally wrenching inner struggle (*Busskampf*) that results in the ravishing, joyous psychological union with God, the inner-worldly mystical "bride of the lamb."[26] Francke speaks of a new being, a new creation marked by existential reorientation, separate from the kingdom of Satan and the world, engaged in a battle to build the Kingdom of God. The new creation adopted the five distinguishing marks of the life of faith: (1) trials (*Anfechtungen*), (2) cross-bearing, (3) obedience to God's law, (4) trust in God, and (5) joy.[27] Finally, the life of faith demanded an absolute faith in God manifested by a childlike spirit. Daily life was to become a witness to joy in life and God—almost a literal song sung by brethren united.

In the eighteenth century, the German Pietist Movement promulgated an experiential religion of the laity whose hallmark was Sophia—affective union with Christ and joy bordering upon religious enthusiasm.[28] Together, the theologies of Spener, Francke, and others in the Halle School and the radical communitarian Pietism articulated by Jacob Boehm and Gottfried Arnold provide the foundation for Eberhard Arnold. From Pietism Arnold appropriated the emphasis upon a sudden, transformative conversion experience redolent with themes of inner-worldly (psychological) union with Christ; the need for a religiously grounded personality forged in the crucible of *Busskampf* (known to English and American pietistic Puritans as *automachia*); and the lifelong struggle against self, pride, and the remnants of sin. Believers embraced a war against the self by attempting to annihilate the self and self-love. Through the practice of daily devotional piety, each person hungered for the selfless surrender to Christ, to recover Sophia, and to surrender to the unity of the church-community to experience the daily infusion of joy. The Arnold church-community, also in the Pietist tradition, viewed creation through the dualism of the two warring kingdoms— God and Satan. Through separation from the world and the external church, by maintaining strict brotherly surveillance, the new humanity strived for perfection and sexual purity as champions of the Kingdom of God. And Arnold, like the Pietists, asserted the centrality of Scripture for his church-community. However, only the living Word illuminated to the prepared heart by the Spirit would reveal the true message of love, the inner meaning of the Christian Gospel. Without Innerland piety, the Word degenerated into dead legalism, an affectively empty moralism.

The doctrines of evangelical Pietism had migrated to America during the First Great Awakening (1740–1760), transforming the character of experimental religion in America. Arnold encountered this Pietism in the writings of the grand nineteenth-century revivalist Charles Grandison Finney and in the later Salvation Army revivalism exported to Europe by American religionists in the closing decades of the century. In a nine-volume collection of courtship and engagement letters written by Eberhard and his fiancée, Emmy von Hollander, in 1907, the sources of Innerland piety guide and sustain the couple in their struggle to ascertain God's will in their lives. Arnold wrote daily letters, acting as soul mate, director of conscience, and teacher to his beloved Emmy. They pledged complete honesty toward one another and shared their hopes, fears, and most intimate concerns about religious vocation, marriage, education, and family matters.

Arnold urges upon his beloved the works of Finney—the call for methodical self-examination, continued evangelical humiliation in repentance to God for sins, and longing for a selfless, ecstatic union with the Holy Spirit.[29] Conversion was open to all who would exercise their will to serve God, who would struggle to annihilate the worldly self, and, in a sudden rapture, receive the Holy Spirit in their hearts. Arnold writes to Emmy on April 28, 1907, of the Holy Spirit: "who makes His dwelling thus in each one who is converted and glorifies Jesus, wants to take possession of him and fill him so fully and utterly that he will be at His constant disposal as His instrument for people. This means being equipped with the Holy Spirit to serve; this was what gave Finney the strength to save so many thousands; through this we have today such powerful awakening."[30]

Arnold's sudden conversion in 1899, and a decade of theological studies and evangelism, provide the model of Innerland piety that he sought to instill in Emmy, those drawn to his lectures, and his disciples who joined the first community at Sannerz in 1920.

The mystical-Pietist strains of Innerland conversion and devotionalism encouraged believers repeatedly to practice methodical self-examination and recover instances of self-love and sin. Lutheran Christocentrism placed a premium upon engendering intense, at times overpowering, emotional states of suffering punctuated by transient times of ecstatic joy. Repentance revealed a sick conscience, self-loathing, and despair. Arnold suggested that such seasons of spiritual desolation are to be expected as normative, almost prescribed, exercises of the soul's pilgrimage away from selfishness and sin. The conduct of self-examination and repentance encouraged the extinction of self-love and the growth of a selfless love to God. In a moment of abject surrender to God and church-community the follower experienced unspeakable joy—ecstatic assurance of being a child of God, and the ravishing mystical presence of the Bridegroom as the Spirit irradiated the believer's heart with God's love.

Evangelical Pietism valued the continued affective union with God and the wrenching emotional cycle of grieving despair as prerequisites to ecstatic union. Not infrequently believers were overwhelmed by the heroic demands of their ethic of conviction, of forging a religiously grounded personality in *Busskampf*, and perpetual warfare against the self. Especially among Pietist evangelicals, Weber noted, "the emotion was capable of such intensity, that religion took on a positively hysterical character, resulting in the alteration which is familiar from examples without number and neuropathologically understandable, of half-conscious states of religious ecstasy with periods of nervous exhaustion, which were felt as abandonment by God."[31]

Arnold's Innerland offered a devotional guide, or handbook, that charted the *ordo salutis* and the progressive sanctification of the regenerate "new creation" in a lifelong glorification of God. As a guide, Arnold helped mediate the theological meanings and understandings of authentic spiritual growth to his congregation. He sought to teach followers what to expect in their inner pilgrimage and encouraged them to undergo experiences of suffering in the interest of spiritual growth. *Busskampf* was the normal, appropriate, and necessary psychological suffering required of those called to a religious vocation. Times of *Anfechtung*, of trial, cross-bearing, and desolation were to be expected as preparatory for joy. They were opportunities to undergo spiritual maturation. However, the other side of joy, as Weber understood, could entail severe spiritual sickness, "nervous exhaustion," or neurasthenia—late nineteenth-century categories for depressive psychiatric disorders. As one abandoned by God and bereft of God's love, the believer was helpless, hopeless, and unloved.

Arnold himself recognized that the other side of joy could produce spiritual sickness, which he termed the unhealthy conscience. He writes: "The unhealthy state of an erring conscience comes to expression in annihilating self-accusations and in hateful reproaches so violent that they derange the mind. . . . Such a sickness fills the whole of life with grievances and dissatisfaction, with self-laceration and injustice."[32]

The spiritual sickness identified by Weber and Arnold was known to previous generations of Protestants as religious melancholy. Evangelical pietists had a special elective affinity for this disorder, as noted by Robert Burton in *The Anatomy of Melancholy*, published in 1621. Burton identified for the first time a form of melancholia that would remain closely connected with Protestantism in Europe and America until the late nineteenth century. Burton called this malady "religious melancholy." It was characterized by extreme guilt and anxiety about salvation, fear of damnation, and obsession with sin. As a subcategory of "Love-Melancholy," persons in the despond of religious melancholy saw themselves as bereft of God's love. Those afflicted were "in great pain and horror of mind, distraction of soul, restless, full of continual fears, cares, torments, anxieties; they can neither eat, drink, nor sleep."[33] The religious melancholiac suffered protracted religious despair and usually made repeated efforts at suicide. Burton's treatise delineated what today would be termed a "culture-bound syndrome," a variety of mental disorder inextricably associated with a specific cultural and historical milieu.[34] Religious melancholia as a culture-bound syndrome reflects the central themes and contradictions of a distinct type of Protestant personality and identity—Calvinist sects that articulated a theology of evangelical Pietism.

Innerland piety produced a religiously grounded personality that was caught between two wrenching contradictions. Followers committed themselves to radical conversion and reconstruction of identity as a childlike new creation enjoying an inner-worldly mystical experience of Sophia and ecstatic joy. However, Innerland piety also bore a special affinity to the other side of joy. Religious melancholy was common among evangelical Pietists at times when God removed his countenance, when the follower lost the assurance as a child of God, and in seasons of spiritual coldness when God's love and Spirit were absent.

In addition, every believer was required to forge a distinctive personality in *Busskampf* and achieve a personal illuminative relationship to Christ and divine mandate. God spoke to each regenerate soul through the illumination of the Holy Spirit that gave new life and meaning to the Word. Each self received direct ethical guidance and revelation of God's will in their lives. Tillich has termed this the religion of the transmoral conscience that frees the self from connection to received tradition, ecclesiastical authority, and political control.[35]

Philip Greven has argued that evangelicals were threatened by the prospect of adult choice and the exercise of agency and individual autonomy. They remained at best semi-autonomous and filled with angst and perplexity when confronted with discerning God's purpose as applied to their lives. Greven writes:

> the intensity of their quest for the precise fulfillment of God's law and word, and their unending efforts to repress the self and self-will as thoroughly as possible, made it impossible for evangelicals ever to be truly comfortable with a sense of individual autonomy. Their personalities were too rigid, too defensive, too systematically repressive to enable them to tolerate much liberty for themselves. By leading lives of rigorous purity and precision, they provided themselves with the assurance, stemming from strict compliance to rules set by someone other than themselves, that they were fulfilling the expectations and commands set forth for them by God. Only then could they feel truly free.[36]

Those who shaped their selves by the demands of the Pietist conversion struggled in search of inner assurance of salvation, mired in *Busskampf*, eager to surrender the burdens of choice and responsibility to the collective will of the group. Those who fashioned a religiously grounded personality from Innerland piety experienced both joy and the other side of joy—religious melancholy. They found an immediate, personal relationship to Jesus to direct their lives and, paradoxically, fled from individual freedom into the security of the community to escape the burdens of self and choice. Bruderhof religious life relied upon fervent devotees who were shaped by Innerland piety. Bruderhof children of God embrace the ceaseless challenge of making their lives in the spiritual hothouse of this dialectic of joy and religious melancholy—freedom as surrender to the collective will.

Religious Rejections of the World and Their Directions: Max Weber and Eberhard Arnold

Innerland piety, that contradictory blend of joy and melancholy, of individuated religious personhood in communal fusion, was one response to the challenge of modernity. Arnold called upon believers to achieve a unified, religiously grounded personality forged in the crucible of Pietist conversion and dedicated to the social ethic of the Sermon on the Mount. Those attracted to this subjectivist religious vocation appropriated an *Innerlichkeit*, an inner, subjective stance that was in dynamic tension with modern society. Innerland piety required a religious rejection of the world, a utopian flight from secular modernity.

Eberhard Arnold's work reflects the most important concerns of the spirit of his time—the question of existential and spiritual authenticity for individuals confronted with the societal transformations of modernity. It is instructive to view Arnold's Innerland piety alongside the pioneering work of his contemporary, Max Weber, who addressed these very questions during the period 1913–1915 in papers delivered at his home before informal groups of intellectuals and artists known as the "Heidelberg Circle." In 1915, Weber published "Intermediate Reflections"(*Zwischenbetrachtung*), translated as "Religious Rejections of the World and Their Directions." Late in his career he delivered the addresses "Science as a Vocation" (1917) and "Politics as a Vocation" (1919), which remain his final statements clarifying the existentialist stance toward the questions of modernity.

Both Weber and Arnold would center their respective analyses upon the question of *Innerlichkeit*, and both were concerned with the religious rejection of the world through an ethic of brotherliness (*Brüderlickkeitethik*). Weber considered any attempt to create a social ethic and community founded in absolutist adherence to the Sermon on the Mount as doomed to fail. The comparison of Eberhard Arnold, the charismatic prophet, with Max Weber, the sociologist and existentialist, offers a critical perspective on Arnold's utopianism.

Early in his career, Weber joined the public debates in Germany regarding social policy, national political unity, and industrial labor and agrarian reform. Beginning in 1891, and for most of the decade, he participated in the Evangelical Social Congress (ESC) and wrote for the journal *Christian World*. In association with Otto Baumgarten, Weber served on the editorial board for a journal devoted to Lutheran social questions. He considered the questions posed by Christian or religious socialists and Lutheran conservatives in their various efforts to recast social policy and reform within the framework of a Christian worldview.[37] He advocated a social policy that recognized workers' rights to trade unionism, political representation, and self-determination.

Weber was sympathetic to the social conscience of German Protestantism (excepting the anti-Semitism and autocratic policy of Stoecker, who founded the ESC). In a letter to Otto Baumgarten in 1891, Weber acknowledged, "There is no doubt that the needs of the time demand that energetic and idealistic young clerics do more than teach and preach on the burning social questions."[38] However, Weber described himself as "religiously unmusical"[39] as opposed to those who lived their lives as religious virtuosi devoted to the daily practice of piety and the fulfillment of religious values. Social conscience concerns were not his central interest. He allied himself with "Cultural Protestants" who separated theoretical inquiry from theological and moral programs. As Rita Aldenhoff writes, Weber presented "himself to some extent as a specialist in law and political economy willing to serve Protestant aspirations by carrying out his work of theoretical 'enlightenment.' "[40]

In 1892, under the auspices of the *Verein für Sozialpolitik,* Weber conducted a survey of landlords to analyze the transformation of the agrarian patriarchal economy east of the Elbe River. The ESC expanded this survey in 1894 to include fifteen thousand rural clergy.

Weber and Goehre collaborated on this larger study, and presented their findings before the 1895 congress. Weber's interests in political economy, theory, and social policy were congruent with those of the Cultural Protestants.

Weber reported profound transformations in the East Elbian *latifundia*, or landed estates. Once the centers of isolated and autonomous political domination, the manors had once recruited garrison soldiers and served as centers of rural administration. The status group of Prussian aristocrats—the *Junkers*—tenaciously clung to their political, military, and economic hegemony despite their declining economic condition. Weber considered Junkers as no longer fit to provide national political and military leadership for the Reich. However, neither a worker aristocracy of unionized and politically organized labor nor a politically mature middle class had emerged to wrest power from them and provide leadership and national unity. Weber analyzed the transformations of the eastern latifundia from this perspective of the political economy of the German nation-state and power politics, and not from the ideal of working toward the realization of a Christian social order.

These isolated domestic economies had once formed natural communities of interest between patriarchal aristocrats and the estate workers; the *Instmann*, who was a small landholder and tenant, kept a small herd and worked the lord's estate with his family and employed day labor. The *Instmann* enjoyed a share of the crop and a threshing share after the harvest. Landlord and tenant had a mutual interest in the crop and prices.

This vestigial patriarchal economy was transformed by capitalist agricultural development, international competition for markets, and the introduction of wage labor. The marginally productive lands of the latifundia could only operate profitably through the intensive cultivation of cash crops and the proletariatization of labor. In the face of deteriorating conditions, estate workers emigrated to western Germany in their wish to be free from patriarchal domination and downward mobility. Thousands of Polish workers migrated into eastern Germany to work for cheaper wages, live in primitive conditions, and further depress agricultural wages. The "Polonization" of eastern Germany raised ominous demographic, political, and military questions for the German nation-state.

Weber presented these findings before the ESC and suggested social policies to address this crisis. Consistent with the political thinking of nineteenth-century Nationalism and Liberalism, he suggested that Germany close its eastern borders to Polish migrants and adopt a government-sponsored colonization program that would purchase the large estates and create self-sufficient peasant farms and organic communities of resettled German workers. These traditional communities would produce for a local market and remain insulated from world market forces and fluctuations.

Weber advanced these findings in "Developmental Tendencies in the Situation of East Elbian Rural Labourers" and in his Freiberg inaugural address, "The National State and Economic Policy," in May 1895. The goal of social policy analysis was to assist in the political unification of the nation won through ceaseless internal struggles for power among competing classes and interests. Those who would tackle the social questions of labor and the working classes from the value-perspective of "universal charity" or "eudaemonism" would be disabused of this illusion. He writes, "the deadly seriousness of the population problem prohibits eudaemonism; it prevents us from imagining that peace and happiness lie hidden in the lap of the future, it prevents us from believing that elbowroom in this earthly existence can be won in any other way than through the hard struggle of human beings with each other."[41]

Weber's early writings in political economy discounted the value-laden perspective of promoting a Christian worldview to alleviate the suffering of the masses, promote social justice, and build God's Kingdom. As Aldenhoff concludes, there is "no evidence that at the beginning of the 1890s, Weber believed in the possibility that effective political action could be conducted on a Christian basis. Rather, his analysis of the rural worker's question had made him aware, at an early date, that modern development tended to replace person power with impersonal domination by a class of property owners."[42] Weber's political sociology "of the possible"[43] embraced a different set of values as its point of departure—the ideal of a German nation-state. "In spite of the great misery of the masses, which burdens the sharpened social conscience of the new generation, we have to confess openly that one thing weighs on us more heavily today: the sense of our responsibility *before history*."[44] The state might sponsor a German worker resettlement program to "Germanize" the eastern provinces against the tide of Polish immigration and subsidize peasant farms and *Gemeinschaft* as a tactic of defense in the national political and economic interest. These policies and proposed communities, in Weber's estimation, had nothing to do with the ultimate religious values of the Kingdom of God.

Weber's sociology of religion, like his early political writings, rejected out-of-hand the ideal of reforming modern society or forging identity guided by the ultimate concerns of the Sermon on the Mount. As Lawrence A. Schaff has argued in *Fleeing the Iron Cage,* the construct "modern society" or "modernity" was synonymous with life in a rationalized, bureaucratized, disenchanted life-order, the "iron cage" of vocational specialization, and capitalist market forces that transformed traditional social structures everywhere. For Weber, like Marx and Nietzsche before him, the question remained: What is the "fate" of men and women in the modern world? Schaff argues, "It is the center of his concerns as a writer whose self-defined vocation was to see whether any meaning at all could be wrested from a postcritical, disenchanted world, an 'age of subjectivist culture.' "[45]

Weber conceived of "disenchantment" as the progressive intellectual rationalization of modern society through science and its allied technologies that produced a fragmented, secularized culture of competing value spheres. The institutional domains of polity, economy, family, religion, art, and eroticism were each rationalized according to their distinctive value positions. Each domain achieved independence and was structured by internal laws of organization. Each institutional domain became a "life-order" that claimed the allegiance of persons who devoted their energies and lives to the fulfillment of discrete values and goals.

Weber understood that the disenchantment of modern culture produced an inward sense of "devastating senselessness." He writes that "the advancement of cultural values, however, seems to become a senseless hustle in the service of worthless, moreover self-contradictory, and mutually antagonistic ends."[46] Thus, in an age of subjectivist culture, the burdens were borne by each individual. What alternatives presented themselves to the seemingly inescapable iron cage of capitalist political economy? Which ethically authentic stances, which existential choices of self-constitution confronted moderns? How could people bear the burdens of their existences, the suffering imposed upon them by the external conditions of life? What inner demon could men and women choose to hold the fibers of their lives together?[47]

"Zwischenbetrachtung," as Schaff points out, "provides a commentary on the relentless struggles waged by those dwelling within the different life-orders and value spheres in their attempt to cope with the historically given 'world' through adaptation, rationalization, manipulation, escape."[48] Weber hoped to elaborate the possibilities available to individuals as each confronted the burden of existential choice in their life. What stance or posture would one embrace—accommodation and world-acceptance, or rejection and world-abnegation? Either choice presupposed that individuals as products of modernity were committed to *Innerlichkeit*. Speaking at the first meeting of the German Sociological Society, Weber argues, "this culture ushers in the reign of assertive subjectivity and 'inwardness,' or 'interiority' (*Innerlichkeit*), with all their hidden and explosive potentialities for both subversion and originality."[49]

The Apostolic Christian Church provides the basis for Weber's model of religious rejection of the world. Here a soteriological community was founded upon the prophetic teachings of a savior offering to the ingathered faithful (*Gemeinde*, congregation) the promise of salvation. Weber argues, "prophecy has created a new social community"[50] that devalued family and marital ties in favor of obligations to the congregation. Here the faithful were enjoined to "stand closer to the savior, the prophet, the priest, the father confessor, the brother in the faith than to natural relations and to the matrimonial community."[51]

The soteriological religion of congregations demanded of each believer an absolutist ethic of conviction that Weber terms the religious ethic of brotherliness (*Brüderlichkeitethik*).[52] Without regard to the cost or consequences, without reckoning self-interest or economic advantage, whatever personal suffering brotherliness might entail, the absolutist ethic required that each believer strive for the fulfillment of these ultimate values. The dictates of the Sermon on the Mount informed the ethic of brotherliness. Brothers and sisters in the faith were obliged to render economic support, mutual aid, interest-free loans, charity, and alms to those in need. Each believer was bound by an ethic of love, "a communism of loving brethren,"[53] *caritas* for all of humanity including one's neighbor and even one's enemy.

The ethic of brotherliness promoted an inner sense of joy and ecstasy. The absolutist stance of the ethic of brotherliness placed each believer in dynamic tension against the other societal life-orders. The rational, depersonalized market economy transformed all human values and institutions through the calculation of money. When values were caught within the web of a cash nexus, reduced to monetary equivalences, this proved the antithesis of acosmic love and the indifference to material things required of brotherliness. In the political sphere, also, the modern bureaucratic state apparatus was equally depersonalized, devoid of brotherly love in the mass administration of government. As Weber argues, "it is absolutely essential for every political association to appeal to the naked violence of coercive means in the face of outsiders as well as in the face of internal enemies."[54] However, the radical pacifism of the Sermon on the Mount enjoined believers to resist no evil.

The religion of brotherliness stood in extreme tension to the irrational force of sexual love and modern forms of eroticism including free-love communes like Asconia and the *Lebenscult* Movement.[55] Weber states that in this age of subjectivist culture, many moderns fled from the iron cage and into the promise of inner-worldly salvation of erotic love.

> the erotic relations seems to offer the unsurpassable peak of the fulfillment of the request for love in the direct fusion of the souls of one to the other. . . . It is so overpowering that it is interpreted "symbolically" as a sacrament. The lover realizes himself to be rooted in the kernel of the truly living which is eternally inaccessible to any rational endeavor. He knows himself to be freed from the cold skeleton hands of rational orders, just as completely as from the banality of everyday routine.[56]

The religion of brotherliness brands this promise of salvation in eroticism and psychological fusion with the other a false idolatry and anathema to the love to God. Only monogamous marriage in fulfillment of the divine mandate to be fruitful and multiply, to place concupiscence under ethical control, is acceptable. Here, too, sexuality is sublimated as an expression of love to God that rejected a concern with erotic technique and suppressed the experience of lust or passion.

Finally, the religion of brotherliness was antagonistic to the aesthetic sphere—the life-orders of modern music, dance, painting, and literature that would each forge a new cultural synthesis and offer the promise of this-worldly salvation from isolation and despair. "Art takes over the function of a this-worldly salvation. . . . It provides a *salvation* from the routines of everyday life. . . ."[57] In this context, Weber refers to the operas of Richard Wagner, the cult surrounding the poet Stefan George, and Georg Luckács's Sunday Circle.

Georg Lukács's "Sunday Circle" in Budapest brought together a remarkable ensemble of literateurs, poets, composers, and critics united in their passionate hatred for materialistic, utilitarian civilization and in search of collective redemption through art. Mary Gluck describes the Sunday Circle as the first generation of cosmopolitans coming of age in modern society, 1900–1918. They included Lukács, Karl Mannheim, art historians Arnold Hauser, Charles de Tolnay, Frederick Antal, and Lajos Fulip, the poet Bela Balazs, and the composer Belah Bartok. They viewed themselves as victims of political liberalism and capitalism. Seeking liberation from bourgeois individualism through flight into a mythical past and escape into the *Innerlichkeit* of subjectivist culture, they looked to artistic forms for redemption. "They were fascinated by primitivism and folk cultures. In primitive African masks, in Chinese paintings, and in the still unspoiled folk music and poetry of the Irish, East European, and Russian peasantry, they thought to have discovered the sense of personal wholeness and communal rootedness they so bitterly lacked in the modern world."[58]

The culture of aestheticism promised the triumph of the inner self liberated from the tyranny of convention. But this also could devolve into narcissistic self-absorption, intellectual sterility, and psychological immobilization.[59] Like Kierkegaard's aesthete, the culture of aestheticism produced an amoral *Gefuhlskultur*, a "culture of 'feeling,' and 'experience,' out of which grew a special sensitivity to art, psychic nuance, emotional states, expressiveness and interiority. It was a marginal, particularizing culture closely linked with the oppositional identity of outsiders or with the sloganeering of 'art for art's sake.' "[60]

The religion of brotherliness, as Weber understood, was antagonistic to *Gefuhlskultur*. The culture of aestheticism reduced questions of ethical choice to matters of artistic taste and license justified in the name of artistic expression. Weber argues: "with this claim to a redemptory function, art begins to compete directly with salvation religion. Every rational religious ethic must turn against this inner-worldly, irrational salvation. For in religion's eyes, such salvation is a realm of irresponsible indulgence and secret lovelessness."[61]

The religion of brotherliness rejected the competing promises of salvation from the independent life-orders of art and eroticism and stood in dynamic tension with the spheres of family, polity, and economy. The new congregations of brethren united by the absolutist ethic of the Sermon on the Mount created organic communities of believers marked by faith, joy, and acosmic love. Weber's ethic of brotherliness provides a sociological counterpart to the world-abnegation of Eberhard Arnold's Innerland piety as the foundation of Christian community. Replace "iron cage" with Mammon, and the two authors appear congruent. Why then did Weber reject out-of-hand the possibility for the success of an experiment in the religion of brotherliness in modern society? Why did Weber feel that Tolstoy's demand that moderns fashion their lives according to the mandates of Matthew 5, 6, 7 or the utopianism of radical syndicalism was doomed to failure?[62] What did Weber mean when in concluding his essay he stated: "in the midst of a culture that is rationally organized for a vocational workaday life, there is hardly any room for the cultivation of acosmic brotherliness. . . . Under the technical and social conditions of rational culture, an imitation of the life of Buddha, Jesus, or Francis seems condemned to failure for purely external reasons."[63]

Weber's abiding cultural pessimism rejected the possibility of a charismatic return to a religion of brotherliness. Instead, he advocated a resigned acceptance of the highly rationalized modern social order and the opportunity to pursue a secular vocation in science, politics, or one of the other autonomous institutional orders. Weber, with Toennies, Simmel, and the emerging German Sociological School, embraced "a heroic ideal of rational clarification in the face of tragedy. They preferred analysis to hypocrisy and destructive despair: they became scientific."[64]

The rationalized social order of bureaucratic statecraft, the ubiquitous techniques of control and administration, and the cold, dehumanized structure of capitalist enterprise, markets, and class divisions undermined each person's capacity for autonomy, power, and self-mastery. Modern social orders with their competing values and autonomous organization effectively fragmented and eroded past forms of individual selfhood and collective identity derived from *tradition, religion, cultivation (Bildung)*, and education.[65] Weber formulated an "individualist metaphysics," a nonsociological, existentialist solution to the problem of modern identity. Each person needed to choose a secular vocation and engage on a mission, a warfare, in pursuit of ultimate values, forging an identity grounded in the consistent realization of one of these ultimate concerns, forsaking all others. Only then could the self stand in dynamic tension with the "world," in a journey and struggle to serve one "god" among the many in the polytheism of modern value spheres. The self on mission, in service to a value sphere, and in dynamic tension with other value spheres provided the inner assurance of this-worldly salvation—redemption from meaninglessness and powerlessness.[66] Scientific knowledge and technological applications could never achieve the comprehensive system of meaning and ethical action that were once offered by the world religions. However, the activities of the scientist—the activist pursuit of this vocation—provided a locus of meaning and self-mastery. Passionate service in one's profession rendered life meaningful.

Weber articulated this idea of the secular equivalent of Protestant inner-worldly asceticism in "Science as a Vocation" and "Politics as a Vocation." Although urging upon each individual the burdens of existential choice and commitment to vocation as if "the fate of one's soul can be imagined to hang in the balance,"[67] he eschewed a vocational "ethic of conviction" in favor of an "ethic of responsibility." An ethic of conviction promoted the unyielding, rigid, and at times fanatical pursuit of ultimate values without consideration of costs, consequences, or effectiveness. Selves constituted by an ethic of conviction welcomed opportunities to be martyred for their cause and expressive action to dramatize their ideals. An ethic of responsibility directed selves to adopt flexible, adaptive tactics that compromised and accommodated to achieve partial, incremental success in the realization of ultimate values.[68]

The religious ethic of brotherliness promoted an absolutist ethic of conviction that could not succeed as a cultural foundation for selfhood (*Innerlichkeit*), identity, or community in modern society. Men and women who gave themselves totally to the ethics of the Sermon on the Mount, who expected the imminent fulfillment of the Kingdom of God, confronted without compromise the objective, impersonal operation of a capitalist market economy, class, and status-group conflict. However, this economic order operated according to its own autonomous principles and generally ignored or stood opposed to values of "economic brotherhood" or "social justice." The ideals of religious-socialism were doomed to fail for external reasons as this ethic of conviction futilely opposed the unyielding ascendancy of world capitalist development.

Weber reflects upon the efflorescence of the Christian Socialist youth groups in the postwar years. He writes in "Science as a Vocation" that this movement represents

> something very sincere and genuine if some of the youth groups who during recent years have quietly grown together give their human community the interpretation of a religious, cosmic, or mystical relation, although occasionally perhaps such interpretation rests on misunderstanding of self. True as it is that every act of genuine brotherliness may be linked with the awareness that it contributes something imperishable to a super-personal realm, it seems to me dubious whether the dignity of purely human and communal relations is enhanced by these religious interpretations.[69]

Weber inserted the fragment "The Market: Its Impersonality and Ethic" after an essay on the world-abnegation of the religion of brotherliness, "Jesus' Indifference toward the World" in *Economy and Society*. As counterpoint to the community of goods, acosmic love, and rejection of Mammon demanded by Jesus' world-rejection stood the organization and imperatives of a market ethic. Weber writes:

The market community as such is the most impersonal relationship of practical life into which humans can enter with one another. . . . Where the market is allowed to follow its own autonomous tendencies, its participants do not look towards the persons of each other but only toward the commodity; there are no obligations of brotherliness or reverence, and none of those spontaneous human relationships that are sustained by personal unions. . . . In sharp contrast to all other groups which always presuppose some measure of personal fraternization or even blood kinship, the market is fundamentally alien to any type of fraternal relationship.[70]

The absolutist ethical demands of brotherliness were possible only to a privileged few—a religious aristocracy independent of the workaday world. The religion of brotherliness proclaimed a radical equality among believers, each in charismatic contact with the Holy Spirit and bound together in an organic community. However, the experience of the "inequality of religious charisma"[71] produced internal divisions, inequality, and stratification between the religiously qualified and the laity. The charisma of the prophet can become routinized and institutionalized in a religious office or in the hereditary succession of religiopolitical power in the prophet's family. Ethnic, racial, social class, language, national, generational, and gender differences can be introduced, thus eroding the unity of organic social community. All of these sources of disunity and division would in fact develop in Bruderhof communities transforming the religion of brotherliness that Arnold proclaimed into an authoritarian religious community.

Weber's problematic identified the rationalized, societal life-orders that produced different types of social actors and social character. Modern social structure, driven by the bureaucratic rationalization in all spheres, produced a "rational *Lebensführung*," or rational conduct of life, of the trained specialist. This modern life-order and "character" type formed the "iron cage" of modernity and, for Weber, excluded the possibility of charismatic transcendence in life-orders where men and women labored in a religious calling to realize the Apostolic vision of the absolutist ethic of brotherhood.[72]

Through the religious rejection of the world and the rationalization of dogma and communal association, Bruderhof primitivism and Pietism would produce a life-order and social character of a kind that Weber distrusted. Arnold's experiment in redemption developed into a religious aristocracy and a community internally divided that would "succumb in the end to the world domination of unbrotherliness."[73]

Two

THE THRALL OF UTOPIAN ILLUSIONS

Seeking the Kingdom of God

The utopian ideals of creating a Christian primordium, of building the Kingdom of God, and implementing an absolute ethic of brotherliness within a harmonious, organic *Gemeinde* served as the foundation of the Bruderhof movement. In this chapter, we retrace the decisive turning points in the formation of Eberhard Arnold's utopianism.

Eberhard Arnold's ideas of Innerland piety, the religion of brotherliness, and an absolutist ethic of world-abnegation reached a decisive turning at the end of World War I. Arnold lived in Berlin from 1915 until 1920 and worked for the Furrow Publishing House, served as general secretary of the German Student Union, and assisted the German Student Service in the care of war prisoners. Until the war, he had devoted himself to the interests of revival Pietism, seeking to rebuild the churches through mass conversion and effect social reform by appeal to the social conscience of the state church.[1] After the war, Arnold was drawn to the emerging religious-socialist movement founded in December 1919 as the Federation of Religious Socialists. The Federation conceived of itself as an association "of all men and women who want to take seriously the principles of Christ not only in private but also in public life and who therefore stand up for the socialist form of life."[2] Arnold advocated communitarian forms of Christian Socialism allied with the youth movement, or *Wandervogel*—especially the radical group of Marburg University students, self-styled Christian revolutionaries who founded *Das Neue Werk* (the New Work) and the New Work Movement. In association with the New Work Movement and the southern German Schlüchtern religious-socialists, Arnold heeded the call for inner renewal issued by Karl Barth at the Tambach Conference in 1919. Innerland piety and the ethic of brotherliness would now find sociological expression of "Christian Revolution" by abandoning social activism within church and society and seeking world-abnegation in the creation

43

of an "organic community" located at the periphery of a faltering civilization.

Arnold had gravitated to the theology of religious-socialism, especially the work of Christoph Blumhardt (1842–1919) and the Swiss religious socialist Leonhard Ragaz (1868–1945). Blumhardt followed in the path of his father, Johann Blumhardt (1805–1880), a Pietist preacher who performed a wondrous exorcism of demons from a servant girl in 1843, proclaiming "Jesus is Victor" and establishing a religious retreat at Bad Böll. The Blumhardts believed that men and women should anticipate the coming of the Kingdom of God in their lifetime, blending a utopian optimism, pacifism, and an abiding concern for the poor. Unlike the inward-looking Pietism of the father, however, Christoph's religious-socialism advocated social activism. He joined the Social Democratic Party in 1899, supported striking workers in Wurtenberg, and gained election as a socialist to the *Landtag*.[3] Political activism put Blumhardt in direct conflict with the Lutheran church, and he was forced to resign his pastorate in 1900.

Ragaz engaged in religiously motivated political activism promoting Swiss workers' rights and strikes, arguing that Christ must side with the oppressed. Socialism thus fostered the ethical ends of those who labored for the realization of the Kingdom of God. Speaking at the end of his ministry in Basel in 1908, he pronounced a theology of hope and collective redemption. "We are to become free children of God, free from guilt, free from hate, free from the tyranny of the world and of death, free from service to Mammon, free from self-service; we are to breathe freely in the freedom of God and become united in a Kingdom of freedom, purity, justice and love."[4]

Ultimately, Ragaz advocated a faith-claim that placed Christians in dynamic tension with the established institutions of church, economy, and state. He proclaimed that Jesus "does not want a religion, but rather a Kingdom, a new creation, a new world. He wants God, the people, the brother, a new justice, the liberation of the world from fear and sensuality, from Mammonism, from despair, from death—and from religion."[5]

Ragaz believed that the world had entered a time of anticipation of the imminent creation of the Kingdom of God, a time of *Kairos*, the special moment of *Heilsgeschichte* when the kingdom of the world was vanquished by divine intercession. Soon all humanity would be transformed into children of God laboring in His peaceable Kingdom.[6] Socialist politics, evangelical conversions, and the outpouring of social conscience represented "signs of the times" that augured collective salvation.

Arnold adopted the Blumhardt and Swiss-Socialist idea of the Kingdom of God as radically distinct from the kingdom of the world. The signs of the times demanded that the faithful renounce the Mammonism of the world, especially capitalist political economy and the established churches. The "Kingdom of God" theology increasingly rejected tactics of political reform and activism and advocated world-rejection and the creation of Spirit-led organic communities of the converted. Only within these alternative communities could believers live in conformity with the absolutist ethics of conviction demanded by the Sermon on the Mount. Arnold appears to have reached this conclusion during the encounter with Karl Barth at the Tambach Conference.

The Schlüchtern Circle of religious-socialists had invited Barth as their keynote speaker to replace the ailing Ragaz. Barth's speech reflected utter disgust with the Bolshevik Revolution and the Communist revolts in Munich, Berlin, and Bavaria earlier in 1919. Barth opposed the Culture-Protestantism of liberals like Naumann, who linked the Gospel with the highest secular ideals of the times. According to Barth, the church must avoid the secularization of religious-socialism. Barth offered Historical Christianity a "theology of crisis"[7] to address what James Luther Adams describes as "the widespread economic distress, demonic nationalism, and scientism; the world war; and the despairing nihilism born of disillusionment."[8]

Barth published *Epistle to the Romans* in 1919, the first essay in a lifelong project of Christian dogmatics, intended to restore God as the center and subject of theology, reaffirming the fundamental truths of the Gospel, the absolute sovereignty and transcendental "Otherness" of God. In Barth's thought, believers were in complete dependence upon grace that God had given freely through the intercession of Christ. In place of an anthropocentric, historical exegesis and hermeneutics of Scripture, and in place of concern with psychologies of religious experience, Barth demanded a return to the fundamentalism of a theocentric theology. The truths of the Bible were knowable only by the faithful who opened their hearts to illumination and guidance by the Holy Spirit, by what the theologian Otto Piper termed "pneumatical exegesis."[9]

Barth's keynote, "The Christian's Place in Society," enunciated this theocentric "Prophetic Theology" in response to the crises of the times. James Luther Adams best defines Barthian prophetic theology as asserting

> that God through Jesus Christ is the Lord of history and of culture. This Lord of history calls men and women into a community of faith. In response to the Lord of history this community of faith takes time and culture seriously, so seriously as to hold that political and social institutions, the arts and the sciences, as well as the individual believer, have a vocation from on high. . . . Accordingly, prophetic theology recognizes the obligation to interpret the signs of the times in light of the End, that is, of the Reign of God.[10]

Reminiscent of Max Weber's "Intermediate Reflections," Barth understood that the institutional orders of society operated according to their own, autonomous inner workings. The Christian should not, indeed could not, avoid participating in society and myriad institutional spheres—family, religion, education, and economy. However, believers must avoid making idols of human values and institutions, such as the Wandervogel's quest for freedom from authority (for its own sake) and the pursuit of experience in religion or art (for its own sake). Barth unleashed a scathing attack upon the modernist search for meaning and personal redemption through the value-spheres of marriage and family life as the "voracious idol of the erstwhile middle classes."[11] Each person needed to seek a place within the social order with the clear inner direction of the God-centered—as one grounded in God.

Those grounded in God avoided both the extremes of world-affirmation and of dynamic world-rejection. Barth rejects as "perfect naivete" the stance of the simple cooperation and unquestioning acceptance of the social order. Absolute opposition to society or "perfect criticism" is equally untenable. He writes: "we must now fortify ourselves against expecting that our criticizing, protesting, reforming, organizing, democratizing, socializing, and revolutionizing—*however fundamental and thoroughgoing these may be*—will satisfy the ideal of the kingdom of God."[12]

The person grounded in God would repudiate the political ideas of "hyphenated" Christians, of religious-socialists, as misguided attempts to mix human activity with "the wholly other" associated with God. Politics, statecraft, revolution, strikes, and street fighting were totally corrupt, did not serve God's sovereign will, and did not build an authentic church or the Kingdom of God. Barth writes, "Clever enough is the paradox that the service of God is or must become the service of man; but that is not the same as saying that our precipitate service of man, even when it is undertaken in the name of purest love, becomes by that happy fact the service of God."[13]

In light of the call to live in society as a believer grounded in God and guided by Prophetic Theology, Barth concludes his talk by posing Tolstoy's question, "What ought we then to do?"[14] Barth's reply left his audience stunned, confused, and immobilized. He completed his address in a cloud of ambiguity, stating, "What can the Christian in society do but follow attentively what is done by *God*?"[15] Thus, the God-centered Christian would seek the leadings of the Holy Spirit by meditations upon the Word of God and work within the church. Those grounded in God, like the seventeenth-century Calvinist, must strive to forge their personalities in systematic obedience to God's will, to act in the world as a theater for the dramatization of God's greater glory, and to avoid all secularization of religious values. In this manner, the Christian might live *in* the world without becoming *of* the world.

Eberhard Arnold attended the Tambach Conference and made a formal comment to this address. Arnold stated that Barth's lecture was "a rather complicated kind of machine that runs backwards and forwards and shoots in all directions with no lack of both visible and hidden joints."[16] Hans Meier, a religious-socialist in attendance, heard Arnold reply to this challenge with the words "Karl Barth is right. Human action goes nowhere. But if God tells us to do something, is that just human action?"[17] Arnold synthesized the ideas of Kingdom of God in religious-socialism and Barth's dialectical theology. Arnold accepted the call to a fundamentalist-theocentric theology, a devaluation of familism and humanistic values, and the urgency of a crisis-driven, prophetic mission to embrace a religious vocation grounded in God. Innerland piety granted that each seeker ascertain the will of God by receptivity to the infusions of the Holy Spirit. For Arnold, the "leadings of the spirit" pointed to Barth's rejection of human intervention in the kingdom of the world, and retreat into an organic community that would serve as a continuing vessel for the Spirit and beacon for the Kingdom of God. Only in retreat from the world and by rejecting the deadening legalism of the established churches could Arnold hope to realize the ideals of the Kingdom of God theology of Blumhardt and Ragaz—freedom from service to Mammon and egoism, and selfless service to God.

Earlier that year, Arnold had addressed the Whitsun Christian Student Movement Conference at Marburg challenging all who would call themselves Christians to devote themselves completely to the absolutist ethic of the Sermon on the Mount and the imitation of Christ. Erwin Wissman reviewed Arnold's address.

> This was the Sermon on the Mount in the full force of its impact, in its absolute and undiminished relevance, its unconditional absoluteness. Here there was no compromise. Whoever wants to belong to this kingdom, must give himself wholly and go through it to the last! To be a Christian means to live the life of Christ.[18]

By forging an absolutist ethic of conviction that would realize the mandate of the Sermon on the Mount, Arnold moved away from the Furrow and the Christian Student Movement and toward more radical Schlüchtern religious-socialists who represented a Christian variant of the German Youth Movement.

Arnold's religious rejection of the world and the ideal of an organic community adopted the central criticisms advanced during the Cultural Crisis (Kulturkritik) in Wilhemite, Germany, the spirit of antimodernity, and the countercultural ideals of the Youth Movement, or Wandervogel. These ideas also formed the core of the ideology of cultural despair for the generation of 1890 and the intermediate generation that came of age during the period between the two world wars. Arnold embraced these ideas with the utopian conviction that their implementation would result in building the true church and God's Kingdom. Instead, Arnold's utopianism bore fruit as an authoritarian sect.

Youth in the first decades of the twentieth century were filled with a sense of dread about the future, anxiety about modern, urban, and industrial society, and rebellion against the rationalization and bureaucratization of society and the vestiges of authority in the patriarchal family. They expressed a wish to be free, to devote themselves enthusiastically to a cult of inner, subjective experience (*Erlebnis*), spontaneity, and emotional fellowship. Youth rejected the depersonalized ethics of mass society[19] and bureaucratic regimentation seeking escape to nature. As Stachura argues, the Wandervogel

> sought through a passionate commitment to rambling and hiking in the countryside and to the untrammelled delights of Nature, to bring the younger generation back to the purer foundations of a society in which human bonds would be restored to their rightful place of priority over machines, factories, materialism, and the impersonalism of urban civilisation. The upsurge of the Wandervogel was an indictment, therefore, of industrial Germany and its value system.[20]

The counterculturalists of the early youth movement idealized a mythic medieval German village life, Toennies's organic community (*Gemeinschaft*) of persons bound by blood and soil, and the idea of the *Volk,* or collective identity, as a people unspoiled by modernism. The early movement advocated a Romantic-Illuminist cult of the past, emulating the heroics of the wandering medieval scholar, seeking simplicity, genuineness, spontaneity, and escape from mundane routine. The early Wandervogel, under the autocratic leadership of Karl Fischer, grew to 25,000 members in 800 local branches drawn largely from Protestant adolescents and college students. The movement split into various factions advocating health reform, school reform, folk music and dancing, political reform, Pan-Germanism, *Weltpolitik,* and militant nationalism during the war. In October 1913, meeting at Hohe Meissner Mountain, 3,000 youths and adults, including Max Weber, founded the Free German Youth, proclaiming autonomy and a revolutionary mission to transform German culture.[21]

Arnold's work for the Furrow Publishing House after the war required that he attend youth conferences of the Free German Youth Movement and the Christian Student Union. Emmy Arnold writes of this period after the war of a crisis of individual meaning and collective purpose faced by working-class and middle-class youth, Christian and atheist.[22] Youth searched for spiritual, religious, mythological answers to the agonizing perplexities of cultural crisis. Piper writes that "the War aroused in the German people the passionate desire for a *religious* explanation of their lives, and specially [*sic*] of the recent period."[23]

The collective trauma of the war proved a watershed in German culture and society. Piper described a mood of anomic disorientation, a sense of dread, irrationality, and loss of security, particularly among young adults. With the loss of faith in the rationalist ideal of progress, science, and nationalism, the fate of postwar Europe appeared uncertain and fraught with peril from mass political movements, economic crises, and the modernism posed by the "Americanization" of mass popular culture—new fashions, commercialized leisure, and mass consumption.[24]

Germany had experienced an increased birth rate in the first decade of the century. Between the staggering war losses of men aged 18–45 and the large birth cohorts of children coming of age in the 1920s, "youth" came to make up a disproportionately large segment of German society. The generation coming of age in the 1920s suffered the protracted absence or death of their fathers and a generation gap as they entered adulthood longing for emancipation from patriarchal authority and the cold impersonality of the pervasive bureaucratization of urban society. Detlev Peukert writes of this "superfluous" younger generation:

> during the 1920s the prewar "bulge" age-groups came flooding into the labour market. The proportion of young people in Germany had never been so high. . . . The labour market in the 1920s was therefore exceptionally crowded. This surplus of labour, and the particularly bleak outlook facing the virtually redundant generation of those born around the turn of the century, lent the nationalist slogan, "*Vol ohne Raum*" (a people without space or territory) a certain specious plausibility.[25]

One response to the alienation of the youth was the creation of the proto-Fascist Bundische Youth Movement—a nationalist, conservative call for spiritual renewal, extolling the heroic ideal of the soldier in defense of the *Volksgemeinschaft*. In response to the fragmentation of modern culture and the recurrent economic and political crises that plagued Weimar, the Bund groups joined together into charismatic fellowships, duty-bound to the hierarchial authorities of their groups and dedicated to the revitalization of the Fatherland.[26] Peukert writes, "The Wandervogel evolved into the *Bundischen*; the war had made them more nationalistic, their organization was now more rigorously committed to the command principle and the youth mystique was blown up into a diffuse ideology of mission."[27]

Eberhard Arnold refused to follow the Wandervogel into a proto-Fascist and quasi-religious mission of national renewal and, in accord with Barth's idea of the God-centered, rejected the socialist youth group's ideology of political reform. Arnold's utopia would never involve German nationalism or a *Volksgemeinschaft* founded upon racial purity, militarism, and state-sponsored genocide, violence, and terror. Rather, Arnold drew upon the elements of the ideology of cultural despair—the utopian primitivist *Gemeinde*, in which believers surrendered their individuality to the organic community—forging a life's philosophy in the face of anomic meaninglessness. Emmy Arnold recounts that her husband had adopted the slogan from the Hohe Meissner

Mountain gathering as a call to action: " 'we want to be free to build up our own lives in a truthful and genuine way.' "[28]

Arnold at first considered collecting a circle of followers and living a countercultural life of roaming. Emmy Arnold describes their search for a solution to the challenge posed by the youth movement. Conventional, bourgeois life was unpalatable and they considered opening a folk school, a cooperative land settlement. Possibly they would purchase a trailer and travel across the countryside as musicians, teachers, and bearers of joy.[29]

Arnold ultimately rejected the neoconservative and romantic life of roaming in communion with nature on a mission to rebuild communities ravaged by war. His association with the New Work Movement and their life devoted to the realization of the Sermon on the Mount within the Habertshof community provided the model he used to synthesize the highest aspirations of the counterculture, religious-socialism, and a spiritual vocation of Innerland piety.

The New Work Movement was a Christian variant of the youth movement that hungered for spontaneous religious fellowship, emotional radicalism or experience of fusion, and rejection of individualism in favor of "an impulsive tendency toward comradeship and group life."[30] Habertshof, founded in 1918, instituted communal property, vegetarianism, life-reform, and healing. They opened a folk school and dedicated their lives to the realization of the absolute ethics of conviction of Christian Socialism and the countercultural ideals of the Wandervogel. Adherents to this movement and community advocated "a revolutionary will against mammonism and capitalism; a decided will to peace and against might and violence; and the recognition of an eschatological tension between the present and God's eternal future."[31]

Emmy Arnold recounts their visit to Hesse and Habertshof in 1920. As residents of Berlin and self-conscious as "town folk," the Arnolds felt trepidation about beginning a new life and community, but they admired the simple lifestyle, the lack of pretension, and the "peasant garb in the style of the youth movement. Eberhard and I felt that our own life in the future should have a similar outward form."[32]

Eberhard Arnold, together with his wife and a small retinue of disciples known as "the Holy Seven,"[33] founded the Sannerz Community in southern Germany in June 1920. In a decisive break with the past, Arnold left his job at the Furrow Publishing House, cashed in his life insurance and other assets, and abandoned middle-class urban life in Berlin for what would become in 1925 an organic community of those united in their seeking for God's Kingdom in life modeled upon the Sermon on the Mount. Arnold received a gift of 30,000 marks from Kurt Woermann of the Hamburg-America Line as a down payment for the farm in Sannerz.

Benjamin Zablocki describes Sannerz as a community lacking in formal organization, normative order, clearly defined criteria for admission and membership, a settled routine, or a secure economic foundation.[34] Arnold directed the New Work Publishing House, and the community subsisted on small-scale farming and gifts from generous guests and friends. During the first two years, the community grew to more than fifty persons and entertained almost two thousand guests from the Christian Youth Movement. The Sannerz and Habertshof communities were utopian models of community living in the spirit of the Sermon on the Mount. They attracted the curious and more casual members of the Schlüchtern religious-socialist movement. Members and guests sought "communion" together guided by Arnold's charismatic leadership. Emmy Arnold remembers the first two years of Sannerz as times of joy, miracles, and celebration.

> Every day that we were able to live together in community was a great day of celebrating, truly a festive day! . . . Whether we picked up stones and rocks from the fields we had rented, whether we hoed beans, peas, or potatoes, or whether we preserved fruit and vegetables or preserved jam—all of these occasions were opportunities for celebrating and for experiencing fellowship together.[35]

The early enthusiasm for the Arnold community shared by various Christian groups waned in 1922. Support for life-reform and evangelical fellowships eroded as youth turned away from the counterculture and returned to the established churches and more settled middle-class lives. The Christian Student Union Conference at Whitsum declined to use Sannerz as their meeting place and denounced Arnold's community as a "fantasy utopia," proclaiming that "People with a new vision should now turn back to the old conditions of life, to be a small light there."[36] As John McKelvie Whitworth describes, "throughout 1921 and 1922 the group at Sannerz received many visits from members of the political youth associations, who variously accused the sectarians of being irresponsible, idealistic, parasitic, and, most wounding of all, of being essentially and inescapably bourgeois."[37] These denunciations produced a schism in the New Work Movement.

By the summer of 1922, the German economy suffered disastrous inflation, straining the New Work publishing business as investors called in their money. Arnold had taken his family for a month-long holiday in Holland and refused to shorten this vacation to attend to the crisis. When he did return, he found the publishing house in receivership and was confronted with the mass defection of forty of the community members. Only the original Holy Seven remained to reconstitute the effort. "Eberhard recounts the crisis of 1922: When the call first came to us, we felt that the Spirit of Jesus Christ had driven us and charged us to live in full community, in communal solidarity, with an open door and a loving heart for all people. It was the word of Jesus Christ, the reality of his life and the fact of his Spirit, that gave us the strength to start firmly. . . ."[38]

The community was reconstituted as a church-community in August 1925. They published a profession of faith, stating: "The community feels that its true calling is to establish itself as a Church, to live together as a commune fully united in daily life on the basis of sharing all property, having surrendered all private property."[39] In 1926 the Sannerz community numbered forty-five persons, publishing as the Eberhard Arnold Publishing House, and remaining ever dependent upon the generous financial support of outsiders. Arnold and the inner circle of full members decided to leave Sannerz and settle on a larger farm in the Rhön Mountains in 1927, establishing the Rhön Bruderhof. The community required a more secure economic footing, an organizational and belief structure that would regularize community life, and a structure of conversion and commitment that would separate the casual inquirer from the committed believer. Arnold initiated the routinization of his charismatic authority by delineating the theological basis of Spirit-led church-community and defending the authenticity of the Bruderhof from an increasingly hostile and indifferent world.

Arnold would renounce the democratic and individualistic expressions of religious freedom found in the Sannerz community and implement the demand that individuals seek self-anihiliation in the organic church-community. The appeal to the mysteries of faith and the workings of the Holy Spirit would obfuscate the more undemocratic and authoritarian elements of the rationalization of the Bruderhof.

The Illusion of Organic Community

Eberhard Arnold felt compelled to write a pamphlet in 1927, "Why We Live in Community," to clarify the motives and purposes that guided the reconstituted community at Rhön following the defection in 1922–1923. The Bruderhof formed a community as an inescapable imperative, overwhelmed by the certainty that authentic Christian vocation compelled them to submit to God-ordained mandates of a life in common.[40] Only in community could the church become a vessel to capture the Holy Spirit, a beacon for the world to see, a "city upon a hill." Only in community could Christians escape concupiscence and the "Mammonistic, unclean, murderous human society."[41] Only in the common life could believers repeatedly recover the exaltation of God's love and joy, the inner-worldly mystical infusion of divine love. But the common life exacted a terrible price upon each individual. Using the metaphor of fire, Arnold proclaims that the spirit of community forms a white heat that burns away individuality. Arnold tells us that suffering is necessarily the other side of joy. "When we follow God's will for community, we are led straight into the reality of a life of work and the struggle for existence, into the reality and difficulties created by human personalities. It is an exceedingly dangerous way, a way of severe suffering."[42]

Community acted as a crucible that re-formed each believer in the white heat of suppression of self-will, pride, and the sinful proclivities of the "natural man." Each believer voluntarily embraced a life of *automachia*, or psychological warfare, against any remnants of the sinful self. Arnold spoke of the "New Man" forged in this crucible of relentless self-torture. "The Spirit of the church takes up a fighting position in each individual and fights the old man within him from the position of the new man."[43]

Arnold defined the attributes of the New Man, in large part, in terms of the negation of the old self. The New Man vanquished the sins of Mammonism—the will to hold power over others, egomania, covetousness, the value of money, wealth, and the calculation of value through the cash nexus of a market relationship. In opposition to the prideful, ambitious, willful individual addicted to "soul-destroying Mammonism," the New Man strived to become poverty-stricken, humble, submissive to God's will, empty of self and pride, and thereby open to the infusion of divine pneuma. With single-mindedness, each believer must find the courage to become small, to find an "inner eye" of concentrated vision that strives for simplicity in all things.[44] Finally, the New Man in community would assume a childlike spirit. Arnold writes in *Salt and Light*, "you will live like children." "A life of this nature is only possible if we can become young, spontaneous, trusting, again and again. Only a life born out of unconstrained feeling, out of childlike, genuine emotion, which wants to love all people the way children do, can be capable of such an attitude."[45]

The concept of the New Man working toward this-worldly salvation can be found in many utopian ventures: the American Adam freed from old-world influences and corruptions; the "New Man in Soviet psychology" or in early Christian Apostolic communities; the utopianism of the Free German Youth Movement after the war; and the murderous manliness of Freikorps soldiers after the war.[46] The idea of a New Man implies key assumptions about anthropology: human nature, personality, motivation.[47]

Without the Spirit-filled community, and absent the baptism and radical restructuring of personality, each person remains trapped in sin, corrupted to the core, motivated by venality and worldly appetites, and alienated from others and from God. With the creation of the New Man in godly communion with others, Arnold perceived the new creation as basically good, motivated by abundant, acosmic love that flowed out from the reborn heart toward brothers and sisters in the faith and outward toward all of humanity. With naive optimism, Arnold believed that the New Man in community would submit willingly to the requirements of an ethic of brotherliness—simplicity, humility, childlike surrender to the fellowship. Old wounds were forever healed; past sins were remitted. Still, a remnant of the old man in each believer persisted. Arnold demanded a continual *automachia*, an inner psychological and spiritual warfare against evil consistent with the logic of evangelical Pietism. He writes in 1927, "The Spirit of the Church takes up a fighting position in each individual and fights the old man within him from the position of the new man."[48] Thus, the new men and women in community experienced the outward joy of fellowship together founded upon the inward struggles against evil and sin of the ever-present vestigial old creation.

The anthropology of a new man also stipulated the sociological conception of a church-community or *Gemeinde*. Arnold always referred to the *Gemeinde* as an organic community organized in the literal fulfillment of the dictates of the Sermon on the Mount—all things in common, a common purse, the eradication of private property, an evangelical witness to the world pointing the way to authentic Christian living. In the early communities, members and guests lived in extended family relationships that minimized social differences and tended toward the radical equality of believers. Only the "natural" distinctions remained between parent and child, husband and wife, member and guest. Even these differences were diminished by the baptismal vows that demanded a believer's complete allegiance to the will of the community and not the needs of family. Factionalism, gossiping, and disunity were prevented by the First Law of Sannerz, which enjoined members to seek out an offending brother directly, without intermediaries, and settle differences. Believers felt united in their emotional devotion as disciples to the charismatic teaching and presence of Eberhard Arnold.

The idea of organic community meant that the whole, the unified community of regenerate believers that formed the vessel to capture the living Spirit, was greater than the sum of its constituent parts—the individual members. Individual members were spiritual material to be fashioned and reshaped by the organic community. Consistent with Innerland piety and New Man psychology, the idea of *Gemeinde* stipulated the constant process of molding individuals to serve the totality. Through an act of faith and love inspired by God and religious brotherhood, individuals would willingly abandon their individual selves and identities. Writing on July 30, 1933, Arnold defines the church-community:

> The Church-community is a living building. The people in it are the living stones. These living stones have nothing perfect in themselves: they must be hewn and trimmed to fit better and better into the building. Yet the building is perfect. . . . Through the fitting together of these stones, spiritually dead by nature, new life is aroused in them, not out of the various parts, but out of the all-comprehending, uniting element, the Holy Spirit.[49]

The early communities before the routinization of charisma achieved by the adoption of Hutterian forms in the 1930s largely ignored the questions of church polity, community power structures, an economic division of labor, or social control. Questions of community organization dissolved before the mysteries of faith when believers received the Holy Spirit in their hearts and responded to this complete love to God by acts of justice and goodness toward others. Arnold viewed social institutions, even established churches, as afflicted with deadening legalism. In comparison to spiritual deadness, the *Gemeinde* began with God's love—the life-giving Spirit. Arnold writes, "a completely different situation is given as soon as people are gripped by God's love. They grow toward one another and become organs of a mysterious unity, of a mystical body which, ruled by a spirit of unity is one heart and one soul."[50]

Eberhard Arnold's sociological vision of *Gemeinde* represents a backward-looking rejection of modernity founded upon two models of community: Ferdinand Toennies's romanticization of the Germanic medieval village (*Gemeinschaft*) and the *ekklesia* of the Apostolic Church. Both models suggested the possibility of creating, separate from the world, an organic community of persons fused in total harmony.

No German sociological work achieved greater popular readership and influence than Toennies's *Gemeinschaft und Gesellschaft*. First published in 1887, this monograph became a best-seller in the 1912 second edition and the succeeding publications in the 1920s.[51] Toennies articulated the malaise and dissatisfactions with modernity codified in the concept of *gesellschaft*, or societal rational association. Modern society was a fragmentation of warring social classes, interest groups, and rational-bureaucratic associations motivated by the logics of reckless capitalism, market forces, and commodity production. Artificial aggregates of individuals abandoning themselves in the reckless pursuit of self-interest and material advantage at the expense of others put each individual in tension with all others. The *Gesellschaft* was organized as a rational will (*Kurwille*) and the instrumental-rational action of individuals in their competition for power, money, and prestige. Modern German society lacked cultural integration and national unity. The parvenu driven by the *Besitz* value of accumulating material wealth and engaging in the vulgarity of conspicuous consumption, supplanted the ideal of the middle-class individual committed to finding ultimate meaning from the materials of high culture (*Burgerkeit*). Now the cultural philistine (*Bildungsphilister*), the career-driven bureaucrat, and the economic ruthlessness and vulgar materialism of social-climbing capitalists dominated the new metropolis of Berlin and other German cities.[52]

Toennies and the generation of Germans who struggled with the idea of modernity after 1890 looked to their past for the resolution to their present anguish. Katherine Roper in her study of the novels of Imperial Berlin, *German Encounters with Modernity*, uncovers this leitmotif of nostalgia for a time of unified purpose and cultural integration. In novels and popular culture, Germans hungered for "images of venerated generations from the past embodying virtues of duty, simplicity, hard work [that] collide with perceptions of modern generations who are self-indulgent, materialistic, or bereft of patriotic commitment."[53]

Toennies harkened to the mythic past, to the sentimentalized idea of a medieval German village organized as a patrimonial household and village-community. This natural community, built upon the affinities of blood and soil, common habits of mind, and common purposes, resulted in a perfect unity of human wills, or *Wesenwille*.[54] People cheerfully submitted to the organic authority of parents over children, husbands over wives, leaders over villagers. Workers submitted to the discipline of labor with the joyful enthusiasm of working in unity with others for common goals. Toennies writes:

> the very existence of *Gemeinschaft* rests in the consciousness of belonging together with the affirmation of the condition of mutual dependence which is posed by that affirmation. Living together may be called the animal soul of the *Gemeinschaft*; for it is the condition of its active life, of a shared feeling of pleasure and pain, of a shared enjoyment of the commonly possessed goods, by which one is surrounded, and by the cooperation in teamwork as well as in divided labor.[55]

Eberhard Arnold was greatly influenced by Toennies's pessimistic critique of modernity and plan for social reconstruction through organic community. Toennies corresponded with Carl Franklin Arnold, Eberhard's father, a professor of Religion at Breslau, in the 1870s and 1880s. Carl Arnold attempted to persuade Toennies that true community and friendship originated with agape, and these discussions informed Toennies's subsequent ideas of mystical friendship and organic unity in *Gemeinschaft*.[56] It remained for the son, Eberhard, to synthesize his father's commitment to a community founded by love to God and Toennies's themes of critique and social reconstruction into the Bruderhof model of organic community. Arnold rejected *Gesellschaft* as a universe of greed, alienation, exploitation, and social conflict as "Mammonism." Eberhard transformed Toennies's concept of the patriarchal village community into a *Gemeinde*—Spirit-led church-community where through the mysteries of faith, individual "I's" would fuse into the organic harmony of the communal "We"; where New Men and Women in a childlike spirit would joyously surrender to work, worship, and association in total unity. Through the mystery of faith, Arnold argued, men and women who had previously desired to free themselves from patriarchal authority in family and community would now joyfully abandon their independence in the anti-individualism of organic community.

Martin Buber introduced Arnold to Gustav Landauer's *A Call for Socialism* (1919), and Landauer provided an important anchor to the utopian idea of a socialist organic community of men and women redeemed from the crisis of modernity.[57] Modern civil societies structured by social class divisions, impersonal market forces, bureaucratic formal organizations, and administrative and regulative law represent Landauer's concept of the "State," and Arnold's idea of Mammonism. Landauer calls for a revolution to transcend the rationalization of the state and to recover the emotionally satisfying primordial relationship of an organic community. A new revolutionary consciousness will bring forth a renewed spirit of community. As Buber argues in *Paths in Utopia*, "this is precisely what will result from the creation and renewal of a real organic structure, from the union of persons and families into various communities and of communities into associations."[58] Arnold accepted Landauer's call to a socialist organic community but grounded this renewal of individual and group in the Holy Spirit and in emulation of the early Apostolic church-communities.

Eberhard Arnold published in 1926 *The Early Christians After the Death of the Apostles* adopting the Apostolic Church as the historical and divinely inspired model of organic community that the Bruderhof would emulate. In the spirit of the early Christians, the Bruderhof would abide by an ethic of brotherliness, reaffirmed in the Love Meal and strict monogamous marriage and sexual purity. Like the early Christians, the community viewed itself as a congregation committed to the equality of believers reborn in baptism, united in the possession of faith and the pneuma of the Spirit. Through the magical properties of the Holy Spirit infused in each believer's heart and in this "charismatic communism of love," the Bruderhof became God's "revolutionaries of the Spirit," hastening the day when His Kingdom would rescue humanity from the nightmare of history.[59]

Bruderhof primitivism embraced irrationalism founded upon a "religiosity of faith"—a nonrational attitude of unlimited trust in God.[60] The religiosity of Christian faith transvalued Pharisaic Judaism's emphasis upon an educated priesthood, upon obedience to divine will through ritual praxis and observance of the law. In place of Jewish rationalism, the Jesus movement called for charismatic devotion and possession of God's pneuma as the irrational path toward salvation. Instead of a deadening "legalism," the followers of the prophet Jesus lived in the Spirit. As Schlüchter argues, "Only those who were ready to trust completely in God, instead of their own intellectual power, who were even willing to sacrifice their own intellect for this relationship of trust, could become disciples of Jesus and children, or servants of God."[61]

The absolute faith in God's love came from within the believer's heart as an experience and expression of unconditional trust not accessible through reason or rational argument. The religiosity of faith promoted an anti-intellectual, nonrational emphasis upon charismatics, gifts of the spirit and prophecy by congregants, magical forces, and spirit-possession.[62]

Benjamin Nelson viewed the Apostolic communities as a break-through to the "faith-structure of consciousness" with important social and psychological consequences for each believer. The faith-structure of consciousness enjoined all individuals and groups to achieve an inward mediative experience of the contents of faith and "to engage in contin-uous purgation and catharsis of evil thoughts and feelings and to discover a way by which they can appropriately conform by being *informed* by the faith-consciousness."[63]

The Pauline *ekklesia* that formed the basis for the Bruderhof model of community was a charismatic congregation lead by the active infusion of the Spirit, committed to intense solidarity or emotional communital-ization of believers.[64] These early congregations combined aspects of the household (*oikos*), voluntary association, and synagogue to create a *Ge-meinde*, a religious congregation of pneumatic, charismatic piety. The Pauline movement created the congregational form and instituted a form of community association marked by emotional intimacy, internal co-hesion, and separation from outsiders and from "the world."[65] According to Wayne Meeks, households provided the "cells" or basic units of church-communities offering privacy, intimacy, and stable meeting places for the diversity of congregants who gathered in prayer. Confront-ing the hierarchy of the pater familias of the *oikos*, the *ekklesia* promoted egalitarianism. Pauline groups adopted many features of the clubs, guilds, and associations of the early Roman empire, including open membership not restricted by birth, and a site for commensality, ritual, and cultic activity. However, unlike voluntary associations, the Pauline groups forged soteriological communities exclusive to the baptized, demanding totalistic commitment of members fused into this organic congregation.

The Pauline *ekklesia* articulated a "language of belonging" with emotion-laden words depicting members as a family of brothers and sisters in faith, children of God, New Humans in Christ. Congregants needed to open themselves to joy and rejoicing, fused into *communitas*, receptive of *charismata*, or the infusion of the Spirit.[66]

Meeks also identifies a "language of separation" that differentiated the Christian from "the world" of nonbelievers and wicked practices. Con-gregants came to expect persecution, martyrdom, suffering, and the ever-present threat of Satan and demonic forces.[67] However, the absolute surrender to faith in God, faith in the mystery of Jesus crucified and resurrected, formed the secret revealed to the *Gemeinde* and the basis of a new salvation community.

Eberhard Arnold's *Gemeinde* mirrored the community of believers in the Pauline congregations: a social diversity of class and status groups reborn as brothers and sisters who dwelt together among the faithful. Guided by the injunctions of the Sermon on the Mount, they adopt a common life of Christian Socialism bound together in the solidarity of emotional communitalization. Arnold depicts the joyous emotional life of the faithful who forge their lives in the *Innerlichkeit* of the imitation of

Christ, purged of sin and separate from the world. He writes of acosmic love, "a life of this nature is only possible if we can become young, spontaneous and trusting, again and again. Only a life born out of unconstrained feeling, out of childlike, genuine emotion, which wants to love all people the way children do, can be capable of such an attitude."[68]

Arnold's *Gemeinde* also emphasized the nonrational elements of magic, spirit forces, demonic possession, and Satanic battle characteristic of the *ekklesia*. In the troubled times between the two world wars, Arnold was preoccupied with the question of the coming apocalypse as geopolitical alliances headed toward destruction. He envisioned a Manichean struggle of dualities: forces of light and forces of darkness colliding, God and Satan, Mammonism and the community lead by the Holy Spirit. Human existence involved cosmic battles unfolding in history over these opposing forces. In a New Year's Day sermon in the year of his death, Arnold spoke of "The Struggle of the Two Atmospheres."

> The spirit of the world contained only death and destruction through war, greed, competition and forces that alienated people from one another and believers from God. In opposition to this atmosphere, the way of Christ allowed believers to breathe an atmosphere of creative life, clear, pure, fresh life alive with joy in all living things. In a mysterious way the atmosphere of the Holy Spirit is present in the unity of believers. This is what makes life in the church-community so important.[69]

By maintaining separation from the atmosphere of the world, by constant vigilance, the *Gemeinde* might escape the ever-present threat of death and destruction. One form of vigilance involved the injunction that each believer grow in faith, grace, and inward piety. Arnold exhorted the brethren to pursue the goals of Innerland evangelical piety by lifelong purgations of sin and reaffirmations of faith through the imitation of the redemptive sufferings of the crucified savior. "Unless you die with Jesus on the cross in such a way that you are no longer part of any other atmosphere, like a dead man on whom that atmosphere no longer has any claim, Christ will have died in vain."[70]

Innerland piety, then, formed the first line of defense against spirit forces, demons, and the threat of Satanic attack on individuals and the community. Arnold warned his followers to beware, as "unclean spirits" were ubiquitous, in the air, poised ready to infect the community and destroy the *Gemeinde* in an epidemic of sin. Arnold preached the following dire warning only a week after his sermon on the struggle between two atmospheres. "Unclean spirits are the really murderous spirits that govern in the air. And if all wars were done away with, pacifists would be forced to realize that the spirit of murder is not done away with so long as the atmosphere in which millions live is filled with impurity."[71]

Each believer's heart and soul provided a microcosm for the inevitable battle between God and Satan. In 1922 Eberhard Arnold and the early community at Sannerz waged such a battle against Satan for Lottchen, a 16-year-old girl. During her novitiate, Lotte suffered crises of doubt punctuated by periods of inner maturation and piety. During her baptismal preparations, a demon personality emerged from the youth. Arnold writes of the successful exorcism and healing of Lotte that this victory meant more than the emancipation of one troubled individual from the forces of evil and Satan. Lotte's cure involved the struggle for supremacy between two spiritual powers; it is the conflict between God and Satan.[72]

Eberhard Arnold acknowledged the theological influence of Johann Blumhardt and his son Christoph Blumhardt. Johann Blumhardt was pastor of the Lutheran church in the village of Moettlingen, Germany. After a two-year struggle over the soul of a demon-possessed servant girl, Gottlieben Dittus, Blumhardt succeeded in 1842 in healing her through exorcism. He proclaimed "Jesus is Victor!" and used this success to initiate a local revival, repeating the course of spiritual healing, conversions, directing the effervescence of evangelical fervor in the community. When the Spirit of God became manifest as Jesus as Victor, then the Kingdom of God appeared imminent. In *Thy Kingdom Come*, Blumhardt depicted the "invisible battlefield" that Arnold would later adopt in the war of two atmospheres. This battle takes place "primarily in inwardness, in the invisible life-impulses of man."[73]

Blumhardt left the church to open a spiritual retreat at Bad Böll. He characterized the retreat as a zion of God where he served as house father, not parson. Gottlieben, the living embodiment of the New Humanity, victorious over Satanic temptations, reborn in Christ, and laboring in expectation of the imminent advent of God's Kingdom, lived with him until her death in 1872. He wrote, "I believe that, here at Böll . . . we do not want simply to learn the churchly conduct of gatherings and sermons. No, in our daily life we want to learn how to be out meeting the kingdom of God in order, thus, to make our way into the will of God."[74]

Blumhardt's son Christoph would write the systematic theology that had eluded his father, and in doing so he helped preserve Johann's charismatic, prophetic vision. Blumhardt maintained that a community founded upon the religiosity of faith needed to harken to three "trumpet calls." First, each believer needed to be cleansed, purged of sin through self-examination and repentance. Second, seekers must tear themselves away from traditional churches and from a selfish search for individual salvation or pursuit of pleasure of the flesh. He urged that "Jesus is the Victorious King, who also *conquers our flesh*."[75] Through the death of the prideful self and by quieting the sensual gratifications of the natural man, Jesus will live in the hearts of believers. The third trumpet call enjoined all to "carry the love of God in your heart!"[76] Through acts of devotional piety, by the imitation of Christ in childlike surrender, the faithful sought the inward mystical infusion of God's pneuma, the contemplation of God's love irradiating their hearts, the joyful fusion into the unity of the *Gemeinde*. Eberhard Arnold consciously adopted the Innerland devotional piety and the idea of *Gemeinde* from Christoph Blumhardt.

The Routinization of Charisma

The early Sannerz and Rhön communities began as small, loosely organized charismatic bands of disciples united in utter devotion to the person and vision of Eberhard Arnold. Max Weber's ideal type of charismatic authority, drawn from the example of the Apostolic church-communities, defines the charismatic community as a *Gemeinde* founded upon the continuing recognition and validation of the extraordinary spiritual gifts of the founder. Disciples entered into an intense emotional relationship of complete personal devotion to the charismatic leader, forsaking rational, mundane life, careers, and economic activity for the promise of salvation.[77] As Weber understood the charismatic church-community, "It is only in the initial stages and so long as the charismatic leader acts in a way which is completely outside everyday social organization, that it is possible for his followers to live communistically in a community of faith and enthusiasm on gifts . . . or sporadic acquisition."[78]

Weber argued that charismatic communities were short-lived and fragile types of social organization, at first resisting mundane social routines but ultimately succumbing to routinization to achieve security in matters of succession, leadership, administration, recruitment of followers, and economic self-sufficiency. Weber's ideal type of the routinization of charismatic authority is a blueprint for Eberhard Arnold's efforts to place the Bruderhof upon a secure economic and organizational footing, and to ensure the institutionalization of an absolutist ethic of world rejection.

Bruderhof primitivism might have developed in the direction of a voluntaristic congregation governed by democratic consensualism with constitutional and administrative policies and procedures for church and community governance. In that model of the routinization of charisma, legal-rational administration in bureaucratic councils and committees administer the daily life and economic-mundane matters of community living while maintaining a separate and sacralized "visible church" of saints that in unity serves as a vessel for the Holy Spirit. The concept of *adiaphora*, or "things indifferent," to the sacred mission of the *Gemeinde* permits the community to foster a diversity of opinion and debate in secular and mundane matters that are differentiated from the fundamentals of the faith.[79]

Bruderhof primitivism rejected democratic consensualism and the compartmentalization of the spheres of life in favor of the model of a high-demand sect that did not distinguish public activity in the prayer meeting, dining hall, school, or workshop from private activity in the intimacy of the family household, or intrapsychic activity—thoughts and desires. The dynamic of this authoritarian community necessitated the production of unity and submission to authority in these three spheres through the practice of church discipline, community surveillance, and the Pietistic practice of methodical self-examination, repentance, and confession. The Bruderhof collapsed public/private-intrapsychic activities into an obsessive compliance with dogma and ethos mediated by the charismatic leadership to the brethren.

Arnold confronted practical issues: How to realize the call to a community of goods and the Sermon on the Mount yet provide a secure livelihood for the community while resisting the inroads of Mammonism. How to implement a division of labor and administration to accomplish the daily work of living without alienating the brethren by creating status differences that jeopardize the equality of believers called to the life in common. How to systematize dogma, ritual, and the orders and rules of spiritual discipline without succumbing to legalism—the anathema of a "Spirit-led" church-community. Finally, how to ensure the orderly succession of the leadership of the Bruderhof in continuity with the charismatic vision of the founding generation. Arnold hoped to resolve what O'Dea has termed dilemmas of institutionalization: (1) the dilemma of mixed motivation, as factions and a diversity of individual motivations take the place of a single-minded devotion to the charismatic founder; (2) the symbolic dilemma that codifies and objectifies the charismatic teachings, opening up the threat to alienating legalism; (3) the dilemma of an administrative order that can separate leadership from the rank and file; and (4) the dilemma of power: conversion versus coercion.[80]

Eberhard Arnold looked to the Hutterite communities in North America and the teachings of Anabaptism for the solution to all of his spiritual and temporal concerns.[81] By adopting forms of Hutterian colony organization and religious orders, he hoped to ensure the continuing survival and institutionalization of his charismatic community.

The Sannerz Community relocated to the Rhön Bruderhof, near the village of Fulda, settling into a dilapidated farmstead that was secured in 1926 with a down payment of 10,000 marks supplied by a wealthy patron, Prince Waldenburg-Schoenburg. From the beginning, the community faced economic crises: insufficient income from their farming, craft, wood-turning and publishing activities; mounting debts to merchants for food and building supplies; and insufficient cash to pay outside laborers hired to rebuild and expand the community. They suffered from hunger and an inadequate diet. Emmy Arnold describes this first winter. "Meat was very scarce, and the rations of bread, fat, and sugar were inadequate. Our best food item was still the potatoes. . . . We had some very tough beef from old cows, and some sauerkraut which had fermented and of which we could have our fill. But there was no fat in the diet."[82] At times the community would kill a "roof hare" (cat) to supplement their diet.[83]

The Bruderhof staggered under growing debts, struggling to keep creditors at bay, unable to achieve economic self-sufficiency or to secure enough cash to proceed with building and missionary projects. Emmy Arnold speaks of the chronic financial crises of 1928 and 1929. "We had hardly started at the Rhön Bruderhof when the whole property was threatened with being sold at auction by court order. . . . Mr. Schreiner, the sheriff, came nearly every Friday to impound either a piece of furniture, a cow, or a hog. . . . All this had a paralyzing effect on our working strength."[84]

Against this backdrop of continual economic duress, in 1928 Arnold learned of the existence of Hutterite colonies in the western United States and Canada. He began an extensive correspondence with Elias Walter, Servant of the Word of the Stand Off Colony in Alberta, Canada, and other Hutterites including Joseph Kleinsasser, David Wipf, and Jacob Hofer. The personal correspondence and community letters, or *Sendbriefs*, made clear Arnold's intentions: to unite the American and German Bruderhofs; to adopt Hutterian belief, orders, discipline, and styles of dress and appearance; to implement Hutterite structures of hierarchial religious authority; to secure Arnold's ordination as a Servant of the Word; and to receive $30,000 in direct financial assistance for the Arnold community.[85] To advance these interests, Arnold traveled in North America and spent a year visiting hofs in South Dakota and Alberta during 1930–1931.

The Hutterian Brethren began in 1528 as followers of Jacob Hutter. Always a minority religion, Hutterites formed a radical sect in separation from the world, practicing pacifism and a community of goods. They suffered unrelenting persecution in the Swiss-Palentine and throughout Europe. The Hutterites migrated to the Ukraine from 1770 to 1790 in search of religious toleration. When conditions in Russia deteriorated, they made a final move to the northwestern United States and Canada from 1874 to 1877. Today, they resemble an "ethicized tribal group,"[86] dividing into clusters of affiliated colonies: the Lehreleut, the Dariusleut, and the Schmiedleut.[87]

In 1928 Arnold had requested to Walter in his first two letters that several "leading brothers" from America "come to us, to be some years with us, and to take over the main responsibility for the development of our Bruderhof."[88] Without doubting the sincerity of this astonishing request, it underscores the economic desperation of the Rhön Bruderhof. The Hutterites declined to assume financial and religio-administrative responsibility for Rhön. Arnold replied to Walter on November 6, 1928, expressing his disappointment, reaffirming the commonality of their belief, and introducing the theme that would come to characterize his dealings with the Hutterites: the unrelenting appeal for money. Only when the Bruderhof had sufficient funds could they realize their mission to evangelize, to serve as beacon on the hill. In a *Sendbrief* in June 1932 after his trip to North America, Arnold presents his community as a source of revitalizing energy for the Anabaptist communitarian movement that the Hutterites must assist.

> Our Bruderhof is then a church with a mission. In spite of poverty, yes, just in this poverty, eyes, heart, and doors must be wide open in order for her to be an ark for all awakened and zealous people in their deepest need. She must let something of the saving community of God's kingdom shine out above the waves of today's flood. In spite of your own need, you, our dear brothers in America, are without doubt appointed by God to help in this task.[89]

Arnold's letters home and his journal report his single-minded and incessant appeals for funds as he visited the many Hutterite colonies. He tells of the small sums collected and sent to Germany, the more ambitious request for tens of thousands of dollars, and the dissembling Hutterian reply. From his journal of October 8, 1930, in Lethbrige he states:

> At West Raley Bruderhof I spoke repeatedly about the $400 journey expenses (to travel to America). . . . I told here, as everywhere, of our selling meadows and of our scarcity of food and milk. . . . Please never think that I forget the economic task for a moment, or put it on one side. . . . Whenever I can, without hurting our cause, I speak of the $25,000 which I would like to bring home at Christmas. Then they would ask in their Hutterian innocence and with earnest eyes, "so much at once?"[90]
>
> You can scarcely imagine how unspeakably hard it is to build up community life and orderly, efficient, common work without money. We began this community work literally without a penny to our name. We trust God, who has often helped us already through the darkest need, to bring us through this winter. Thanks to the harvest, if we exercise the utmost economy and simplicity, we will not starve. But our debts press heavily upon us, and it is to be feared that some to whom we owe money may deal harshly with us, bringing our community life into danger. We ask you from our hearts to intercede for us, so that through your help it might be possible for us to pay off this winter at least 30,000 marks, that is, about 7,000 dollars. If that could be given through God's grace, our hands would be free to work effectively in spreading the gospel of the church in the German lands and gathering upright men into the common life.[91]

Eberhard Arnold returned to Germany in May 1931 as an ordained Hutterite minister, having joined his community with the Hutterian church and in possession of a modest sum of money. Until his unexpected death in 1935, as the Arnold community experienced ever-worsening finances and Nazi persecution, he pursued this connection with the Hutterites, always in need of protection and financial assistance.

In a talk delivered upon his return to Germany in July 1931, Arnold urged his followers to accept the Hutterian orders. "We are duty-bound to adopt mandatory rules and precepts. Yes, like those of religious orders. That is the only way to survive."[92]

The Arnold community and the Hutterite bruderhofs shared the Anabaptist vision of a community of goods, pacifism, and separatism in a church-community to recreate the Kingdom of Christ in dynamic tension with the carnal kingdom of the world. Hutterite colonies are organized as inclusive church-communites, hierocratic associations in which the exercise of administrative and religious power is concentrated in the hands of church leaders who interpret the Spirit and Word of God.[93] The spiritual and administrative leader of all colonies, the *Vorsteher* or bishop, interprets divine mandate, applying a pneumatical casuistry—an inspirational guidance of the Spirit to discern the meaning of God's mandate with respect to contemporary matters of colony administration, arbitration of disputes, and determining the future direction of the congregation. Individual colonies are led by a Servant of the Word, a combination preacher and chief executive officer, elected by the consensus of all baptized men. A council of five to seven Witness Brothers serves as an administrative council to assist the Servant of the Word. Witness Brothers include the community Steward, or controller, various work department foremen, and elderly spiritual leaders.[94]

Hutterites have thus routinized charisma in the direction of traditionalist hierocracy, patriarchal charisma of the office, and gerontocracy. This traditionalism is legitimated as emanating from the will of God, whose divine order created a hierarchy of patriarchal relations between husband and wife, parent and child, leader and follower. Authority patterns originated with God; leaders served as His instrument providing spiritual and temporal "rulership" over the congregation. God also decreed an organic social order in which men exercised authority over women, and parents over children.[95]

The Bruderhof adopted this Hutterian hierarchy and added their own gradations, differentiating Brotherhood members into classes that include *full baptized members*, who enjoy participation in prayer circles and vote in Brotherhood decisions; *single members*, who do not participate in discussions that touch upon sexual questions; and *non-decision-making Brotherhood members*. Members of this last class, known as *"weak" brothers*, suffer from emotional instability, invalidism, or the infirmities of old age and senility. The Bruderhof shields them from the burdens of participating in controversial decisions.[96]

Hutterite teachings instilled in members a willingness for self-surrender, self-denial, humility, and submissiveness. Each person adopted the inward struggle of Pietist *Busskampf*: remorse, self-abasement, and self-loathing for sin, beseeching God for the saving intercession of Christ's mercy and spirit.[97] John A. Hostetler has written about the relationship of Hutterian "individuals" to the totality of the community and the experience of fusion with divinely ordained structures of hier-archial authority.

> Since "God worketh only in surrendered men," the individual will must be "broken" and fused with the will of the community. Just as the grain of wheat loses its identity in the loaf of bread and the grape is lost in the wine, so also the individual must lose his identity in one corporate body. . . . Only unconditional obedience (*Nachfolge*) and self-renunciation (*Gelassenheit*) permit the gifts of God to take effect in man.[98]

The promises of salvation are inextricably tied to surrender to God's will and the believer's submission to divinely legitimated hierocratic authority. Hutterite traditionalism instills habits of unquestioning obedi-ence to the authority of Witness Brothers and the Servant of the Word. As Weber argues, hierocracies like the Hutterites and the Bruderhof cannot concede freedom of conscience to their members. They adopt the credo "We must obey God rather than men," self-assured that the Servant of the Word and Witness Brothers derive their authority from God. The religious office, not the occupant, holds considerable charis-matic authority. Members nevertheless learn to submit with unquestion-ing obedience and reverence to persons because superiors occupy char-ismatic leadership roles.

Zablocki writes of the Bruderhof's reliance upon the Hutterian Or-ders, the hierocracy of leadership, and a set of escalating sanctions delin-eating degrees of exclusion from the community. In a church-community that would remain free from sin and in fervent conformity to a single belief system, the Orders enjoin the congregation to exclude the offending and sinning brother or sister who would not or could not reform. The Bruderhof acknowledges the importance of Hutterian Or-ders, "Our debt to the Hutterites is beyond measure. They gave us the Orders. Before the Orders we had the Spirit but we always floun-dered."[99]

The exclusion system derives from the Book of Matthew, enjoining brothers, motivated by love, to engage in fraternal correction and ad-monishment of the offending member, seeking repentance, reform, and return to good standing within the community. However, those persons whose ideas, thoughts, or individual conscience endanger doctrinal or-thodoxy; those who would stand in opposition to the leadership and threaten unity; those who cannot or will not repent and reform from sinful thoughts and conduct must be punished. First offenders or mem-bers who commit minor infractions are prohibited from attending the *Gemeindestunde* prayer circle. The small exclusion, or *Kleiner Ausschluss*, allows the offending member to remain in the community but under extreme social ostracism. The Great Exclusion, or *Grosser Ausschluss*, involves expulsion from the community.

The threat of exclusion is a powerful and dreaded method of social control in the Bruderhof. A Brotherhood member's baptismal vow to the community takes precedence over any natural ties of blood and marriage to spouse, children, or kin. Exclusion of a kinsman invariably disrupts families, since those who remain in the community must shun the offending brother or watch helplessly as their loved one is forced to depart the community. The trauma of ostracism, exclusion, family disruption, and shame is shared by family, falling most heavily upon children.

The threat of exclusion into a sinful world stained by Mammonism weighs heavily upon Bruderhof members. Exclusion signifies a personal failure of religious vocation, a public certification of spiritual inadequacy and sin, and banishment from what the Bruderhof consider to be the only possibility for the pursuit of an authentic Christian life. The prospect of traumatic family disruption and the dramatization of spiritual failure exacerbates the emotional suffering imposed by the exclusion system. Paradoxically, the Bruderhof stresses joyful surrender and abiding acosmic love, yet they appropriate social sanctions that impose the most severe penalties of civic-religious "death," mental suffering, and unbrotherly rejection of the unrepentant sinner.

Why did Hutterite traditionalism appeal to the Arnold community? Sannerz and Rhön attracted religious-socialists, young men and women from the Wandervogel and Christian Youth Movement who rejected vestiges of patriarchal authority and family patterns, who joined together as equals in their mission to reconstitute a modern church-community in conformity with the absolutist ethic of the Sermon on the Mount. A hierocracy that removed women from spiritual and administrative authority—a divinely ordained patriarchalism—should have been inimical to those committed to greater spiritual and social equality for women.

The early Sannerz and Rhön communities were organized as charismatic sects—small groups of the religiously qualified, a visible community called to religious vocation in the Lutheran-Pietist tradition. Arnold guided his flock to the "pneumatical ability to experience ecstacies" through the "struggle for penitence" (*Busskampf*) until the experience of breakthrough (*Durchbruch*), or joy.[100] The charismatic congregation adopted a direct democratic administration of the *Gemeinde*, advocating freedom of conscience for individual believers and voluntarism for the self-selected faithful who joined the community and who could choose to leave as a matter of conscience. Zablocki describes the early communities as founded upon spiritual-emotional relations and governed by a democratic centralism.[101] The first crisis and mass defection in Sannerz in 1922 was an expression of this congregational democracy in action, calling into question Arnold's charismatic authority and making him directly accountable to the membership. Why did a charismatic sect with an elective affinity with democratic principles, individual

freedom of conscience, and the equality of believers embrace a patriarchal and authoritarian structure of church polity?

When Arnold reconstituted the Sannerz community after the first
crisis with the New Work Movement, he moved away from congregational democracy and toward a hierocratic sect governed by a single-
belief system that prevented the formation of factions or individual
claims founded upon conscience. Toward this end the Bruderhof devised
the First Law of Sannerz, inspired by "abiding and joyful brotherly love,"
prohibiting gossip and secretive factional dissent. This central normative
code states that

> words of anger and worry about members of the brotherhood are out of
> the question. In Sannerz there must never be talk, either open or hidden,
> against a brother or sister, against individual characteristics—under no
> circumstances behind their back. . . .
>
> The only possible way is direct address as the spontaneous brotherly
> service to the one whose weaknesses cause something in us to react
> negatively. The open word of direct address brings a deepening of friend-
> ship and it is not resented. Only when one does not find the way together
> immediately in this direct manner is it necessary to talk together with a
> third person whom one can trust to lead to a solution and uniting in the
> highest and deepest.[102]

The First Law of Sannerz effectively prevented the formation of
intracommunity divisions and factions that would divide the colony over
matters of theology or leadership. Only single individuals who labored
under troubling differences could come forward to air their grievances.
Individuals were isolated, prevented from forging alliances and thus easily
admonished, stifled, brought back into conformity, or banished through
the exclusion system. In this manner, the Bruderhof transformed Hutterian Orders into a more authoritarian commune exercising complete
control over the lives of committed members.

The First Law of Sannerz, together with the modified Hutterian
Orders and the transcendent appeal to the fusion of individuals into an
organic church–community, justified the formation of authoritarian controls over members in the name of the work of the Holy Spirit, the
experience of collective joy, and bearing witness to the world.[103] Francis
D. Hall, a Quaker and Bruderhof apostate, argues for the inevitability of
an authoritarian attack upon individualism for an intentional community
that hopes to routinize the message of the first generation. Bruderhof
leaders must fight the inroads of pride, sin, and factionalism by a regime
of fear of Satanic or worldly contamination. Those who willingly submit
to the controls of a single-belief system are forced to spend great amounts
of time and energy to attempt to resolve personal differences, bringing
the wayward back to orthodoxy, purifying the tainted, and "breaking
the spirits" of those who deviate from community standards.[104] The

security interests of the *Gemeinde* necessitate continual surveillance and control of thought, experience, and behavior. Hall concludes, drawing upon his knowledge of the Woodcrest community: "The main consequence of all of this is tragedy: the group which had set out to be a witness for a unified love becomes a force of division achieving its unity only by sending away everyone who disagrees with its authoritarian directions, separating itself from all men who are not part of it."[105]

The Undemocratic Fate of Religious Brotherhoods

The routinization of Eberhard Arnold's charismatic vision illustrates a doleful irony common among groups who would restore biblical primitivism. New religious movements arise—new soteriological communities of faith emerge where prophets and their disciples envision a return to the radical equality and emotional communitalization of the Pauline congregation. However, within a generation of the founding, these religious brotherhoods routinize the charisma of the prophet, restoring patriarchal and traditional hierarchies and abandoning democratic ideals. This would be the undemocratic fate of Arnold's vision of the ethic of brotherhood.

Early Bruderhof primitivism emulated the Pauline congregation committed to equality and emotional communitalization while at the same time embracing the contradictory ideal of organic community. The organization of the Apostolic congregation (*Gemeinde*) was radically different from the *Gemeinschaft* of the Bruderhof church-community with its undemocratic requirements of self-annihilation and surrender to the dictates of the United Brotherhood as mediated by the commune's leadership. Arnold wrote *Early Christians After the Death of the Apostles* in 1926 and then *Why We Live in Community* in 1927 without any notice that the first essay extolled the antipatriarchal brotherhoods of the Pauline *ekklesia* , while the second advocated the restoration of the patriarchal inequality of the *Gemeinschaft* organic community.

In an atmosphere of recurring crisis, material deprivation, and alternating exhilaration and exhaustion, Arnold attempted to mix antithetical ideas into his wildly eclectic vision. Writing in April, he recalls this time of crisis, 1926, fraught with danger both from without and from the demonic within his commune. "In the winter of 1922 we faced two difficult challenges: economically, our existence hung by a thread and this struggle exhausted us and left its mark on all aspects of our work. The second and more difficult challenge was the spiritual struggle. We were fighting the dark demonic forces of mammon which had penetrated into our midst and afflicted our life that winter."[106]

Arnold routinized his personal charisma into the office charisma of a bureaucratic hierarchy, transforming the prophetic personalism of his leadership of the commune into a hierarchically structured world-rejecting sect that in many ways resembled a monastic "association of convictions" of the Rule of Benedict.[107] He never acknowledged the contradiction between the egalitarian emotional communitalization of the Apostolic congregation and the patriarchal and hierocratic religious order and brotherhood of the *Gemeinde*.

From a variety of sources—the political romanticism of Toennies's *Gemeinschaft*, the image of the new congregational forms of the Pauline church, the inner-worldly mysticism and retreat of the Blumhardts at Bad Böll—Eberhard Arnold crafted his utopian vision of church-community. Here, through the mystery of faith and the operation of the Holy Spirit, individual differences would gently merge into loving unity; individual "I's" would fuse into the organic harmony of the "We." Arnold characterized the *Gemeinde* as the experimental implementation of the ethical mandate of authentic Christianity. "No one is in opposition to another here and no one is condemned. No one is coerced here; and no one is despised; no one is violated. And yet love rules as truth. . . ."[108]

The concept of *Gemeinde* is one of the most important culturally supported "illusions" in Judeo-Christian thought. The organic community founded upon a single-belief system, total unity, and fusion into the collective implies the existence of an illusory pre-established harmony of interests, cosmic philharmonism, unanimism, or undivided oneness. Of the utopian communities like the Bruderhof, Benjamin Nelson says:

> these attempts have repeatedly run into difficulties either because they have assumed the absolute necessity of single systems of belief or utter unity in organization of motivations. I know of no modern or recent experiment in community, however elevated its articles of faith, which does not have totalitarian features or propensities. . . . It makes no difference whether these schemes of total integration take the form of a vision of cosmic brotherhood, a totalitarian race-nation-state, or consecrated sectarian brotherhood within the pores or on the frontiers of a hateful civilization.[109]

Nelson identifies Primavera, the Paraguayan Bruderhof then affiliated with the Hutterite movement, as a recent experiment in community with troubling features. He writes:

> Anyone who wishes to discover for himself how difficult it is to reconcile individuality with social order, stability and progress, tradition and innovation . . . has only to read recent writings by sympathetic participants and reporters concerning the Hutterites in the Dakotas, Montana, Canada, and Paraguay, and the experiment now being conducted by the high-minded American veterans in Macedonia, Georgia.[110]

The Bruderhof's mission to establish a *Gemeinde*, a charismatic and pneumatic congregation separate from the world in expectation of God's

Kingdom, is founded upon, in Nelson's estimation, utopian illusions. Three important sociological consequences often follow. We might call them "utopian disillusionments."

First, the demand for total unity and total religious commitment tends to devolve into a moral absolutism. If the operation of the Spirit does not foster spontaneous and loving unanimity of thought and practice, then coercive methods enforce unity and abridge freedom of conscience. The routinization of charisma in this community founded upon an ethic of conviction and brotherliness has unbrotherly results. Personal, doctrinal, and policy disputes lead to draconian measures of social control in the cause of harmony and unity. Individual and collective exclusions, defections, and apostasy are the result of a community obsessed with total unanimity.

Second, the faith structure of consciousness demands periodic acts of individual and collective purgation, "clearings and clearances" of brothers and sisters who confess their sins. Only after community-wide purgations can they partake of the sacrament of Holy Communion or join together in unity at Easter free from any blemish of sinfulness. Rituals of purgation, confession, and clearance can lead to obsessions with purity. Normative codes of thought and conduct become ossified and repressive, especially in matters relating to sexuality and the protection of childhood innocence.

Third, the emotional communitalization and irrationalism of the Bruderhof *Gemeinde* produce feelings of joyous fusion, childlike elated expectation, and a sense of wonder, awe, and marvel. Brothers and sisters are blanketed in the warmth of God's love, ravished by the Spirit, transported by the inner-worldly mysticism of their faith. However, those who pursue joyous transcendence of self also encounter the other side of joy in a variety of culture-bound syndromes. A religiously grounded personality founded upon the principle of inner pilgrimage away from sin toward the fulfillment of divine mandate, and ceaseless warfare against the residues of sin and pride, frequently succumbs to spiritual discouragement—religious melancholy. A community forged as a vessel to capture the Holy Spirit and admonished to expect and repel attack by Satan and demonic forces from without and from within will periodically bring forth cases of demonic possession.

Eberhard Arnold's experimental community of those called by an ethic of conviction to Innerland piety suffered these inevitable utopian disillusionments. Those who answered the ethical mandate of living a life in common, in response to Arnold's challenge of "why we live in community," discovered that the quest for an authentic Christian experience was a difficult pilgrimage, riddled with contradiction and struggle. A panoply of benefits and consequences marked their lives—the joyful *Gemeinde* and the other side of joy.

Religious brotherhoods like the Bruderhof can emerge to provide new forms of spiritual life and new democratic forms of association at the boundaries of church hierarchy or patrimonial (feudal) authority, or rationalized bureaucratic authority of the modern state. These experiments in religious brotherhood and democratic association can also return to undemocratic polities. Lay confraternities in late Medieval and Renaissance Italian and French cities provide examples of the undemocratic fate of religious brotherhoods. The emergence of these urban, oath-bound associations in Perugia in 1260 corresponded to recurring crises of European society, marked by times of plague, chiliastic predictions of the end of history, and battles between Guelf and Ghibelline groups in Italy following the war between Frederick II and the papacy.[111] *Laudesi* confraternities were devoted to the exaltation of divinity, of Mary, and of city patron saints, who would intercede with God in the remission of sin. *Disciplinati* associations emphasized human degradation, penitence, and the imitation of Christ's humility and suffering by means of austerities of the body, such as flagellation. Particularly within the Lombard cities, confraternities functioned as democratic ritual brotherhoods operating in parallel with the urban communes.[112] Ronald F. E. Weismann says:

> in organizational structure the typical late medieval Florentine confraternity was a miniature commune. The city's religious brotherhoods employed, in essentials, the methods of election and governance of the commune of Florence, including extensive rotation of offices, and temporary disqualification of individuals in order to diminish the possibility of monopolization of office by cliques.[113]

Confraternities promoted an enhanced devotional life of piety, meditation, and the contemplation and imitation of Christ for the laity, serving as alternatives to the local parish or monastic orders.[114] In addition to observing the communal and calendrical rituals of the Catholic Church, and a rich ceremonial life of feasts, processions, and festivals, confraternities offered care for the dying, burial rituals, private devotions or "mental confessions" of sins with God, and intensified penitential acts of individual and collective flagellation.

Weissman argues that within Florence in the republican period (1250–1449), ritual brotherhoods permitted men to transcend the social fragmentation and particularisms of social class and status groups bound to the geography of neighborhood and parish social networks. Every week, within confraternal ritual process, members suspended mundane social relations and forged true brotherhood, "social pacification," without the normal agonistic social relations of duplicity, and dramatizations of honor and shame. Under the illuminated image of Saint Anthony, the patron and symbol of unity, brothers experienced individual and collective penance.

> Leather whips were then distributed, and after the governor exhorted the *fratelli* to practice a true penance, a penance of lamentation and tears, the

remaining light of the chamber was put out. The members, now cut off totally from the social structure . . . offered silent prayers. Flagellation began, accompanied by a responsive liturgy of humiliation and debasement, focused on the Passion of Christ, death, and the evil and brevity of earthly life, drawn from the penitential psalms. Having temporarily dissociated themselves from the social structure, the members, at that moment, were able to see themselves as part of larger, all-inclusive communities and offered prayers on behalf of such communities: the church, Christianity, dead souls. The members washed their wounds. Having scourged, humiliated, and debased themselves, the brothers now underwent the symbolic death of sleep.[115]

Confraternities established chapels, elected officials, enacted their own statutes of membership, internal order, and fraternal discipline, and appointed their own priests and functionaries. They performed acts of private and public charity, founding hospitals and caring for the poor. However, in Bologna and in other cities the ideal of autonomous and democratic lay brotherhoods was transformed in the fifteenth century into oligarchic and authoritarian rule by patricians who directed the rationalization and bureaucratization of charitable institutions.[116]

Andrew E. Barnes notes that lay confraternities in Marseille in the early modern period came to rely upon bequests, endowments, and income from aristocratic groups who usurped control of the governing councils and ended the coalition of cliques of these formerly democratic brotherhoods.[117] With the restoration of the Medici in Florence in 1530, confraternities became elite assemblies controlled by the Duke of Tuscany celebrating particularistic ritual brotherhoods of specific social class alliances and aristocratic culture.[118] It appears that democratic brotherhoods did not survive in the early modern period. These lay confraternities, like the early Sannerz Community, demonstrate that new forms of democratic associational and community participation are fragile and can easily revert to traditional, patrimonial structures of authority.

The search for the New Jerusalem by Jean de Labadie (1610–1674) offers an example of authoritarian Pietist and primitivist community that predates the Bruderhof. Labadie began his education at the age of seven at the Jesuit Collège de la Madeleine in Bordeaux. By 1622, he had completed his basic education and received the tonsure. He joined the Society of Jesus in December 1623. As a young priest and emerging theologian, Labadie was attracted to the Jesuits' renewed emphasis upon the traditions of Apostolic and contemplative spirituality of their founder, Ignatius Loyola. Labadie also immersed himself in the works of the mystics Saint Theresa and Saint Catherine of Sienna and longed for devotion to Jesus and mystical union.[119] He left the Jesuits in 1639, abjured Catholicism in 1651, and embraced Calvinism. Throughout his life, his writings and preachings inspired religious controversy. T. J. Saxby explains that Labadie's "intractability and his unshakable faith in visions and inner promptings as valid forms of guidance allied with a sense of vocation so strong that, in the last resort, it overrode submission and denominational affiliation."[120]

Labadie's charismatic visions and writings called for the creation of a primitivist New Jerusalem, restoration of the Apostolic Church, separate from the world, where regenerate men and women could surrender in discipleship and promote the glorification of God. In 1669, in *Manual de Piété*, he demands the death of the criminal, worldly, sinful self. Through mortifying the flesh, repentance, and the practice of piety, a new self might emerge, purified of concupiscence and engulfed in the rapture of God's love. "We lose ourselves in thy vastness; we plunge into thy depths; we are dazzled by thy light and are blinded by thy infinite brightness. We are absorbed into thy ocean!"[121]

From the 1660s Labadie gathered a small group of disciples, forming primitivist communities in Utrecht, Amsterdam, Herford, and Altona. Pierre Yvon succeeded Labadie after his death in 1674 and rationalized his dogma into a primitivist and Pietist New Jerusalem at Wieuwerd in Friesland. Here, three hundred fifty men and women of diverse nationalities and social classes joined together in a community of goods in radical separation from the world. Two hundred men worked in cottage industries: textiles, printing, a metal foundry, tannery, bakery, brewery, corn mill, apothecary, a medical laboratory that manufactured fever remedies, and gardens and a farm.

The ascetic discipline of work allowed the community to achieve self-sufficiency and promoted the mortification of the flesh and the transcendence of self-love. For men and women alike, the imposition of arduous menial labor and frequent job rotation prevented the mastery of any one craft and thus helped eradicate any vestiges of worldly pride. Community leaders imposed disciplines and mortifications as a test of spiritual growth, and meted out harsh punishments (reduced rations and public confession) for sinful conduct and worldliness.[122] As Natalie Zemon Davis writes, "In this spiritual economy of love and punishment, some members felt remade and joyous—'How good to be among the children of God'—while others began to resent the mortification."[123]

The community came to be divided into two distinct classes: (1) elect brothers and sisters who were baptized members with detachment from pride and world, and (2) "*corps mystique*," or novices who were progressing toward rebirth and away from self-love and self-interest. Yvon required complete community unity, guided by the Holy Spirit, as mediated by the elect leadership.[124] Labadie and his core group of disciplines formed a special cadre of the elect, the "holy family," or elders, of the community. All were called to adopt a humble, childlike spirit and to live in purity in all things. The holy family administered church discipline and supervised the witness to the fivefold denial of discipleship (denial of self, of Satan, of the world, of attachment to the earth, of flesh and blood not of Christ).[125] As in the Bruderhof, discipleship to Jesus and commitment to community took precedence over attachments to kin, marriage vows, or the intimacy of the family.

Saxby explains the more coercive aspects of the discipline of children in the New Jerusalem.

> Children were seen as the fruit, and therefore the responsibility, of the whole community, and parents were forbidden to be possessive and even overtly affectionate. Adults were called Uncle and Aunt, and each child received a personal tutor or governess, who was responsible for its education in community ways and good manners. . . . The constant attempts to "bring out the sheep" in the children and to "deny the wolf" by restraint and regular corporal punishment meant that they lived in constant **fear**. They could be given a good thrashing by tutor or parent, and were expected to thank God for having blessed them with parents and others who loved them enough to save them from the world.[126]

Yvon's rationalization of Labadie's primitivism and Pietism constituted an authoritarian, hierarchal community of goods devoted to the absolute unity in the Spirit. The Labadists institutionalized an authoritarian primordium with striking similarities with the Bruderhof. Both the Bruderhof and the Labadie Pietist primordia required the mortification and death of the worldly self and the rebirth of the New Man. Both prescribed multiple denials of self through discipleship to ensure godly living in purity as structured by the pervasive system of church disciplines and austerities. Both employed evangelical nurture by imposition of strict, authoritarian child-rearing to forge a religiously grounded self weaned from worldliness and pride. Like the Bruderhof, the Labadists aggressively proselytized their movement and established overseas colonies in Providence Plantation, Surinam (1683–1719) and in Bohemia Manor, Maryland (1697–1722).

The Labadists, like the Bruderhof, produced career apostates who openly criticized the coercion of these primitivistic communities, most notably Petrus Dittlebach. Dittlebach and his wife and children spent five years in Wieuwerd from 1685 to 1690. He published a diatribe against the community, charging the holy family with abuse of power and bringing to light many domestic scandals. He accused the Labadists of abusive child discipline and "high-handed authority, unequal distribution of benefits, financial mismanagement and a stubborn refusal to be guided by anyone with greater knowledge than they."[127] The success of Dittlebach's book precipitated a community crisis that ultimately resulted in the end of the common purse and the demise of Yvon's primordium.

The Labadists had financial difficulty supporting the mother colony in Friesland and the colonies in Surinam and Maryland. Yvon depended upon the income and support of a surgeon and obstetrician, Hendrik van Deventer, who contributed an estimated 10,000 guilders to the community. When he withdrew his support, the common fund faced bankruptcy. This resulted in the liquidation of Friesland assets, the flight of three hundred of the elect, and the formation of a congregational church polity of fewer than fifty members who lived separately in private households.

Eberhard Arnold knew about Labadie's and Yvon's writings and their short-lived experiment in New Jerusalem and self-consciously emulated this seventeenth-century primordium.[128] The Labadie community illustrates, like the Bruderhof, how the charismatic teachings of a founder who hungered for the expression of his individual freedom of conscience and for the restoration of the authentic Apostolic Church can be rationalized into moral absolutism and the authoritarian suppression of religious individualism. These examples show that primitivism and Pietism have an elective affinity for high-demand church-community and illustrates the undemocratic fate of religious brotherhoods.

Three

THE REVITALIZATION OF
BRUDERHOF PIETY

Eberhard Arnold routinized his charismatic community by seeking financial assistance in 1931 from the Hutterian churches and by adopting their traditional, patriarchal, and hierocratic doctrine and community organization. The Bruderhof became an authoritarian sect and thus achieved the doctrinal and organizational stability necessary to survive the episodic crises and deracinations of the 1930s and World War II.

Table 3.1, Bruderhof Communities, 1920–1997, lists the communal settlements from the founder's era, 1920–1937, through the relocation during World War II and the sojourn in South America. Included are the European and American hofs that characterized the revitalization of the Bruderhof under the leadership of Heini Arnold during the Great Crisis, and the contemporary expansionism guided by Johann Christoph Arnold.

When National Socialism came into power in Germany in 1933, the Bruderhof resisted, refusing to surrender draft-age men for compulsory military service, denying the right of Nazi schoolteachers to educate their children, and flaunting their allegiance to the Kingdom of God through conscientious rejection of Hitler's salvation state. Hans Meier describes how Arnold deliberately called attention to himself, inviting Nazi repression and reprisals. Persecution would fulfill Arnold's millennarian and apocalyptic prophecies, reaffirming the community as a vessel for the Holy Spirit and as a beacon pointing toward the Kingdom of God. Meier explains:

> in many letters to the government and even personally to Hitler, Eberhard expressed the united determination of the Brotherhood to stand for and represent only the Gospel and the discipleship of Jesus Christ. . . . Eberhard warned all the members of the Bruderhof either to be ready for persecution or else to leave. A few guests and novices left the Bruderhof, and the rest of the members united in faith for the task of giving a living witness for God's Kingdom in contrast to all the kingdoms of this world.[1]

Table 3.1
Bruderhof Communities 1920–1997

Hof	Country	Dates	Theme
Sannerz	Germany	1920–1926	
Rhön	Germany	1927–1937	Founder's Era
Alm	Liechtenstein	1934–1937	
Cotswold	England	1937–1941	War Resettlement
Primavera	Paraguay	1941–1961	
Sinnthal	Germany	1956–1961	International
Wheathill	England	1942–1961	Socialism
El Arado	Uruguay	1952–1960	
Woodcrest	United States	1954–Present	
Forest River	United States	1956–1957	
Bulstrode	England	1958–1966	Pietist Revival—
Deer Spring	United States	1958–1997	Great Crisis
Macedonia	United States	1958– Merger	
New Meadow Run	United States	1958–Present	
Darvel	England	1971–Present	
Pleasant View	United States	1985–Present	
Spring Valley	United States	1990–Present	Contemporary
Michelshof	Germany	1989–1995	Expansionism
Catskill	United States	1990–Present	
Palm Grove	Nigeria	1992–1994	
Beech Grove	England	1995–Present	

The Bruderhof sent their children to study in Switzerland and formed the Alm Bruderhof in Liechtenstein in 1934 as a haven from Nazi persecution. Meanwhile, in Germany the Third Reich prohibited visits to the community by guests, forbade the sale of books and handicrafts, increased taxes, and in November 1933 sent 150 armed troops to the Rhön community, searching for weapons and incriminating documents.[2]

Eberhard Arnold died suddenly and unexpectedly in 1935 from complications following surgery to repair a broken leg. The loss of the founder compounded the atmosphere of crisis. Finally, the Gestapo closed the German Bruderhof on April 14, 1937, seizing the land and property under the pretext of criminal fraud and bankruptcy. Several Witness Brothers were jailed for three months and narrowly escaped removal to a concentration camp. The presence and witness of two visiting North American Hutterian elders, David Hofer and Michael Waldner, probably deterred the Gestapo from sending the members to extermination camps and permitted the community to flee en masse to

England, where they had secured a farm in Ashton Keynes, Wiltshire, as the site for the Cotswold Bruderhof.

This English community grew to 300 members, mainly consolidated from the German, Swiss, and Liechtenstein dispersal. They added a second farm in 1938, revived their publishing work, producing a quarterly magazine, the *Plough*, and aggressively recruiting converts from among European refugees, Quakers, and pacifists.[3]

The Bruderhof published an English edition of Eberhard Arnold's 1927 tract, *The Individual and World Need*, to promote their religious mission. In this essay, Arnold decries egoistic individualism and the secular pursuit of happiness: "The overall misery of this world today is inextricably connected with the feeling of guilt in each individual for his own dividedness. The deadly weakness of sin as separation consumes the vital energy of love. The curse of half-heartedness and disunity stands in the way of decision and fulfillment. World suffering in public life is consonant with the sum of personal guilt."[4] Arnold proclaimed that an Innerland piety of selfless surrender to the church-community would answer the individual need for salvation and escape from the impending cataclysm of a world gone mad in totalitarianism, militarism, economic collapse and war. In the first years after Arnold's death, the movement cleaved to his doctrine, while refusing to accept the hereditary succession of his sons into leadership positions.

The entry of Britain into the war in September 1939, brought the Bruderhof sojourn in the Cotswolds to an end. The British government wanted to register and sequester German nationals as "enemy aliens."[5] To avoid this division, in 1940 the Brotherhood sent Hans Meier and Guy Johnson to New York with the hope of securing permission to emigrate to Hutterite colonies in Canada or to arrange immigration to the United States under the sponsorship of the Mennonite Central Committee (MCC). Instead, the MCC provided assistance in arranging the immigration to Paraguay, a country ever eager for European settlers and investment.[6]

In 1941 the community made the transatlantic passage, avoiding the hazards of German submarine wolf packs. The immigrants purchased a 20,000-acre cattle ranch in East Paraguay, north of Asunción. Primavera grew to include three villages: Isla Margarita, Loma Hoby (1942), and Ibaté (1946). The El Arado community was established in Uruguay in 1952. Durnbaugh characterizes this time of expansionism as one of outreach, social mission, and dynamic growth.

By 1953 the three colonies harbored 700 inhabitants. From the first the community gave medical assistance to their Indian neighbors, using its three physicians and other trained personnel. By 1954 a 29-bed clinic was treating over 10,000 patients per year. The service committees of the three Historic Peace Churches—Friends, Mennonites, Brethren—raised funds for this project. . . . Extensions of the Primavera settlement were established elsewhere: a center in Asunción for government liaison and student housing and a similar urban center in Montevideo, Uruguay.[7]

The Mennonite historian Joseph Winfield Fretz studied Primavera in 1950 and was struck by their rapid growth, which he attributed to large families that averaged 4.7 children per household.[8] Fretz reports that the Bruderhof were not financially self-sufficient but survived on the charity of friends and contributions from the service committees of the Church of the Brethren, the Society of Friends, and the Mennonites. He writes that unlike the ethnic and national homogeneity of North American Hutterites, the Arnold communities are extremely heterogeneous.

> Eighteen different nationalities and ninety family names are found among the Hutterites in Primavera. About half of the members are English, a portion are German, and the rest are made up of a sprinkling of Swiss, Austrian, Dutch, Scandinavians, and others. Furthermore, the population is predominately made up of younger people; practically all married couples are under fifty years of age, most of them between the ages of twenty-five and forty. Children constitute a high portion of the total population and there are comparatively few old people. The diversity of backgrounds has provided new blood and invigorating spiritual and intellectual stimulation in the brotherhood.[9]

A small group of English Bruderhof who had remained behind to settle financial matters formed the nucleus for a new English hof in 1943, Wheathill, on a farm in Lower Bromdon, Shropshire. In the 1950s, they added a second community, Bulstrode, near London, and a German hof, Sinnthal.

The authorized history of the community—the official collective memory—characterizes the period between the close of the Rhön community in 1937 and the opening of the first American hof, Woodcrest, in Rifton, New York, in 1954 as a time of sojourning in a spiritual wilderness, a period of declension from the authentic vision of the founder. I term the doctrinal innovations of the 1940s the "Spirit of Primavera." This refers to an abiding concern for humanitarian outreach, international activism, and a pacifist community of goods based upon Christian tenets. The "Spirit of Primavera" has been condemned by the Brotherhood in their revisionistic history, *Torches Rekindled*, as representing an inauthentic "atmosphere" of worldliness that crept into the community. By this account secular humanism and the ideal of brotherhood could never serve as the authentic basis for a community that aspired to build the Kingdom of God. The "Woodcrest Spirit" of the American hof rejected outreach and social activism and demanded the restoration of the fervent inner-worldly mysticism and evangelical Pietism of Arnold's Innerland piety.

Fretz describes this tenor of Rifton community life in 1954 as a "spiritual radiance and missionary concern."

> Members of the Brotherhood are concerned with a prophetic Christian Gospel. Practical religion is strongly emphasized. The writer was told that most members joined the Brotherhood not to find personal salvation, but to join in the struggle for righteousness in the kingdom of God. Each man is encouraged to yield himself to God's direction as manifested through the Holy Spirit. One senses a strong element of Christian mysticism in colony individual and collective life.[10]

Under the charismatic leadership of Heini Arnold, the Bruderhof experienced a shattering revitalization of Pietist dogma, a recentering of the movement to the United States. The Bruderhof communities of Primavera, El Arado, Sinnthal, and Wheathill were closed and more than six hundred baptized members were expelled or resigned. This reorganization of the commune has been termed the Great Crisis of 1959–1961.

The Bruderhof movement was turning inward, to become an introversionist sect. Introversionists manifest absolute withdrawal and separatism from the world, defining their religious community as the sole avenue for individual and collective salvation and the repository for the Holy Spirit. The church-community becomes the basis for total allegiance and participation of true believers who are enjoined to purge themselves of sin and maintain a purified fellowship.[11]

Beyond this inward turning, the Woodcrest Spirit also needs to be understood as a variety of Fundamentalism; a world-rejecting, charismatic, utopian renunciation of modernity informed by an apocalyptic vision of approaching crises in world history.[12] Eberhard Arnold's tract, *The Individual and World Need*, informed the Woodcrest Spirit's vision of the institutional and individual moral decay of modern secular egoism as evident in the growth of substance abuse, sexual deviation and excess, Mammonism, and concupiscence. As Martin Riesebrodt explains in *Pious Passion*, this religious rejection of the world emerged in the American Fundamentalist Movement in the first quarter of the twentieth century and revived during the Fourth Great Awakening in America in the decades following World War II. Like the European "culture of despair"[13] in the interwar period, America in the 1950s experienced cultural malaise over the emergence of suburbia, mass culture, consumerism, and the amoral conformity of the "organization man" in the burgeoning white-collar service economy.[14] The Bruderhof seemed to provide an answer to this postwar culture of despair. Strong family and community social structures and a strong church and authoritative moralism offered an antidote to excessive individualism and the alienation of mass society. Bruderhof doctrine also attracted many American converts in the 1950s because of its affinity with American salvation history—the idea of America as a chosen nation and people elected to convert the masses, to struggle against individual and collective evil, to vanquish Satan, and to help bring about the millennial Kingdom of God.[15]

The revitalization of an introversionist and Fundamentalist theology and the full institutionalization of the Bruderhof primordium as an authoritarian and introversionist sect would have profound consequences that would prove deleterious to the psychological well-being of apostates and true believers alike.

Arnoldism

From his youth, Heini Arnold[16] was drawn to the Protestant mysticism of the Blumhardts, and the Pietism of his father's *Innerland*. In the fall of 1941, as a young adult and Servant in Primavera, he attempted, without success, to implement his vision of enthusiastic fervor—inner-worldly mysticism, collective purgation of sin, and Pietistic devotionalism.

The early Primavera community labored under frontier conditions with members struggling to build housing and facilities, secure water, plumbing, and electricity, and provide adequate food and medical care. Heini's call to renewed fervor occurred in the context of a heroic struggle to provide basic material needs and an economic foundation for this community of three hundred and fifty European refugees. They endured tropical diseases, eye infections, malnutrition, and the death of five children in the first year of settlement. Heini himself contracted a life-threatening kidney infection. From August until October he languished, fevered, emaciated, and confined to bed. When his physicians warned him that he had only six hours to live, he assembled the *gemeindestunde* in a death-bed vigil, calling for collective purgation and repentance.

Someone recorded what was feared to be his final words. Heini spoke words of admonishment to the community. Merrill Mow reprinted these instructions to the Bruderhof as part of the official history of Heini's mortal crisis and the call to redouble their love to Christ, their efforts to build God's Kingdom and the true church of the ingathered faithful. He pleaded: "What I have to say to you is this: the fight against Satan comes first. It comes every time Christ enters into our midst. Then comes repentance, and then the future kingdom."[17]

Roger Allain was also present at this scene and offers a divergent account in his remembrance, *The Community That Failed*. He writes that Heini

> thanked the commune for their love and prayers, and then added that his heart was deeply troubled. He had prayed that this hour might be spared him, but he could no longer remain silent. God had bade him speak. The attacks of illness and death against the Church has weighed heavily on his

heart. They could not be explained away in medical terms but must be seen for what they were—the fruits of evil. If God no longer heard our prayers, it must be because Evil had gained a hold on us, and we must seek repentance. Had we not been concerned with the practical work, our lack of money and food, our fears, instead of being concerned first for God's Kingdom? . . . Then despondency and evil had run through the veins of the commune like a subtle poison. Had it really been eliminated in every single heart? We must seek repentance and not come to common prayer until each one of us hearkened to the voice of God, examined himself and confessed whatever was not of God in his heart.[18]

Heini understood the Bruderhof's travail in Paraguay as the special providence of God who would chastise His chosen people, warning them to return to the path of righteousness. Speaking as a prophet of doom, he hoped to lead the community toward a Pietistic revitalization.

Both Mow and Allain identify in this community crisis the key elements of Arnoldism: the belief in the ever-present danger of satanic attack from without and of sin and impurity from within; the crisis-call to interpret adversity as the special providence of God visited upon the community as chastisement for individual sin and collective declension into Mammonism; and the obligation for all believers to renew and deepen their faith and reappropriate a Christocentric religious enthusiasm through repentance, confession, and purgation. Allain recounts the exhausting time of collective crisis and renewal that followed Heini's "death-bed" exhortations. He writes that Heini

stood before us night after night like John the Baptist, his full black beard fluttering in the breeze, his eyes shinning with fever, his voice drawing strength from castigating our weaknesses. Night after night we sat on hard wooden benches, listening to the sermons of Blumhardt, Andy's [Allain's pseudonym for Heinrich Arnold] favorite author, on driving out of demons, of fiery challenges and self-flagellations, and yearning for the end of the meeting and the whole clearance.[19]

It became apparent to the Brotherhood that Heini's mental condition had deteriorated. Mow argues that the community dispensary did not have the proper medications and Heini was given a drug that produced serious side effects, including hallucinations. Elizabeth Bohlken-Zumpe, daughter of Hans Zumpe, writes in her memoir, *Torches Extinguished*, that Heini had become dehydrated, feverish, and racked with pain. "When Heini's sickness reached a critical point, the doctors gave him morphine injections for his pain. Brothers went to Friesland [Mennonite colony] to buy beer especially for Heini. . . . The medical staff had agreed to give him as much drink as he could tolerate. They wanted to stimulate his will to take fluids."[20]

Bohlken-Zumpe also recalls that "much later he confessed that he kept on asking for morphine injections although he was no longer in pain. His call for repentance no longer was a message from God, but more and more just Heini circling around himself."[21]

Whatever the cause of this mental alienation, he could not continue as Servant, and by late fall Hans Zumpe was confirmed as Servant of the Word. Heini was relieved of his service and hospitalized in Asunción for an extended medical leave.

Upon his return in 1942, Heini discovered that Zumpe was advocating a continued moratorium on his leadership, arguing that "Heini should have a rest from all spiritual work because he was not recovered and had lost so much weight."[22] In fact, Heini did not resume a leadership position as Servant of the Word for ten years, until his reconfirmation on September 26, 1951.[23]

During this decade-long hiatus, Heini made two unsuccessful efforts to take over the community's leadership, precipitating two community-wide crises. In 1942 he was posted at the second Paraguayan community, Loma Hoby, where he worked as a geography teacher and conducted a Bible study *Sonnentrup* club for adolescents in baptism preparation. The Servants and Witness Brothers at Loma Hoby eagerly embraced Arnold-ism, calling for repentance and a return to Christocentric piety. The Isla Margarita Servants, lead by Hans Zumpe, rejected this appeal and admonished Heini and his brothers Hardy and Hans-Herman Arnold, punishing them with the small, or internal, exclusion. As Bohlken-Zumpe remembers, the wider Bruderhof felt a spiritual arrogance coming from the Loma group. The wider community "had been through so much hardship, burying some twenty children. They felt " 'Let's get on with the work ahead and not lose ourselves in constant soul-searching!' " The school and the hospital had to be finished, the housing was still poor, wells had to be dug for drinking water. Many brothers and sisters were grieving for the loss of their babies."[24]

Heini waited two years before making his next bid for power. In 1944 he joined a cabal of sixteen brothers who secretly conspired to assume control, writing to the American Hutterites with accusations of the Bruderhof's spiritual declension and asking for their assistance. The Brotherhood was stunned when this intrigue came to light. Allain relates that

> a joint Brotherhood meeting was suddenly called and a report given about a plot hatched to overthrow the leaders. . . . The accused acknowledged the main facts and recognized their responsibility. Short work was made of them. They were condemned to the Great Exclusion, away from the commune, while their respective wives and a few brothers who had been approached but not dared to join were condemned to the Small Exclusion for having failed to report the plot. Well do I remember the ominous atmosphere of the meeting in which the wicked were excommunicated in the harsh words of the Hutterian formula, consigned to Satan for the destruction of their flesh in order that their spirit might be saved on the Day of the Lord. True, they were challenged to seek repentance and

the way back to the fold, but it was made clear that is would be a long, arduous road.[25]

Heini was sent away for a two-year exclusion during which he worked as a farm manager on a leper colony in southern Paraguay. As the official Bruderhof history relates, Heini sojourned in the wilderness, isolated from family, consumed with anguish and inner torment. The authorized history explains that this time of humiliation and banishment reaffirmed Heini's faith and brought him closer to the Kingdom of God. But as a condition for his return to the community, he had to disavow mystical enthusiasm and emotional Pietism. "He was told that he had to give up his ideas or not return. He was told that his love to Jesus had no place in our community life."[26] Heini would dissemble adherence to the community consensus and bide his time.

What was this community consensus that Heini found so abhorrent, so redolent of sin—the essence of the "atmosphere" of this world and the antithesis of an atmosphere centered upon love to Jesus? Community life was now founded upon "the social ideal of brotherly community,"[27] an ultimate commitment to pacifism and social justice. This humanistic call for peace and universal brotherhood, which devalued the evangelical Pietism of Eberhard Arnold's theology, stood in diametrical opposition to the theocentric vision of Arnoldism. When the Hutterite church sent emissaries to Primavera in 1953, they decried the Bruderhof apostasy and formally dissolved their fellowship with the Arnold communities. Seeing this as mounting evidence of the betrayal of the founder's vision, Heini added restoration of Hutterite unity to his personal goals.

Mow relates that "a bureaucratic approach to community life had gained control, a humanistic approach not centered on God but on the brotherhood, not on the united church but on the 'will of the people,' and not on the leadership of Jesus but on that of Hans Zumpe."[28] The community spirit was marked by an internationalist, pacifist, and brotherhood witness. They actively proselytized the Primavera ideal of Christian community and waged an unsuccessful effort to convince the German government to resettle war orphans. Primavera did sponsor over two hundred displaced persons but failed to recruit any from the group to convert and join their Christian community.

The Bruderhof had greater successes with their appeals to American Protestants, attracting many guests and seekers. Bob and Shirley Wagoner visited Paraguay in 1953 and kept a journal of their experience of the Primavera community spirit. They left Chicago, where Bob had completed his first year at Bethany Theological Seminary, and began a two month overland journey to Primavera. What they sought in this adventure, and what they were predisposed to find, shapes the tenor of the first chapters of their work, *Community in Paraguay*. Bob was searching for an alternative to the declension from Anabaptist tradition in the Church of the Brethren—the apparent concern with getting children into membership rather than focusing upon adult conversion, the absence of close-knit fellowship, brotherly admonition, and conscientious objection to war.

Bob explains, "While it seemed like the New Testament message required some kind of 'communism of love' among believers, to use Ernst Troeltsch's term, I did not see how it was possible. I was on the verge of accepting human divisiveness as normative and believing that an individual could only do his solitary best in compromise with the evils around him."[29] The Bruderhof presented themselves as an alternative to this declension. Bob and Shirley began their travels with the intention of examining an experiment of how a church-community operates when disciples renounce their more worldly selves and commit themselves totally to the way of Jesus. Bob explains, "while Shirley had not my initial interest in the Bruderhof, she did come to share my concern as we began searching together for the meaning of the Christian life for us."[30] The promise of a community of like-minded Christians dedicating their lives to the practice of agape and brotherly and sisterly fellowship acted as a magnet for the Wagoners, bringing these high-minded people into the Bruderhof orbit.

Arriving the day after the death of a child, an event that in any community raises questions about how a loving God can allow the suffering and death of innocents, the Wagoners experience their first irradiation of blanketing love. Bob writes, "We began to see that evening, and are seeing more clearly every day we are here, the true meaning of agape—Christian love."[31]

The Wagoners immersed themselves in the public life of the community, with Bob undertaking hard physical labor in the fields and dairy. Shirley worked at first in the sewing room and later, with Brotherhood approval, taught in the school. Bob assures the reader that they were not casual visitors or what might be termed "religious tourists." Their long stay allowed them to go behind surface appearances and dispel any idealistic notions that Primavera was utopia. Bob writes:

> It was certainly no utopia in any sense of the word; this notion should be dispelled entirely. The work was hard, there were disagreements and even occasional personality clashes, and the children could be as naughty there as anywhere. In a word, we found them to be heir to all the usual human frailties. Their uniqueness was not in this but rather that in the common spirit of love among them they have a way of meeting these weaknesses and overcoming them. The longer we were there, the more we saw how necessary to their way of life a complete receptivity to the spirit was.[32]

While the Wagoners could see abundant love—feel the public tones and textures of this spirit—they also reported a rejection of Pietistic individualism and emotional fervor, the doctrinal key to Arnoldism. Bob writes: "I never heard the topic of salvation discussed or very often

mentioned while we were at the Bruderhof. It occurs in some of Eberhard Arnold's writings but never in a position of great prominence. One
could say that the topic is so taken for granted as to be ignored. They
do not live as they do to better insure their chances for salvation. They
feel that their life is the logical and inescapable outcome of accepting the
fact that God has an intention for mankind. . . ."[33]

Guests like Bob Wagoner reported the absence of a Pietist morphology of conversion. This is consistent with the reported experiences of
Primavera's young adults who took their baptismal vows. Elizabeth
Bohlken-Zumpe was born in 1935 in the Alm Bruderhof and came of
age in Primavera. In 1951, at the age of 16, she asked to join the
novitiate and a baptismal preparation group. She recounts her spiritual
itinerary toward conversion and lifelong commitment to the church-
community in a mundane, matter-of-fact manner. There is no suggestion of a protracted, painful, or intense inward struggle to relinquish the
carnal self and find rapturous surrender as a child of God. She describes
an adolescent sense of rapture with nature bordering on pantheism,
stating that "I was still writing religious poems and talking to the moon,
the trees and flowers. I felt that each person, as part of the creation,
should be at peace with their heart and with all mankind."[34]

Bohlken-Zumpe progressed through her baptism preparation with
little sense of urgency, save for the ominous reminder of her own
mortality that was repeatedly dramatized by the deaths of children and
young adults in Primavera. She waited three years, relocating with her
family to Wheathill and beginning her nursing training in England
before she took her vows in the week before Easter 1954. She explains,
"I wanted nothing more than to surrender my life to the cause of love
for my fellow men, to give my life to Jesus and let him alone lead my
way in the future."[35] Without inner torment or selfless surrender, she
wrote a poem of joy and praise for God:

> With my God—
> I can conquer
>   the highest mountain!
> Joy must fill
>   my whole being!
> That all nature
>   will resound
> from the song
>   of my praise!
> With my God—
> every task can be done—
> Night must flee away—
> sunshine fills the air—
> All life is joy again!
>
> Because my God—
> takes from me

all trembling fear,
he sees my heart's desire—
forgiveness is entire—
in the promise for eternal life!
This through his son
who became man
like us—a man on earth![36]

The Primavera and Wheathill community spirit emphasized acosmic love, a religious ethic of brotherhood, and an international peace witness that stood as a beacon after World War II for a world in the throes of nuclear rearmament and the Cold War. The Bruderhof was a Christian community devoted to the this-worldly fulfillment of the dictates of the Sermon on the Mount. However, at this time commitment to community did not entail Pietistic devotionalism or enthusiastic religious fervor. Immersing oneself in community and voluntarily embracing the rigors of the pioneering generation in Primavera were implicit avowals of the depths and sincerity of a believer's faith. Given this tacit understanding of religious identity, believers need not undergo self-torturous repetitive cycles of death and rebirth of the spirit as a seal of a covenant of grace or a certification of growth in religious maturity. By a decisive act of will—by choosing a life in religious community and forsaking the secular world of Mammon—each member found the ready assurance of God's love and the promise of salvation.

Heini abhorred this "Arminian" variation of the Bruderhof community spirit and waited impatiently for an opportunity to revitalize the evangelical Pietist doctrines of his father. He worked indefatigably to "rehabilitate" himself, win community favor, and regain his leadership role. Allain remembers that after Heini's "erratic first years in Primavera, he had fully 'proved himself' for a long time in Ibaté, where he worked in the horse stable in the morning and in the school in the afternoon."[37] In 1950 Heini traveled as a missionary to the United States. The success of his mission and fund-raising provided the grounds for his reinstatement as a Servant and for the possibility of revitalizing the Bruderhof. To understand how this remarkable return to favored status occurred, we must first understand the Bruderhof tradition of "missionary fund-raising."

Fund-raising tied to missionary outreach had long characterized the Bruderhof communities, who suffered chronic money shortages and had never developed a stable and self-sufficient economic foundation for their communities. Ever dependant upon the capital that new members brought, inheritances received by existing members, and donations from outsiders, the Bruderhof welcomed infusions of money that passed "from the service of Mammon into the service of God."[38]

Like the communities that preceded them, the Paraguayan communities never achieved economic self-sufficiency, and their construction projects, resettlement of DPs, establishment of a full-service hospital, and extension of medical care to the indigent led to perpetual money problems. Primavera came to rely almost exclusively upon missionary fundraising, known as *Werbung*, defined as wooing or winning someone over to one's cause. Allain translates this term to mean begging in the mendicant tradition of evangelicals or Franciscans who, devoted to God's service, could beg without shame. He describes the mixture of religious and practical concerns as believers wooed wealthy Quaker friends and identified begging as the most profitable work department or enterprise. *Werbung* had "acquired truly amazing proportions, in comparison with our small numbers in Paraguay in 1949."[39] Allain writes:

> We begged from business firms by correspondence (and for the commune's use we had specific expressions such as *Sachwerbung* for begging [for] things and *Geldwerbung* for begging [for] money, etc.). We begged from benevolent associations and from the Hutterian communes in North America. We begged from old friends and made new friends in order to beg from them. We begged from old aunts and grandparents, and asked them to help the education of our children or with some relative's costly operation.[40]

The theology of Arnoldism would enjoy a warm reception from American intentional communities, Anabaptists and Friends committed to the New evangelicalism of the Fourth Great Awakening in America. In 1954, the Bruderhof established the Woodcrest community in Rifton, New York, taking members and resources from the Macedonia Cooperative Community in Georgia and the Kingwood Community in New Jersey. Woodcrest acquired the principle assets of Community Playthings, a quality wooden toy manufacturing business, from Macedonia. In 1958, Woodcrest auctioned off the Georgia farms, liquidating all of Macedonia's assets and absorbing all but one member of this community.

For the first time in Bruderhof history, the community achieved economic self-sufficiency. In addition, several wealthy Americans responded to the *Werbung* appeals with astounding generosity. John and Josephine Houseman, members of the Kingwood community, gave $20,000 for the down payment and almost half the $57,500 purchase price of the Woodcrest property.[41]

As Woodcrest's Servant of the Word, after decades of humiliation, Heini finally possessed the economic, political, and theological foundation for the control of the Bruderhof Movement. Allied with a retinue of American converts, themselves fervently committed to his charismatic leadership and the tenets of Arnoldism, Heini fostered what we shall term "the Woodcrest spirit," in dialectical opposition to the spirit of Primavera.

The Woodcrest spirit included (1) a Christocentric evangelical Pietism that demanded a sustained religious enthusiasm; (2) Insistence upon absolute doctrinal and practical unity within and among the Bruderhof communities; (3) repeated outreach toward and attempts at reconciliation with the Western Hutterite colonies; (4) an aggressively expansionist policy of building new American hofs, seeking out other Christian communities and challenging them to merge with the Bruderhof in God's revolution; and (5) the perception that Woodcrest constituted the authentic center of the movement.

In the name of doctrinal unity and purity, Heini and his disciples would ultimately disband brotherhoods, liquidate six hofs in South America and Europe, and exile over six hundred persons. Arnoldism promoted an evangelical and theocentric vision of community as the only authentic foundation for a common Christian life. Mow explains, "it is very clear that our communal life is not founded upon a social ideal of brotherly community. It is founded upon love to Jesus."[42] Heini condemned the spirit of Primavera as a declension bordering upon heresy, blaming Hans Zumpe above all others as the author of the Bruderhof's spiritual descent into sinful error.

Heini cherished Eberhard's last letters, including one written to Hans Zumpe in 1935. Heini viewed them as the definitive charge from the charismatic founder to his disciples. Eberhard reaffirmed Bruderhof theology: "I hold firmly to the inward and outward uniting of *genuine old Hutterianism* with the *attitude of faith* of the two Blumhardts and with the life-attitude of the true *Youth Movement* as a real and wonderful providence for your future; whereas I regard a merging of Hutterianism with modern pietism as a misfortune."[43] Here Eberhard recounts the doctrinal basis of his theology and warns of the routinization of the Spirit into deadening forms of legalistic doctrine or bureaucratic church polity. He reiterated the now familiar theme that the Arnold communities of the Bruderhof could offer a fresh and inspiring challenge to the North American Hutterites whose spiritual fervor had grown cold.

Months after Eberhard's death, his sons Hardy, Heini, and Hans-Hermann angrily confronted Zumpe in Zurich where they lived as refugees from Nazi persecution. Known as the Zurich *Handel* (clash between opposing directions), this succession conflict resulted in Heini's first exclusion and the lesser discipline of Hardy and Hans-Hermann.[44] Thus began Heini's lifelong enmity toward Hans Zumpe and his nearly twenty-year struggle to revitalize the Bruderhof in fulfillment of Eberhard's final charge. Woodcrest provided the vehicle for Heini's vindication as he sought to redeem the movement from the decades of declension and restore a Pietist primordium.

Heini's special gifts rested upon the theological foundation of Eberhard Arnold, whose theology legitimated the charisma and authority of the son. Heini used sermons and private exhortations to teach the long-neglected Bruderhof canon. Later, he committed the *Plough* to the English translation and publication of Arnold's major writings, official Bruderhof history, and his own practical theology. Beginning with *When*

Time Was Fulfilled (1965), and followed by *Salt and Light* (1967), *Why We Live in Community* (1972), and *Seeking for the Kingdom* (1974), Heini published the crucial works that supported Arnoldism.

Older members from the early Sannerz, Rhön, Cotswold, and Primavera Bruderhofs had known Eberhard, found edification in his sermons, and read his works in German. The recent American and English converts lacked this connection with the founder and his teachings. Heini lamented the sad fate of *Innerland*, which remained untranslated and out-of-print.

Heini remarked that the English Bruderhof members of the 1940s and 1950s "somehow did not feel the depth of the book speaking to them at this time."[45] Preaching, catechism, and religious instruction would now proceed from the writings of Eberhard Arnold, of Blumhardt and Bonhoeffer, and from the Hutterian and Anabaptist tradition that formed the Bruderhof canonical texts. Bible study and preaching from the scripture were de-emphasized.

Heini, like his father before him, promoted a pneumatical exegesis of Scripture and other confessional literature. Only the penitent seeker, humbled before God as a poor and wretched sinner, could open his or her heart and receive the Spirit-filled illumination in the printed page or spoken word. Pneumatical exegesis of the Word devalued intellectualism, systematic theology, and rational discourse, and encouraged fervent emotionalism and the inward piety of a believer who yearned for a personal connection with God's love and mandate. This was essential to Arnold's evangelical Pietism.

The example of Merrill Mow is instructive. Mow came to Woodcrest as a baptized member of the Brethren Church. He and his wife Shirley accepted Heini's invitation to join a baptism preparation group in 1956 and participate in a week-long retreat in the Pocono Mountains. Mow reported that he had to unlearn and discard the intellectual traditions he had acquired during his years of seminary training, dispensing first with Bible commentaries.[46]

Arnoldism did not rely upon or encourage Bible reading among the faithful. Rather, the canonical Bruderhof texts formed the basis for reading, meditation, and instruction. The Servant of the Word might begin a prayer group or assembly with a line from Scripture, but the exegesis proceeded from the Bruderhof canon. The most important truths were revealed to the charismatic Witness Brothers and Servants of the Word, who discerned where the Spirit would lead and direct the community. As one visitor noted in 1956,

> The traditional conservative Christian often gets something of a shock in visiting Woodcrest and observing the apparent cavalier treatment of the Bible, for there is no formal use of the Bible there on any fixed occasions. The Servant, for example, may bring a Bible with him to a funeral, or he may not. I can recall no single guest or Household meeting during my

visits where the Bible was read from—or even quoted from for more than a single phrase or two.

Members say that they respect the Bible but oppose literalism, the taking of a single verse and making it authoritative. I have seen Bibles in members' apartments in places indicating that they are probably read as time permits, but the all-important things at Woodcrest again and again is said to be the living of the daily life in obedience to the leading of the present Spirit.[47]

Heini simplified and systematized his father's ideas into an inner-worldly Pietism, adopting the German evangelical Pietist theology of assurance—the necessity of an intense, emotionally wrenching inner struggle (*Busskampf*) that resulted in the ravishing, joyous psychological union with God, the inner-worldly mystical "bride of the lamb."[48] Each new being was marked by an existential reorientation, separate from the kingdom of Satan and the world, engaged in a battle to build the Kingdom of God.

The life of faith was not easily won. Arnoldism appropriated the Lutheran concept of Christocentric faith—the imitation of Christ's cross-bearing and his redemptive suffering. Heini frequently directed his followers to Dietrich Bonhoeffer's *The Cost of Discipleship*, which spoke against "cheap" and freely proffered institutional grace and salvation of the churches. Disciples who emulated Jesus, who devoted their lives completely to the teachings of the Sermon on the Mount, were destined to suffer. "Suffering, then, is the badge of true discipleship."[49] The life of faith alternated between joyful surrender to Jesus—the rapture of assurance as a child of God, fulfilled by His love—and the seasons of abject suffering—cross-bearing, self-accusations of sinfulness, and religious melancholy.

The new person in faith possessed a renovated heart receptive to the living word of God, not the dead letter of Biblical legalism. Heini Arnold's charismatic genius manifested itself in the gifts of discernment—of seeing into the hearts and minds of believers, ascertaining the depth or superficiality of his or her faith, and guiding each person's spiritual pilgrimage. He mediated to community members the cultural meanings and "cues" of authentic spirituality—what to believe, how to feel, how to think, how to perceive, what was the agenda or order of things, and whom to emulate.[50]

The complete unity of regenerated souls who surrendered their lives to Jesus, and who continually accepted the challenge of living in community and building the Kingdom of God in spiritual warfare against Satan, constituted the basis for true community according to Arnoldism. With this doctrinal foundation, enthusiastic converts went forth into the world, aggressively converting the unbelievers and challenging other Christians to join them, especially the Western Hutterites whom Eberhard Arnold had hoped to evangelize with Bruderhof spiritual vitalism.

Heini would complete his father's unfinished work. Ironically, this "striving for" unity and brotherly outreach led to disunity, schism, and unbrotherly consequences as exemplified in the Forest River debacle.

Woodcrest began construction of Forest River House in 1955, named in honor of the Forest River Hutterite colony in North Dakota. Five Hutterite carpenters traveled east to assist in this project: Paul and Darius Maendel from Forest River colony itself, Sam Hofer from Bloomfield colony, Fred Kleinsasser from Sturgeon Creek colony, and Dave Waldner from Milltown colony. Heini used this visit to "challenge" the guests to embrace a more profound devotional piety, to seek inner illumination of a Spirit-directed identity. Arnoldism now won its first Hutterian converts, in the shape of the Forest River guests, who accepted the premise that the Arnoldleut (Arnold communities of the Bruderhof) had rekindled the founding Anabaptist spirit. This spirit had grown cold and distant in Forest River, a colony troubled by factions, internal divisions, and unresolved grievances among the brethren. Forest River would prove receptive to the evangelical message of Arnoldism.

Merrill Mow arranged a meeting in his parents' home in Chicago in July 1955 between representatives from Forest River and the Bruderhof leadership, including Heini Arnold and Alan Stevenson. Hans Meier traveled from the English hof to attend. The Forest River brothers invited the Bruderhof to visit North Dakota and proselytize the colony. This invitation did not reflect a vote from the congregation or church ministerium, however, and bypassed traditional Hutterian authority. The Forest River Servant of the Word, known by the honorific title "Vetter," and many of the congregants would view the subsequent Bruderhof invasion as an arrogant and a scandalous attempt to usurp ownership and control of the colony.[51]

Within weeks, Woodcrest had sent Heini and his wife, Annemarie, Hans Meier, Arnold Mason, and Bruce Sumner to Forest River along with a dozen young families. Heini found fertile ground for a religious revival. He discovered that the Hutterites had fallen away from the joyful community of goods and allowed Mammonism to enter. Brothers and sisters had grown cold toward one another. Mow relates that "Consciences were struck: by accumulation of possessions like the yearly allotment of cloth, material, or shoes, which was often more than was needed in a family. . . ."[52]

Heini exhorted and promised a return to love, to Jesus, a warm-hearted ethic of brotherliness, a revitalization of the Sermon on the Mount, and the call to brotherly reconciliation found in Matthew 18. Heini's challenge to return to the original spirit of the Hutterite founders era struck a responsive cord in Forest River. One elderly sister invoked the spirit of Peter Reidemann, one of the early founders of the Anabaptist Movement. She exclaimed in the midst of the revival, "Peter Riedemann came alive!" The evangelism brought dramatic and sudden results: the removal of the Forest River servant, Andreas Hofer, and a vote to unite with the Bruderhof and exclude the sixty Hutterites who opposed this change. While true believers of Arnoldism welcomed these events as wondrous signs of the times, the excluded colony members reacted in dismay to the loss of everything that they had worked to achieve. In the midst of this revival and crisis, Andreas Hofer and his supporters requested assistance from the wider church. The James Valley Hutterian Brethren from Starbuck, Manitoba, sent eleven ministers to investigate. They arrived at Forest River in late August and issued on September 6, 1955 a 20-page report on "the Forest River Affair," charging Heini Arnold and the "Paraguay people" with misbehavior: "Andreas Hofer, who for over 30 years has been in service and is the leader of this Bruderhof, knew nothing of what was happening, not even until Sunday, August 28th did he know anything. The Paraguay people had so persistently undermined Andreas Vetter's leadership. They talked behind his back to the people and mislead them. It is abominable."[53] The Woodcrest Servants began evangelizing other Hutterite colonies. Heini had usurped total control of Forest River—ownership of the property, spiritual leadership of the church, and administrative control of daily affairs. The James Valley report denounced the Bruderhof in their chronicle of the vote to unseat the Servant and unite with Woodcrest: "Hans Meier, Bruce Sumner, Heini Arnold, [Arnold] Mason, men, women and children seated themselves in the presence of the preachers. Peter Vetter asked them to leave, but Meier got up and started to talk and Bruce got up and started to talk too. Peter Vetter got up and with the eleven other preachers walked out and left them sitting there. This is how the split took place in this church. . . ."[54]

The Forest River debacle resulted in a schism between the Arnoldleut and the Western Hutterites that lasted from 1955 until 1974. Forest River remained an Arnoldleut hof until 1957 when the colony disbanded, assets were sold, and most of the personnel were reassigned to the Eastern communities.

Heini's evangelical enthusiasm propelled him to convert the Hutterites to Arnoldism and to forge unity on his terms alone. The result was disunity and acrimony. Nevertheless, Heini remained undaunted by this setback and immune from Hutterian admonishment. As a charismatic visionary, he looked forward, not backward; the conversionist logic of Evangelical Pietism pushed him onward to challenge new groups—to convert the world.

The American Bruderhof expanded rapidly, opening two additional communities—Oak Lake (New Meadow Run) near Pittsburgh in 1957, and Evergreen (Deer Spring) in Norfolk, Connecticut, in 1958. With three growing hofs, the Woodcrest leaders were able to absorb members from the closed European and South American communities, welcome returnees from the Forest River colony debacle, and effectively promote Woodcrest as the new center of the Bruderhof movement. Woodcrest leaders actively proselytized other intentional communities (such as

Celo and Koinonia), seeking formal union and the exchange of personnel. Repeatedly, Woodcrest looked to "absorb" the assets and personnel from these allied groups.

The Reba Place Fellowship (RPF) offers a case in point. In 1957 a group of young Mennonite men and women, under the leadership of John Miller, began the Reba Place Fellowship in South Evanston, Illinois. The early urban community, under Miller's charismatic leadership, had much in common with the Bruderhof. RPF created a church-community of Christian Socialism open to the guidance and illumination of the Holy Spirit regarding how to implement the ethical mandates of the New Testament. All members must dedicate their lives totally to the fulfillment of God's will. God's mandate became manifest, not through church tradition, ecclesiastical institutions, or hierarchial authority but through two or more gathered together in Christ's name. This counterinstitutional interpretation of Matthew 18 was the foundation and vessel for the Spirit-led fellowship that RPF hoped to establish in their church-community. Through the unified will of the church-community, individuals would surrender to the Lordship of Christ; God's will would "ruthlessly emerge—ruthlessly because it will very soon be seen that areas of our own lives that we had hitherto considered our 'own business' now turn out to be anything but private."[55] Like the theology of Eberhard Arnold that called for a fusion of individual I's into the Spirit-directed harmony of a collective We, so RPF called for the renunciation of individual self and identity. Dave and Neta Jackson have written a critical history of RPF, *Glimpses of Glory*. They argue that Reba Place misinterpreted key passages from Matthew 18, "Though every person's input on a matter is valued, such a high premium is placed on complete agreement that long term differences of opinion are seen as profane individualism."[56]

Heini proposed a merger between the RPF and the Bruderhof. The story of Reba Place-Bruderhof relations centers upon the dealings between John Miller and Heini Arnold. Miller first visited the Woodcrest Bruderhof in 1956, which paved the way for exchange visits from members of Reba Place to several Bruderhof communities in 1958, 1959, and 1960. Mutual admiration and cordial relations characterized these early contacts. The Bruderhof was intrigued at the success of an urban community. Reba Place was considering a new religious affiliation after they had separated from the Mennonites. However, troubling stories of community crises in Forest River and Primavera, and accounts of excluded ex-members and their unbrotherly treatment made Reba Place proceed with caution. When Miller and Arnold did begin formal discussion of merger in 1960, the questions of Bruderhof treatment of excluded members and the causes of these community crises were put to Heini. Miller was also troubled by what can be termed Bruderhof Fundamentalism—the self-righteous belief that they alone possessed God's literal truth. Others who differed, regardless of how well meaning or ethical their conduct, remained trapped in error. The Jacksons state: "Relations with the Society of Brothers . . . had been warm and very influential in the formation of Reba, but there was always the hint from the Bruderhof that a *better way* might be to somehow unite with them fully. Though there was some attraction to this option, it also made people at Reba nervous that unity would equal assimilation."[57] Would uniting mean full surrender to the Bruderhof? Heini argued that should the Bruderhof ever encounter a group that better embodied the ideal of Christian love, then they would willingly surrender and fuse with this superior group. Heini challenged Reba Place as to the depth of their Christian love, implicitly urging them to accept the superiority of the Bruderhof community. He exhorts Miller, "My question to you is: Are you not too early satisfied, and does God not want to give so much more in this?"[58]

Miller's reply rejected any Bruderhof claim of superiority and raised concerns about groups that demanded total unity of belief and practice. Historically, such demands had often produced a dreadful history of crises, schisms, and divisions. Miller replies:

> It is still not clear to me exactly what you mean by "one in everything." You may know that Mennonite history in recent times presents a dreadful spectacle of division over trivialities. There are those who have arisen under the motto of "one in everything" to try and stamp on the whole people one type of dress, one style of hair, one color of bumper and many other ridiculous things. . . . But this does indicate that sometimes when we speak of "one in everything" we can include some things that do not really belong there.[59]

Woodcrest leaders, including Hardy and Heini Arnold, worked indefatigably to proselytize the spirit of Woodcrest and the doctrines of Arnoldism, challenging Mennonites, Friends, Church of the Brethren— sister Anabaptist conventicles—to visit Rifton and experience the joyous rededication of the founding spirit of the movement. Articles in the *Plough* and pamphlets extolled Woodcrest as the realization of salvation promises enunciated in the Sermon on the Mount. Many responded to this outreach, visited the Bruderhof for extended stays as guests, and returned to their home churches with glowing reports—advertisements for the authenticity of the Woodcrest spirit.

David Eiler, a professor of theology at Bethany Theological Seminary, affiliated with the Church of the Brethren, spent six months (accompanied by his wife, Ruth) at Woodcrest in 1956. The Eilers wrote a short paper, "Impressions of the Woodcrest Bruderhof," and presented their findings at a Bethany faculty retreat in January 1957. After recounting the history of the Bruderhof and the details of daily life in the community, the Eilers devoted the remainder of their essay to a defense of Bruderhof religious practice. They justified Woodcrest's introversionist and sectarian retreat from the world, the demand for total unity of thought and action, and the struggle to rid the church-community of individualism. The Eilers described the explicit faith commitment that served as the foundation for community participation:

> The inner motivation and power rest entirely upon a deep faith in God and on the experience of his presence in the gathered fellowship of the faithful. They believe that God seeks to gather a people completely surrendered to his will and, through this people to lead all mankind to redemption. . . . Thus, the basis of membership is a total dedication and commitment to life—one's whole mind, strength and will—to Christ and the Brotherhood. This total self-surrender means that there is nothing experimental or tentative about membership.[60]

The Eilers urged others in their confessional group to examine the Bruderhof challenge. Words did not capture the textures of the lived experiences of the Woodcrest Spirit.

> The Bruderhof has already made an impact in this country all out of proportion to its size. And there is little question but that this impact will become much wider and more significant in years to come unless the whole movement somehow gets "off the track." The deep inner power and dynamic of the whole thing is amazing. Its uniqueness actually makes it difficult to communicate one's impressions and experiences to anyone who hasn't been there himself.[61]

David S. Tillson, a friend and colleague of David Eiler, accepted the challenge to come and experience the Bruderhof Christian witness. He made five visits to Woodcrest from June 1956 through June 1957, living in the community for a combined total of forty-nine days. Tillson conducted participant observer research and produced a doctoral thesis, "A Pacifist Community in Peacetime," a comprehensive community study with chapters devoted to history; community organization and economy; education and child-rearing; and the "religious basis of life." Tillson's background in divinity tempered his social science, and he offers a celebratory depiction of the early Woodcrest hof. He never observed, did not inquire, and did not realize that Heini had already begun clearances, expulsions, and the extensive use of church discipline to reshape the movement.

Tillson's final chapter discussed Woodcrest's possible problems and their probable future. He discounted the likelihood of internal divisions, citing their single-belief system and sensitivity to disunity. He quoted at length from a personal letter that he received from David Eiler, who remarked that the Bruderhof "have been through enough crises to be able to discern hidden inner threats to this unity long before any outsider would be able to detect anything amiss. Whenever any such threat appears they exert every ounce of energy and go to almost any length to overcome it. Maintaining unity takes precedence over every other community effort and over all individual impulses. . . ."[62] Tillson explained that "Woodcrest and the Bruderhof Movement as a whole offer great contributions to the social life and the spiritual dedication of members of Western society and our world at large."[63]

In an unbroken chain of religious "intelligence," of published reports by visitors who accepted the Bruderhof challenge, Dave and Neta Jackson report on their stay at New Meadow Run in the mid-1960s. The Jacksons' search for religious answers to the perplexities of modern life is recounted in *Living in a World Falling Apart*. The Jacksons discovered an authentic alternative as searchers for a high-commitment Christian group who wanted to dedicate their lives to an absolutist ethic of brotherhood, surrendering to the leadings of the Holy Spirit. Their description of work and fellowship in New Meadow Run reads like a passage from utopian fiction.

> All around the Society of Brothers we saw the expressions of lives lived for others. A walk around the community was literally filled with joyful surprises—the abundant flowers and rock gardens planted by the young people as a "gift" to the others; carefully carved steps in a steep path; beside the land a spring someone had landscaped with beautiful pools, waterfalls, moss, and flowers. In each family apartment we visited we saw paintings, trinkets and crafts that various community children had brought. Everyone stayed after lunch one day to help the vegetable-garden people snap beans. On another occasion, the young people painted a beautiful mural and sang specially practiced songs to welcome their parents and other adults home from an outing. Each aspect of their lives seemed not a private gratification but a gift to others.[64]

Pitirim A. Sorokin, sociologist and director of the Institute for Applied Altruism at Harvard University, captured the tenor of Primavera and Wheathill in his paean *The Ways and Powers of Love* (1954). Arguing that the Bruderhof held the answers to the crises of modernity and had successfully institutionalized agape and altruism in their community, Sorokin extols their communal life:

> They realize that voluntary poverty and simplicity, a harmonious and pure common life, with an open door for all, irrespective of nation, creed, race, age, sex or wealth, is the answer to the confused and frustrated condition of contemporary man, who faces the problem of spiritual and physical survival in a state of utter bewilderment. They know from experience that the need of modern man is as much spiritual as economic, as much emotional as physical, as much personal as social.[65]

Sorokin, Eiler, Dave and Neta Jackson, and Bob and Shirley Wagoner eagerly and uncritically embraced an idealized vision of Bruderhof life, as published in the *Plough*, in promotional pamphlets, and through the reprinted canonical works. Each new American seeker in turn published a personal testimonial of their own vital experiences of agape and brotherliness as a guest in this Spirit-led church-community. They discovered in the Bruderhof answers to the religious crises of their generation.

Thomas O'Dea traced these crises of contemporary religious consciousness in America after World War II to alienation from mainline denominations that failed to provided satisfying answers to the questions of "authentic transcendence and genuine community" in the lives of the laity.[66] He writes that religionists from many denominations confronted times of anomic disjuncture when "existence tends to be experienced in terms of its manifold contradictions. People neither have the noetic capacity to integrate an organized outlook nor the psychological ability to achieve a sense of meaningful participation in their society."[67] The quest for new forms of religious identity and community offered one resolution to the postwar crisis of religious consciousness in America for many in the throes of alienation and anomie. Revivals would also address these issues. As William G. McLoughlin argues in *Revivals, Awakenings, and Reform*, "Awakenings begin in periods of cultural distortion and great personal stress, when we lose faith in the legitimacy of our norms, the viability of our institutions, and the authority of our leaders in church and state. They eventuate in basic restructurings of our institutions and redefinitions of our social goals."[68]

The appeal and success of Arnoldism among the Western Hutterites and other Anabaptist groups, Friends, and communitarians, needs to be understood in the broader context of the American religious scene in the decades following World War II—a time of institutional transformation and restructuring.[69] In one sense, America emerged from the war as an increasingly secular mass society driven by the core values of consumerism and championed by the upwardly mobile white-collar middle class—the conformity of the "careful young men" and other-directed corporate managers who celebrated a common civic and "culture religion." Will Herberg's *Protestant, Catholic and Jew* discovered that religious differences, like ethnic or national origins divisions, diminished as Americans entered the melting pot of coequal denominations that celebrated the American way of life. Gone were sectarian controversies, religion as a radical critique of social conditions, or religious commitment as an exercise of vital personal piety. Culture religion promoted a gospel of happiness, peace of mind, personal adjustment, and material success bestowed upon all believers by "the man upstairs." Norman Vincent Peale, Fulton Sheen, and many others preached culture religion to mass audiences on radio and television.

A. Roy Eckardt offers this withering portrait of the new American culture religion:

A rhapsodic inquiry greets us from the TV screen and the radio: "Have you talked to the Man Upstairs?" God is a friendly neighbor who dwells in the apartment just above. Call on him anytime, especially if you are feeling a little blue. He does not get upset over your little faults. He understands. We have been assured by no less a theologian than Jane Russell that the Lord is a "livin' Doll," a right nice guy.[70]

Eckardt objects to what he perceives as a tendency to trivialize the doctrinal truths of Scripture. He rejects out-of-hand the banality of the gospel of happiness and well-being and would restore the centrality of evangelical Pietist conversion. Eckardt challenges Christians from all denominations to embrace a religious life-order and commitment to ultimate values to accept a life of spiritual pilgrimage replete with opportunities for redemptive suffering and spiritual trials as each pilgrim stands conscience-bound in tension with secular society. He concludes his article in *Christian Century* (1954) with this challenge:

> Against all human idolatries we may set the peace of Christ which passes all understanding. We have not earned this peace. It is a gift we have received. It does not center in the self or the group. It centers in the cross and the empty tomb. . . . It is the peace of disturbing forgiveness. God ceases to be fashioned in our image; we are made over into his. We are granted not a short-cut or trivial solution to our anxieties but the grace to laugh and to know that our anxieties are of no ultimate consequence. The peace of Christ comes, mysteriously, when we forget all about our peace, when we prostrate ourselves before the holiness of God. . . . [71]

The dissatisfaction with culture religion went hand-in-hand with a deeper rejection of the mainstream Protestantism. W. H. Auden captured the malaise of the postwar era in his phrase "the age of anxiety," anxiety associated with the collapse of a worldview. The ideals of Liberalism, the Social Gospel faith in science and technological progress, and melioristic activism to solve societal problems had faded in the face of total war, totalitarianism, and the coming of the nuclear age with the specter of world annihilation and geopolitical Cold War against godless communism. Increasingly, conservative Protestants like Eckardt called for reform and revitalization of American religion—a return to Pietism and "religious individualism." As Robert Wuthnow explains, "Against cold intellectualism, popular sermons advocated a religion capable of expressing deep inner emotions; against an outmoded social gospel, a message of personal redemption; against ineffective concern for social ills, the need to care for individual souls."[72]

The mass revivals in America during the 1950s signaled the emergence of a "progressive evangelicalism" that eschewed the militancy, doctrinal controversy, and isolation that marked earlier Fundamentalist groups.[73] Under the auspices of the National Association of Evangelicals, founded in 1943, evangelical Pietist groups formed nonsectarian coalitions, what Wuthnow terms "parachurch" organizations designed to win America for Christ. Harold John Ockenga called the movement the

New Evangelicalism, refering to the inclusive nondenominational mix of evangelical Protestant churches and charismatic, Pentecostal, and healing sects. Fuller Theological Seminary, recently founded and under Ockenga's leadership, offered theological direction and intellectual rigor to the movement. Carl Henry, a Fuller scholar, assumed editorial direction of *Christianity Today*, a popular journal that would spread the new evangelical message. The Billy Graham Crusades brought the message to the urban masses through revivals and print and electronic media: Americans needed to make a decision for Christ. Neo-evangelicalism could win American society for Christ.

The new evangelicalism created what Henry Van Dusen called a "third force in Christendom"[74] that was marked by the exponential growth of Pentecostal, holiness and Adventist new religious groups such as: the Churches of Christ, Assemblies of God, Church of God in Christ, Seventh Day Adventists, Church of the Nazarene, and Jehovah's Witnesses. McLoughlin argues that these "fringe sects" or new religious movements displayed emotional and missionary fervor, demanding of adherents a high level of self-sacrifice consistent with the tradition of American Pietism. "Americans have always measured faith in terms of the activistic, enthusiastic self-commitment to their faith that the third-force believers displayed."[75] Third-force groups rejected culture religion in search of an authentic Christian option for personal identity, fellowship, and community in opposition to the challenges of secular, mass society.

The founding of Woodcrest Bruderhof as a third-force sect coincided with the Fourth Great Awakening, Billy Graham's urban Crusades, and the new evangelicalism appeals for a revitalized American piety. The emotional fervor of a Christ-centered and "surrendered" life formed the marrow of Heini Arnold's evangelical Piety and appealed to many Americans seeking an alternative to the seemingly secular culture religion.

Dean Kelley reports in *Why Conservative Churches Are Growing* that during this period Americans defected from established, mainline denominations and affiliated with conservative churches and high-commitment Pentecostal and evangelical groups like the Southern Baptist Convention, Assemblies of God, and Church of the Nazarene. Kelley argues that Americans hungered for a comprehensive worldview that provided emotionally satisfying and compelling answers to the existential questions of human existence. They fled the religious and ethical relativism and pluralism of "weak churches" in a quest for absolute and Fundamentalist doctrine. Believers wanted to immerse themselves in high-commitment, integrated church-communities. Americans joined "strong" religions characterized by moral absolutism, a closed belief system, and high levels of conformity. Kelley explains that strong religions like the Bruderhof required "firm adherence of members to the group's beliefs that they would be willing to suffer persecution, to sacrifice status, possessions, safety, and life itself for the organization, its conventions, its goals."[76]

Heini Arnold enjoyed charismatic, almost hypnotic, appeal among his retinue of American converts and devotees. They emulated his mannerisms and closely identified with his life story as a man made to suffer repeated injuries—uprooted from his homeland and made to wander as a stranger in the South American wilderness. They accepted Heini's self-pitying account of betrayal by Hans Zumpe after Eberhard Arnold's death, Heini's near-death experience in Primavera, and the cruel injustice of his several exclusions and banishment. In the Great Crisis the American disciples eagerly identified and punished Heini's "enemies," the spiritually lax, and those who had criticized him and injured him. Heini served as a model of redemptive suffering that resulted in spiritual quickening.

The new American converts joined the Bruderhof in their disillusionment with postwar American society and the "weaknesses" of American cultural religion and denominationalism. Like the previous generation of European seekers, who responded to their era of cultural despair with adherence to the charismatic magnetism of Eberhard Arnold, so too this postwar American generation sought transcendence of their milieu of cultural despair. Arnoldism would resolve the troubling questions of alienation, anomie, and the disappointment of cultural religion. They were drawn into the orbit of Heini's charismatic leadership by their future-oriented optimism and decision to pursue a risk-filled, vital Christian vocation. Charles Lindholm explains that in America during the 1950s (and the subsequent counterculture of the 1960s) disaffiliated middle-class youth were drawn to charismatic groups. They harkened to the message "that the important world is in the future, and the future is to be newly created by the young."[77] In addition, charismatic sects like the Bruderhof appealed to young Americans who evidenced a "willingness to risk the self . . . [and] who find the world they live in to be suffocatingly safe, morally corrupt, or simply dull. They are ready to give up that world not because of desperation or marginality, but because of an adventurous urge to live more vividly and fully."[78]

The Inner American, a survey of Americans from 1957–1976, found a weakening of status-role and institutional ties that had previously bound individuals to family, work, and community. Family disruption caused by the divorce revolution and the decline of a vocational work ethic in favor of leisure and consumer ethos attenuated the inner direction and stability of work and family life. Where Americans could once forge a coherent and structured sense of self and identity through institutional affiliations, they now confronted anomic disjuncture. The authors of the survey argue that "without these easy guarantees, we have become a somewhat more anxious people. We see more problems in many parts of our lives. As many people have learned, it is often difficult to discover the authentic self. Freedom from a constraining authority often becomes a burden; the freedom to choose often a haunting personal problem."[79]

The Woodcrest Spirit

Arnoldism elaborated a comprehensive religious worldview—a symbolic map that mediated cultural cues and meanings to believers, directing them about the order of things, individual and collective identity, and the prescribed and proscribed thoughts, perceptions, emotions, and actions of their single-belief system. As David Chidester has noted, a religious worldview affords a "comprehensive, totalizing capacity to organize every aspect of human belief, action, and experience in terms of a system of symbolic classification and a sense of symbolic orientation."[80] The religious worldview of the Bruderhof under Heini Arnold reanimated the emotionally charged anticipation of the Kingdom of God. David Eiler terms this belief an "experiential eschatology." Through joyous surrender in unity the

> power of the Holy Spirit is experienced so powerfully in their life together, particularly in worship, that the coming of the Kingdom in its full glory miraculously transforming the earth and putting an end to all evil becomes a vividly real expectation and hope. Thus they feel that all life is to be ordered here and now on the basis of the absolute demands of the Kingdom as proclaimed by Jesus.[81]

If we are to understand the Woodcrest Spirit and the lived experiences of adherents of Arnoldism, we must attempt to peer through the lens of their worldview. They turned their sights to the Kingdom of God and the necessary measures taken to hasten the advent of millennium. Ironically, the measures adopted to usher in a time of peace and brotherliness led to division and ruthless unbrotherliness.

The ardent struggle to vanquish sin in individuals and the church-community and to unite as a vessel of the Holy Spirit was the central organizing principle of the Woodcrest Spirit and worldview. This struggle involved a cosmic battle between the forces of God and Satan. True believers waged ceaseless warfare against Satanic attack; they believed that the Devil looked to make inroads against the Bruderhof by turning spiritually weak brethren. The spiritually weak and vulnerable included: emotionally unstable members—those tempted by sins of the flesh, those haunted by obsessive guilt and blasphemous thoughts—and religious melancholiacs who believed themselves to be forsaken by God. And each person, weak or strong, faced the ever present danger of demonic possession. The community confronted the perils of Mammonism from without and disunity and Satan-haunted sinners from within.

In *Freedom from Sinful Thoughts, Christ Alone Breaks the Curse*, Heini Arnold taught that "there is no doubt that the Devil tries by every means to suggest to us human beings proud, evil, impure, even blasphemous feelings, ideas or thoughts—even the urge to commit suicide or murder."[82] Only a Christ-centered psychology and a religiously grounded personality founded upon evangelical Pietist principles could end the curse of obsessional thoughts and actions. According to Heini, the power of Christ alone could break Satan's hold, releasing frail men and women from the hypnotic power of autosuggestion whereby the mere thought or temptation of evil produced the compulsion to commit the evil act. The sick in spirit must surrender to Christ, bear the cross, purify the heart and mind, and separate from the kingdom of sin to cleave unto the Kingdom of God—to the Bruderhof church-community.

Freedom from Sinful Thoughts delineated the doctrines that buttressed the Woodcrest Spirit and addressed an unanticipated consequence of the evangelical Pietist conversion ideal of Arnoldism—the vulnerability of the faithful to spiritual obsessions.

The Woodcrest Spirit entailed securing and maintaining the unanimity of thought, sentiment, and action of all believers. Honest differences of opinion, criticism of Servants, of Heini, or a natural diversity of ideas appeared as dangerous openings to Satanic attack, blasphemy, and an intolerable affront. The preoccupation with unity brought inevitable disunity as errant individuals or families received admonishment, exclusion, or expulsion. When members failed to convince the leadership that they conducted their life sufficiently surrendered to Christ and founded upon piety, right action and the avoidance of sin, the church-community cast them out to preserve the purity of the *Gemeinde*.

Mary Douglas's *Purity and Danger* offers an important insight into the concerns with sin and pollution, dirt and disorder found in all cultures. Ideas about pollution have an instrumental dimension by delineating a sanctioned moral code and charging men and women with the commands of good citizenship. At the expressive level, pollutions create symbolic classifications of social order. Douglas explains that "ideas about separating, purifying, demarcating and punishing transgressions have as their main function to impose system on an inherently untidy experience. It is only by exaggerating the difference between within and without, above and below, male and female, with and against that a semblance of order is created."[83] Dirt, sin, and pollution offend our sense of social order and must be kept separate from the group. The instrumental expulsion of the offending body or polluting action, concept, or expression prevents the contagious spread of this impurity and reaffirms (at an expressive level) a sacred moral code and the collective representations of social order.

Anabaptist and Pietist sects like the Bruderhof created exclusive church-communities restricted to the ingathered faithful—religiously qualified believers who embraced the doctrine and moralism of an absolute ethic of brotherliness. This ethic demanded a radical separation from the world and the emulation of the Apostolic Church. The faithful were enjoined to engage in a brotherly watch and fraternal correction to ensure that believers remain free from any stain of sin. Consistent with this sectarianism, Heini emphasized a renewed introversion and separation from the polluted secular society, sharp boundaries between the "brother" and the spiritually dangerous "other," and unrelenting surveillance for any evidence of sin within the community.

Sin would invite Satanic attack. Sin would alienate the community from God, rupture the unity requisite to the infusion of the Holy Spirit, and prevent the advent of the millennial day. Heini was haunted by the specter of sin. Not infrequently in the late 1950s, he and his retinue of American Witness Brothers descended upon Primavera, the English hofs, Bulstrode and Wheathill, Sinntalhof in Germany, and Deer Spring and New Meadow, demanding self-examination, collective humiliation, repentance, and confessions. Known as clearances or clearings, these collective exercises of community renewal were derivative of the American revivalist tradition in which itinerant evangelists traveled to local communities to awaken slumbering sinners and reanimate religious fervor among the already churched and converted. By some accounts, Heini was influenced by the mass evangelicalism of the Billy Graham Crusades that excited American Fundamentalists in the 1950s.

Elizabeth Bohlken-Zumpe relates a clearance in Bulstrode in August 1958. Heini and Wendel Hinkey confronted the Brotherhood during a Morning Meeting, charging the English communities with accepting "social cases," spiritually weak members, people with chronic diseases, invalids, or those who came without true religious vocation in search for a more comfortable life. The executive leadership of Bulstrode was told to exclude these weak members who were not called "for a life of true brotherhood."[84]

In her autobiography, *Free from Bondage,* Nadine Moonje Pleil describes the clearances initiated by the American Brothers in Wheathill in 1961, immediately following the closing of Primavera and the mass expulsions of the membership. She writes without concealing her sarcasm that

> the wonderfully "perceptive" American brothers came like a whirlwind to set us straight and to purify the English Bruderhofs. . . . [They] dissolved the existing brotherhood, the circle of baptized members and said that a new brotherhood would have to be formed. All the baptized members would have to rededicate themselves individually and the American brothers would decide who was worthy to take part in the new brotherhood. They made all the decisions in small meeting groups among themselves and started expelling scores of people.[85]

Clearances created emotional earthquakes that, on the instrumental level, excluded and punished those identified as guilty of sin, disunity, and secret crimes now brought to light. At the expressive level, clearances redefined policy, doctrine, and the correct "spirit" that bound them together. Clearances redrew the symbolic boundaries of brother and outsider and of *Gemeinde* and world. Those sent away into the corruption of Mammon no longer qualified as "good citizens," brothers and sisters surrendered to Christ and living in the right spirit. Clearances took the measure of a person's inward piety and intentionality. Moralism and correct action mattered less than piety.

Clearances were demoralizing and traumatic for those cast out. Zablocki argues, however, that "these mass confessions are often followed by intense euphoric experiences."[86] After the travail of collective confession, evangelical renewal, and the expulsion of corruption and impurity, the community experienced rapturous exuberance and joy. Believers readily accepted the need for clearances when brothers and sisters grew contentious or cold-hearted. Clearances provided an exercise of *Gelassenheit*—surrender or yieldedness to God's mandate as mediated through the *Gemeinde*.[87] When they succeeded, these times of mass confession, individual exclusion, and spiritual renewal reanimated the doctrinal ideals of the community and reassured individual believers that they were children of God and collectively working toward the realization of God's Kingdom.

The crucible of clearance purified their church-community and brought renewed experiences of acosmic love. Thus, motivated by this outpouring of joyous love in new-found unity, they could cast out the polluting sinner. Those shunned in "disfellowship" experienced traumatic loss and disorientation, at first blaming their fate on their own spiritual inadequacies. Later, when confirmed as apostates with no way back, they came to view exclusion as a callous act of unloving, unbrotherly cruelty.

The most dangerous threat of pollution and sin came from unregulated sexuality. Eberhard Arnold addressed these questions in a series of talks and writings from the period 1920–1935 translated and published by the *Plough* in 1965 under the title *Love and Marriage in the Spirit*. He pleaded for all believers to devote themselves, without reservation, to the pursuit of agape, or love to God. This expression of love pours over the faithful without bounds, directing them to the imitation of Christ, the purified, unconditional, and absolute struggle to find adoption as a child of God. From this acosmism of love, brotherly love among the church-community and erotic love restricted to lifelong monogamy achieved a sublimated spiritual purpose.[88] Without love to God guiding their thoughts and actions, believers would succumb to idolatry of the flesh, "degrading animal sensuality," or "demonic self-destruction" through the fulfillment of lust and sexual desires for their own sake.[89] Arnold banished anything that would enhance sexual pleasure or draw attention to the erotic sphere, including nudity, sex education, fantasy, autoeroticism, and premarital and extramarital sexuality.[90] The Bruderhof moral code systematically repressed erotic action and thoughts by instituting an asceticism that prohibited surrender to the sensuous pleasures of the body. The Bruderhof championed a childlike spirit of innocence. Sexual intercourse and knowledge of carnal matters were to be restricted to conjugal couples, themselves baptized members of the commune, who sublimated their passion in the interests of God-willed action enjoined to bring forth children and love one another as an expression of God's sacred affection and mystery.

Children, adolescents, and young single adults proved particularly dangerous with regard to pollution. Constant vigilance and sexual moralism were required to ensure their safety and purity. As Mary Douglas explains, these groups were in transition to new statuses, moving toward definable roles. "Danger lies in transition states, simply because transition is neither one state nor the next, it is indefinable. The person who must pass from one to another is himself in danger and emanates danger to others."[91] Groups mitigate this danger by ritual: rites of passage, the segregation of children, novices, or unmarried adults. Nevertheless, categories of persons in the Bruderhof who were marginal and in transition represented a constant threat of pollution, sin, or openings for Satanic advance.

This sense of danger is apparent in the Bruderhof ambivalence toward children and childhood. Bruderhof orthodoxy adopted both a sentimentalized, angelic image of the child and, simultaneously, the fear that Satan used the weakness of children as points of entry for demonic attack. The issue of demonic attack and possession of children and adults was introduced to Bruderhof orthodoxy in the writings of Eberhard Arnold through his reading of Johann Christoph Blumhardt and Christoph Friedrich Blumhardt. The Blumhardts counsel loving, gentle treatment of troubled children, hoping that such care will bring the child to Christ in spiritual battle against Satan. However, they understood the dangers of rearing "problem" children and write, "There are times, too, when a child is as though possessed by an evil spirit or at least as though an evil spirit were working in him and making him stubborn and resistant."[92] This idea of the child as vessel for the evil spirit received great emphasis in Bruderhof thought and practice.

Eberhard Arnold romanticized childhood. *"Each child is a thought in the mind of God"*[93] "In every child there is love for the earth."[94] Writing on the mission of education in community, he states that each child must be shaped to conform to the needs of the group and awakened to their indwelling spirituality: "it is trust in the voice of God rising in every child as a desire for community and as joy in purity, truth and love. We show this trust in our daily dealings with the children through respect and reverence for the essential good that is alive in all children. . . . For us, education means awakening the child to the essential and ultimate thing that lives in the depth of his heart."[95]

But Bruderhof orthodoxy held an alternate image of the child as one who easily falls prey to evil, as "naughty," egotistical, selfish creatures prone to "chronic indifference and dull ingratitude."[96] Arnold writes: "it would be wrong to suppose that there is no struggle in a child's life, no temptation to evil. That insight into the nature of a child which we owe to Jesus only, shows us how terrifying it is when the will to evil appears in a child and urges him on to action. This is why children must be led to arouse and strengthen their own ability to give themselves to the good."[97]

Some Servants of the Word and community leaders were preoccupied with issues of sexuality, seeking to repress all sexual impurity from this age of innocence. Eberhard Arnold speaks clearly to the issue of sexual impurity and the dangers to children and adolescents.

> Sexual impurity is the most dangerous poison of untruthfulness and deceit. It robs us of our freedom. . . . Purity is the essence of love and, like truth, it is the secret of the life which is God himself. The life of God is love in purity and truth.
>
> The deepest thing that we can ask for our children is that while they are still at the innocent age when they cannot yet distinguish between good and evil, the whole atmosphere in which they live may be filled by the Holy Spirit of purity and love. That must be our chief concern, otherwise we shall be guilty of a crime against the children.[98]

Young children who were reported to the Servants for taking an "excessive" interest in the opposite sex or having mentioned the mysteries of reproduction have been subjected to interrogations and clearings, forced confessions, and purifying exclusions. Roger Allain reflects upon his experience as a Servant in Primavera:

> Some servants and educations were so sex-obsessed that they smelled the slightest whiff of sex, impurity and sin in the most natural and harmless situations. A young man and a girl could be kept apart or sent off to another hof if suspected of an undue attraction, official engagements were broken off in case of the slightest intimacy before marriage, brothers confessing masturbation were repeatedly humiliated and excluded; but much worse still, even very young children were punished and/or excluded if convicted or even suspected of "impure" play or curiosity.[99]

The case of an 11-year-old girl typifies the Bruderhof moral code of sexual repression and the expulsion of pollution. She lived with her family in Primavera in 1950. One Sunday while on an outing with her mother and a school friend, the girls happened to observe donkeys mating. She writes "Now I knew this male donkey was less than a year old, so I casually remarked to my friend, 'Gee, I didn't know that donkeys did this at such a young age!'"[100]

The next day the housemother and later the servants began their interrogation. The leadership assembled a dossier of the girl's sexual transgressions that included lewd conversation and "dirty poems." They accused the girl of writing a limerick that branded her as a sinner and resulted in her temporary removal from her family and exclusion to Ibaté. Public degradation and exclusion were the punishments meted out for the chance comment of a curious, independent, and rebellious girl who delighted in sharing forbidden knowledge with her peers and reciting "scandalous" lines of verse, such as

> My bonnie lies over the ocean
> My bonnie lies over the sea.
> I gave her a kiss on her bottom,
> Oh bring back my bonnie to me.[101]

Several months later, she was brought before Ibaté Servants. "I was asked what I could do to get out of this mess. I sat in silence, shaking my head. The silence of the group hit me back. I was asked again and again. I realized there had to be a 'right' answer. My father started to weep. He sobbed. . . . After what seemed hours, I finally said, 'I must ask God for help.' "[102] After eight months of repentance and correction, she was returned to her family and life regained a semblance of normality.

Allain explains Bruderhof practice.

> We were incredibly prudish, avoided all reference to sex and repressed it as "impure" in its most harmless manifestations. Of course there were degrees in our condemnation of "impurity," but our puritanical code made us condemn and severely punish even young children caught in sexual games or exhibitionism. At the age of six, our own Simon had been excluded from the family and the school for several weeks, along with other playmates, for just such an offense.[103]

One ex-community member relates her childhood in Primavera as a time filled with recriminations for her purported wickedness and sexual misdeeds. Her parents would leave her in the evenings at age five in the care of the Night Watch to attend evening Brotherhood meetings. She remembers being awakened one night. "It was a hot night, and in my sleep my nightgown had moved up my little body exposing my bottom. I woke up in terror, and this woman . . . [the Night Watch] said to me, 'You filthy, dirty girl!' "[104] During her childhood in Primavera she received many admonitions, clearances, and punishments, and was locked away in a small room for hours to correct childish misdeeds. Her family moved to Wheathill in 1957. There the Servants of the Word interrogated her about a special friendship with a boy. She explains:

> I saw a group of Servants of the Word sitting in a semi-circle. I had to stand in front of my judges, and they proceeded to accuse me of sinning

against God. I was a dirty girl, a disgrace to all. Lots of questions were asked, but I could not talk because I was so terrified and felt so humiliated. I was 15, and my breasts were showing through my blouse, and these men sat there and accused me of sinning. They kept this up for almost an hour. All I did was cry constantly and I peed my pants. Then I was told I was not to return to school, to have no contact with anyone. For three weeks I had to peel spuds and sprouts in the little hut across from the kitchen. . . . I was branded UNCLEAN and the whole community knew this.[105]

As a Servant in Primavera, Allain heard the confessions of unmarried men who felt tormented by the sin of masturbation, a married man living in separation from his wife and guilt-ridden over nocturnal emissions, cases of conscience involving premarital sexuality and adolescent sexual daydreams. He eventually would conclude that "collective sexual repression leads to sexual obsession. The fear of sin hung over the thoughts and sleep of unfortunate brothers who had succumbed to 'impurity' at one time or another."[106]

Throughout Bruderhof history, Servants of the Word labored to repress masturbation among adolescents and single brothers, interrogating offenders, asking about the frequency of this "self-abuse," and urging boys and girls to pray to Jesus for strength to resist temptation. One youth coming of age in Primavera experienced the onset of puberty as convincing evidence of Satan's influence. Nocturnal emissions and awakening sexual feelings filled him with shame. He was convinced that he and he alone harbored these impure and evil inclinations and practices. He attempted suicide after his family removed to Woodcrest during the Great Crisis and explains:

"I remember how often I envied the natives of Paraguay their carefree ways. There was that incredible sensualness of the Paraguayan women and I viewed my sense of being drawn to them as a sign of the evil in me. Even after I had been sent away I saw the great relief I felt as part of Satan's work—he was seducing me to like the free world even though I did not participate in the 'sexually liberated' American ways."

Another single American brother observed this situation among brothers in Primavera.

Of course some people had more masturbation problems than others. There were a couple of guys whose lives were ruined by it. They became hangdog burned out personalities from having to get up and confess so many times. I particularly remember one of them, this poor little bald-headed bookkeeper, who lived where I lived. He had to get up and confess to it so many times that he was numb about confessing. . . .

It seemed to me, the older one got, the nastier this sin seemed to the other Bruderhof members. We had a paraplegic guest, an old guy who had been hit by a car in Buenos Aires, and could barely shuffle around, an old German. The only work he could do was peel the skin off garlic, all alone . . . I noticed that some important people had a hostile attitude toward him. I asked, "What's the matter? I know he isn't very bright, and he doesn't seem to be all to with it as the requirements of faith." "He's nasty. He's a dirty old man." So they apparently knew . . . probably from his laundry.

These concerns about sexuality and purity continue unabated today. Johann Christoph Arnold, Eberhard's grandson and the third Arnold to lead the movement, has recently written *A Plea for Purity* (1996). This dogmatic plea for purity provides a long list of impure beliefs and practices that members must avoid. He explains, "I have counseled many young people who are enslaved by masturbation: they earnestly desire to be freed from their habits, but they fall into it again and again."[107] Other impurities include feminism and belief in the equality of women, reproductive rights of women (abortion and contraception), sex education in public schools, homosexuality (conduct and lifestyle), pornography and sexually explicit mass culture, transsexualism, sexual perversion, divorce, and remarriage.

Andrei Codrescu visited Woodcrest in 1990, doing research for his film and companion book *Road Scholar*. He relates a conversation with several Bruderhof teenagers.

> TEEN 1: "I don't know of any boy that's ever felt attracted to me, but when I feel attracted to a boy I just try and not show it because there's nothing . . . I won't . . . it won't . . . there's nothing I can do about it. . . . [Codrescu] While I was talking with the young people, an elder who was listening admonished them: "Speak of Jesus or it's meaningless!" I bet. God forbid they should inadvertently succumb to a rock star younger than Jesus.[108]

Questions of sexual purity and rituals of purification reached their extremes during episodic community crises. One ex-member remembers the creation of a "children's clearing house" in the Forest River community in 1956 during a time of community turmoil. He relates the imposition of religious discipline when he was seven years old. The Bruderhof used a basement to separate the offending children from their parents. He writes:

> We who were spied upon and reported to be engaging in various pro-scribed activities, such as watching each other pee or daring to take off our shorts under the covers when we went to bed at night, were isolated from the rest of the children for months, and taken from our normal families. . . . I remember enduring interrogation sessions during which I could only cry and sob. All my normal relationships were suspended as I

was kept isolated from the rest of my family and the extended family of which I was a part in the colony.[109]

The issues of sexual purity and purification of children coincided with the harsh adult spiritual politics of community-wide purges during the Wheathill Crisis of 1948. Several English community members had remained behind in 1941 during the South American diaspora and they formed the nucleus for the Wheathill community, begun on two economically marginal farms. The Bruderhof's principal community, Primavera, could not easily coordinate and control satellite hofs like Wheathill because of problems in communication and the great distances that separated the settlements. Inevitably, "Word Leaders" or Servants of the Word and Witness Brothers in the satellite English hof would develop extracanonical or idiosyncratic interpretations of Arnold theology and church discipline.

Llewelyn Harries assumed spiritual direction of Wheathill in the late 1940s. He interjected into Bruderhof belief archaic ideas about good and evil spiritual forces that reside in nature and come to possess the souls of children and men and women of faith. Harries claimed that he and he alone enjoyed the gift of discernment, of harkening to God's holy voice that spoke to him and identified the evil spirits that threatened the community. He discerned who among the community had succumbed to the contamination of evil spirits. Unbaptized, innocent, and corruptible children were most vulnerable to the lure of evil spirits and sexual pollution.

Harries began purging those defiled by evil spirits. Elizabeth Bohlken-Zumpe provides this account of the crisis:

> "Evil" began to be seen everywhere, and the whole community busied themselves fighting against it. Marriages were separated, and the men sent away. The children were sent to Cleeton Court [one of the two Wheathill farms] to ponder their sexual sins. Some children were interrogated in such a way that today they have not overcome the abuse. One boy my own age was born before his parents were married, so he was suspected of having inherited an evil, dirty, sexual spirit. . . . A sister was asked to ring the big bell on the hill to drive away the demons overshadowing the community.[110]

One ex-Bruderhof woman remembers the crisis of the Spring of 1948, when she was 11 years old. She overheard two of her schoolmates discuss "sexual play." When she refused to turn in her classmates or discuss this "guilty knowledge," the leadership began interrogating her and quickly imposed church discipline. She was excluded from her family for ten weeks. She explains:

> I was interrogated by a group of mothers in the black hut as to why I did not report on the two children. They ordered me to stand, and tried to

force a confession out of me, surmising that a wrong doing on my part was the reason I had not talked. Again and again I said that I had done nothing. They were very hostile. . . . The next day my mother told me Llewelyn had said in the brotherhood that my situation was very serious and that he decided that I was to be excluded, not only from the children's community, but also from my family. The shame and pain of that moment is still with me. I asked my mother how long. I protested, "Not my family too!"[111]

The Primavera Bruderhof regained control of Wheathill by sending two Servants of the Word as emissaries. They managed to freeze bank accounts, seize ownership of the commune's assets, and challenge Harries and exclude him for heretical conduct. Previously excluded children and adults returned to their families and community, and Wheathill regained a semblance of normalcy.

The eleven-year-old girl quoted above explains that after reuniting with her family, she was questioned by the new Servant of the Word, who asked:

"Did I still have anything on my conscience?" That question was such a blow. It implied that I had been bad, but had been overly punished. Still very burdened and confused, I was allowed to rejoin my family in Clee-ton Court. . . . The kids figured out that the Harries were in exclusion and [that is] where they were. A year later, we were told that the brotherhood had reunited with Llewelyn and that he had been sick and forgotten everything. But what about us kids? It was as if the evil done to us were grown-up business. Even though we were children, we deserved a full explanation, a complete taking back of things we were accused of, a full apology from everyone involved. . . . [112]

Llewelyn Harries had been discredited as a mentally ill man who committed outrages against children during his breakdown. However, Harries's use of folk religion and belief in spirits resonates with Pietist and mystical doctrines articulated by the Blumhardts and long accepted by Bruderhof orthodoxy. This theology envisions a cosmic battle against the forces of evil and the ever-present temptations of Satan who would infiltrate the community through it's most vulnerable members— women and children. Blumhardt cast out a demon at Bad Böll, and through exorcism proclaimed, "Jesus is Victor!" Eberhard Arnold re-peated this victory over the Devil within the early German Bruderhof.

Harries's behavior during the community crisis reflected prevailing European attitudes about children that were derived from nineteenth-century Protestant doctrines of evangelical nurture. These doctrines in-cluded will-breaking and corporal punishment to facilitate unquestion-ing obedience and submission to parental authority and hierarchial church authority, analogous to the surrender of each Christian to God's will. Without intending to injure children, motivated by the most elevated religious ideals and guided by long tradition and theological mandate, Bruderhof parents attempted to "win their children for the community" and to "win their children for Jesus." Parents and community leaders, acting in the name of these highest ideals, employed corporal punishment, excluded children, conducted protracted interrogations and clearances, and suppressed and punished masturbation and adolescent sexuality. In this view, children do not represent an end in themselves but a means to an end, an instrument or tool that parents shape, transforming the natural, sinful creature into a new creation molded in the image of God.

The Bruderhof has not suffered persecution or martyrdom in pursuit of the primordium during their sojourn in America. The leadership has needed to "manufacture" the attacks by the forces of evil. Church discipline and the obsession with purity are inextricably linked to the need to battle the enemies of faith. As Franklin H. Littell observes about the Great Crisis, 1959–1961: "Smaller and more deliberately intense churches may also experience the same transmutation when their eschatology flags and fails. The present crisis of discipline within the Bruderhof movement may be taken as a contemporary illustration of the spiritual problems that arise when martyrdom is far distant and a seductive general culture is very near."[113]

Heini Arnold stressed childhood purity, precocious spirituality, and childhood piety, creating a childhood ideal fashioned from the remembrance of his own early conversion. Beginning in the 1970s, he held yearly interhof conferences for schoolchildren and adolescents. As Nadine Moonje Pleil recounts: "Heini wanted the children to make some sort of commitment to Jesus. He told them about his 'Jesus Experience' as a twelve-year-old. Some children felt very moved by this and wanted to start what Heini called a 'Sun Troop.' They came together to sing songs and talk about Jesus."[114]

Pleil and her husband engaged in a seemingly endless series of confrontations with Servants and teachers who criticized her "problem children," who admonished her for failing to win the children for Jesus, and who insisted that the Pleils administer beatings while the Servants used interrogations and exclusions to correct the children's errant behavior and attitudes. The Pleil children blamed their parents for failing to protect them from the Servants' discipline. Nadine Pleil describes one incident with her son Amadeus.

> When Amadeus was twelve, he was once again called into the Servant's office and this time it was serious. He was told that he had touched a twelve-year-old girl. We were also called in.
>
> "Your son has been told so many times to leave the girls alone, but he doesn't listen," one of the Servants told us. "What are you, his parents going to do?"

All Amadeus had done was to jump out at the girls [*sic*] when she went into the dining room and yell, "You're it!" and touch her on the shoulder. This incident was observed by one of the women walking behind the girl and who reported our son. Amadeus was very upset because once again too much had been made of a small playful prank. Then suddenly both Servants began to speak at the same time. "If Amadeus were my son, I would beat him." . . . So against our better judgment, we applied that type of punishment. Of course it did not help, but only alienated Amadeus from us.[115]

The Servants of the Word and community leadership moved quickly to punish "problem children," rebellious and stubborn children, and those judged to be evil as a result of precocious sexuality.

The Woodcrest Spirit placed renewed emphasis on the moralism of sexual repression, the obsessive concern with purity, and the exclusion of those judged guilty of sexual pollution. Under Heini's leadership, the *Plough* published Eberhard Arnold's work on sexual purity in 1965 and Heini's own treatise *In the Image of God, Marriage and Chastity in Christian Life* in 1977. These talks and sermons borrowed heavily from Eberhard's teachings. Heini proclaimed that men and women created in God's image, living in the imitation of Christ, needed to sublimate their fellowship and marital sexuality in the name of love to God and directed to God's glorification. In this manner, each conjugal couple finds a "marriage in the Holy Spirit," a unity of heart, soul, and body, and a purified sexuality informed by religious meanings and ends.[116] Absent this marriage in the Holy Spirit, individuals fall victim to pollution, opening their hearts to impure spirits, demons, and "an abyss of sinfulness."[117] Heini excoriated the abuse of sex by the impure: "He surrenders his secret, delivers himself over to base flesh, and desecrates and violates what God gave to man alone as His image, thereby separating himself in a terrible way from God."[118]

Heini sought to deal with the problem of sexual impurity by stressing the Innerland piety of his father's devotional theology and the inner-worldly mysticism of Meister Eckhart. In *Man The Image of God And Modern Psychology*, Heini embraces Eckhart's detachment from the erotic and all worldliness. "He seeks the relationship of man to God only; that is the center point. And Eckhart believes that if we detach ourselves from all things for the sake of God, then we do not need to suppress our nature: we find fulfillment in God, even if some urges of the animal in us are still in our subconscious."[119] Heini maintained, citing Eckhart, that a regulated, sublimated sexual moralism could prevent any expression of the socially disruptive and spiritually destructive erotic sphere.

One important regulation for single young adults involved the engagement *Gemeindestunde*, or prayer meeting, at which single men and women came forward and asked the assembled Brotherhood for permission to marry. This public testimony placed each petitioner's motives and spirituality under collective judgment. Only those couples who voiced a pious, Jesus-centered love toward each other passed public scrutiny by the Elder, the commune leadership, and the assembled church-community. Heini published numerous accounts of engagement prayer meetings as models for all communities to emulate. One of these, *Jesus Calls Each One by Name*, reports public testimonials of April 1977 made by Stephen King and Lucille Ehrlich.

> STEPHEN KING: I have very great love for Lucille Ehrlich, and I would like to ask the Brotherhood if I could go this way with her. I just want while I have a chance to thank you all very much. . . .
>
> HEINI: Lucille, would you like to say something?
>
> LUCILLE EHRLICH: Stephen and I are just very happy in Jesus and we want that Jesus Christ is always first and central, and this is the sense in which we ask.
>
> HEINI: Also here the parents are very much in agreement. Is the Brotherhood in agreement with that?
>
> ALL: Yes![120]

The punishment for adultery was harsh. In June 1960 in a letter to his wife, Hans Zumpe confessed to a protracted adulterous relationship while acting as Servant to the Wheathill community in the 1950s. Long seen as Heini's nemesis, Zumpe had been retired from service in 1958 and resided with his wife and children in Woodcrest at the time of this disclosure. Zumpe's transgression left him broken, depressed, and suicidal. Heini excluded Zumpe and returned him to Germany where he lived until his untimely death in a plane crash in 1973. Mow related the official Bruderhof account of the exclusion, stating that "it was impossible to come to church discipline and forgiveness because his attitude was not one of repentance but even one of resistance. . . . In the following years there were many attempts to reach out to him by letter, by phone, and by visits. He was asked to seek repentance in order to find reconciliation, but he never did. . . . [121]

In fact, Heini intercepted all correspondence between Hans Zumpe and his wife Emi-Ma, preventing her from ever knowing the depths of her husband's anguish and contrition. There would be no way back for a member of thirty years who had committed a grievous sexual sin, despite evidence of sincere repentance and his desire to return to his family and Bruderhof, as evidenced in a letter dated July 9, 1960:

> Dear Emi-Ma, in my mind and spirit I keep writing long letters to you, but in reality I have been writing this over a couple of days. I would just like to tell you in very simple words how very ashamed and sorry I am for what has happened. . . . Humanly speaking, there is no forgiveness for me, because I can never make undone what I did. I feel with grief in my

heart that I have broken something that can never be the same again in the future.

Therefore there is just one way of deep repentance—the grief about my own sin and search and turning to Jesus alone in complete trust and surrender. He does not want the death of the sinner, but wants to awaken something new where everything seems lost![122]

How can we explain Heini's complete rejection of a repentant sinner when the logic of Bruderhof church discipline should actively seek to reform and return the wayward member? Zumpe's disgrace and exclusion removed an irritant personality who had opposed Heini Arnold. Zumpe's ouster and the fiction of his unrepentant heart dramatized the conflict between two atmospheres contesting the spirit of Primavera and the Woodcrest Spirit, setting the unassailable virtue of Heini over against the concupiscence of Zumpe. In addition, this morality drama provided expressive and symbolic support for sexual regulation and purity, casting out the impure, dangerous, contagious, and dirty adulterer. In this manner, Arnoldism vindicated the regimen of sexual repression and the denial of erotic. Should even an important Servant surrender to loneliness when separated from his wife while traveling on community business, should he betray his faith by indulging in the secret desires of the heart, he would suffer certain banishment.

Jesus Is Victor!

As Heini Arnold and his retinue strained to identify and purge sin from the church-community, evidence of ever greater and more ominous transgressions came to light. Sexual impurity, disunity, pride, and a plethora of other sins had opened the door to Satan. Heini knew that "Jesus is Victor over devils and demons. But the Brotherhood must be so deeply bound together in Jesus that no evil spirit can grieve Jesus at the Lord's Supper."[122] When Heini confronted what he perceived to be a case of demonic possession, he used this powerful symbol of the cosmic struggle between good and evil to transform the Bruderhof movement. Official Bruderhof history describes this time as the struggle between two atmospheres, one Christ-centered and authentic, the other humanistic and wayward. I have termed this the contest between the Spirit of Primavera and the Woodcrest Spirit.

Johann Christoph Blumhardt had exorcised a demon from a servant girl, Gottlieben, in 1842, proclaiming "Jesus is Victor!" Eberhard Arnold was profoundly influenced by Blumhardt and himself cast out demons in Sannerz in 1925. Heini Arnold fought the Prince of Darkness who had entered the Woodcrest Bruderhof in 1959, through the possession of a young novice, the pseudonymous Miriam Way. This episode lasted six months without a clear resolution to her spiritual crisis. The struggle for the soul of Miriam Way became the metaphor for the collective renewal of the Bruderhof movement. As Mow relates: "Even though the battle for this one person did not seem to end in a full redemption for her personally, it began a breakthrough in our Bruderhof struggle for renewal in a return to Christ as Center."[123]

Heini had committed the Plough Publishing House to translate and publish an English version of the Blumhardts' theology, then little known in America. Miriam Way worked in the Servant's Office in Woodcrest and was permitted to read the Blumhardt manuscripts. She soon manifested symptoms of possession. Ramón Sender, another novice who was in a baptismal preparation group with Way, describes her personality change, from outgoing and given to light-hearted remarks to withdrawn and hostile.

> Late one night, I received a call to come to Heini's apartment. I arrived to find twenty brothers and sisters gathered around Miriam who was lying on the bed thrashing around strangely. We sang hymns at Heini's request to drown out the obscenities that she was screaming. Her behavior resembled the possessed young woman in Blumhardt's book.[124]

The community segregated Way, removing her to special rooms in the Baby House and putting her under around-the-clock surveillance. Heini hoped to cure Miriam through exorcism, but he failed to achieve a victory for Christ and the crisis continued for many months. Sender writes:

> During intervals of lucidity, Miriam appeared at meals seated beside Heini, with a sweet, faraway expression on her face. . . . When not "under attack," she was, according to Heini, very perceptive on religious matters. However she was taking up a great deal of his time. One night there was a flurry of activity and the sound of a car leaving the parking lot. In the morning, I heard that Miriam had thrust both her arms through a window and severely cut her wrists. She was stitched up by a friendly doctor who promised not to report the matter to authorities. That same day, a work crew replaced all the glass panes in her room with unbreakable plexiglass.[125]

According to Sender, some members disagreed with Heini's diagnosis and treatment of Miriam's disorder, and they were excluded for questioning his authority in these matters. The community even took Miriam to visit a house that was purportedly the source of the spirit-force (poltergeist) that harassed her.[126] However, after a constant strain on personnel and many months of unfruitful pastoral care, Way's case proved intractable to religious cure. Heini equivocated about treating the case as demonic possession, and the Brotherhood decided in favor of psychiatric institutionalization. Mow writes, "she had to be hospitalized for her own protection, and as with Lotte Henze, we never did come through to a full freeing."[127]

The religious worldview of cosmic battle was useful in legitimating the consolidation of political authority. Using his gifts of the Spirit of discernment, Heini distinguished believers who manifested an evil, impure, insincere, and egocentric spirit from those souls who enjoyed the authentic Christ-centered Spirit. In 1959, during the spiritual battles for the soul of Miriam Way, Heini removed long-term guests and prospective members who did not manifest the emotional fervor and "warmth of heart" requisite to the Innerland piety that now served as a distinguishing mark of conversion and community membership.[128] He expelled guests, novices, and weaker members as a threat to the collective, as an opening to Satanic attack. Confronted with devils and demonic possession, he reaffirmed the absolute necessity of unity among the Brotherhood as the only defense. Those brethren who raised questions, challenges, or grievances against Arnoldism and its adherents opened the door to the Devil. Brethren who promoted disunity had no place in the Gemeinde; they faced expulsion.

Warmth of heart came to characterize younger and more zealous members in contrast with the sedate, cold-heartedness of the parental generation. And the possession of a warm heart separated nationalities in the community. Benjamin Zablocki explains: "some of the German members harbored a feeling that the English, and to a lesser extent the Swiss, were cold-hearted, while the Germans and the Americans tended to be warm-hearted. . . . This diversity, which for a quarter of a century had been proclaimed as one of the finest aspects of Bruderhof life, suddenly became, in 1960, an intolerable source of disunity."[129]

The interhof conference held in 1953 began the process that eventually resulted in the schisms of the Great Crisis. Acting in conformity with a group that was in Heini Arnold's words "authoritarian with respect to Christ,"[130] Arnold and his American converts reaffirmed the Innerland piety and pneumatical exegesis of the founder's era. Those who championed the Woodcrest Spirit would actively discredit the Spirit of Primavera as a declension. The Bruderhof expansion in South American and Europe had never achieved economic self-sufficiency but made a livelihood by Werbung, or begging, in the mendicant tradition. The Woodcrest Witness Brothers repeatedly challenged Primavera to abandon their agricultural project of commercial rice production and adopt a manufacturing-industrial enterprise. A second interhof conference was precipitated when Bud Mercer in Primavera wrote to Mark Kurtz in Oak Lake in the fall of 1959, questioning the propriety of spending $250 to send Eberhard's widow, Emmy Arnold, to visit England. Charged with a "lack of love," Servants from Primavera, Wheathill, and Bulstrode traveled to Oak Lake in May 1959 for fraternal correction and the restoration of interhof unity. Mow relates the shared understanding that Woodcrest would assume leadership of the movement, that South American hofs would close and the Bruderhof would be consolidated and unified consistent with the Woodcrest Spirit.[131]

The interhof conference unleashed a series of clearances in Primavera that culminated in a request for Woodcrest to send leaders to assist in the reconstitution of the Brotherhood. Zablocki quotes one ex-member at length:

> A little cloud no bigger than a man's hand grew to a storm of self-criticism, fault finding, confession, near hysteria, and more confessions, as Primavera gave itself a house-cleaning that went on night after night in all three villages for three months. Two women had to be taken to Asunción for electric shock treatment. Sins, prides, and hostilities emerged that had been covered over as long as fifteen years. . . . The American Brotherhoods sent members to help with what amounted to setting up community life on a fresh basis."[132]

In late January of 1960, Heini, Art Wiser, and Doug Moody traveled to Paraguay, followed a month later by Merrill Mow and Gert Wegner. The Americans reportedly discovered cold-hearted declension, confessions of enmity toward Eberhard Arnold, remarks disparaging Eberhard's children as the "royal family," and an admission that Emmy Arnold's writings and diaries were taken from her and locked away in a "poison cabinet."[133] Others confessed and accepted responsibility for Heini's "betrayal" by Hans Zumpe. During this first month of collective clearings and revival, the Brotherhoods were near collapse. Mow writes on February 7 describing collective anxiety that bordered on bedlam, with some members remaining immobilized in stunned silence, fixed on the spot like statues, while others protested in vociferous anger.[134] One former Servant wrote that Heini "has been yelling at the circle there telling them they were never Christians. The whole Brotherhood weeping and sobbing and confessing sins. Heini says we were never a Christian community in all the twenty years in Paraguay."[135]

Robert N. Peck, who had joined the Bruderhof in 1948 and suffered exclusion during the Great Crisis, characterizes the Primavera clearance in the following terms:

> one of the founder's sons was raised to virtual sainthood status in the resuscitation of a decades old leadership struggle. He was backed by a number of recent American converts, who with the overzealousness of the newly converted represented a narrow-minded evangelical strain sometimes found in American Protestantism. In a specifically Christian group it was peculiarly difficult to resist the accusations of one who laid claim to religious experience and wielded his sword in the name of Jesus. It was equally difficult to resist the claim that the community had fallen from its true origins and must go back to them.[136]

After two months and under Heini's direction, the American Witness brothers had dissolved the Primavera brotherhood and examined each member to ascertain whether or not they manifested a warm heart, fervent piety, and reverence for Eberhard Arnold and his successor, Heini Arnold. Thus began the mass exclusion of people who previously enjoyed full membership but who could not qualify under the stringent spiritual tests of the new brotherhood lists organized according to the standards of the Woodcrest Spirit. Roger Allain, who rejected the new brotherhood and left voluntarily after two decades of service, writes of the "morass of frenzied clearances and collective introspection."[137]

> In the meetings that now followed, dozens of people accused themselves or were accused of coldness, lack of faith, or irreverence. A wave of guilt feelings, confessions and mutual recriminations was unleashed. Some of those who had accused themselves were absolved, those who tried to justify themselves were attacked from all sides. Every meeting ended with one or two, then three or four exclusions.[138]

In the name of the Holy Spirit and love to God, the American Witness Brothers worked enthusiastically to fight the pollution of the Spirit of Primavera, to punish those who stood accused of causing past injuries to Heini. Dr. Cyril Davies, who had treated Heini for his debilitating kidney infection in 1941, was charged with deliberately prescribing improper medication. Made to shave his beard as an act of public humiliation, Davies returned to Isla Margarita for continued admonishment. Following the closing of the Loma Hoby community and hospital in 1959, "Cyril was sent to Isla Margarita where the stones from his dismantled hospital were arriving by the wagonload. He was asked to clean the stones so they would be ready for sale. Cyril did that. He stood in the burning sun cleaning the stones and grieving for all the years and years of work that was being destroyed. . . ."[139]

Davies and scores of other members excluded in the Great Crisis never recovered from the involuntary and traumatic separation. As new apostates, they suffered shock and disorientation at having been judged spiritually inadequate, evil, and unfit for community membership in the new brotherhood—cast out into the sinful world of Mammonism. The Bruderhof showed extreme indifference to the material welfare of the apostates by providing little or no economic assistance. After years of hard work and service to the commune, many were cast out without passports, with uncertain immigration status, without money for travel or resettlement, without references, marketable job skills, or sponsors.

Elizabeth Bohlken-Zumpe recounts:

> I remember one of the [witness] brothers telling us at the Arnold home. "It was so difficult to keep to the strict line of the spirit. There was this elderly couple imploring us to be taken into the new brotherhood, almost begging on their knees, saying, 'All we have always wanted is to live this life of brotherhood and love. What have we done? Tell us, what have we

done to be sent away? Where shall we go? What shall we do? We gave our word at our baptism to be loyal, and that is what we want to be! Please, please don't send us away!'

"But it was evident that they were not in the new spirit," continued the brother. "So they were sent away."[140]

The Great Crisis proceeded with clearances in the English communities after Heini received, in June 1961, a remarkable letter of confession by Gwynn Evans (later repudiated as a statement given in a time of madness). He admitted to many wrongs: fostering an anti-Arnold spirit, personal attacks on Heini and the Arnold children during the Primavera crises in the 1940s, an unholy alliance with Hans Zumpe, and repeated criticism of Arnoldism and opposition to the Woodcrest Spirit. Evans would write, "It makes me shudder now to think of the hard things that I allowed myself to say and to do in this mood—let alone the dreadful perversion of the gospel message and the harm done to people's souls through this."[141]

The pattern of clearance, mass expulsion, and community closing and liquidation proceeded in Wheathill, Bulstrode, and Sinnthal. As Zablocki notes, "by 1962, the Bruderhof had undergone a major change in value orientation, and a purge of top leaders; the number of hofs had been reduced from nine to four, and half of the membership had quit or been sent away."[142]

Arnoldism as a worldview justified the mass expulsion of members found wanting in the Spirit and religious fervor. Roger Allain maintains that groups committed to the realization of absolute principles frequently resort to extreme methods to achieve their religious ends as in the absolute principle of clearance and purification of sin, purging the Spirit of Primavera regardless of the human cost. Allain quotes a letter from Gwynn Evans before his June confession:

Art [Wiser] spoke of it as the time of harvest when the grain was being sifted from the chaff. The same analogy was used in Geneva when the Calvinists were seeking to make it the Holy City, and all who did not match up to the requirements were sent to the stake or hurled out of the city. The comparison between Geneva at that time and the Bruderhof in this present time has often struck me forcibly."[143]

Conclusion

Arnoldism rationalized the Bruderhof movement as a primitivistic and Pietistic spiritual hothouse and successfully implemented Eberhard Arnold's mature vision of an authoritarian community marked by the indoctrination and conversion for adults and the evangelical nurture for children and adolescents. The community mechanisms of social control through church discipline of individual members, and the collective rituals of purification and purgation promoted collective unity. Maintaining the United Brotherhood became an end itself. Once this mechanism of spiritual polity was fully institutionalized, it mattered little if the direction of group unity was the Spirit of Primavera, the Woodcrest Spirit, or Harries's (neo-Pagan) shamanistic spiritualism.

Louis Dumont considered communities that require surrender of the individual to the group and suppression of freedom of conscience as "the totalitarian disease." He writes, "totalitarianism is a disease of modern society that results from the attempt, in a society where individualism is deeply rooted and predominant, to subordinate it to the primacy of the society as a whole."[144] Among the Bruderhof, the spiritual polity of the founder's era, long suppressed by the democratic humanism of the Spirit of Primavera, was revitalized during the succession crisis and the ascendancy of Heini Arnold's Woodcrest Spirit.

Those who rejected the Woodcrest Spirit or were excluded in the Great Crisis charged Arnoldism with authoritarianism and the suppression of religious individualism. Bob and Shirley Wagoner, who visited Primavera in 1953, decided not to join the Bruderhof, despite their ebullient endorsement of Primavera written from Chicago after returning in 1954.

> there is no doubt in my mind that we saw there the fullest expression we have ever seen of the New Testament life. . . . This same incarnation of love can and does happen when persons do choose and accept Christ's lordship over their life. Their life then becomes at once a revelation and a command. It demonstrates what God can do with lives under his dominion, and it is an imperative summons to discipleship. This is what happened to us at the Bruderhof. We saw and were pulled. It spoke to our condition in an unforgettable manner.[145]

Bob performed alternative service in Puerto Rico as a conscientious objector to war, but he never returned to the Bruderhof. Heini corresponded with Bob and Shirley, exhorting them to recommit themselves to the challenge of Christian communalism and addressing their concerns and objections regarding Bruderhof authoritarianism. Writing on October 21, 1955, Heini seeks to assuage their doubts about Bruderhof spiritual polity. Heini explains that "There were one or two sentences in your letters where I had the feeling that you think of the Bruderhof as authoritarian; I am not sure if my impression is right. In a certain way we are authoritarian (with respect to Christ). . . ."[146]

Bob and Shirley Wagoner ultimately rejected the authoritarianism of the Woodcrest Spirit. Others who shared the Wagoners' objections published personal accounts of the Great Crisis. Francis and Pearl Hall were Bruderhof members in Primavera and El Arado for seven years until their removal in 1961. Writing in the *Christian Century* in August 1963,

Francis Hall argued that intentional communities founded upon the promise of a community of love frequently devolve into authoritarian suppression of religious individualism and freedom of conscience. Hall enumerates three tensions between individual freedom and the totalistic demands of individual surrender and unity within an organic community.

> First, there is the inordinate amount of time consumed in attempts to solve these personal differences. Second, the desire to make the community succeed opens the door to exaggerations of all types: taking itself as a group too seriously; obsessions with orthodoxy or with purification from all traits of sin; enthroning of people into places of exalted religious authority; subjecting the individual to corporate values, breaking the spirits of those who do not come into the united image. Third, the attempt to save the community can lead to the building of a wall between it and the world and to dominance by fear in protecting itself against contamination from the world. The main consequences of all this is a tragedy: that group which had set out to be a witness for a unified life of love becomes a force of division, finding its unity by sending away everyone who disagrees with its authoritarian directions. . . . [147]

Four

SURRENDERED TO JESUS

Varieties of Religious Melancholy

Dear God, what do you have in mind for me? Why do I live in such unreality? I am also Thy child and belong to Thee and Thou willst help me. But the days drag out and I do not see my way in front of me, but am only anxious about them. Help me to step out of myself and into Thy hands. Amen.

Prayer of a young
Bruderhof woman

Bruderhof social structure and high-demand church-community create a regimen of ceaseless stress for devotees. Believers must work hard to remain within the orthodoxy of communal unity, struggling to ensure that their actions, utterances, thoughts, and intentions reflect religious authenticity in "the right spirit," as judged by the leadership. Members must willingly submit to admonishment, fraternal correction, and escalating forms of church discipline. They are enjoined to experience spiritual humiliation as an outpouring of brotherly love. Indeed, believers must ask for discipline or assist in administering discipline to others in the name of Christian love. The faithful ardently desire redemptive suffering. Members must mobilize considerable anxiety and emotional energy in the constant struggle against Satanic attack from without and within, purging the unworthy, purifying the sinner, and hating the outsider who they believe seeks to destroy the Bruderhof because of their commitment to Jesus. They live with chronic anxiety, at the edge of enthusiasm, in dialectical opposition with the perceived enemies of faith.

Corresponding to their spiritual polity, Innerland piety requires that believers achieve an intensive, contemplative experience of regeneration, conversion, and assurance as children of God. The social-psychological dimensions of a Christ-centered, "surrendered life" create fervent devotees who eagerly embrace the travail of Bruderhof existence. Elements of social structure, particularly sexual repression within authoritarian-patriarchal families, create authoritarian temperament or social character.

Each Bruderhof religious personality needed and expected to receive Christian love through the punishment of church discipline and, in turn, to give others love by the methodical administration of parental or church discipline. Trapped in this psychic economy of love, parents used corporal punishment with their children as an act of love in submission to the leadership's orders. Children were expected to receive church discipline, however harsh, and thank their parents and elders for these acts of love. In this manner, Bruderhof religious personalities were marked by a transvaluation of desire as redemptive suffering. The introjection of this expression of Christian love and the externalization of these toxic introjects upon the enemies of faith constituted an organizing principle of Bruderhof personality and interpersonal relations.

Through the administration of church discipline, the leadership mobilized true believers in ritualized purges and purifications characterized by cathartic abreactions, ecstatic fusions, and childlike joy. Thus, their psychic economy needed enemies of the faith–Satan, "persecution" by unbelievers, and, from within, the sinful impurity of weak brothers and children and adolescents who were not yet "formed" as religious personalities. In the blink of an eye, a child, adolescent, or adult baptized true believer could be transformed from a person in good standing into a demonized and impure enemy of the faith.

Not infrequently, believers found themselves overwhelmed by the tyrannical burdens of their religious vocation, succumbing to spiritual desolation, and convinced that they were unworthy of God's love. Others have been beset by temptations, obsessions with sinful thoughts, and compulsions to commit blasphemy or impure acts.

Heini Arnold addressed the burdens of Bruderhof spirituality in his pastoral theology. In his published writings and sermons, he taught that men and women in a "natural" and unconverted state existed in a tension field caught between animal and spirit, mired in a neurotic attitude, a *Geisteskrank*, or sickness in spirit. "Apart from Christ, in every one a neurotic attitude is to a greater or lesser extent inborn. The extreme case of this attitude is a complete inability to find oneself, which is complete derangement."[1] Conversion purportedly brought new life, mental health, and an abiding sense of purpose and fulfillment through surrender to Jesus. And for many of the Bruderhof faithful childlike submission to Christ conveyed the salvation promises of release from suffering. They successfully forged a religiously grounded personality devoted to the fulfillment of the absolute ethic of brotherliness through religious authoritarianism, renunciation of an autonomous ego-identity, the punishing Bruderhof experience of love through church discipline, and the dialectic of opposition.

God's children in the community, however, frequently succumbed to sickness of spirit—the very malady that afflicted unconverted men and women. Wayne E. Oates defines spiritual sickness as "specific situations in which particular people suffer major failures of functioning in the conduct of their lives because of religious preoccupations and stumbling blocks."[2] On the one hand, Heini set before believers the very religious preoccupations and stumbling blocks that produced life crises. He understood that the trials of faith would engender redemptive suffering in the sick in spirit and foster their spiritual growth. On the other hand, Heini recognized that protracted and unrelieved episodes of spiritual sickness trapped devotees in religious obsessions and produced clinical depressions among the Bruderhof faithful.

Heini needed to guide believers through these trials but prevent the onset of religious obsession, mental illness, and emotional breakdowns. A Christocentric faith should protect believers from the anguish of the existential condition of unregenerate humanity and promote a this-worldly salvation through the health and emotional balance of believers committed to a world of total meaning.

Heini recognized the prevalence of spiritual sickness, "cramped wills," and obsessive sinful thoughts and temptations among those youths and adults who struggled ceaselessly to embrace Pietistic conversion—surrender of the individual self to Jesus. As a charismatic director of souls, he was prompted to write a pastoral guide for the perplexed (a companion to his father's *Innerland*), seeking to assuage the spiritual predicaments of the Bruderhof faithful. Heini explains why he wrote *Freedom from Sinful Thoughts*: "I have put this book together because there are some in our households and even some who grew up in the communities who are really tormented against their will by evil thoughts, images or ideas."[3]

Heini explained that the Devil caused this torment, afflicting the faithful with sinful thoughts, temptations, and seemingly overpowering urges to commit blasphemy, to renounce God and rise up in cold-hearted rebellion against God's laws. Akin to Christ in his travail in the desert and at Gethsemane, the spiritually sick person felt beset by evil spirits who urged the believer to abandon faith in God.

Citing the work of Charles Baudouin, *Suggestion and Autosuggestion*, Heini argues that an initial sinful thought quickly develops into an irresistible compulsion to commit the imagined transgression. Thus, the spiritually sick believer found himself or herself haunted by evil thoughts, compulsions to sinful acts, in the throes of devilish attack, and bereft of divine comfort. In this predicament, the believer was immobilized, fearful of committing unpardonable sins, languishing with a cramped will.

Those suffering from the sick soul could find healing, purification of the heart, and agency to act with renewed powers of volition by following Heini's regimen of spiritual direction for troubled souls. He prescribed the practice of daily devotional piety—prayer, meditation, and reading from the published works of the Arnold canon. He advised sick souls to learn the technique of inner-worldly mystical "inner detachment"—silencing the ego and the creature so that the heart may open to receive the Spirit and love of God. He urged upon the afflicted a meditation and contemplation of Jesus derived from Meister Eckhart's inner-worldly mysticism of inner detachment.

> It is a daily necessity for every Christian to drop all inner tension so that he can experience inner detachment and thus be able to hear what Jesus is saying to his heart. . . .
>
> It will be of critical importance for one who is particularly tempted, therefore, always to concentrate his inward vision completely on Jesus. Absolutely everything possible must be done to find inner quiet and to drop the cramped "will" so that what is deepest in the heart can speak in all quietness, in all stillness and inner peace; so that the heart can find detachment in faith.[4]

When the supplicant emptied his or her heart to God and adopted a child-like faith, then the work of healing might begin. "Here, at the Cross, every soul can find peace. Those deep words which say that the blood of Jesus Christ purifies us from all sin indicate that it is in order to be purified that we go through this suffering with Him."[5] In selfless and absolute surrender to Jesus, the faithful purified their hearts from sin, found new powers of godly volition, and understood that Jesus is victor over Satan. Christ alone breaks the curse.

But who could say whether the newly converted or the already converted who exclaimed "Jesus is Victor!" would continue to enjoy this-worldly salvation as believers "immunized" against repeated episodes of religious melancholy and soul sickness? Was Christ's victory abiding? Did not Satan repeatedly challenge the church-community? Did not human frailty, even among the converted and godly, subject them to renewed temptations of the flesh or even more heinous sins? *Freedom from Sinful Thoughts* implied a life of travail replete with seasons of childlike joy and communion with Jesus and the church-community and punctuated by times of soul sickness and spiritual desolation. The very structure of evangelical Pietism adopted by Eberhard and Heini Arnold ensured the repetition of religious melancholy among the Bruderhof faithful. Heini knew and acknowledged what the contemporary Bruderhof leaders deny: the affinity of Christocentric piety and the absolute ethic of brotherliness with the sick soul.

The heady emotionalism of Innerland piety with its strains of mystical-illuminism encouraged Christocentric conversion. Conversion here means a radical transformation of identity, an existential restructuring of self that marked a break with one's past life and the beginning of life as a new creation.[6] Conversion required a protracted time of preparation during the novitiate, religious instruction, and testing in baptism preparation groups. The ultimate ritual of immersion and the public ceremony with the profession of a lifelong vow to God and the community marked the rite of passage into full adult status within the community. The authenticity of each conversion was certified by public validation of the Brotherhood and its leaders. However, the certainty of conversion was ultimately knowable only to each devotee by the inner, subjective sense of the assurance of God's love and grace. In each person's heart, the solitude of prayer or meditation brought the conviction that he or she had received adoption as a child of God and enjoyed the continued grace of God. Only the abiding presence of the abundant love of God and repeated infusions of the Holy Spirit gave compelling evidence of spiritual maturation and continuance in the grand scheme of salvation.

Eberhard Arnold's model of Pietist conversion (revitalized by Heini) emphasized the experience of *Anfechtung*, or trials of faith—religious melancholy. Believers who entered a spiritual pilgrimage in search of salvation and who subsequently struggled to make a godly life, would periodically encounter times of despair and spiritual desolation. It would prove impossible to sustain indefinitely the emotional intensity attendant to the single-minded pursuit of the imitation of Christ and the mystical-illuminist quest for the Holy Spirit. Not infrequently, devotees fell into periods of spiritual lassitude, times of personal or collective adversity, and crises of conscience. They would feel abandonment as though forsaken by God, or rise up in cold-hearted rebellion and enmity toward God.

In his theology Eberhard Arnold held up Luther's experience of *Anfechtung* in the Black Tower as a model of conversion and the making of a Christian life. Although the trials of faith afflicted all believers, these spiritual crises augured a positive opportunity to deepen one's faith, to appropriate the joyous promises of Scripture, and to secure the restorative infusions of the Holy Spirit.

> This distress of conscience is the deepest, most crucial affliction. The indescribable agony that Luther experienced in his Black Tower could not be expressed in words. Unless we know what Luther suffered in his isolation and despair, we cannot grasp his faith. Only this agony under God's wrath and remoteness makes it possible to understand the certainty and joy of faith which was awakened in Luther as an entirely new experience.[7]

Luther's Theology of the Cross provided the foundation for conversion and postconversion Bruderhof spirituality. From the depths of doubt, inner conflict, and warfare against the natural or carnal self, through *tentatio* (doubt and loss of subjective certitude about one's state of grace) the seeker struggled to achieve a renewed apprehension of faith and the truth of the Gospel. The trials of spiritual doubt and despair were necessary, inevitable, and ultimately beneficial. Believers needed to embrace their *Anfechtung* as an opportunity to undergo a moment of redemptive suffering, an opening for spiritual quickening and maturation. Between 1513 and 1518, Luther developed this experiential theology founded upon his own personal struggles. Won Yong Ji writes:

> After years of uncertainty and terror of conscience, internal trauma, a deep sense of being lost, cast off in sin, and being disconnected from "the Vine" (John 15:6), the Reformer was led to a new understanding of the Gospel of the grace of God on account of Jesus Christ. . . . Only the humbled sinner, struck down by the experience of *Anfechtung*, that is, spiritual assaults and conflict, can know God who for his justification underwent the humiliation and condemnation of the cross.[8]

Heini taught his followers to expect even the most extreme manifestation of religious doubt and *Anfechtung*, abandonment by God and the attendant religious melancholy. The faithful could succumb to a crushing sense of alienation from God that resulted in debility and mental illness.

> Mental illness is an abnormal inner attitude toward God, toward fellow human beings, and toward one's own self. To feel that one is without God is not a proof of ungodliness. It is an accepted fact that many serious Christians have suffered severe inner pain because they often felt they were without God for prolonged periods of time. On the Cross, Christ himself had to experience this state of darkness, a darkness so terrible that we men cannot comprehend it. This is expressed in His words: My God, my God, why hast Thou forsaken me?[9]

Wayne E. Oates's *Anxiety in Christian Experience* (1955) explores what he considers the most profound of anxieties, the "holy dread" and "anxiety of the cross" that believers had to confront as they prepared for conversion and a rebirth of self. Drawing upon his work as a pastoral counselor and his knowledge of doctrine, Oates presents clinical case histories as unfolding spiritual pilgrimages in which the faithful succumbed to times of desperation, hopelessness, and immobilizing anxiety. He quotes the diary of one patient who felt forsaken by God.

> I wonder why this soul is left on earth to wander alone through its hidden valleys of self-torture, for one soul can torture itself to destruction.
> I wait each night for that lost feeling, until its thoughts and weariness embezzle themselves into the brain of my being, I feel it again, and I die a thousand deaths as one who has tasted love and found it has suddenly lost its savor, not understanding where it has disappeared.[10]

Oates acknowledges the psychological dimensions of Christocentric conversion—the propensity for adherents to suffer anxiety, religious melancholy, and clinical depression. He validates as the "brilliant heroes of faith" Christians who embrace the inner torment of the anxiety of the cross as a purposeful, creative moment, a prerequisite to conversion. Those, however, who would flee from the demands of the Theology of the Cross he likens to the rich youth who came to Jesus only to reject his teachings and pursue the idolatries of wealth. Oates presents a contemporary version of worldliness, what I have elsewhere termed "life as therapeutic renewal—the promise of a future-oriented, power of positive thinking optimism where the abundant love of God and mercy of Christ will solve all personal trials."[11] Oates writes:

> Today he would probably have turned to a barbiturate religion that soothed him away from the necessity of a cross, a new birth, and the courage of the unknown. He may have bought and worn out books on "the power of positive thinking." He would certainly need these, because in fleeing from the anxiety of the cross, he had shrunk back into the narrow resting place of a smug safety and under the shivering covers of the insatiable worship of finitude![12]

Clearly, Oates seeks to universalize the piety and conversion derivative of Luther's Theology of the Cross as the only authentic Christian experience. Ideally, the crisis of anxiety of the cross proves to be only a transient moment in the passage of the heart to grace, and the healing embrace of "the cross-bearing fellowship of like-minded persons in the church."[13] Oates, like Heini Arnold, championed an evangelical piety that brought believers repeatedly back to the crux of faith.

Given the rigors of Christocentric piety, with the proclivity to suffer spiritual trials, religious melancholy, and even mental illness, what attracted and sustained adherents to this life-order? The Bruderhof answer lies in the capacity of the faithful for self-torture as an expression of love and desire, and in the complex reciprocal relationship between charismatic leader and enthralled follower.

Heini's charismatic gifts of the spirit and discernment and his leadership role as Servant and later as Bishop legitimated his public exercise of power. However, the dynamics of Heini's power far exceeded the formal-structural concentration of authority within the Bruderhof hierocracy. Heini served as a director of the soul and spiritual advisor and forged intense affective relationships with the membership, who grew to love and revere him. Plain and weak brothers and "ordinary" sisters emulated his mannerisms, style of speech, and posture, identifying with Heini as the embodiment of the highest ideals of spiritual perfection. Relatively powerless brothers and sisters, and members from other hofs who were personally unknown to Heini, wanted to be like him and to win his notice and approbation. He exercised a compelling personal influence over members who desired, above all else, to express their love to Jesus and to Heini and to receive love from him. They wholeheartedly submitted to Heini's criticisms and accepted arbitrary, extreme, and, at times, abusive treatment.

Heini's frequent and capricious use of exclusion and church discipline would create an immediate and overwhelming trail of faith and experience of *Anfechtung* in the "offending" brother or sister. In the blink of an eye, a person was transformed from a baptized member in good standing in the community to a person who possessed an impure spirit, a dangerous attitude, a selfish, prideful enmity to the leadings of the Holy Spirit. Heini used *Ausschluss* as a tool to force evangelical humiliation and the trials of faith upon his followers.

Dick and Lois Ann Domer were part of the group of new American converts at Woodcrest. The Domers received exclusion and forced separation from their children in 1960, ostensibly because they had manifested sympathy toward Hans Zumpe (a self-confessed adulterer) and had been found wanting by Heini and the Brotherhood in the education and discipline of their children. After punishing them for many months, Heini decided to re-admit the Domers the day before he departed for Europe. Elizabeth Bohlken-Zumpe, who lived in Heini's household, remembers:

> Heini leaned over to [his wife] Annemarie and said, "I would very much like to take Dick and Lois Ann back into the brotherhood before I leave!"
>
> "Heini, that's impossible," Annemarie said. "Your airplane leaves at 4 p.m. How do you think you can do that?"
>
> . . . "But Amela, (diminutive of 'Annemarie') actually they have not done anything!"[14]

From Bohlken-Zumpe's account, the evangelical humiliation, exclusion, and traumatic family separation appears to have been an arbitrary exercise of charismatic authority. The Domers had neither transgressed the *Gemeinde's* orders and normative code nor espoused blasphemous or heretical beliefs.

Throughout Bruderhof history, church discipline and the exclusion system had been the remedy of last resort to punish known sinners who committed serious offenses and to maintain political and doctrinal unity. The leadership of the Woodcrest Bruderhof, however, employed exclusion as the first and principal technique of solidifying Arnoldism and eliminating the last vestiges of heterodoxy from the movement. Heini excluded those judged as spiritually lazy, cold, and lacking in fervor, or those whom he considered disloyal. For both the leadership and the ordinary laity, periodic exclusion was an expected and accepted, albeit traumatic, aspect of their religious vocation.

Servants of the Word and the Brotherhood routinely challenged excluded members to "fight your way back into the brotherhood," to seize upon humiliation as an opportunity for spiritual growth, and to accept chastisement as an outpouring of collective love. Many brothers and sisters later expressed gratitude for the spiritual quickening and hardwon piety achieved through exclusion. Others, however, remember their separation as an act of meaningless cruelty and a time of unnecessary injury inflicted upon their children and family.

Heini transformed church discipline by joining the issues of political loyalty with evangelical Pietistic fervor. Should individuals or emerging factions openly question community policy and Heini's leadership, they received exclusion for disloyalty, branded as sinners who had fallen prey to diabolical influences. In 1974, Servants of the Word in Evergreen (Deer Spring) and Woodcrest challenged Heini's decision to seek a "reuniting" with the Western Hutterite colonies. In a *Sendbrief* to the Hutterites on June 10, 1975, Heini wrote:

> The sin that was revealed in a special way was that several were against the uniting with *you*. This happened under the leadership of Mark Kurtz, who had appeared to us as the most trustworthy brother. There was unfortunately a lot of talk about this in Evergreen. It was especially evil how Mark Kurtz misused his Service to have power over souls, to hurt them, and to bring them into need. In this connection Mark Kurtz, Ben Zumpe, and Georg Barth were removed from the Service of the Word. It was a demon that wanted to use the dedication to Christ and the Church to gain power. My beloved brother Hardy and Art Wiser also fell into this sin. They too were removed from the Service of the Word and together with those mentioned above were placed under various forms of Church discipline.[15]

Thus, the exclusion system was used to intimidate opposition to Heini's charismatic leadership and ensure that the Bruderhof faithful would suffer the trials of faith as pilgrims who endured redemptive suffering in search of spiritual deepening.

Bruderhof apologists Merrill and Kathy Mow express profound gratitude to Heini for the hardships and deprivations that he endured to render charismatic service to the Bruderhof. Any errors, excesses, or acts of unkindness represented lapses on the part of the lesser leadership who acted without Heini's wisdom and discernment during times when Heini was forced, periodically, to retreat from service due to illness or exhaustion. Kathy Mow explains that the Great Crisis was not directed against people but against spiritual declension.[16]

Bruderhof apostates remember Heini as a complex, divided man, at times capable of acts of kindness, loving concern, and empathetic communion with ordinary brothers and sisters. However, they also recall the cold, cruel, calculating, unforgiving, and ruthless Servant driven by obsession with internal enemies. If Heini's followers committed injustices during Heini's frequent retreats, they did so with his clear knowledge and approval.

Janet Liebman Jacobs's important study, *Divine Disenchantment, Deconverting from New Religions*, examines the leader-follower relationship from a psychoanalytic perspective. Jacobs interviewed apostates from a variety of high-commitment New Religious communities including charismatic Christian and Eastern mystical groups. These groups share much in common with the Bruderhof. Both the New Religions studied by Jacobs and the Bruderhof organize their common life as an extended patriarchal family under the guidance of a charismatic elder. As sectarian communities in dynamic tension with the world, they impose a rigid and comprehensive normative code that regulates all aspects of a believer's life. The hierarchial and authoritarian power structure divides believers from both groups into unequal classes and relegates women to subservient positions. Ultimately, the apostates that Jacobs studied became disenchanted with the social and sexual inequalities and the heavy demands imposed upon members by the leadership.

Jacobs captures the attractiveness of these worlds of total meaning. Clearly, from her perspective, New Religions, like the Bruderhof, present their common life as the fulfillment of the highest ideals of Christianity articulated in the Sermon on the Mount. Adherents strived to realize the absolute ethic of brotherliness through participation in a loving family life and organic community. Their experiences in natural families and more worldly communities had failed to gratify their need for unconditional love, but the new families and communities constituted in faith promised abundant joy and love.[17] In addition to meeting the salvation needs of followers, these groups met the devotee's profound intrapsychic longings, "the secret needs of the heart."[18]

Jacobs adopts Kohut's relational psychology of the self. She argues that followers have internalized an object relationship of infantile dependence and surrender to an omnipotent father. Through the process of transference, believers continually repeat this pattern and recreate this relationship established in childhood by projecting this integral aspect of their adult selves onto their relationship with the charismatic leader. They long for union, the merging of ego boundaries, and participation in the leader's special gifts and spiritual perfection. Projective identification with the charismatic ego-ideal and absolute surrender and devotion to the leader produce in followers states of joy and the experience of unconditional love—the recovery of infantile satisfactions. The psychic "costs" of the gratification of infantile needs are loss of autonomy, dependency, and unquestioning submission to authority that can include acceptance of psychological abuse.[19]

Innerland piety enjoined believers to achieve a childlike spirit by pursuing evangelical piety and the humiliation requisite to selfless surrender to Jesus. The central doctrines, social structure of patriarchal hierocracy, and child-rearing and conversion practices produced (or attracted) believers with a distinctive, religiously grounded personality. The dynamics of Bruderhof life under Heini's charismatic rule structured (during crises and purifications) individual and collective moments of fusion with the transcendent "Other," and with the charismatic leader as the embodiment of the transcendent. Here, culture and social structure coalesced to support a personality constituted by the wish to cast off adult autonomy and to regress to infantile helplessness and dependency.

These aspects of Bruderhof selfhood, supported by religious belief and community social structure, valorized dependency and helplessness among believers such as Nadine Pleil. Pleil acted in conformity with Christocentric piety and the imitation of Christ when she relinquished her capacity to choose for herself. She writes in a "Bruderspeak," a rhetorical style that depicts her self as an object acted upon by external forces. She employs intransitive and passive constructions, such as "it was decided." This denotes how others made critical life decisions for her, or her passivity and failure to act to protect her children from community discipline. Despite the pain and conflict engendered by such renunciations, she did enjoy fleeting moments of joy, fusion, and the experience of unconditional love. Paradoxically, the tyrannical, judgmental, punishing father or God alternated with the image of an all-loving, nurturing, forgiving and accepting God. One needed to appease the tyrannical punishing father image to enjoy the contemplation of abundant agape.[20]

Religiously grounded personalities and religious commitments are not inherently pathological and do not necessarily require regression to infantile process or the formation of malintegrated selves. Heinz Kohut argues that religion can play a vital part in the construction of "selfobjects"—significant object relations that are constitutive of an integrated and healthy personality.[21] Varieties of religious practice can satisfy what Kohut defines as the three fundamental relational needs—the need for connection to the transcendent, the need for recognition and acceptance, and the need for mutuality in our associations.[22]

Arnoldism during Heini's charismatic regime (1951–1982) did not encourage the formation of coherent, religiously grounded selves who could act with agency. The renunciation of religious individualism requisite to Christocentric conversion, the prescription to undergo the *Anfechtung* patterned after Luther's Black Tower crises, the use of church discipline to engender the travail of redemptive suffering, and the captivity of the charismatic relationship—all of these processes prevented some of the faithful from achieving stable and integrated selfhood. The psychic economy that encouraged self-blame through the evangelical humiliation of church discipline made religious melancholy a recurring psychological and religious experience within Bruderhof Pietism. It is not surprising, then, that Heini needed to write *Freedom from Sinful Thoughts* to address the religious melancholy, obsessional ideation and conduct, demonic possession, and clinical mental illness that afflicted true believers. Heini mediated to his followers a model for the religious life, offering a spiritual template, a morphology of conversion that would guide the faithful through a torturous and joyous pilgrimage.

An Arnold Family Legacy: Two Case Histories

Two of Eberhard Arnold's granddaughters, Elizabeth Bohlken-Zumpe and Miriam Arnold Holmes, were expelled from the Bruderhof during the 1960s. Both women were born in Europe, reared in Primavera, and spent their last years in the community in the new American hofs. Both women had made their baptismal vows and had committed their lives, without reservation, to the Bruderhof. However, each suffered a spiritual and psychological crisis during young adulthood, and each woman struggled with the questions of autonomy, independent action, and the seemingly stifling demands of Bruderhof piety.[23] Ironically, at the moment when each woman found the courage to act, Heini and other Servants of the Word expelled them as spiritually inadequate backsliders.

Authentic spirituality, as judged by the Bruderhof leadership, had become the principal test for continued membership. Spirituality that was judged inauthentic prompted collective discipline and exclusion. Only those true believers who exhibited authentic spirituality, who demonstrated spiritual reanimation and maturation by appropriating the Theology of the Cross might remain in good standing. Each member had to submit willingly and repeatedly to mutual criticism, and to impose upon himself or herself techniques of evangelical humiliation (self-examination, confession of sin, and repentance) designed to foster spiritual quickening.

Heini Arnold waged a wider religiopolitical conflict between the Spirit of Primavera and the Woodcrest Spirit—a contest for the future of the Bruderhof movement. He employed the doctrines of evangelical Pietism as weapons in this struggle. The willingness to embrace *Anfechtung* and evangelical humiliation served as the line of demarcation between authentic and profane belief. And the telling question, "Do you resent the Arnold family, do you harbor jealousy and enmity toward Heini?" initiated the test of spiritual adequacy as administered by the leadership during the Great Crisis. The "correct" response required confession, purgation, self-examination and humiliation before the Brotherhood and God, which reaffirmed the psychological captivity of the believer to Heini's charismatic authority.

The contrite and selfless believer might find forgiveness and collective assurance of abiding brotherly and divine love. The refusal to undergo evangelical humiliation and adopt the trials of faith put the member outside of the doctrine and fellowship founded upon Luther's Theology of the Cross.

Elizabeth Bohlken-Zumpe, aged 26, single, trained as a nurse, and admitted to full membership as a baptized sister, lived with Heini's household in Woodcrest in 1961 after her father's disgrace and exclusion. By her own account, she turned away from the enormity of Hans Zumpe's sin as an adulterer and grew to love and admire her uncle Heini. In the course of the Great Crisis, however, she stood accused by another Servant, Dwight

Moody, of secret jealousy toward Heini's family, of resenting the special loving connection Heini shared with his daughters.

Bohlken-Zumpe wrote a letter of confession, admitting these sins and asking for forgiveness. The Brotherhood wanted a deeper and more profound expression of evangelical humiliation, repentance, and abject selflessness. Seemingly, she possessed an unclean and evil spirit, a contamination from Paraguay, an emanation of the Spirit of Primavera in their midst. The Brotherhood meeting regarded Bohlken-Zumpe as a profanation of all that they held sacred. She remembers: "The brotherhood looked at me in such staring disbelief! How could they have harbored such a spirit amongst them? They even had let me look after their babies. . . . This terrible spirit, which they believed to be far away in Paraguay, now was amongst them in the flesh! I could feel all this as a certainty."[24]

Bohlken-Zumpe received the small exclusion—shunning and internal banishment to an isolated cabin on the hof—and the loss of the right to practice her profession as a nurse or to attend Brotherhood meetings. She cleaned toilets by day, and spent her evenings in enforced solitude in the sewing room mending piles of clothing and knitting sweaters for others. The menial and demeaning labor of cleaning toilets symbolized her impurity and defilement. During her six months of public humiliation, from April until September, she grew increasingly depressed, avoided the public dining hall, and went without food for days until she eventually weighed only ninety-three pounds.

The Servants wanted evidence of progressive evangelical humiliation. She needed to practice a daily piety of self-examination, methodically reviewing her past life for evidence of sin. As a penitent she needed to catalog these transgressions and beseech Jesus and the church-community for forgiveness. But Bohlken-Zumpe could not, or would not, undergo this incremental self-mortification. She did not understand or would not submit to the test of spiritual authenticity. She had only begun to test the limits of what she would endure through the required experience of church discipline as love. Bohlken-Zumpe writes: "They told me that it was quite obvious that I was hiding some sin of the past, and as long as I did not clear that up, there could not be a reuniting of any sort. BUT THERE WAS NO SIN, AND ALSO I COULD NOT THINK OF ANY SIN TO CONFESS!"[25]

In her study of deconversion from New Religions Jacobs provides an example of pastoral guidance that resembles Bohlken-Zumpe's crisis. Jacobs considers the exercise of evangelical humiliation a form of psychological abuse that produces feelings of low self-esteem, especially among women. She describes one Christian group where

a female devotee was told that she needed to be delivered of her sins. Following this declaration, she was chastised publicly for having "the spirit of homosexuality" because of her close relations with other female members. A few weeks later, she was again called before the group and this time she was delivered from the "spirit of lust" because she had been seen talking to too many male devotees. When this young woman sought to leave the group, she was told that Satan would do terrible things to her family and when she finally made the break, she described herself as suicidal, confused, humiliated, and depressed.[26]

Like this woman, Bohlken-Zumpe succumbed to disorientation and suicidal depression.

From the perspective of evangelical humiliation, she exhibited a cold-hearted refusal to employ self-examination to uncover hidden sin, an obstinate refusal to repent and to restore a relationship of childlike faith and obedience to God and to the church-community. Her willfulness confirmed the judgment that Bohlken-Zumpe was at best spiritually inadequate and at worst a manifestation of an evil and impure spirit. Most community members avoided her, looking through her as if she were invisible. Others sought her out to denigrate her, to dramatize community standards by public criticism of her faults.

The combined effects of the small exclusion—public stigmatization and separation from routine community life—proved devastating.[27] She bided her time hoping that the troubles would pass, but she became increasingly depressed and disconsolate. After several months of this torment, she attempted suicide. Bohlken-Zumpe explains:

> Life was grim. At one point I decided it wasn't worth all the struggle and effort. I still had a key to Milton's [Zimmerman] medical office, and one day when I was forbidden to talk to my grandmother because this would upset her, I went to the office during the meeting and took a handful of sleeping pills. I wrote a little farewell note to the brotherhood and swallowed the pills with a glass of water to make an end to my miserable life. Then I thought of my poor mother and Oma [grandmother], would be the victims of my actions. I stuck a finger down my throat and vomited all the rubbish out again.[28]

Bohlken-Zumpe was expelled from Woodcrest in September for committing the "independent act" of pursuing a marriage proposal with an expelled member, Hans Bohlken. She never returned to the common life of the community.

Heini and the Woodcrest leadership wished to purge the community of any vestiges of the spirit of Primavera. Baptized members in good standing who could not or would not embrace the fervent piety of Arnoldism and reap the spiritual benefits of evangelical humiliation could not remain within the reformed and revitalized Bruderhof. Apostates came to the crushing realization of their manifest spiritual inadequacies when measured against the standards of Lutheran piety.

Miriam Arnold Holmes was born on December 17, 1939, at the Cotswold Bruderhof to Edith and Hardy Arnold. Her father was the eldest son of Eberhard Arnold, and her status as an Arnold would always mark her life in the community. She grew up in Primavera. The austerities and ruggedness of her childhood in these pioneering conditions matched her spirited, adventurous, and indomitable personality.[29]

When Holmes was three years of age, her mother died. Six years later Hardy married his second wife, Secunda, and blended her sons and daughters with his own children. Miriam quickly learned to love her second mother and her new siblings. She established a particularly close relationship with her younger stepsister Heidi. Secunda also encouraged Holmes to study the violin and the classical music that was an important part of community life in Primavera.

Holmes's abiding intellectual curiosity, her struggle for autonomy, and her open, honest style of address and stance as a free spirit would bring her into repeated conflict with Bruderhof authority over the issues of sexuality. She was accused of "pride" and "selfishness." During her childhood in Primavera, she tested the limits of permissible conduct and flirted with disaster on several occasions. She knew firsthand the mental anguish occasioned by church discipline.

Holmes emigrated with her family to the Oak Lake Bruderhof (New Meadow Run) in 1957 when she was seventeen and a high school senior. She quickly adjusted to the North American winters and the youth culture of American high schools. In the summer of 1962, Art Wiser and Heini Arnold invited her to join a baptism preparation group, and by August she had taken her vows. That fall she entered her freshman year at West Virginia University and pursued a major in music. By community standards, she had progressed, without difficulty or delay, assuming the spiritual and temporal roles and responsibilities of young adulthood.

Holmes's experience in living independently from the community, and her first extended exposure to the outside world through college courses, concerts, friendships, and extracurricular life produced conflict and dissonance. She had expected to encounter Mammonistic, selfish, unbrotherly, and sinful people ensnared in iniquity and blinded to the light of Gospel truth. The Bruderhof anticipated that she would long for the community and suffer from intense homesickness. Instead, she enjoyed college and savored the new experiences of life on the outside. She writes:

> The three (Bruderhof) girls who had gone to the university the year before came home weekends [and] always talked about how difficult it was out there and all the struggles that were going on. They said how wonderful it was to come home, and how great it to be in the loving Bruderhof atmosphere. I did not feel that way, but I understood that I

should feel that way. There must be something wrong with me that I enjoyed myself so much in the "outside world."[30]

Holmes describes feeling out of place and alienated during weekend visits to the Bruderhof. She failed to utter the expected profundities during the *Gemeindestunde* (prayer meeting) to give evidence of her continued piety and spiritual maturation. She began to withdraw from community participation in Brotherhood and prayer meetings, singing, and music programs. Clearly, her life had reached a turning point. On the one hand, as the granddaughter of the founder, born and reared in the community, and having recently taken baptismal vows for life, Holmes remained committed to the church-community. On the other hand, her newly found autonomy as a college freshman opened up possibilities for education, work, and personal satisfactions independent of the Bruderhof. Had the Bruderhof encouraged and supported her incipient adult autonomy and powers of agency, she might have actively chosen one of these alternative paths. Instead, she asked Mary Wiser (the housemother) for permission to leave college, hoping, with passive dependency, to be directed to continue with her studies. Holmes relates, in the convoluted logic of this "suspect autonomy," how she asked for the "right" thing by abandoning the secret desires of her heart.

> The year was coming to a close, and my discomfort at the Bruderhof became more intense. That spring I felt I should tell Mary Wiser that I didn't think I should go back to school the following year. That was not really what I wanted. Of course I wanted to go back. But I felt that they wanted me *not* to go. Sure enough, when I made the announcement, she said, "Well, that's really a good idea." Secretly I was hoping she would say, "Oh, silly, of course you will go," But no, she said, "Well, we think you're right. You shouldn't go. It's not a good influence on you," or something to that effect. I guess they were concerned that I enjoyed it so much.[31]

Holmes returned to community routine after completing her first year of college. She worked with children, gave music lessons and organized a chamber ensemble. Her passion for music proved trouble-some when, on a visit to her mother at Woodcrest, she sought insistently to borrow a recording of "Judas Maccabeus" from a reluctant age-mate, Dan Maendel. She persisted, saying "Come on, Dan, don't be so selfish. You should share." He refused, and she let the matter pass.

Upon her return to New Meadow Run, Servant of the Word Art Wiser called her into his office and accused her of misconduct at Woodcrest. " 'I had a phone call from Heini,' he said. 'He was very very shocked that you, Miriam, had asked for a record from Dan Maendel. That was very very selfish, and you even put pressure on him. There is something drastically wrong with you, and Heini was absolutely horrified about what you did. He wants you to give an explanation in the brotherhood meeting tonight.' "[32] Heini had arranged for a stenographer to record Holmes's account of this incident.

Her offense pertained to the unfettered exercise of will, the capacity to act and make requests to satisfy her personal needs, and her uncontrolled passion for music. Holmes explains in her memoir that this admonishment served as a pretext for Heini to humiliate his brother Hardy by imposing church discipline upon Hardy's daughter. The ramifications of the internecine struggles for power and control of the movement between the founder's sons were visited on the grandchildren.

Despite her apology and public confession of sin, she received the small exclusion which lasted from late summer 1963 until November 1965 when the community expelled her. During this period she suffered from stigmatization and depression. Holmes explains, "I was feeling disgraced, and worthless, almost dirty and having those feelings reinforced by being treated as less than human. People stopped talking to you. When you went to second breakfast, people left you out of the conversation."[33]

Many of her peers eagerly seized public opportunities to stigmatize her as a sinner. Johann Christoph Arnold, Heini's son, always found something blameworthy in her conduct. She writes: "Either I was calling attention to myself or I was not participating properly or something. He always found some fault with my behavior. I could do nothing right."[34]

Denied the right to work with children and teach music, Holmes cleaned bathrooms in the common areas. Both Holmes and Bohlken-Zumpe cleaned countless dirty toilets, areas polluted by the profane needs of the body. Both young women understood that they shared in this impurity, in the excrement and abhorrence of the respectable members in "good standing." Church discipline reduced these talented young women, one a trained nurse and the other a gifted musician, to the status of charwomen, suited only for menial labor. In this manner, the small exclusion and shunning effectively curtailed and mortified their sense of self-worth and dignity.

Evangelical humiliation demanded that each penitent sinner accept the mortification of the prideful self as a technique to recover God's grace. Holmes endured unceasing humiliations. She gave away her radio to Merrill Mow, one of the community elders. She reasoned, ". . . I really loved this radio. Maybe if I give it up, they will see that I really mean business and am really repentant and have the right spirit and they'll let me back into the brotherhood."[35] She explained to Mow, "I spend too much time listening to it, and I really want to give my heart and soul to the church, so I'm giving up this radio."[36] But the Brotherhood did not forgive her, and she did not experience divine forgiveness or irradiations of the Holy Spirit. Instead, she lived with this additional mortification, denied the daily contact with the outside world through radio broadcasts that had sustained her.

Finally, after almost two years of the small exclusion, the new house mother, Noranne Blough, ordered her to attend a Brotherhood meeting where the Servants informed her of impending expulsion from the community.

> "What do you think of that?" they asked.
> "Whatever the brotherhood feels is right is what I will do," I said.
> . . . I remember Norann shouting, "Don't you have a mind of your own? Can't you think for yourself?"
> "Whatever the brotherhood says," I said.[37]

On November 22, 1965, one brother took Holmes to the nearby town of McKeesport, Pennsylvania. There she secured room and board in a private household and worked as a waitress in a local bar/restaurant. Several months later she found a job as a nurse's aid at McKeesport Hospital and rented a small, unheated attic apartment.

Holmes lived in limbo, struggling to adapt to life on the outside independent of the community while at the same time accepting the challenge to fight her way back to the Bruderhof. She was marginal to both worlds, rejected by, and expelled from, her natal community and maintaining a reserved distance as a stranger in the secular society. For several years she would suffer the torments of this double marginalization, immobilized and unable to decide which world to embrace. Her powers of agency faltered and she grew increasingly depressed, anoretic, and suicidal.

Hardy Arnold arranged for his daughter to see a psychiatrist at Bruderhof expense. The alienist, a strict Freudian, was not interested in learning about the community or the social and cultural aspects of Holmes's life crises. She benefitted little from the psychotherapy.

After two years of exclusion, Holmes was hired to manage the household and supervise the children of a recently widowed physician, Dr. Smart, who lived in Pittsburgh. She visited New Meadow Run on the weekends:

> My life during that time consisted of visiting the Bruderhof on weekends and feeling like a fish out of water, taking care of the Smart household, taking some courses, going to the psychiatrist, going to recitals. . . . My inner conflict became more and more acute. I grew thinner and thinner, I was not interested in eating. . . . I think I just wanted to wither away. My subconscious desire was to disappear so that I would not have to worry about the Bruderhof. All those crazy conflicts! On the one hand, I could not go to the Bruderhof. It was impossible. They were terrible. It was awful there! I couldn't stand it! At the same time, I couldn't stand the

thought of hurting my father and not going back. I think what worried me the most was being unfaithful to my father.[38]

By her own admission, Holmes remained mired in a suspect, semi-autonomy, unable to accept the conditions of life in the church-community and unwilling to break her ties of filial piety to her father. Coming of age and choosing a life course as an adult frequently necessitates disappointing one's parents and rebelling against aspects of one's past. Holmes lacked the capacity to decide and extricate herself from this conflict. Instead, she responded by punishing herself, turning her anger against community and family inward in depression, attempting to disappear by regimes of starvation and attempted suicide.

Holmes was admitted in 1967 and again in 1969 to a state psychiatric hospital for treatment of depression and attempted suicide. Holmes recoiled from the harsh repression and joyless lovelessness of the Bruderhof. However, she could not make the break from her previous life and identity. Starvation and attempts at suicide ended the impasse and transported her into what Susanna Kaysen calls the parallel universe—the world of the institutionalized insane. Kaysen writes in her autobiography, *Girl, Interrupted*, of her own season of madness in McLean Hospital as a young woman in the late 1960s. She explains, "it is easy to slip into a parallel universe . . . most people pass over incrementally, making a series of perforations in the membrane between here and there until an opening exists. And who can resist an opening?"[39]

Kaysen, like Holmes, fell into the crucible of identity formation and autonomy dilemmas. These tribulations involved issues and conflicts surrounding the patient, her family, and the wider sociocultural milieu.[40]

During Holmes's first confinement, the Bruderhof arranged for her to visit Woodcrest at Christmas. There, Holmes entertained thoughts of making a permanent separation from the community after her father confided in her that the Bruderhof leadership had labeled her as a "weak" member. "I would not be allowed to participate in the brotherhood meetings because I was a 'weak person.' Attending the brotherhood meetings would be too burdensome for me. . . . Why would I want to come back to the Bruderhof if I couldn't even come to brotherhood meetings? That's silly! [Holmes told father], 'Gee, I dunno about that. I don't know. That doesn't sound right to me.' "[41]

During her second institutionalization in March 1969, Holmes worked in the hospital accounting office and began an intensive therapeutic relationship with one of the staff psychiatrists. Dr. W. helped her resolve this eight-year conflict by urging her to abandon the community. After several months of therapy, she accepted his guidance. Holmes explains:

I will never forget the moment when that clicked in my head. I was so relieved! It was such a burden off my shoulders, that I did not have to go back.

"Okay, I won't go back," I said to Dr. W. "I'll just go on with my life and make myself a real life out in the world. No shadow life."[42]

After Holmes's release from the hospital, she separated from the Bruderhof and has lived independent of the community for the last twenty-five years.

Elizabeth Bohlken-Zumpe and Miriam Arnold Holmes discovered that for them the costs of Innerland piety, evangelical humiliation, the transvaluation of love as punishment, and surrender of the individual to the collective that characterized the Bruderhof temperament meant suicidal depression and unrelenting inner torment.

The "Bruderhof Syndrome"

In 1989, a group of ex-Bruderhof began circulating a monthly newsletter and formed the Keep In Touch network, or KIT. The first KIT reunion of apostates from the Great Crisis and subsequent Bruderhof purges and expulsions convened at the Friendly Crossways Youth Hostel in Littleton, Massachusetts, in August 1990. With forty people in attendance, the KITfolk, as they called themselves, conducted meetings to share their experiences, externalize the unresolved traumata of forced separation, and recover the collective memories of their previous life in the community. As later reported in *KIT*:

> a special concern was brought up about the treatment of children within the Bruderhof, and the Sunday morning meeting focused on this issue. Many incidents were reported of young people experiencing deep depression and a conviction that they were harboring an "evil Spirit." Opinions were expressed that these seem to be an inevitable outcome of their doctrinal belief in their negative obsession with sin and in the devil as an actual entity who can possess or inhabit individuals. . . . Now that the Bruderhof has its own doctors, many of these cases are now treated inside the community with antidepressants.[43]

The possession and exorcism of Miriam Way, discussed in Merrill Mow's *Torches Rekindled*, and Heini's admission in *Freedom from Sinful Thoughts* of cases of religious melancholy, suicidal crises, and obsessions with unpardonable sin that afflicted many Bruderhof youth lend credence to the KIT collective memories. Coming of age in the Bruderhof often brought with it protracted and unresolved spiritual crises of conversion. When pastoral care failed to cure these spiritual sicknesses, Bruderhof elders would turn in desperation to a system of thought and therapeutics that they had long disparaged—secular, humanistic psychiatry.

The young people presented as case histories in this chapter experienced religious and spiritual crises of conversion and crises of adolescent adjustment in the Bruderhof during the late 1950s and 1960s. These cases suffered from what I term "the Bruderhof Syndrome"—a culturally specific expression of depressive disorder, a "culture-bound syndrome" associated with Arnoldism and Bruderhof spiritual polity in the time of Heini Arnold.

At this time, the *Diagnostic and Statistical Manual* (*DSM*) of the American Psychiatric Association (APA) did not include diagnostic categories that focused upon the peculiar illnesses that beset distinct cultural, ethnic, or religious groups. Indeed, as Hans Küng argued in a 1986 address to the APA, psychiatrists after Freud have tended to "repress" the religiosity of their patients, relegating this dimension of human experience to the status of immature, infantile needs that mature, ego-integrated personalities learned to fulfill through sublimation in work, aesthetic expression, and other secular endeavors.[44] David Lukoff, Francis Lu, and Robert Turner describe this inattention to the religious concerns of their patients as a "religiosity gap." Clinicians have tended to dismiss, pathologize, or reduce religious symptomatology as simply the expression of underlying mental disease.[45]

The *DSM-IV*, revised and adopted in 1994, addressed these issues and has included a new category, "Religious or Spiritual Problem." Today, unlike in past decades, psychiatrists are encouraged to "perceive" the role that religion plays in the lives of patients, to cultivate a new appreciation for the religious and spiritual commitments, expressions, conflicts, and symptoms of patients.

The Bruderhof presents itself to the world as the answer to the vexing problems of modernity, and it promises adherents the opportunity to realize an absolute ethic of brotherliness and the joyful fulfillment of this-worldly salvation. It will not readily acknowledge the propensity of believers to suffer conversion crises and religious melancholy. Despite Heini Arnold's admission of these realities in his published pastoral literature, the Bruderhof steadfastly denies the existence of religiously grounded depressive disorder among their devotees.

Drawing upon KIT interviews and informal discussions at Friendly Crossways KIT reunions, I have developed a more systematic definition and discussion of the Bruderhof Syndrome. The case history excerpts that follow have been altered to protect the anonymity of respondents. Changes in identifiers, the use of pseudonyms, and the blending of the particulars from different cases allow the researcher to remain faithful to the syndrome without compromising the confidentiality of respondents.

The Plough Publishing House has recently published pastoral letters written by Heini Arnold to members who languished in spiritual desolation. This gives additional support to the existence and pervasiveness of the Bruderhof Syndrome. Heini writes to one disconsolate believer,

"Every serious Christian must go through hours of godforsakenness; even Jesus himself did."[46]

Writing to another person, one obsessed with sin, Heini encourages him to view this distress as a consequence of temptations of the flesh (lower nature) and the temptations of Satan to renounce Jesus. He explains, "Until Jesus comes back and frees us completely, we will always have to fight sin on this earth. The fight is first a struggle against the lower nature. Second it is a battle of spirits, a battle against Satan and his demons. Your fall was not only a matter of your lower nature; it was also satanic. . . ."[47]

Hela Ehrlich and Christopher Zimmerman have written an Introduction to a posthumous compilation of Heini Arnold's teachings, *Discipleship*. They describe him as "a true *Seelsorger* or 'spiritual guide' who cared deeply for the inner and outer well-being of the communities entrusted to him."[48] Indeed, Heini possessed extraordinary gifts of discernment and excelled as a spiritual healer. The following undated letter attests to the power of autosuggestion to create ever-worsening obsessions. Here, Arnold offers a gentle consolation.

> I have heard your desperate cry for help, and I have great understanding for you. Your thoughts frighten you so much that they gain power over you. You must turn from this fear. Through it you yourself suggest these thoughts into your heart, and then even more desperate and terrible fears, anxieties, and needs enter you.[49]

In fact, Arnoldism articulated a Christocentric, contemplative, and highly emotional doctrine of Pietistic conversion and discipleship to Jesus that many believers found arduous to fulfill. Arnoldism structured a self-torturous spirituality for many devotees that motivated Heini Arnold to devise a system of spiritual healing in response to the widespread affliction. The Bruderhof Syndrome represented a "psychic cost," or one travail, for true believers who attempted to find a selfless surrender to Jesus but stumbled along the way or failed in their inner journey.

The Bruderhof Syndrome manifests the familiar behavioral signposts common to affective disorder everywhere: chronic fatigue, listlessness, malaise, and sleep and appetite disorders. Patients complained of mood and ideational problems: profound sadness bordering upon despair, an abiding feeling of hopelessness, helplessness. They felt unloved and undeserving of love or consideration by others. In this state of fugue, life was a torment, an ordeal in which suicide appeared as a possible escape.

The Bruderhof Syndrome shared these dimensions of depressive illness. But this cluster of symptoms constituted a distinctive depressive illness peculiar to the collective religious milieu of the Society of Brothers. The patients, especially the young women, spoke of their spiritual inadequacies, their pervasive sinfulness. They felt unworthy to stand before God or their parents and friends in the Bruderhof religious community. The adolescent girls interpreted their first sexual awakenings as sin-pollution, manifestations of the demonic or Satanic enemy in their lives. They had committed sins that cast them beyond the pale of human or divine forgiveness. They felt polluted to their very marrow, beset by ontological guilt and convictions of wormlike worthlessness.

Heini Arnold's obsession with purity, chastity, and virginity encouraged adolescent girls to view their nascent sexuality with alarm, as can be seen in the excerpts from two letters reprinted below:

> Dear Sister, it seems to me that there is an atmosphere of eroticism around you, and I want to warn you about this. There is nothing surprising about the fact that the powers of eroticism and sex are problems any person has to face, and you are no different from anyone else. But I plead with you to value the gift of purity—the light of absolute chastity and virginity. Do not let the smallest shadow of an overly casual relationship with boys or men come into your life, also not in the way you dress or the way you walk. Please take this advice from someone who loves you.[50]
>
> Your question, "Why do I feel attracted toward this boy if he is not meant for me but for someone else?" is a bit of a rebellious one. It accuses someone higher than yourself. Ultimately it accuses God. Human nature being what it is, we often feel attractions that we have no choice but to reject. That is simply part of our human weakness. . . . The important thing for you is to give your life to Jesus.[51]

Two adolescents, Miriam Arnold Holmes and Joel Clement, whose cases are presented in this chapter, fasted excessively as rituals of purification from sin, seeking the moment of joyful surrender to Jesus. These heroic regimens of fasting developed into a religiously motivated "evangelical anorexia nervosa."[52]

Secular developmental psychology and popular culture have long accepted the "natural" adolescent processes of sexual awakening and masturbation, of testing newfound powers of autonomy, iconoclasm, rebelliousness as the turbulent crucible of identity formation. The Bruderhof, however, imposed a Fundamentalist Protestant framework of interpretation when faced with these "natural" developments of adolescence. Bruderhof evangelical Pietism endeavored to crush willful autonomy by instilling a childlike spirit. Any expression of sexuality before marriage was sin. Temptation to sin was the active work of Satan. Rigorous sexual repression would prevent sexual thoughts, sexual impulse and desire, and the commission of sexual acts such as flirtation, sexual experimentation, or autoeroticism.

Overzealous spiritual guidance, harsh discipline, and sexual interrogations by elders convinced many Bruderhof-born seekers that they had sinned beyond the bounds of repentance or remission. These youths lapsed into spiritual desolation and religious melancholy. Baptismal aspirants were caught within a classic trap, in an agonizing vocation crisis. Unable to move forward toward conversion, church membership, and the rites of passage to adulthood, they faced the prospect of being asked to leave. Each quaked before the possibility of exclusion from friends and family into the sin-ridden outside world that they lacked the resources to understand or negotiate. Yet they felt sinful, creaturely, unworthy of community membership, and hopelessly lost.

One current Bruderhof member wrote to *KIT* to offer her own life as an example of reconciliation and healing following years of exclusion, a Bruderhof childhood, and a young adult life filled with injury. She left Woodcrest in 1974 as a broken youth and spent the first month of her *Ausschluss* in a mental hospital. She describes herself in terms evocative of the Bruderhof Syndrome:

> I left in 1974 with a lot of unresolved feelings of anger and bitterness towards my parents and others whom I felt had hurt me in one way or another during my childhood and early adult years, but was afraid of facing those feelings. I didn't want to admit that I harbored hatred, resentment and fear towards the very ones who were the closest to me and loved me the most, so I began my time away in a mental hospital for a couple of weeks.[53]

When this woman reflects on the nature of her life crises she describes an obsession with spiritual perfection, purity, dread of her emergent sexuality, and spiritual inadequacy—the key symptomatology of the Bruderhof Syndrome. She writes of the unbearable burdens of self-renunciation and the unattainable standards of Christocentric conversion, and the crushing realization of her spiritual inadequacies: "Basically, I thought I have to be PERFECT: always loving, thinking of others, giving up feelings of attraction for young men. In short, I was trying to be what is impossible for a human being, so of course I despaired of ever coming up to 'the mark.' "[54]

Another case history is that of Elizabeth, who joined the Woodcrest Bruderhof in 1957 with her husband and one child. As an American raised in the Quaker tradition, she followed her husband's lead to this Christian Socialist community. However, Elizabeth's gifts involved music, not religion. She would never know spiritual fulfillment or peace at Woodcrest. She gave up her music and allowed the housemother to cut off her long, luxuriant auburn hair as two mortifications intended to satisfy the demands of Arnoldism: Christocentric conversion, *Gelassenheit*, and unquestioning compliance to patriarchy. With the birth of each additional child (six children), she grew increasingly overburdened and despairing.

Elizabeth's oldest son remembers his mother's depression:

> They did try to get her to teach music, but she couldn't cope; she started crying several times in front of the children. She felt that she didn't have proper discipline and that she wasn't living up to community expectations. She wasn't good enough. . . .

I used to see her with one of the brothers wandering around the community in the evening, deep in serious, quiet talk. I can remember hearing my father's voice through the bedroom wall when I was going to sleep. He used to read to her from Bonhoeffer, Eberhard Arnold, and Blumhardt.

Elizabeth never completed the spiritual passage to conversion. One day in the spring of 1961, she refused to get out of bed, distraught, weeping over a joyless and loveless existence. The brotherhood removed her to a state mental hospital for the first of several confinements.

Elizabeth's hospitalization devastated her son. He explains:

I grew up with an overwhelming sense of being insignificant, with no contribution to make, and having no importance to anyone or anything. I experienced terrifying psychotic episodes of leaving my body and abandoning it to function in the pre-programmed, robotic manner expected of it. . . . The only person for whom I was real was my mother, and she was sent to a mental hospital for over a year without being allowed to even say good-bye to me first. After she returned, I felt she was too fragile to be burdened with anything I might say.

After electroconvulsive shock treatments and a regimen of antidepressants, Elizabeth lived out her life in Woodcrest as a weak sister, well-medicated, compliant, and chronically mentally ill. Her son bears the psychic scars of a Bruderhof childhood replete with exclusions, family disruptions, and a vibrant mother reduced to invalidism through the persistence of religious melancholy.

Fredrick was born in the Cotswold Bruderhof in 1940 and came of age in Primavera. He made his baptismal vows in 1958 and survived the purge of the Great Crisis, arriving in Woodcrest in 1961. He came to be accused by Heini and the American Servants of the Word of sexual impurity for confessing to the sin of masturbation. The Brotherhood charged him with disloyalty to his vows to Jesus. Fredrick writes: "They began to hold it against me that I was baptized but not loyal to my brothers and sisters. I was not loyal to God, to Christ, or my brothers and sisters. I went around feeling awful. They sent me to a psychiatrist in Rifton who told me after several sessions, 'There is nothing wrong with you. You need to leave that community.' "

Fredrick's depression did not respond to therapy or antidepressant medication. The pastoral sessions with Heini and other Servants exacerbated his sense of humiliation and worthlessness. "They yelled at me, shouting at the top of their lungs, 'You are evil!' "

He lived for a time in the small exclusion in the cabin at the base of the hill at Woodcrest. In 1964, Fredrick was expelled and eventually severed his association with the Bruderhof.

The Bruderhof Syndrome also includes two known instances of religiously motivated crises of anorexia nervosa where an adolescent girl and boy engaged in food refusal and excessive fasting during protracted spiritual crises. Evangelical Pietist groups in Europe and America from the sixteenth through nineteenth centuries employed excessive fasting as a technique of practical piety. This fasting involved self-imposed redemptive suffering to purify the sinner of sin, to demonstrate the sincerity of repentance, and to recover the ravishing of the Holy Spirit in the believer's heart.[55]

Religiously motivated anorexia nervosa has assumed a variety of forms and has also provided effective strategies for the usurpation of personal agency for people in relatively powerless conditions. Caroline Walker Bynum examines the *anorexia mirabilis* of European religious women in the thirteenth and fourteenth centuries. These women championed the cult of eucharistic devotion, investing the sacrament of communion with magical and miraculous powers. I have argued elsewhere, following Bynum, that

> Believers fasted and mortified their bodies and approached the rite in a heightened state of anxiety and spiritual expectation. Not infrequently, the faithful experienced visions, frenzies of excitement, and miracles of food multiplication. In the eucharistic encounter the penitent affirmed the excruciating bodily pain of the crucified Christ (*imitatio crucis*) and the unspeakable pleasure of union with God. Eating God through the transubstantiation of wine and bread would sustain the faithful. . . . The appropriation of severe discipline motivated by higher ethical purpose and spiritual perfection conferred opportunities for self-assertion, self-control, and autonomy for women in largely patrimonial households where status, honor, property, family title, and political authority were vested in men.[56]

Secular and medicalized forms of anorexia nervosa, first identified in the 1870s, offered adolescent girls a technique of covert rebellion against maternal overinvolvement and suffocating love in the emergent affectionate family. The meanings of food refusal have varied in anorexia mirabilis, evangelical anorexia nervosa, and modern anorexia nervosa. However, the underlying desire of relatively powerless, dependent persons to employ the highest cultural ideals of their sociocultural milieu to forge a self that can act with agency and autonomy characterizes all forms of purposeful food refusal. As we have seen, Miriam Arnold Holmes fasted excessively, hoping to waste away and to end her life and thus resolve the seemingly interminable conflict between her attachment to her family and community and her "suspect" autonomy and wish to be free of the Bruderhof.

Joel Clement also suffered anorexia nervosa. Clement was born in the early Woodcrest community in 1955, the sixth of seven children in a Quaker family with roots in Pennsylvania and New Jersey. He describes an idyllic childhood that lasted until age 6 when his father was excluded for four months during the Great Crisis in 1962. As a young child, Clement could not comprehend why the Brotherhood would take away his father and disrupt his family in the absence of a heinous crime and venial sin. The elder Clement stood charged with the sins of pride and ambition, of having criticized Heini during the fateful 1959 visit to New Meadow Run. The son was overwhelmed by feelings of anxiety, anger, and abandonment. He explains that "from this point in time on, the Bruderhof was no longer a safe place, particularly for a child. There existed an underlying element of fear that overshadowed all the good aspects of communal life. . . . The fear was systemic rather than acute. . . . You learned to live with it because you had no choice, but it could come back later in life to haunt you."[57]

Joel Clement entered eighth grade in 1968. There he read about the President's Council on Physical Fitness in a national current-events weekly. The seventh and eighth grade classes wanted to participate; a Woodcrest leader refused permission because, in his estimation, athletic competition might encourage the more gifted athletes to feel superior to the less talented children.

During the spring of 1969, Clement began to train as a runner, increasing the distances and the severity of his workouts.

> Without expressly asking my parents' permission I began to run—every evening after supper around the big circular driveway which encompassed the Schoolhouse and the Schoolhouse lawn. I had heard that six times around was equivalent to one mile. Now there was a challenge—to run one mile. I was fairly chunky at the that time and not in tip-top shape, so I would huff and puff a couple of times around the circle and be quite winded. But I was accomplishing something and wasn't harming anyone and it felt good.[58]

Clement's father soon forbade his son to run, offering no explanation for this prohibition. Now, instead of running, he walked obsessively, logging mile upon mile at the noon hour rest period, in the mornings before school, and in the evenings. The Servants and Clement's parents could not prevent him from walking, and they could not force him to eat. Fasting, carefully monitoring his food intake, and walking to burn off the calories tallied, he continued his covert rebellion against Bruderhof authority. He likens his plight to that of a caged animal, pacing back and forth, refusing to eat what the keepers tossed into the prison.

Clement suggests that running served as a metaphor of escape—running away from the irreconcilable conflict between community standards and adolescent sexual awakening, between the obligation to undergo selfless submission to parental and hierarchial authority in the brotherhood and the emergent sense of rebelliousness and self-assertion.

> The onset of adolescence and its inherent sexual awakening and personal identity awakening proved too much for me and I took it out on myself

in the form of self-starvation. The conflict between my sexual awakening and the religious community's ideals of absolute purity seemed irreconcilable. The same held true for my awakening sense of identity and the community's ideal of complete selflessness—of complete self-surrender. I was a good Bruderhof child with good Bruderhof parents and I wanted to be good, which meant following the Bruderhof principles absolutely. My parents said that of their seven children they thought I would be the easiest to get through adolescence.

"But you were our easiest child!" my mother has said—almost in protest.[59]

Clement and his family visited New Meadow Run in August 1969 where Dr. Milton Zimmerman examined him for symptoms of diabetes or other wasting organic illnesses that would explain the appetite and weight loss. He had gone from 140 to 105 pounds, starving himself with a pleasing determination, celebrating each pound shed. He secretly exalted in transforming himself into a listless, emaciated skeletal form.

He had gained important insights in the contest for the determination of his religious and personal identity. By obstinacy and willfulness, he could thwart parental and community efforts to control him. He experienced the paradox of self-assertion in a hierarchial social and cultural milieu where children and adolescents were powerless in the face of parental and church authority. Acts of covert rebellion and self-assertion produced clear evidence of nascent autonomy. Ironically, his acts of self-assertion were self-destructive regimens that could result in suicide.

Clement ended his private hunger strike in the fall of 1969 when he matriculated in ninth grade at a public high school in Kingston. He explains: "The noise, the profanity, the mind-blowing diversity, and the horrible (and wonderful) reality of the real world probably saved my life. At this point the seeds of understanding were sown that my physical and psychiatric salvation lay in getting out of the Bruderhof. From the very marrow of my bones I knew that one day I would have to leave the Bruderhof."[60]

Clement finally left the community at age 22 in 1978, but not before suffering many personal and family crises. Throughout his adolescence, he alternated between striving for the realization of Bruderhof spiritual ideals and sexual repression and surrender to his seemingly overpowering sexual desire. He recounts one incident:

I went to the Servant of the Word in 1974 and confessed to a minor sexual infraction and to having feelings for a Bruderhof girl. Perhaps in bringing these two things together I set him up, in a sense. Why is it that having feelings for a girl is made out to be bad? He could have assured me that this was normal. Instead, he said something to the effect that "the basic law is: Thou shalt not commit adultery." Then he read me something which Eberhard Arnold had written on the subject, a text which I already knew, and gave me Blumhardt to read, something rather complex about Creation.[61]

The burdens of bearing Bruderhof religious personality proved too onerous for Clement, who wished to be free from the experience of punishment as love and the anxiety he felt by the relentless oppression of an authoritarian community.

Faith was a child of the Bruderhof, coming of age in the late 1960s in the recently opened hof at Oak Lake. A vivacious, athletic, beautiful and bright senior at Uniontown High School, she excelled in school and set her sights upon college and medical school. Above all else, Faith wished to work as a physician in the Primavera hospital and to devote her life to the Bruderhof movement. However, she soon discovered that Bruderhof elders would quash these aspirations. Faith explains:

> The school sponsored a Parent's Open Evening. The brochure given to each parent that night reprinted an award-winning essay that I had written in my literature class. I was also listed as an honors student. Many Bruderhof parents attended and news of my accomplishments got back to the community which created undercurrents of disapproval. A Witness Brother met with the Principal and made it quite clear that the community would decide the right future for me.

A community leader informed her that the Brotherhood would decide her future and that she needed to submit to their collective spiritual wisdom. Faith replied, "My only desire was to devote myself completely to the community, and I accepted this wholeheartedly."

When Faith read excerpts from a popular novel, *The Catcher In The Rye*, she shared her find with another highschooler, Hope, the daughter of a Servant of the Word. Faith recounts the interrogations, clearings, and draconian church discipline that followed the discovery of her sin.

> After graduation Hope confessed to her father that both she and I had read and shared erotic excerpts from *The Catcher In The Rye*. I was summoned to speak with a Servant and immediately confessed my sin, admitting that I felt defiled and ashamed by my actions. He asked me to describe this forbidden material, but I was too embarrassed to comply. He asked intimate questions and accused me of having improper motives for wanting to become a doctor. He continued his interrogation by asking specific questions about the novel's plot, about many episodes that I had not even read. He asked sexually explicit questions using words that I had never heard before. (Later, when I looked up these words in a dictionary, I didn't think that I could look this man in the eyes again.)
>
> This interrogation was horrible and proved more sexually revealing than the few paragraphs that I read from the novel. I made a confession of personal sin which was to be used repeatedly against me in future interrogations as evidence of my depravity.

Faith was prevented from entering a baptism preparation group, from proceeding with college, or from working in the baby house or with children. She joined the cleaning crew and later endured months of social ostracism and the small exclusion at another hof. Another community leader continued the clearance, probing for more evidence of eroticism and sexual sin. Faith explains:

> He asked me to open up and confess about wrong relationships as others, unnamed, had confessed to impure feelings about me. He always spoke in such nebulous language.
>
> I admitted that I had sat next to a boy on the coach trip back from summer camp. We had talked quite a bit and then dozed, leaning against each other. I liked the boy a lot and fantasized that one day we might be married. (I learned that he too had been interrogated after my confession. He ran away from Oak Lake. I felt absolutely dreadful. It seemed to be my fault.)
>
> I sank deeper and deeper into despair. I could barely sleep or eat or speak. It was decided that I was to spend some time away. I was petrified. I was taken to a cheap hotel next to the railroad. All night long, loud, raucous voices filled the air. I was too frightened to step outside my room, even to go to the toilet or to find something to eat. The next day I went to the Social Security Office, where someone from the hof would help me sort out my papers and find work as home-help caring for two young children. I spent two months in this outside family. I was somehow able to convince the Witness Brother in my letter and after his visit, that I had truly repented and was now able to renew my faith and commitment to Jesus and the community.

Several months later, she was invited to join Woodcrest where Heini Arnold joined the interrogation. During a prayer meeting, she fainted, convinced that God had stricken down so great a sinner. "That night in the *Gemeindestunde* someone suggested the song 'Now passed is the darkness, the night is overcome.' The despair and turmoil and now this song. It was just too much! Suddenly, the room darkened and I fainted. I found myself coming round in a lobby outside the meeting. Surely God had struck me down for my sins."

In the weeks that followed, Heini Arnold continued the clearances.

> I sobbed and begged for forgiveness. I said I wished I were dead. Life held no future for anyone as wicked as me. He told me to kneel down and he prayed for me to be given the strength to open up and to be totally truthful. This was demeaning, frightening and unpleasant. I was overwhelmed by anxiety and felt a sick, churned up feeling in the pit of my stomach.
>
> These sessions seemed to drag on interminably. There were such long silences between his utterances. I felt that I was drowning in the silence, gasping for breath, but unable to speak.

Faith entered a clinical depression and was treated by a Kingston psychiatrist who prescribed major tranquilizers and sedatives. She became increasingly depersonalized and suicidal. She refused to submit to electroconvulsive shock therapy. After she had suffered from intractable depression for months, Heini sent her, unaccompanied, to the Bulstrode Bruderhof in England. The interrogations continued. After one devastating round of clearances, Faith attempted suicide. She explains:

> I sank into the "Slough of Despond." My situation seemed irretrievably hopeless. So many people knew the dreadful truth about my childhood. I couldn't face meeting any of them! I wanted to die. I managed to swallow a bottle of liquid chloral hydrate sleeping medication that was kept near the wash-up sink. By morning my miserable existence would be at an end. I lay down on my bed, my body racked by sobbing. I had no moment of regret or uncertainty.
>
> I came round hours later, retching uncontrollably, covered with my own vomit. My head was exploding and I was unable to move my body. My attempted suicide ended my life with the Bruderhof. They informed me that because I had rejected psychiatric help and had rejected their attempts to cleanse myself of sin through confession, then clearly I must leave and find my own way of reaching out to Jesus for help. I was accepted as an auxiliary nurse performing general cleaning duties and meal service at a small maternity hospital. Thus, began my separation from and new life outside of the Bruderhof.

Bruderhof adolescents and young adults did not escape the commonplace social and psychological issues of development of late twentieth-century Western societies. Coming of age in the community did not protect these young people from confronting the issues of sexual maturation, the struggle to forge a separate identity, and the propensity for self-expression, idealism, and rebellion from authority. While the Bruderhof did organize adolescent youth groups for work, charitable service, and religious instruction to channel the idealism and energies of adolescents, the community did not demonstrate any special awareness of, or toleration for, the normal conflicts and identity concerns of youth. Those who did not make successful adjustments and exemplify community models for living received temporary or permanent *Ausschluss*.

Successful passage through youth in the Bruderhof entailed surrender of independence, autonomy, and self-expression through the protracted stages of Christocentric conversion. The curtailment of self, the abandonment of autonomy, and unquestioning compliance to community dogma and authority marked the model for living that evidenced personal and spiritual adequacy (progressive sanctification) in the church-community.[62]

Those who manifested the varieties of depressive illness brought together in the Bruderhof Syndrome resembled what W. I. Thomas has termed the "unadjusted." The emergent individualization of identity and behavior strained at the limitations of received tradition. Writing in the 1920s about the generation gap between Jazz Age youth and their parents who held tenaciously to nineteenth-century values, and about acculturated immigrant girls who rejected the urban ethnic enclaves and cultural traditions of their southern, central, and eastern European families, Thomas explains:

> The modern revolt and unrest are due to the contrast between the paucity of fulfillment of the wishes of the individual and the fullness, or apparent fullness, of life around him. All age levels have been affected by the feeling that much, too much, is being missed in life. The unrest is felt most by those who have heretofore been most excluded from general participation in life—the mature woman and the young girl. Sometimes it expresses itself in despair and depression, sometimes in breaking all bounds.[63]

Many Bruderhof youth were unadjusted to the received tradition of the *Gemeinde* and the powerful renunciations demanded by Bruderhof religious personality. Even after years of struggle, these willful, bright, and creative individuals could not stifle themselves to fit the model of community identity. They suffered religious melancholy, at times stung by unresolved guilt and anger at the betrayal of their sense of self, while at other moments grieving over their inability to embrace Bruderhof identity. Ultimately, they would leave the community or be cast aside through the exclusion system.

The Burdens of Gelassenheit

Contemporary Bruderhof theology, revitalized by Heini Arnold, fostered a renewed appreciation of the Anabaptist concept of *Gelassenheit* and the inner-worldly mystical elements of conversion and religious identity. Arnoldism and the Woodcrest Spirit imposed heightened expectations of devotional piety, self-abnegation, and the contemplative possession of the Holy Spirit. *Gelassenheit* became the foundation for Bruderhof spirituality, the basis for childlike joy, and the source of the varieties of religious melancholy that afflicted the faithful.

Originating among thirteenth century mystics in South Germany, the idea of *Gelassenheit* assumed critical importance in the early Reformation, especially in Luther's *German Theology*.[64] Meister Eckhart called for an inner detachment from the world and created things, bringing the believer closer to God—renunciation of self-will. Johann Tauler (ca. 1300–1361) envisioned the application of the soul to God mediated through self-abnegation and suffering. This inner-worldly mysticism entered the Hutterite tradition in Ulrich Stadler's writings on the community of goods in 1537. Walter Klaassen explains, "a heart that is egocentric and *Ungelassen* must submit to the patient endurance of suffering

God's will. It needs to be shaped and trimmed . . . like a piece of timber to fit for use in the building of God's house."[65]

Self-denial and surrender to the will of God also demand the willingness to suffer martyrdom, persecution, and profound inner struggle as the way of the cross and a radical discipleship of Christ. During the sixteenth century, the continued persecution of Anabaptists, external crises, and the threat of imminent death heightened believers' fervor to pursue an ethic of self-abandonment to the will of God.[66] However, as Robert Cornwall explains, believers have found it difficult to sustain the demands of mystical renunciation of self and world in the absence of continued persecution. "Perhaps one reason for the waning of the level of enthusiasm may be that a theology born in the midst of severe suffering could not sustain itself on such a high plane once toleration was granted."[67]

The Bruderhof has needed external and internal crises, perceived threats, and enemies from within and without to sustain the church-community's call for the willingness of God's elect to suffer and die for their faith. Bruderhof faithful internalized the dynamic of *Gelassenheit* as central to their spirituality.

The church-community has precipitated an unending repetition of clearances, purifications, purges, and internal crises that continue to this day. Benjamin Zablocki has identified the "crisis-euphoria cycle" as a form of collective behavior initiated by a "triggering process"—the discovery of internal threats, sin, evil, impurity, and disunity. The church-community mobilizes for action, entering a crisis mode of operation, eradicating the threats, and restoring the unity of the Brotherhood. The resolution of the crisis produces a cathartic release of social tension and a collective emotional effervescence. If we place Zablocki's insight about Bruderhof collective behavior in the theological context of *Gelassenheit*, the propensity for the Bruderhof to engineer crises assumes new meaning. At the resolution of each crisis, the irradiations of the Holy Spirit fill the hearts of the faithful who have reanimated their self-abnegation and surrender to God and resolidified the solidarity of the *Gemeinde*.[68] The natural history of the crisis-euphoria cycle demonstrates the institutionalized processes whereby the contemporary Bruderhof periodically revitalizes the efficacy of *Gelassenheit* and, correspondingly, each devotee's fervent commitment to Christocentric conversion, inner-worldly mystical contemplation, and surrender to the discipleship of Christ.

While community-wide crisis involved the collective dramatization of the surrendered life of faith, the willingness to accept family disruption brought the theology of *Gelassenheit* into each member's "private" life. Families were disrupted when the commune's leadership, with the approval of the Brotherhood, excluded a family member found wanting in spiritual devotion, judged prideful and unbending (*Ungelassen*). These forced exclusions invariably created traumatic stresses for the remaining kin group who mourned the loss of a mother or father, sibling or child cast out into the world and cut off from the soteriological community and the kin network.

Gelassenheit provided a comprehensive system of meaning that defined self-abnegation within a theological context of faith and ultimate religious values. Suffering was not meaningless, and thus the faithful could endure heroic levels of redemptive suffering, quietly carrying the burdens of the cross that Bruderhof theology and practice placed upon their shoulders. Through long years of piety and evangelical humiliation, the heroes of Bruderhof piety bore the marks of surrender and self-mortification in their faces and demeanor.

The themes of struggle from within and without, warfare against the natural self, and the search for repose through the humble surrender to the cross, made realization of the ethical demands of *Gelassenheit* an arduous, heroic travail. Many who found themselves attracted to the community, or who came of age in the Bruderhof, could not bear these burdens. Indeed, the many forms of maladjustment to Bruderhof life—the adolescent crises of the Bruderhof Syndrome and individual cases of religious suicide—were evidence of *Gelassenheit*'s psychic costs.

The lives of Fred Goodwin and his daughter Hannah exemplify these burdens. Fred Goodwin (1914–1973) received his education at Cambridge University, taking a degree in civil engineering in 1936 and beginning a promising career in England. He was a cultured man who avidly read history and enjoyed classical poetry; he was also a gifted musician who performed Bach and other classical works for the keyboard. Goodwin joined the Student Christian Movement in the late 1930s and worked in the British peace movement on the eve of World War II. Learning from a friend of the existence of a pacifist Christian community of goods in the Cotswolds in 1939, Fred Goodwin and his fiancée, Margaret, visited the community and eventually remained as guests for four months. They married in 1939, formally joined the Bruderhof, and made their baptismal vows in 1940. The Goodwins emigrated to Primavera in February 1941, where they lived for more than a decade until the family returned to England and Wheathill in 1951. In the early 1960s during the Great Crisis and the closing of Wheathill, they joined the New Meadow Run community. Margaret Goodwin bore nine children, of whom eight survived.

Fred Goodwin died suddenly of a heart attack at the age of 58 in 1973. The Love Meals and Burial Meeting provided opportunities to commemorate his life, to grieve the untimely loss of a brother who died in the faith, and to reaffirm family and church-community values and bonds of solidarity that bind Bruderhof members to one another and sustain them in times of adversity. The Bruderhof recorded and transcribed the proceedings of these rites of passage that were convened in

New Meadow Run, Woodcrest, and Deer Spring in a small booklet for the family, entitled "Memories of Fred."

"Memories of Fred" recounts the life of Fred Goodwin as captured through the remembrances of family and co-religionists. In this memorial, Goodwin emerges as a model and representative life deserving of celebration and emulation by all. The memorial depicts Goodwin as a superbly trained engineer who willingly and eagerly took upon himself the most menial, unpleasant, dirty, and demanding physical labor at construction sites. He lived as a humble brother, sacrificing himself for others. Indeed, Goodwin copied a Hutterite tract on *Gelassenheit*, "Surrender and Genuine Submission," written by Tobia Bertsch in the seventeenth century, and hung these words in his apartment as a constant guide and reminder:

> Now if the whole work of God is to germinate and shoot up in a man, that man must trust God from his heart and commit himself to obedience to Christ. . . . A man must present himself to the Lord, free, empty and surrendered, denying himself, hating himself, sacrificing himself body and soul and all that he has, silent before the word of the Lord, patiently suffering his discipline, parting with everything human, all subtlety and lust, everything that the flesh and the seed of the evil serpent stirs up in him. It means dying to his own wisdom and his own will . . . taking up his cross and truly following CHRIST.[69]

Fred Goodwin was selfless in his devotion to the community. One brother from New Meadow Run remembers an incident that preceded the fatal illness. During a day set aside for rest, "he was in his best clothes with one of the boys, but there he was bending down in one of the manholes of the drainage there, attending to something that needed doing."

Hannah Goodwin was born in Primavera in 1950, the fourth child in the family. She spent, by her own account, an exceptional childhood in Wheathill, free from care, frolicking on the heaths and fields of the English countryside as "nature's child." Hannah Goodwin formed a loving and deeply felt relationship with her father, seeking his attention and approval. She describes herself as a "pushy brat" with her father. Fred Goodwin was playful and adventuresome, and he delighted in the company of his children.

During her adolescence in New Meadow Run, she chafed against community authority and expectations, first by refusing to attend household meetings at age 14. At age 15, she experienced the trauma of her mother's exclusion after the involuntary removal of her older sister. Hannah Goodwin resented the apparently arbitrary exercise of church discipline that cast out her mother and sister. She could never accept the community standards that required her to submit to the commercial (secretarial) track in Uniontown High School while her abilities in art, mathematics, and science, although identified, went undeveloped. Unlike her father, Hannah Goodwin would not embrace the burdens of *Gelassenheit*, refusing to hammer out a Christocentric conversion on the anvil of self-abnegation, submission, and surrender. For a self-described wild, unruly, problem child, the powerlessness and strictures of a patriarchal hierocracy proved stifling. She became incensed at the Bruderhof's obsession with sexual purity, repression, and female virginity. By late adolescence, the New Meadow Run servants cast her aside into exclusion as an apostate.

Like Miriam Arnold Holmes and so many other Bruderhof youth, Hannah Goodwin found it difficult to abandon her attachment to the community, the challenge of making a Christian life, and the enduring emotional relationship with her father. She remained in limbo, on leave from the community, but always haunted by the commitments she left behind, never free of the gravitational pull of family and community. She explains that she still embraced Bruderhof values while at the same time longing for her parents to disown her and cut her ties to family and community. She writes: "The way I felt as a virgin and wanting marriage more than a career was, I wish[ed] my parents would just disown me and then being on my own would be justified."

Hannah Goodwin left the Bruderhof without taking her baptismal vows and moved in with Rebecca, another Bruderhof apostate in Morgantown, West Virginia, in the early 1970s. Rebecca was living on welfare with her small child, and she was depressed and suicidal after aborting an earlier pregnancy. Her rebellion would provide a model for Hannah Goodwin, who would later reenact these themes of sexual activity, depression, and attempted suicide. She explains that "my suicide attempts were attempts in my friend's face. I was very angry about her deserting me that way."

At first Hannah Goodwin worked as a maid, but after Rebecca's attempted suicide she moved into a communal apartment and joined a New Left student group devoted to peace and justice, where she fell in love with Patel, an Indian exchange student and a Hindu. She lived with Patel and became, in her own words, a "child of the sixties," a flower child seeking refuge from the harsh discontinuities of youth and transition to adulthood.

The counterculture of the 1960s provided an ideal institutionalized avenue for youth rebellion against the demands of Protestant biblical religion and secular utilitarian individualism. In *Getting Saved from the Sixties*, Steven Tipton argues that Baby Boomers fomented a cultural divide and generation gap. Youth culture extolled the values of universal love, pacifism, and noninjury to all living things based upon a syncretic blend of Eastern and Christian mysticisms. The counterculture valorized the immediacy of inner experience, spontaneity, self-expression, drug-induced ecstasy, and communion with others.[70] In addition, the youth rebellion championed free love—open, unrepressed and polymorphous sexuality—as a cultural therapeutic to liberate people from the "uptight," conflicted and neurotic sexual double standard and pattern of female virginity before marriage. Marriagelike behavior before marriage promoted cohabitation and sexual activity without affection or emotional commitment. In place of sexual naivete and virginal innocence, women were expected to cultivate sexual sophistication, knowledge of technique, and the ability to prolong pleasure and to give pleasure to a lover. The ethos of free love envisioned sexual pleasure as a natural, desirable, and expected dimension of casual and intimate relationships. For youths like Hannah Goodwin, the combination of eroticism and romantic love crystallized as a gnostic salvation in a lover's arms.

Tipton explains that "the counterculture's ideal society is exemplified by a small-scale, intimate, collegial, and relatively self-supporting commune."[71] The youth rebellion offered a *Gemeinschaft*-like ethos that was tolerant of the body and sexual desire and that supported individuated identities. Permissiveness reigned as each youth "let it all hang out," sought to "do your own thing" and allowed "different strokes for different folks."[72] Goodwin's private rebellion coalesced with what Marcuse called the "great refusal" of the counterculture and the generational rebellion of 1960s youth culture. Supported by these social movements, she experimented with sexuality and hallucinogenic drugs. She reveled in the expressive ethic of hippie self-culture and flaunted her worldliness before her father and natal community.

Hannah Goodwin periodically visited her family at New Meadow Run during the first three years of her exclusion. However, she informed her father of her love affair with a Hindu in a series of letters sent to Fred in the spring of 1973. She openly admitted her love for Patel. She had found someone to share her bed and life who represented an affront to her father's lifelong faith. Unmarried, unsanctified, and not a Christian, her relationship with a foreign lover represented the antithesis of Bruderhof belief and practice.

She confessed her sins, worldly adventures, and youthful rebellion, and explained, "Dad wrote to me that a woman has something to defend and died of heart failure. . . . How will I [why] go on living if I cannot express my devastation?" The daughter accepted responsibility for breaking her father's heart and causing his sudden and untimely death. He died before Hannah could reconcile their differences. In her fantasies she longed to return as a prodigal child seeking and receiving forgiveness, solace, and guidance.[73]

The father's sudden death left her immobilized in shock, grief, and self-torture. In this fugue, Hannah Goodwin made the mistake of taking LSD. Her subsequent "freakout" and bad trip resulted in a psychiatric hospitalization and later a suicide attempt. The romantic illuminism of the counterculture with the emphasis upon drugged ecstasy as the foundation for loving community proved illusory. The search for completion through romantic love and polymorphous and free eroticism dramatized the paradox that desire produces suffering. The love affair ended when Patel returned as a dutiful son to resume his life in Calcutta.

Goodwin returned to New Meadow Run as a failure. She writes, "When I confessed sexual activity to a Bruderhof servant after my Dad died, I was told, 'You play with fire and you get burned.' So I was wrong and deserve to be punished?" The Bruderhof reaffirmed the burdens of *Gelassenheit* that enjoined renunciation of the flesh, and constant warfare and vigilant battle against the powerful natural drives of sexuality. However, she refused to stifle her deliriums in an expressive ethic of individuality and would not sublimate eroticism as a manifestation of piety and love to God. Erotic love for Hannah Goodwin meant acceptance of techniques of the body and admission that intense physical pleasure was a natural human expression. The erotic was wholly separate from agape and religious piety.

Hannah Goodwin employed eros as a weapon, as an affront to Bruderhof purity, and an avenue for a powerless young woman to confront the patriarchy. Sexual passion and promiscuity openly affirmed were fighting words against the Arnold canon of sexual repression. She adopted these tactics of rebellion, stating "I mean really, would it be more proper to feel multiple or extended climatic sensations or must I hold out by the forces of mind over matter because to come when Jesus comes is the ultimate in proper orgasm?"

However, Hannah Goodwin has never freed herself from the internalized standards of the commune, from self-torture and self-condemnation characteristic of the transvaluation of love. She alternates between proclaiming her emancipation from family and the Arnold theology and voicing harsh denunciations in the rhetoric of Bruderhof moralism. Fred Goodwin demanded an account and a defense for her worldliness and erotic sins. And Hannah Goodwin has labored to defend herself, to provide accounts and rationales for her actions. She has punished herself for more than twenty years, repeating an unending litany of blame. Convinced that she broke her father's heart, causing his heart attack and death, and prevented by death from receiving forgiveness or reconciliation with her father, she obsesses each day over her guilt. Her sleep is broken by anxiety, by dream scapes created to dramatize her sense of betrayal and "murder" of her father.

Hannah Goodwin spent nearly four years in and out of psychiatric wards, following her father's death, for treatment of depression and mental illness. She married a former patient and gave birth to two children before the marriage foundered in constant conflict. Today, she lives as a single parent, dependent upon income transfer programs, with unfilled blocks of time that she devotes to penitential remembrance of her sins against her father. She writes, "I cannot forgive myself for using Patel to get back at Dad." At times speaking in the voice of Bruderhof moralism: "No one would listen to me if they knew how I dishonor my parents."

She continually searches for words of consolation and prayers of absolution. Where the father lived by the words of *Gelassenheit* posted on his wall, the daughter copies prayers of forgiveness. But Hannah Goodwin appears unable or unwilling to forgive herself for the past. She has no way back to a community that has rejected her; she has not proceeded in a secular life to find satisfactions with work or love relationships.

Fred Goodwin lived as a "surrendered" and broken man, abandoning his Bible classes when Arnoldism demanded that devotees should teach only from the Arnold canon, at times depressed by the oppressive expectations of self-abnegation and the hurtful exclusions of his wife and children. But he chose this life of community of goods and the absolute ethic of brotherliness. He lived surrounded by people, enmeshed in the continuous social networks of communal living. His daughter describes her chosen life as that of a recluse, a solitary individual, separated from extended family and community ties—by her own account, a misfit lacking social graces. While the father worked methodically and ceaselessly for the community, reluctant to take even a day's rest on the Sabbath, the daughter scoffs at this "workaholic" ethic and has purposefully avoided a career or socially useful and remunerative labor, successively abandoning careers in nursing, accounting, and commercial art. She endures the persistence of memory of unfinished business with her deceased father and unresolved anger toward the Bruderhof about their demands of Christocentric surrender and *Gelassenheit*; Hannah Goodwin stands as a remnant of a now-defunct counterculture that could not sustain a romantic-illuminist vision of life or the salvation promises of inner-worldly mysticism.

Peter was born into a large Hutterite family who joined the Bruderhof in the late 1950s during the merger with the Forest River Colony. After the demise of this hof, Peter's family removed to the New Meadow Run Bruderhof where he completed high school at Uniontown, Pennsylvania. He joined a spirited adolescent peer group of youths from Forest River and Pennsylvania. They immersed themselves in athletics, auto mechanics, car culture, ham radio, and spelunking. They attended interfaith work and peace camps. Granted more freedom from adult supervision than is typical of Bruderhof youths, they formed an adventurous, informal friendship group that probed the interstitial boundaries of adult control and authority.

One summer evening, without adult supervision or permission, they piled into a car and headed off to explore a local cave. After several hours of walking in circles in search of the exit, one of the group exclaimed, "Hey guys, I think we are lost!" They eventually found their way to the surface, but this phrase served as the aphorism and reminder of the perils of adolescent passage, and as a warning to all when one of the group appeared overconfident.

"Hey guys, I think we are lost!" well described Peter's protracted conversion crisis after he graduated from high school in 1960. The community excluded him, as he had failed to fulfill the spiritual requirements of Arnoldism. He failed to embrace the burdens of *Gelassenheit* and progress from preparation group, to baptism, to full community membership and marriage. Instead, he drifted for more than a decade, attending college and then dropping out, taking up a demanding musical instrument and flying lessons but never seeing any project through to completion.

During the middle 1960s Peter purchased a Triumph sports car and joined a road rally group. He affiliated with several Bruderhof apostates, joining them for weekend camping trips, peace marches, and Quaker-sponsored antiwar activity. However, Peter's unresolved Bruderhof exclusion and internalized community standards continued to haunt him. He could not accept the counterculture's ethos of sex, drugs, and rock and roll and soon alienated his new friends.

He wandered across western Pennsylvania and Ohio, living as an unattached boarder and moving on through a chaotic assortment of dead-end factory jobs. At times he drove a taxi in Pittsburgh, alienated from family and church-community. Occasionally, Peter would return to the Bruderhof and attempt to forge the conversion experience demanded of members, but in later years the community refused him access to family who remained at New Meadow Run.

Like so many Bruderhof youth in exclusion, he could not free himself from the ties of family, community, and spirituality and make a fresh start in the world. He had internalized Bruderhof spirituality and felt an overwhelming spiritual inadequacy. He could not measure up to the weighty standards of Christocentric conversion. As one of many former Bruderhof youth frozen in liminality between two worlds, Peter's mental health began to deteriorate, and he started exhibiting serious psychiatric symptoms by age 30. He made a final attempt to contact Servants of the Word and rejoin the Bruderhof, meeting with several community elders in February 1972, at a location several miles from the hof. The meeting did not pave the way for Peter's return.

During the ensuing two months, Peter became increasingly disconsolate, antisocial, depressed, and immobilized with anxiety. He suffered from episodes of vertigo, disorientation, and fainting spells. During a blackout, he fell down a flight of stairs and required hospitalization. Writing to a Bruderhof Servant in 1972 after leaving the hospital, Peter mentions his past religious crisis and blackouts and indicates that he will attempt a Christian life independent of the Bruderhof. He explains:

> It has become very clear to me that even in the lower regions of hell we belong to God and can again come to Him. I feel that Jesus has overcome

the darkness and now stands between it and me. I have been cut off so completely from my past life that all I have here is a few belongings and clothes, and some money, but no job. There is really nothing that I want in a worldly sense but to just turn toward the light and be open to God's will in a complete commitment to Jesus. I don't know how this will happen but I look to the future with hope and faith.

Two weeks later, police found him dead, a suicide.

Ruth was born in the community in 1960 to parents who had joined the Bruderhof in the late 1950s from the Church of the Brethren. She came of age in Deer Spring. Friends and classmates remember Ruth as a quiet, compliant, and pleasant child who did not question authority or get into trouble. However, one elder in Deer Spring made an example of Ruth during a children's clearance. The culprits in the class had confessed their guilt about some wrongdoing, but Ruth and another girl resisted, claiming that they had not participated in the sinful conduct and had nothing to confess. The Servant methodically wore the girls down until he had broken them. Weeping before their classmates, they confessed to misbehavior and to additional sins of pride and deceit.

During her late adolescence and twenties, she joined the Woodcrest *Gemeindestunde*, enrolled in Hudson Valley Community college, and prepared for a career within the community in dental hygiene. Only later, when she was in her middle twenties did she succumb to unremitting religious melancholy. We may never know the incidents that precipitated this crisis. Ruth never succeeded in baptismal preparation and never took her vows. She remained obsessed with scrupulosity, admitting in her diary to having blasphemed against the Holy Spirit—committing the unpardonable sin and thus placing herself beyond the protection of Jesus and divine mercy.

After years of pastoral guidance, the systematic practice of piety, and evangelical humiliation (self-examination, confession, and surrender to God's will), Ruth never enjoyed the moment of inner-worldly mystical rapture, the seal of grace in her heart. When she could not receive this contemplative moment of ecstatic selflessness, she could only conclude that her unpardonable sin prevented the workings of God's grace.

The Servants confirmed Ruth as a "weak sister," psychiatrically impaired, and confined her to an apartment in a building on the periphery of New Meadow Run. Weak members and those punished with the lesser exclusion were placed on the margin, geographically segregated from the mainstream of community life. On Christmas eve in 1988, when the church-community commemorated the birth of a savior who would redeem the sins of fallen humanity, Ruth, whose heinous sins could never be washed clean by the blood of the Lamb, attempted suicide by hanging herself with Christmas tree lights. With impeccable timing and symbolism, she chose to express the unbearable agony of her religious crisis. Fortunately, a passerby heard the crash of her body and rescued her from death. The Servants sent her to live with a brother on the outside who was affiliated through marriage with a Pennsylvania Mennonite community. Ruth did not improve despite their efforts to minister to her spiritual concerns. She remained depressed, suicidal, and tormented, telling her brother that she had not suffered enough for her sins and did not deserve reinstatement at the Bruderhof.

Sarah came of age in the Bruderhof and made a successful religious and social transition to adulthood. She married and enjoyed her life in Woodcrest working in the sewing room, laundry, and community kitchen. Sarah found the burdens of *Gelassenheit* insupportable only after she had given birth to five children in six years. She describes a life of maternal depletion as one pregnancy followed upon the next. Always pregnant, nursing a new infant, physically exhausted, and overwhelmed with maternal responsibilities and work for the community, she pleaded with a local physician for a prescription for birth control. But Sarah could not bring herself to use contraceptives, citing the Arnold canon that likens birth control to concupiscence. Confessing her sin to a community leader, Sarah was urged to embrace the cross as a symbol of *Gelassenheit*. Each child represented a gift from God and a special blessing for parents and the church-community.

She grew increasingly dissatisfied and angry at her status as a submissive wife and follower in a patriarchal hierocracy. Sarah could not control her body and reproduction, she could not devote enough time to her children given her work group obligations. Male elders disciplined her children and usurped her authority. Finally she reached the breaking point and rebelled: pregnant with her seventh child, she refused to acquiesce to what seemed to her a needlessly cruel public humiliation of her three-year-old son who was made to confess before an interhof telephone conference heard simultaneously among the brotherhoods of New Meadow Run, Woodcrest, and Deer Spring. The preschooler stood accused of asking sexually precocious questions in the children's group and proclaiming that he knew where babies came from.

Sarah's willfulness and open affront to the authority of her husband and church elders resulted in church discipline. She was cast on the margin in the lesser exclusion, placed in an isolated cabin, separated from her children, husband, and the community. She recalls visits from elders, her parents, and husband who repeatedly insisted that she confess, repent, and submit to God-ordained authority.

After Sarah gave birth to her last child she suffered postpartum depression, panic attacks, and obsessive thoughts that God wanted her to take her life and to murder the infant. She confessed to her mother, pleading, "I'm trapped between heaven and hell; I can't be a wife or a mother. God has forsaken me! My husband, family and community have abandoned me."

When she informed her husband of the murder-suicide plan, he interceded with the Servants and arranged to have his wife committed to a state mental hospital. Today, after ten years, Sarah and her family remain in exclusion. She has joined an evangelical church and has found spiritual fulfillment in a different religious tradition.

The spiritual logic of *Gelassenheit* promised joyful surrender and gracious repose in the contemplation of God. No one can doubt the authenticity of this euphoria among the Bruderhof faithful. But what cost does this joy exact? Joy always attends the resolution of individual and collective crises. Without the ruthless pursuit of self-annihilation, the devotee cannot enjoy selfless ecstasy. In the name of *Gelassenheit*, young men and women relentlessly quashed their suspect autonomy, at times striking out with independence and agency only to return broken in the childlike spirit. Wives and mothers encountered the compound demands of spiritual surrender and sociopolitical submission to the patriarchy. Some contemplated or attempted suicide, "on the heights of despair."[74] E. M. Cioran understands this despair. "To be obsessed with suicide, there must be such inner agony that all self-imposed barriers break and nothing is left but a catastrophic dizziness, a strange and powerful whirlwind. . . . Essential to suicide is the belief that you can no longer live, not because of a whim but because of a terrifying inner tragedy."[75] These are the burdens of *Gelassenheit*.

Apostates and True Believers

The Bruderhof has, with few exceptions, refused to permit sociologists or other trained observers to conduct in-depth studies of their religious community.[76] They steadfastly deny the existence of religious melancholy or other mental health issues created by individual religious conflict or collective crises. The evidence presented in this study was obtained from published Bruderhof sources and from the writings and attestations of ex-members. The relationship between Bruderhof "orthodoxy" and apostate "heterodoxy" remains controversial, with each side accusing the other of falsehood, deception, and un-Christian conduct. Given the dynamic of religious controversy, claims made by either side require independent corroboration. In many instances, in the absence of supporting evidence, the "truth" about Bruderhof history may never be resolved. The dialectic between apostate and apologetic writings tells us more about the uses of history and the methods and purposes of historical memory adopted by each group than about the claims for "objective" truth. In this section, we consider the continuing war of contested collective memory waged by apostates and true believers.

All groups, including nation-states, ethnic and tribal groups, status groups and families, and churches, sects, and confraternities, confront questions of collective memory. How does each group constitute itself as a community of fate and memory? What collective representations does the group elaborate to "reconstruct" their history? Upon what basis do members identify with one another, remember and commemorate a reconstructed past, delineate the standards for inclusion and full participation, and accommodate new and diverse members or exclude others deemed unworthy or deviant?

Sociologists and historians have examined the question of how nation-states and other collectivities deliberately articulate commemorative histories and celebratory rites[77] as part of what Robert Bellah refers to as civil religion, or what Eric Hobsbawm terms the "invention of tradition."

> "Invented tradition" is taken to mean a set of practices, normally governed by overtly or tacitly accepted rules and a ritual or symbolic nature, which seek to inculcate certain values and norms of behaviour by repetition, which automatically implies continuity with the past. In fact, where possible, they normally attempt to establish continuity with a suitable historic past.[78]

National holidays to commemorate military victories, social justice for labor, the inclusion of previously excluded minorities who once suffered oppression; the creation of symbols such as flags and anthems; national shrines, cemeteries, battle grounds, and museums; the mythic representation of national heroes and the "charter myths" of the new nation—all of these examples are a partial list of invented traditions. Hobsbawm explains that the invented traditions of modern societies provide the symbols of social cohesion and membership, legitimate established social orders, and assist in socializing new members into the desired meanings of group participation.

Maurice Halbwachs, working in the Durkheimian tradition, formulated a theory of collective memory by identifying the dynamic where individual actions, within the context of sui generis collectivities, produced both individual memory and the collective representations of group memory. He writes:

> As soon as each person and each historical fact has permeated this [collective] memory, it is transposed into a teaching, a notion, or a symbol and takes on a meaning. It becomes an element of the society's system of ideas. This explains why traditions and present-day ideas can exist side by side. In reality present-day ideas are also traditions, and both refer at the same time and with the same right to an ancient or recent social life. . . . From this it follows that social thought is essentially a memory and that its entire content consists of collective recollections or remembrances.[79]

Halbwachs argues that contemporary actors, living in present time, recast the group's collective representations and reinterpret the past in light of current concerns, social issues, and the spirit of the times. This cultural sociology of knowledge conceives of collective memory as the continual symbolic reconstruction of the past through an alternation of interpretations by each succeeding generation—a radical perspectivalism and presentism. Collective memory has another dynamic, as factions within groups or conflict between groups invariably creates disputations of received tradition, official history, or the canon of religious orthodoxy.

Halbwachs's essay on religious collective memory suggests that the process of contested memory is inextricably tied to the history of Western Christianity. Religious collective memory provides collective representations systematized in the canonical texts that represent the ancient history of a people, the stories of migrations, fusion with new groups, and the narrative of sacred history during the time of the origin of the religion. With the routinization of the charismatic founding group in the direction of hierocracy, the church effectively closed the canon and defined dogmatic collective representations as the eternal and immutable truths that believers commemorated in an unending series of calendrical rites. Halbwachs explains:

> The Church repeats itself indefinitely, or at least claims to repeat itself. The Church gives a privileged status to the early years of Christianity and to the acts and words that had the most impact at that time. What the Church now sees as outside of time in the form of eternal truths took place during a very delimited historical period.[80]

However, religious collective memory can never remain immutable and outside of time. New prophets emerge, mystics eschew dogmatic legalism of Church dogmatics and seek inner-worldly illuminations of the Holy Spirit, and new heresies arise. The contested collective memories of heterodox groups, according to Halbwachs, accuse the Church of declension, and they advocate reforms, revitalizations, and return to their vision of the founders' spirit of the Apostolic Church. All primitivistic groups, including the Bruderhof, employ contested religious collective memory to justify their separation from the "dead hand of legalism" found in established churches. Bruderhof collective memory would also seek to legitimate the moral absolutism and authoritarianism of total community by appeal to the restoration of the true Apostolic primordium.

Religious groups also develop contested collective memories and schismatic conflicts regarding recent developments in group polity, doctrine, and liturgy. Halbwachs identifies this second aspect of contested religious collective memory as the charges and countercharges made by the orthodox against those branded as heretics. He states: "What distinguishes heresies from more or less orthodox doctrines is not that the first are inspired by the present or the recent past while the others draw on an ancient past; rather it is the way in which each recalls and understands the same period of the past which is still close enough for there to exist a great variety of remembrances and of witnesses."[81]

Halbwachs's discussion of religious collective memory, although a one-sided cultural analysis that neglects materialist and structural explanations of intragroup and intergroup controversies, does offer fresh insights into the ubiquity of contested collective memory that has characterized the evangelical and schismatic tradition in Protestantism, the numerous reform movements and variegated monastic innovations during the long history of Catholicism, and recurring periods of religious effervescence and the appearance of "new religious movements" (e.g., seventeenth-century England, nineteenth-century America, post–World War I Europe, the 1960s counterculture, etc.). Invariably, protest movements will arise that legitimate their vision of reform by appeal to the spiritual authenticity of the time of origins. Within all religious groups, factions emerge to contest the recent collective memories, to challenge the official history of the movement, claiming that the full truth can now be told.

The Bruderhof offers an interesting case study of the dynamics of contested religious collective memory. The Bruderhof offer their account of orthodoxy through a series of publications following the Great Crisis. These works include *Innerland* (1963); *Eberhard Arnold's Life and Work* (1964); *Children in Community* (1963); *When Time Was Fulfilled* (1965); *Salt and Light* (1967); *Why We Live in Community* (1972); and *Seeking for The Kingdom* (1974). The community also published several authorized histories of the movement, beginning with *Torches Together* (1963) by Eberhard's widow, Emmy Arnold, followed by Merrill Mow's *Torches Rekindled* (1989) and Bob and Shirley Wagoner's *Community in Paraguay* (1991). In addition, the *Plough* published Heini Arnold's pastoral theology, *Freedom from Sinful Thoughts* (1974), and scores of his sermons, tracts, and teachings during the period 1965 until Heini's death in 1982.

From their founding, the Bruderhof proselytized their primitivist and Pietist commune in their publications and by sustained and effective public relations outreach to the wider society. Many journalists, visitors, and guests have extolled the virtues of this Christian community in uncritical accounts. Articles in national publications such as *Sojourners*, *Christian Century*, and even the *New York Times* have presented an idealized and sentimentalized portrait of the community.[82] The Bruderhof journal the *Plough* and the Plough Publishing House, continually publish endorsements from conservative Protestant national leaders like Senator Mark Hatfield, Anabaptist scholars including John A. Hostetler and John Howard Yoder, and the renowned Catholic theologian Henri J. M. Nouwen. Local newspapers in communities adjacent to Bruderhof settlements print a seemingly endless series of human interest stories that, for example, portray blond and fair children weaving garlands of flowers in celebration of nature and the coming of spring. Somber, bearded men in plain shirts, suspenders, and trousers march in a "peace witness" against nuclear war or the death penalty. Women with heads covered in polka-dot kerchiefs and attired in long, modest dresses go about their daily routine with heads bowed in humility.

In 1996, the Bruderhof hired (but no longer retains) the Manhattan public relations firm the Weiser Walek Group, who succeeded in securing uncritical articles in the *Wall Street Journal*, the *New York Times*, and *Life* magazine.[83] The Bruderhof public relations efforts promote a climate of opinion that sees the Bruderhof as a prosperous, quaint, minority religion, akin to the Amish but willing to accept modern technology. Here, high-minded men and women voluntarily join together in Christian community as seekers of God's Kingdom.

The publication of the official histories and the canonical texts constituted a Bruderhof apologetic—or defense of the faith—and a rationalization of the collective memory of the time of origins and subsequent history of the church-community. Emmy Arnold's remembrance, *Torches Together*, provided the defining collective memory in 1963, after the Great Crisis, serving to mythologize the founder's era. Mow's *Torches Rekindled* voiced the Bruderhof account of Arnoldism and the charismatic leadership of Heini Arnold, who ostensibly saved the Bruderhof movement from declension into secularism and humanism. Bruderhof collective memory, their attempt to write their own history and to control the public's perception of their movement, is born out of the crisis and turmoil that rocked their church-communities. Michael S. Roth observes, "the use of history writing to shore up the collective identities or memories of groups under enormous economic, social, and cultural pressure signals the fragility of their solidarity."[84]

During the nearly thirty-five years since the Great Crisis, Bruderhof public relations and apologetic writings have attempted to provide convincing accounts of the necessity of the mass exclusions. The apologetic gave theological legitimation to the rejection of the inauthentic "spirit" or "atmosphere" of Primavera, the exclusion of "spiritually weak" brothers and sisters, the changed basis for community membership and participation, and the rapprochement with the Hutterite Church in 1974. In his commemorative history, Mow justifies the Great Crisis and the harsh treatment of excluded members as a struggle—between the forces that promote brotherly love and love to God and those that seek to destroy those surrendered to Jesus. He writes, "On this earth there is always a spiritual struggle going on; *the two atmospheres are always in conflict.* . . . There is a spirit in this world that wants to destroy the brotherly life based on love to Jesus. . . ."[85]

Recently, Bruderhof apostates have formed a group and begun to contest the Bruderhof apologetic collective memory of the Great Crisis and the charismatic usurpation of the movement by Heini Arnold. During the late 1980s, Ramón Sender, an excluded novice who had to leave his wife and young daughter in Woodcrest in 1957, discovered by happenstance that the daughter had recently died. The community had for decades denied him the right to visit, telephone, or correspond with his daughter. He learned of her death a month after the funeral. Sender wished to learn more about the daughter that he had been prevented from knowing, and to write a book to commemorate her life. In this quest for what Halbwachs's would term family collective memory he was repeatedly hindered by Woodcrest. Sender turned to Bruderhof apostates living in San Francisco, who put him in contact with other apostates. Soon, the ex-members began corresponding with one another in a round-robin letter that Sender and a small editorial group instituted as a monthly newsletter, *KIT* (Keep In Touch). As Sender explains:

> The KIT newsletter started as a modest two-sheet page sent to thirty or so names, but within four months it expanded to ten-thousand word issues mailed every month to over one hundred addresses. As the volume of incoming mail grew, four Bruderhof graduates and survivors formed the newsletter staff. By 1990, the newsletter grew to 20,000 words per issue and was mailed to over 450 addresses. Most of the copy consisted of letters received from ex-Bruderhofers scattered all over the world.[86]

KIT now operates under the umbrella of a tax-exempt Peregrine Foundation. KIT sponsors annual reunions at the Friendly Crossways Youth Hostel in Littleton, Massachusetts, site of an earlier Bruderhof search for asylum in America. In 1992, KIT added a summer reunion in England for European ex-members. KIT also publishes book-length memoirs of apostates under the imprimatur of the Carrier Pigeon Press. Since 1992, the press has published Roger Allain's *The Community That Failed*; Elizabeth Bohlken-Zumpe's *Torches Extinguished, Memories of a Communal Bruderhof Childhood in Paraguay, Europe and the USA*; Belinda Manley's *Through Streets Broad and Narrow*; Nadine Moonje Pleil's *Free from Bondage*; and Miriam Arnold Holmes's *Cast Out into the World*.

The letters printed in *KIT* express the opinions and sentiments of each correspondent, not an apostate editorial policy. Nevertheless, one theme predominates. KITfolk feel compelled to express their outrage at the official Bruderhof apologetic and to recount events leading to the Great Crisis that differ from Bruderhof history. KITfolk are bearers of a contested collective memory, having witnessed and remembered the traumatic events of the Great Crisis and more recent Bruderhof history. Many define themselves as survivors, "graduates" and exiles who are compelled to remember and inform an indifferent world that the truths about the Bruderhof must now be told. These truths have to do with abuse of church discipline resulting in the disruption of families, and refusal by the Bruderhof to permit family reunions and visitation by former members. KITfolk cite the exclusion of large families who are forced onto public assistance. They recount during Heini's regime the trauma of their own lives and exclusions, and remember those who succumbed as religious suicides and the emotional breakdowns of troubled souls who tried and failed to achieve the degree of devotional fervor he then required. There are also allegations of the physical discipline of children, the repression of sexuality as evidenced by "clearances" and interrogations of young children accused of sexual impurity.

The most cathartic events at KIT reunions are group sessions where each participant in turn rises to remember and commemorate the life of a deceased friend or relative—to recount their heroic stance in the face of injustice and their contributions to the group, and to recall poignant anecdotes about the person's life. These "memorials" honor the lives of past members who died largely in ignominy, in exclusion from the Bruderhof.

KIT and the Bruderhof Plough Publishing House wage a war over contested collective memory. The *Plough* publishes *Torches Rekindled* as a defense of Heini Arnold, and KIT publishes the counterclaim, *Torches Extinguished*. This battle continues over the Internet with competing Bruderhof and KIT home pages on the World Wide Web.[87]

Benjamin Zablocki relied upon apostate accounts to reconstruct the dynamics of Bruderhof community life, interspersing interviews with former members who left in the Great Crisis with statements by present Woodcrest devotees in the 1960s. Zablocki described their early experiences in separation as an ordeal of involuntary expulsion marked by the inability to relinquish the Bruderhof worldview and identity, and ambivalence about their past. Apostates felt conflicting emotions—anger at the betrayal of a dream alternating with staunch defense of Bruderhof fundamentalism as the only authentic Christian life. He viewed them as a tragic group, "those who have dared to overreach themselves, those that have striven mightily and failed, conquered not by what is worst in human nature but by what is best, broken by the inability to bend."[88]

Susan Rothbaum's study of disaffiliation from alternative religious groups adopts the metaphor of the craftsman taken from the writings of Saint John of the Cross. Like the Bruderhof, successful members needed to fashion their souls and lives according to religious ends. Apostates would not or could not make these accommodations.

> You should engrave this truth upon your heart . . . that you have not come to the monastery for any other reason than to be worked in virtue, that you are like the stone that must be chiseled and fashioned before being used in the building. . . . Thus you should understand that those who are in the monastery are craftsmen placed by God to mortify you by working and chiseling at you. Some will chisel with words, telling you what you would rather not hear; others by deeds, doing against you what you would rather not endure."[89]

High-commitment religious movements like the Bruderhof and monastic orders elaborated theological rationales for crafting a religiously grounded personality founded upon the ideals of contemplative surrender to God and yieldedness to God-ordained hierocratic authority. The contemporary Bruderhof and monastic orders each elaborated a world-rejecting mysticism and created an exclusive life-order for the religiously qualified—religious virtuosi who embraced the transformation of self guided by ultimate values. Rothbaum explains:

> This "chiseling away" at the personality is neither a secret nor an unintended consequence; it is predicated in the belief system and institutionalized in the structures and practices of a wide variety of groups. In many religions, the individual ego is viewed as an island of selfishness, a delusion that separates seekers from God or prevents them from realizing their true nature. Members join groups because they are deeply dissatisfied with their faults and limitations; they *wish* to be remade in an ideal image.[90]

Apostates, from the perspective of the Servants of the Word and the Bruderhof faithful who remained in good standing, have failed in their religious vocations. Failure epitomized spiritual inadequacy. Apostates have abdicated their vows to God and the religious community, and they justly deserve church discipline-expulsion into the Mammonistic world. From the viewpoint of Bruderhof orthodoxy, *Ausschluss* functions as a ritual that purifies and solidifies the Bruderhof unanimity of belief. Those ruthlessly cast aside must perform penance for their sin and must accept the stigma of church discipline as an opportunity for redemption suffering, to fight their way back into the true church and the only authentic Christian life. Recently expelled Bruderhof apostates, well-schooled in evangelical humiliation and methodical self-examination, have internalized the Bruderhof ideal image of religious personality. They feel consumed with self-loathing, depression, and cultural disorientation. Many live with the expectation that they will someday return to the church-community. They might sojourn temporarily in the world, but they must remain aloof from worldly values. However after several years, what first appeared to be a brief separation from the community becomes a permanent break. Not surprisingly, the process of making a long-term adjustment to the secular world entails a protracted and traumatic "deconversion," and many apostates require psychotherapy for clinical depression and religious melancholy.[91]

A middle-aged mother of eight children who lived in the Wheathill, Primavera, and Deer Spring communities for eleven years admits to being depressed for more than a year following the final exclusion of her family. She faced poverty and material hardship, culture shock and disorientation, and a devastating sense of rejection and personal inadequacy. She explains, "we were not coming up to their expectations of how individuals should act if they were really committed to God. It was our commitment to God that they were finding fault with."

Apostates in the beginning of their exile struggle with the indeterminacy of their status. They anticipate an eventual return to the community but simultaneously savor their new life and begin to imagine a future independent of the Bruderhof. At times they employ evangelical humiliation as penitents seeking their way back to the true community, languishing in blame and self-loathing for their sins and failures before God and God's community of the faithful. They alternate the exercise of evangelical humiliation with a heightening awareness of betrayal by the Bruderhof. In this manner, early exiles suffered religious melancholy, immobilized by the fateful decision of whether or not to return, mired in self-torturous guilt.

Zablocki notes the case of one teenager, born into the community but expelled with her family, who said:

> The worst part of the community is the way they torture people's minds. Like they can actually make you believe that you're bad. . . . That's what they did to my sister. When she came out of there, she really believed that she was evil. When you hear nothing else all day. When our parents came back, my sister was close to a nervous breakdown. She was just crying and crying all day and we couldn't stop her. She used to get up at twelve o'clock at night and talk with my parents. She couldn't sleep.[92]

We may speak of the "natural history" of deconversion or "apostate career" as a sequence of stages in which former members incrementally separate from the commune. The first stage of exile is characterized by marginality, indeterminacy, and immobilization. During this first stage, exiles alternate between embracing the Bruderhof moral code and worldview that engenders feelings of hopelessness, sadness, and anger for lost family and community, and plunging forward, out-of-control, in anomic normlessness. One ex-member, a young woman exiled from the community in the 1960s, is remembered in *KIT*. "[She] has suffered the most horrific psychotic illnesses, drug dependency, desperate loneliness and endless nightmare of broken friendships, unhappy lodgings, unemployment and hateful jobs—you name it and it's happened to her."[93] Other apostate women, cast adrift in secular society without knowledge of dating and sexual etiquette, have written or shared at KIT reunions accounts of rape where they were victimized after they had left the Bruderhof.[94]

With the passage of time, apostates increasingly distance themselves from Bruderhof social ties and religious worldview and become acculturated to the wider society. Many successfully complete their education, enter careers, begin friendships, marry, or renew extended kinship ties, and make religious and spiritual decisions distinct from the obligations of the Arnold canon.

As apostates move away from community influences, attenuate social and familial ties to the commune, and embrace the secularized culture of American society, they also undertake the psychological work of reinterpreting their past life and reconstructing their sense of self and identity. Peter Berger calls this process the "alternation of biography" where social actors routinely rethink their past lives within the context of their present beliefs and identity. He explains that "we change our worldviews (and our interpretations and reinterpretations of our biography) as we move from one social world to another."[95]

Conversion and deconversion require a radical and comprehensive alternation of worldviews. Just as the newly reborn member of the Bruderhof reinterprets his or her past life as a time of error, sin, and the pursuit of egoistic and prideful Mammonism, so the successfully deconverted apostate recasts his or her Bruderhof experiences with an angry and critical eye. One KIT correspondent writes: "I can't give you a simple *Weltanschauung* the way the pious or religious types can do. What I do know very well is that the language so easily used by those who "have given their lives to Jesus" is a language I do not understand . . . especially when precisely that kind of claim was made by those who screwed up hundreds of kids on the Bruderhof."

Apostates search for psychotherapeutic, sociological, and theological explanatory models and rationales to understand their Bruderhof past. The *KIT* newsletter, from its inception, has functioned as a forum for apostate accounts of deconversion and healing from the trauma of forced exile. *KIT* contributors and editors have mediated to the readership a variety of perspectives by which to understand their past lives in the community. These models include (1) Zablocki's explanation of Bruderhof religiosity as a hybrid form of collective action based upon Robert Lifton's analysis of thought reform and the psychology of totalism; (2) the Cult Awareness Network's controversial denunciation of minority and high-commitment religious groups; and (3) John Bradshaw's notions of religious addiction. Thus, what was formerly accepted, according to Bruderhof doctrine, as the only true or authentic church-community and Christian vocation is now perceived as a discredited form of spirituality and religious life. Apostate letters published in *KIT* accuse the community and Bruderhof leadership of abridging the free exercise of individual conscience, of abusive treatment of children in church discipline and clearances, and of causing the traumatic disruption of families through the use of church discipline.

Affiliation with KIT provides many ex-members with the opportunity to pursue an identity as a "career apostate." Lawrence Foster defines this term to refer to those who devote themselves wholeheartedly to the goals of destroying a faith that they at one time had embraced.[96] KIT career apostates occupy a broad spectrum of views and objectives. While a minority would eagerly rejoice at the destruction of the movement, most KITfolk seek Bruderhof reform, reconciliation, and renewed privileges to visit family who remain in the Bruderhof.

The monthly *KIT* newsletter and the annual apostate reunions in England and at Friendly Crossways Hostel in Littleton, Massachusetts, create a "recollectivization" and group reunion that facilitates the formation of reconstructed collective memories of their Bruderhof past.

From the vantage point of many years of separation, after completing the difficult emotional work of forging new occupational, family, and religious careers and identities, KITfolk provide public testimonials of their communal past lives before a circle of supportive fellow apostates who offer unquestioning and unconditional affirmations. In this milieu, apostates relate the "sad tale"[97] of their Bruderhof past in the familiar, almost formulaic recital of abuse received in the community. They characterize themselves as victims of religious abuse and survivors. When they relate the details and rationale for their final expulsion, many apostates confess with a sincere bewilderment, "I have no idea why I was asked to leave." One ex-member muses: "before I left New Meadow Run, I was out of the brotherhood for some reason—for the life of me, I've never been able to recall why. Maybe there was no 'why'. . . ."[98]

During Arnoldism and the predominance of the Woodcrest Spirit, people found to be wanting in religious fervor or committed to the Spirit of Primavera did not satisfy the exacting standards of religious vocation. They had done nothing wrong and had not committed a serious sin or violation of the Bruderhof orders. Rather, these members could not make the transition to the enhanced spirituality requisite for continued membership. After decades in exile, apostates have reinterpreted the conditions of their exile, with the assistance of the collective memory work of KIT, and have achieved a "reconstructed denial" that allows them to forget the more traumatic and judgmental indictments of their relationship to God made by Bruderhof elders.

The existence of hundreds of apostates forcibly expelled or in voluntary exile from the community as a consequence of the Great Crisis and subsequent purges during Arnoldism has proved a constant irritant and embarrassment for the Bruderhof. The commune views apostates as persons who failed to fulfill their lifetime commitment to Jesus made at baptism, as those burdened by unresolved sin, whose judgment is impaired by a guilty conscience. From the perspective of Bruderhof orthodoxy, apostates have refused to live a surrendered life and have turned their backs upon the challenge, imposed in loving concern, to fight their way back into the community. Although the community must ruthlessly reject the sinner to protect the unity and purity of the church-community, they must also keep a door open for the sincere and repentant wayward soul to rejoin God's true elect. They must hate the sin but love the sinner. Thus, the Bruderhof has extended an open invitation for all individuals who feel that they have suffered injury at the hands of Bruderhof elders, and those with unresolved issues who are at "unpeace," to return to seek reconciliation.

The recent publication of Merrill Mow's *Torches Rekindled, the Bruderhof's Struggle for Renewal* was motivated by a desire to justify the mass expulsions during the Great Crisis, to defend Heini Arnold before the court of public opinion, to justify Arnoldism as a return to the authentic spirit of the founder, to celebrate the "reuniting" with the Western Hutterites in 1974, and to invite apostates to return to the ways of the faith. Mow quotes Heini's rationale for the founding of the Darvel community in England in 1971. Here Heini speaks of the need for a charitable outreach, for gentle and humble mutual repentance of apostate and community member that results in joy to God.

> The main reason for starting a Bruderhof in England was to find the way to those who once belonged to us, to find a new relationship. We felt our door should be open to everyone who is really called by God. . . .
>
> We will need a deep inner clarity and leading from God for this task. In many places we felt that God had worked in the hearts of people. It was quite surprising and touching to see Ria Kiefer. When we first saw her again, she shook all over and said that she had had a terribly bad conscience but had experienced repentance and was asking to return to the English Bruderhof. . . .
>
> Repentance is not something that is **forced** in the heart . . . but repentance brings joy even in heaven. So when we call one another to repentance, we do not call to self-circling and self-torment, but to something that leads to the greatest joy, and this is also a joy to God.[99]

KIT–Bruderhof relations, from 1989 through the spring of 1992, can be characterized as a search for reconciliation of past injuries by mediation and dialogue. The Bruderhof proclaimed a willingness to meet with apostates on an individual basis to seek forgiveness of past wrongs and to make peace. Early in 1990, Doug Moody and his wife visited San Francisco and met with three members of the KIT editorial board. Moody committed the Bruderhof to outreach and open communication with ex-members. Sender published a statement of hope following the meeting. He wrote: "If the attitudes of openness and reconciliation prove, on our impending visits this summer to both Woodcrest and New Meadow Run, to be 'more than words,' I feel that I may well have a final happy ending chapter to my book.[100] Moody paved the way for negotiations at the highest level between KIT and the Bruderhof. Johann Christoph Arnold, leader of the Bruderhof communities, together with Sibyl Sender (Ramón Sender's ex-wife) and a retinue of top Bruderhof Servants and their wives, met with Ramón Sender (and his wife and mother-in-law) in San Francisco on February 11, 1990. As a result of the meeting, Arnold instituted a policy that permitted communication and visitation between ex-members and their family members living in the Bruderhof. In addition, the Bruderhof leadership pledged not to punish ex-members who actively participated in KIT by writing for or reading the newsletter or by attending the annual reunions. This opportunity for reconciliation was short-lived as KIT correspondents and Bruderhof members escalated their conflict, trading charge and countercharge.

Yaacov Oved suggests in *Witness of the Brothers*, a recently published and "authorized" history of the Bruderhof, that the increasingly hostile tone of KIT remembrances that were critical of Heini Arnold undermined any basis for dialogue or reconciliation. Oved presents the Bruderhof leadership's view of the KIT editorial board: "The editorial board neither filtered nor edited the material in an appropriate manner, and the bulletin's issues became a platform for personal attacks, defamation, and slander."[101]

Johann Christoph Arnold responded to the attack upon his late father, Heini, and defended his leadership of the commune. With growing defensiveness and acrimony, he stated in an interview with Oved:

> I do not deny that there were some harsh deeds committed in the past, but to lay all the blame upon my late father, Heini, and upon the present Bruderhof leadership is totally unacceptable. Those who are at present outside the commune and who filled central offices during that period acted no less harshly. . . . In general terms it is irresponsible to judge events which took place thirty years ago in articles published in a bulletin like KIT and which rely solely on personal memory. . . . A large part of what KIT publishes is at best half-truths. . . . There are also deliberate lies and distortion of the facts.[102]

The first two Friendly Crossways Conferences each produced an "Open Letter to the Bruderhof Communities" that called for the reform of the use of church discipline, financial assistance for recent apostates, the right to contact with family members, and a liberalized system of child rearing free from physical punishment or coercion. "Children must be educated and acculturated so that they may easily leave if they choose. They need to be able to make meaningful choices, get training in a field of their choice, and know that if they choose to leave the Bruderhof, they will still be respected and will not be cut off from family and friends."[103] The second Open Letter reiterated these appeals in thirty points and refocused the reform as a call for the civil and religious liberties of current and former members and their children. By November 1991, Benjamin Zablocki had systematized this statement into a "Bill of Rights for Religious Communities and Their Members."[104]

The publication of the "Bill of Rights" escalated the controversy with KIT. Christoph Arnold stated:

> I think that it is a ridiculous proposal, but if one examines it seriously it is both degrading and inflammatory. What right do people who no longer live with us have to impose a set of rules upon us? Does it not hint that the commune infringes the laws of the land? We live in a country in which the citizens enjoy the basic right of choosing their way of life according to the dictates of their conscience, and this is what we do. . . . We ask for nothing but to be left alone to live our lives according to our beliefs.[105]

Although KIT is not a membership organization and does not espouse an official policy toward the community, a majority of the readership accepted the appeal to civil and religious liberties. Zablocki identified ten rights, which included the right to leave, the right to maintain contact with the outside world, the right to health care and education, the right of children for a future of self-determination, the right to humane treatment, and the right to freedom from sexual or marital compulsion.

The movement toward dialogue, mediation, and reconciliation proceeded with the initiative of Art Rosenblum, an ex-member who had spent nearly two decades in the Primavera and Woodcrest communities. Rosenblum lives with his family on a meager trust income, devoting himself to the editorship of an alternative-living newsletter, investigating global problems as a self-proclaimed seeker who would save humankind and the planet from ecological and military destruction. Rosenblum contacted Ramón Sender and the Bruderhof leadership in Woodcrest to arrange a fair-witness arbitration of their differences. This was to be conducted by representatives from Reba Place Fellowship and was scheduled for April 1992 at a Boy Scout camp in western Pennsylvania. The negotiations proceeded by electronic mail, fax, and telephone until the Bruderhof abruptly withdrew two weeks before the scheduled meeting.

The Bruderhof refused to host the meeting for two stated reasons. First, the Woodcrest elders learned about the public testimony made by David Maendel during the 1991 Friendly Crossways Reunion. Maendel was born into a Hutterite family who joined the Bruderhof in the late 1950s. In his public statements at the reunion, he spoke of a childhood and adolescence marked by physical abuse, clearances, separation from his family, and his final exclusion in the late 1960s. Maendel told the KITfolk of his hatred of Heini Arnold that culminated in an incident where Maendel positioned himself on property adjacent to Woodcrest and waited until he had Heini in the crosshairs of a rifle.[106] The Bruderhof published the following version in *KIT*. Maendel "trespassed onto Woodcrest, up to a hilly area overlooking the central and residential area of Woodcrest, with a high-powered rifle and telescopic sight, at which place he waited three to four hours for an opportunity to draw a killing bead onto Heini Arnold."[107] Sender emailed Woodcrest that the editorial board of KIT would not condone illegal acts, and Maendel was not considered to be a threat to the Bruderhof.

Second, the Bruderhof had discovered Rosenblum's involvement as an Internet forum leader on the commercial service Compuserve, where he conducted advice and chat groups with adolescents. He counseled them to join "love groups" and practice "safe," nonpenetrative sexual activities to avoid unwanted pregnancy or sexually transmitted diseases. The Bruderhof harshly condemned Rosenblum, and withdrew from the scheduled meetings. Despite Rosenblum's offer to excuse himself, the

Bruderhof communities sent the following email to Sender on March 23, 1992: "We want Christian and reconciling contact with each and every one of you. We have just been informed of 'love groups.' . . . We have been informed that such groups included minors (people under the legal age of adulthood—in other words; [sic] children). Such a matter is a question not of politics or even just law but one of a Christian's stand to immorality as Christ has taught us."[108]

Bruderhof relations with KIT became increasingly confrontational after the aborted meeting. From 1992 to 1996, the policy of open communication and visitation ended between those on the inside with those on the outside. Inside family members required that their apostate relatives pledge, as a precondition for continued relations, never to read *KIT* or to associate with KITfolk. The Bruderhof declared that KIT and Sender were interested in destroying their religious community. Dick Domer, a powerful elder without "portfolio" within the official hierarchy and former Servant of the Word in Woodcrest, alleged that Sender had issued this threat in a telephone conversation in 1992. Despite repeated published denials by Sender, the Bruderhof persisted in their view of KIT as bent upon the destruction of the Bruderhof. Writing to KIT in May 1994, Domer confronts Sender. "You have apparently been complaining about the fact that word is going around that you have said, in effect, 'as long as the Bruderhof represents faith in Jesus, I will try to destroy it.' . . . You can't hide behind a denial, Ramón. It was quite clear that it is our faith in Jesus that drives you against the Bruderhof."[109]

How can we understand the escalating confrontation between KIT and the Bruderhof? What accounts for the paranoid style of Bruderhof spiritual politics? By 1992, KIT had become an institutionalized and permanent apostate interest group with a newsletter sent to a growing list of apostates, libraries, schools, social service agencies, and Anabaptist scholars. The newsletter published scathing reviews of Merrill Mow's *Torches Rekindled*, which provided a hagiography of the late Heini Arnold. KIT correspondents told chilling accounts of their past lives in the community that vilified Heini Arnold. For the first time in America, the Bruderhof faced an informed and articulate challenge to their published history and collective memory.

Beginning in 1992, KIT sponsored a EuroKIT conference in England, began publishing book-length apostate memoirs under the imprimatur of Carrier Pigeon Press, and produced public relations and media packages to counter Bruderhof public relations. To their chagrin, the Bruderhof leadership realized that, even with reconciliation and mediation of individual disputes with ex-members, KIT as an organization would not go away. Increasingly, Western Hutterite ministers, Mennonite publications, and other sister churches read and reviewed KIT publications.

Within the Bruderhof communities, things turned sour for Arnold and his retinue. From 1990 to 1995, the three factions of the Western

Hutterites divorced themselves in renewed schism from the Arnoldleut, with all sides issuing bitter recriminations over allegations of backsliding, spiritual pride, abuse of power, and finger-pointing about the gross financial mismanagement of Schmeidleut assets resulting in the loss of millions of dollars. After a sixteen-year reuniting effected by Heini Arnold in 1974, the Bruderhof emerged in schism, isolated and discredited with the dissolution of the joint Hutterite-Arnoldleut hof in Palm Grove, Nigeria (1994).

In 1993, a number of highly placed Servants and leaders in Woodcrest and their families, including several in-laws of Johann Christoph Arnold, received the great exclusion in the aftermath of a devastating "palace coup" which unsuccessfully challenged the direction of the movement and Arnold's charismatic vision. Perceived "attacks" from KIT and the Western Hutterites, and threats from within among his most trusted lieutenants, apparently, made Arnold feel insecure and threatened.

From a Bruderhof perspective, Satan employs his minions—KIT, Hutterites, sociologists and journalists, and even baptized members who have risen to positions of authority—to destroy God's authentic church-community and those devoted in discipleship to Jesus. The Bruderhof conditions believers to anticipate persecution and attack from the impure, from sinners, and from those addicted to pride and power.

Wayne Chesley, a recent apostate who has established his own World Wide Web page independent of KIT, was a member of the Catskill Bruderhof in 1995. As a former insider who observed the escalating animosity toward KIT, he explains, "You wouldn't realize from casual contact with the Bruderhof how much emotional energy is spent by the members on their enemies. Sometimes brotherhood meetings (open to members only) are taken up with nothing more than tirades against one enemy or another. . . . To have any contact with particular enemies can result in your being quickly expelled and barred from even seeing your family again, until such time as the brotherhood feels you may come back."[110]

Different types of persons enter into the *KIT* orbit: those who have moved on but read KIT for news of family and past associates; those committed to civil and religious liberties; those who seek reconciliation and dialogue; those traumatized by their Bruderhof past who seek healing; and activists who want "to do something now!" to effect change.[111] In the spring of 1995, a small group of KIT activists formed a membership organization, "Children of the Bruderhof, International" (COBI). They initiated a toll-free telephone number intended to assist persons inside and outside of the Bruderhof who wanted information or assistance. COBI's help line appeared in the Rifton telephone yellow pages nestled between Bruderhof and Hutterian Church numbers. The community responded with more than two thousand harassing telephone calls, including, it is alleged, several death threats in May. The billing records reveal that these calls originated from Bruderhof community telephones or public telephones adjacent to their hofs. Printed fluorescent bumper stickers with the COBI Help number were printed and distributed at several airports, giving the mistaken impression that this number was a free telephone sex line, "SWEET TALK—Joella and Karen are Waiting FOR YOUR CALL—24 Hours—7 Days."[112] Bruderhof spokesperson Joseph Keiderling attributed the phone calls to Bruderhof adolescents acting outside of the control of the leadership.[113] Bruderhof officials deny making death threats and deny responsibility for the SWEET TALK advertisements.

Chesley explains the motivation behind the harassment campaign. "It is a given at the Bruderhof that there is a great conspiratorial organization (KIT) that is out to destroy the Bruderhof and its life 'as long as we follow Christ.' Whoever does not speak well of the Bruderhof is involved in KIT and is of the 'KIT' spirit. It is for this reason that the Bruderhoffers felt actually obliged to make thousands of harassing phone calls. . . ."[114]

COBI held an Open House and press conference at the Trinity United Methodist Church in Kingston, New York, on July 27, 1995. This public meeting and press conference brought the escalating apostate/Bruderhof confrontation home to the local community adjacent to Woodcrest. Local television and newspaper coverage chronicled the religious controversy and added a new allegation that a young couple driving a car licensed to the Bruderhof had attempted to place a listening device in the church several days before the Open Meeting. One press account states how the man and woman gained access to the church, and "while the woman played the church organ after the Sunday evening service, her partner was seen carrying electronic equipment in a bag, Breithaupt [president of the church Board of Directors] said."[115] When the minister questioned the man about what he was doing with the equipment, the couple fled.

The Bruderhof/COBI confrontation escalated in September 1995 when the Bruderhof filed a civil lawsuit in federal district court in Albany, New York, charging COBI with trademark infringement over the use of the names "Bruderhof" and "Hutterian" in their Yellow Pages Help-line advertisement. The Bruderhof sought $50,000 in damages and hoped to compel COBI to change their name and refrain from using the Bruderhof trademark. The Bruderhof reached an out-of-court settlement with COBI in the summer of 1996. The settlement protected the Bruderhof trademark, ended COBI and the Help telephone line, and dismissed any Bruderhof claim to monetary damages.

The appeal to the right of armed self-defense and self-defense through recourse to the police and court system of the state constitute direct violations of the central tenets of Eberhard Arnold's doctrine and Peter Riedemann's Hutterian Confession that has served as a Bruderhof chartering doctrine since 1931. Riedemann states unequivocally:

That Christians must not go to law is shown by Christ in the words, "if any man will sue thee at the law, and take away thy coat, let him have thy cloak also," as though he would say, "Sooner let him take all than quarrel with him over it and on its behalf go to court that is foreign to thy nature." All this is Christ's will, that we may thereby show that we seek not what is temporal and foreign to us, but what is divine and our own. Thus it is evident that a Christian can neither go to law nor be a judge.[116]

Despite their confession of faith the Bruderhof has sued the COBI leaders and members and Sender. Contrary to the prohibition against the employment of agents of the state, Bruderhof leaders at Deer Spring had the Connecticut State Police arrest a former member for criminal trespass, during a public open house in the fall of 1995. When asked about this incident, Joseph Keiderling stated, "are we supposed to just ignore him?" Christian Domer immediately added, "After the police warned him twice, and by the way, we do not feel it is wrong to use the authorities that God gave in this world for our protection. . . . He broke the laws of the land, and we protect ourselves."[117]

The war of words continued in the fall of 1995 when television reporter Mary Richardson of WCVB (the American Broadcasting Company affiliate in Boston) aired an investigative report critical of the Bruderhof in the show "Chronicle," broadcast on October 11, 1995. Richardson had taped interviews during the Friendly Crossways Conference in August, interviewed additional KITfolk in September and traveled to Woodcrest to confront Johann Christoph Arnold with allegations of weapons and COBI harassment.

The KIT-Bruderhof confrontations continued when the Bruderhof sponsored a public hearing on the death penalty in Philadelphia in 1996. Prior to this confrontation, the Bruderhof leadership met in New York City, on September 13, 1995, with attorney Leonard Weinglass and Ben Chaney, brother of slain civil rights leader James Chaney, to form an ad hoc coalition under the umbrella agency, the National Commission on Capital Punishment (NCCP). The NCCP advisory committee included such notables as Sr. Helen Prejean, of *Dead Man Walking* fame, actor Edward Asner, former Attorney General Ramsey Clark, and numerous organizations that promote social justice for the poor and advocate for minority rights. The NCCP's mission was to revisit the question of capital punishment, twenty years after the Supreme Court allowed states to resume executions. The commission hoped to educate the public and foster a national conversation and debate that would lead to legislative efforts to end what the Bruderhof considered to be "the ultimate revenge." The Bruderhof formed a tax-exempt Bruderhof Foundation to solicit contributions for their Death Row Inmate Legal Defense Fund. The community formed a youth folk band, "Just-US" (pronounced "justice") and produced a first album, "Within the Justice System." Most important for the Bruderhof, they scheduled the first of a series of regional hearings under the auspices of the NCCP in Philadelphia on March 25–27, 1996, centered, in part, upon the controversial case of Mumia Abu-Jamal, who was convicted in 1982 of the murder of a Philadelphia police officer, Daniel Faulkner, and has spent more than a decade on death row, appealing the conviction and awaiting execution. He has written his memoirs and become a national *cause célèbre*.

Ramón Sender contacted Philadelphia media and the Fraternal Order of Police (FOP) before the hearings, providing them with the KIT public relations packet. Sender argued that the Bruderhof, as an authoritarian group, does not respect the individual rights of its members and does not value democratic process. They should not mediate the public debate over the controversial issue of capital punishment. The Bruderhof had scheduled the first hearings in Philadelphia City Hall, which gave the appearance of official, political endorsement of their stand in the Jamal case. The FOP, under the leadership of Richard Costello, held a news conference on the morning of March 25, airing the video tape of Richardson's Chronicle report and calling the Bruderhof a "cult." Local newspapers, television stations, and a late-night radio show recounted KIT allegations. News accounts with interviews of Bruderhof leaders counterpoised by questions raised by Sender and other KITfolk, and by sociologists Zablocki and Rubin, made the Bruderhof religious controversy, not capital punishment, the center of public debate.

With this type of social activism, Johann Christoph Arnold and the Bruderhof leadership have moved away from the isolation and world rejection of an introversionist sect, which had characterized Eberhard's and Heini Arnold's vision, into a public denominationalism. The vicissitudes of contemporary Bruderhof policy directly contradict the founding vision of Eberhard Arnold. He advocated on March 26, 1933, refusal to embrace social activism or enter into the public and political issues of the wider society.

> We have to find a different way. It is a very modest way because we refuse to attempt the reform of social conditions by political means. We abstain from all efforts to improve conditions by legislation; we refrain from playing any kind of role in the civic order of society. It may look as though we were withdrawing and isolating ourselves, as though we were turning our backs on society. In fact we are building up a life that is disengaged from the established Churches with their autonomy and self-sufficiency. We want to free ourselves of all these things . . . to follow Christ by living like the early Church in Jerusalem. Such a life means that a quite new reality has to determine everything in social, economic, and religious affairs, a new reality based on the unity and unanimity given by the Holy Spirit.[118]

In recent years the Bruderhof has sought involvement with Roman Catholicism, creating a joint religious community with the *Integrite Gemeinde* (a Catholic religious community) at Castle Bobbit on the Elbe River in Germany in 1995. The *Plough* has featured essays by leading Catholic theologians, and the publication of J. Heinrich Arnold's *Discipleship* included a preface by Henri J. M. Nouwen. The reissue of Eberhard Arnold's *Why We Live in Community* in 1995 includes transcribed interviews with Robert Merton. With the publication of Johann Christoph Arnold's *A Plea for Purity* in March, 1996, and the World Wide Web "Bruderhof Communities" site published in English, German, and French, the community hoped to proselytize their dogma and project an idealized public image of their movement before growing publics in America and Europe. *A Plea for Purity* includes a Foreword by Mother Teresa; a picture of Arnold's recent audience with Pope John Paul II in October 1995; a letter from Joseph Cardinal Ratzinger; and a promotional section "About the Bruderhof." Arnold hoped to contribute to the public debates about sexuality, family life, morality, divorce, and teen pregnancy, as he did about capital punishment.

The contemporary Bruderhof under Arnold's leadership has formed ad hoc alliances with the new Religious Right over questions of sexuality, abortion, and morality while simultaneously seeking outreach to New Left groups over questions of social justice for the poor, racial justice, and repeal of the death penalty. In late summer of 1996, the top leadership accepted an invitation to meet with Minister Louis Farrakhan of the Nation of Islam, an African American separatist group that has been associated with racial polarization, anti–Semitism, and religious controversy.[119] Johann Christoph Arnold and several of his subalterns traveled to Chicago to attend a planning meeting for the "Day of Atonement," scheduled for October 16 in New York City. As reported in the *Plough*, Arnold was deeply moved by Farrakhan's appeal to reconciliation. Arnold concludes, "Only time will tell whether our impression of Farrakhan holds true. In the meantime, however, no matter how deeply we might disagree with him and the Nation of Islam's political and religious leanings, we have heard him speak out on behalf of repentance and reconciliation. We know that both are the seeds of true renewal, indeed, the most powerful forces for lasting change. Can we ignore him?"[120]

The new denominational outreach seeks to frame the debates on capital punishment and other social issues, contradicting the primitivist and Pietist sectarian separatism of their charter doctrines. The appeal to the right of self-defense contradicts the radical pacifism of Arnoldism. Their consistent Anabaptist belief and practice had until recently created crucial doctrinal and practical differences—issues such as adult baptism, the priesthood of all believers, and the rejection of sacraments—that outweighed any superficial similarities with Catholicism. Today, however, the Bruderhof flirts with Catholic theology and religious praxis, seeking an international stage for Bruderhof self-promotion.

How can we reconcile the Bruderhof's avowed ethic of brotherliness, acosmic love, and requirement that they love their enemies with the escalating conflict with KIT? In the psychic economy of the Bruderhof and their spiritual politics, they need to constitute a demonic, persecuting enemy with whom to do battle so that true believers might someday exclaim, "Jesus is Victor!" Many career apostates also cannot move on in their lives. They too are obsessed with the Bruderhof, haunted by memories of their past association with the commune, held hostage by family on the inside, and committed to telling the world disquieting truths about Arnoldism. True believers and career apostates remain trapped in this cruel embrace, which has grown increasingly confrontational with ominous possibilities for continued escalation.

Five

RELIGIOUS MELANCHOLY AMONG
OTHER ANABAPTIST SECTS

It is instructive to compare Arnoldism with other primitivist, Pietist, and Anabaptist sects, and see how these movements address issues of religious freedom, unity, purity, and religious personality. Do primitivism and Pietism give rise to coercion? What factors lessen the moral absolutism in these religious communities? Do the faithful in other primitivist and Pietist total communities also suffer religious melancholy?

Congregational polity in church-communities among the Mennonite, Brethren, and Amish permit private household economies that mitigate the tendency toward religious authoritarianism and moral absolutism. Schism among these sects affords the expression of individual religious conscience and other differences through rebellious division of the church-community. Factionalism and the frequent division and creation of new colonies among Western Hutterites lessen the severity of social controls of church-community. The toleration of factionalism, the Hutterite practice of splitting of colonies to keep communes no large than one hundred twenty-five persons, and the dynamics of schism serve as institutionalized safety values.

Arnoldism, however, has no room for these safety values. The Bruderhof has steadfastly rejected private household economies and private spheres of life that might be kept separate from the spiritual politics of enforced unity. In the First Law of Sannerz, the Bruderhof effectively concentrated leadership and authority among the Servants, Witness Brothers, and an administrative elite who have prohibited the creation of factions or internal divisions. The use of church discipline quieted the voices of protest and the expression of individual religious conscience among the plain brothers by the threat of exclusion and disfellowship.

Table 5.1 Authoritarian Polity within Anabaptist Church Communities, identifies those aspects of belief, practice, and ecclesiastical polity that promote authoritarian social structure. These variables include community of goods, religious rejection of the world, brotherhood enforcement of absolute unity, and the implementation of a total religious ethos that seeks to impose the public morality of a single-belief system upon members of the *Gemeinde*. The Bruderhof, Hutterites, and Amish are clustered in the top half of the table and represent the most authoritarian church-communities.

Variables associated with more open, democratic, and consensual church polity include congregational ecclesiastical polity, private householders formally separated from the church-community, denominational accomodation with the world and worldliness, the proclivity to employ schism or factionalism over issues that divide the congregation, and toleration of moral pluralism and individual differences in morality and matters of conscience. Contemporary Mennonite and Brethren denominations are represented on the less authoritarian bottom half of the table. Key aspects of the Amish *Gemeinde* also promote less authoritarian polity.

The Bruderhof offers the strongest example of an authoritarian church community. As we have seen, Bruderhof authoritarianism and the Woodcrest Spirit results in periodic clearances, purges, and ritualized purifications of the brotherhoods. Bruderhof religious personhood, as a variant of authoritarian character, demands that believers introject the toxic brotherly love of the Woodcrest Spirit, resulting in a transvaluation of love and desire. (Those who exercise power and those who enthusiastically rise up to cast out the sinners and the impure externalize the toxic introject of "love" to purify the church-community.) Many followers have suffered reactive depression and religious melancholy, perceiving their traumatic separation from the commune to be clear evidence of their personal spiritual inadequacy. Arnoldism and the Woodcrest Spirit have created a unique form of religious melancholy

Table 5.1

Authoritarian Polity within Anabaptist Church Communities

	Bruderhof	Hutterite	Amish	Mennonite	Brethren
Community of Goods	X	X			
Dynamic Tension with World	X	X	X		
Brotherhood Enforcement of Absolute Unity	X	X	X		
Total Religious Ethos & Enforcement of Public Morality	X	X	X		
Congregational Polity			X	X	X
Members Reside as Private Householders			X	X	X
Denominational Accommodation with World				X	X
Safety Valve of Schism & Factionalism			X	X	X
Toleration of Moral Pluralism & Individual Differences				X	X

produced by the operations of ecclesiastical polity—clearance, crisis, exclusion, and expulsion—and by the intrapsychic dynamics of Bruderhof spirituality.

Pietist theologies of conversion and doctrine, as distinct from church polity, engender religious melancholy among the faithful. We have examined the nature and varieties of religious melancholy among Bruderhof apostates, demonstrating an affinity for religious despondency among those committed to Anabaptist and evangelical Pietist doctrines of self in surrender to Jesus. The Bruderhof is not unique in their emphasis upon the devotional life. Other Anabaptist groups, most notably Hutterites, Mennonites, Amish, and Brethren, have similar traditions and experiences with religious melancholy derived from common religious doctrine and practical divinity. Like the Bruderhof, these Protestant sects draw upon the tradition of the Radical Reformation and embrace a morphology of conversion fraught with inner struggle and temptation (*Anfechtung*), the abyss of the soul forsaken by God (*Seelengrund*). Here the faithful adopt a patient expectation in waiting for the gifts of the Holy Spirit (*Langweil*), and make an absolute commitment to God through self-renunciation (*Gelassenheit*). Martin Luther's German Theology and Theology of the Cross, and Thomas Muntzer's practical divinity envision a religious experience replete with religious melancholy.

> Dirtied and besmirched by longings, wishes, desires, and human reason, all of which draw man away from God, the *Seelengrund* awaits the activity of the Holy Spirit to set the process of salvation into motion. Man becomes restless and afraid, assailed by doubts about God and himself. He falls into an unendurable distance from God to the point of despairing of himself so that his will to live is broken. In the process of suffering—a mysticism of the cross—man is separated from his worldly desires. He loses his being; his abyss becomes "empty"; he permits the Spirit working in him to have his way; "yielded" (*Gelassen*) he awaits what comes. . . . The divine birth in man takes place in suffering and pain and the infilling of the Holy Spirit.[1]

These Protestant sects have attempted to mitigate the intense, subjective inner devotional life demanded by Radical Pietism by accentuating the sober moralism of a voluntary "believer's church" bound together within a *Gemeinde*—a redemptive community.[2] Carl F. Bowman describes the Church of the Brethren's amalgam of Anabaptism and Pietism. "The 'inner ear' of personal inspiration, devotion, and the workings of the spirit was echoed by the 'outer ear' of obedience and accountability before the gathered body of the church."[3]

In the twentieth century, Mennonites and Brethren notably have focused upon service and outreach in the interests of social justice, human rights, and world peace. In addition, these groups have been transformed by incremental incorporation of the mainstream American

Protestant tradition of revivalism, from the First Great Awakening in the eighteenth century until the current Fourth Great Awakening. Evangelicalism called these Anabaptist groups to harken to their Radical Pietist origins, to reaffirm and renew the evangelical Pietist fervor of personal religious identity. One contemporary Brethren writer explains:

> As Brethren, as Christians, we are called not only to follow the incarnate Christ, but also to live in intimate relationship with him. . . . We must not only be willing to go into the world, even to the far corners of the earth to teach and preach and care, but also to journey inward and to assist others in such a journey. As the late Anna Mow wrote nearly fifty years ago: "There is an inner realm, the country in which the true self grows, that is more important than the things that can be seen and handled."[4]

Hutterites and Amish sects reject evangelical Pietism but continue to emphasize the spiritual and social dynamics of *Gelassenheit* in their respective church-communities. Hutterites conceive of themselves as God's chosen people living on an ark or vessel surrounded by the sin-ridden world. Only the religiously qualified who have overcome the depravity of the flesh and temptations of Satan can live a holy life in the spirit of God. Only through self-renunciation and yieldedness can the believer overcome the weaknesses of the natural man. Hutterites learn to look inward for signs of sin and guilt rather than to find fault or blame others. Their extreme moralism and comprehensive religious ethos provides believers with many opportunities for self-reproach.[5] Michael Holzbach, a German journalist, spent a year among the Wilson colony and discovered the burdens and joys of *Gelassenheit*. He writes that "the reward for this complete self-sacrifice by man, however, is as high as the price, for he who overcomes himself and kills his nature will be born again in the spirit of God and thus attain immortality."[6] Like the Bruderhof, so too within these redemptive communities many devotees struggle with the burdens of self-renunciation marked by the inner turmoil of Hutterite *Anfechtung* and affective disorders among *Gelassen* Amish and Hutterite believers.

Anfechtung *among the Hutterites*

In 1951, a group of social scientists began the ambitious research project of investigating all known cases of mental disorder among a sample of 8,542 Hutterites. The results of this survey were published in two monographs: Joseph W. Eaton's and Robert J. Weil's *Culture and Mental Disorder* (1955) and Bert Kaplan's and Thomas F. A. Plaut's *Personality in a Communal Society* (1956). Hutterites provided an ideal laboratory to study the relationship between the sociocultural environment and mental illness. As an ensemble of largely homogeneous ethnic and religious communities that demanded the strict conformity of adherents to the normative demands of a single-belief system, and provided social isolation from secular society and economic security for members, the Hutterites have enjoyed a reputation for mental health and "peace of mind."[7] However, the Hutterites knew "no immunity from a troubled soul,"[8] as Eaton and Weil discovered. They ascertained from the onset of their research that the Hutterites had no utopia.[9] They explain:

> The strong social cohesion and clear-cut expectations which tend to protect Hutterites from having to face the uncertainties of life unaided and without normative guidance, can also be a source of psychological stress. Strong guilt feelings were found in Hutterites who feared that they might be unable to live up to the expectations of their group. Severe depressive moods were the most common psychopathological symptoms in neurotic and psychotic members of the sect.[10]

The Hutterite Mental Health Survey uncovered 199 cases of mental illness: a rate of 1 in 43 members. This compares with 1 person in 10 in the United States who will suffer from a debilitating mental disorder at some time in their life.[11] Of the 199 cases 53 involved psychoses, including 9 persons suffering from schizophrenia and 39 cases of dysthymia, or *Anfechtung*; 25 women and 14 men were found to be suffering from this depressive illness.

When compared to trends in American society at large, Hutterites suffered from an unusually low incidence of schizophrenia but a larger than expected incidence of major depressive disorders, or dysthymia, that Hutterites term *Anfechtung*. These investigators uncovered what we would today term a culture-bound syndrome, a form of dysthymia associated with a distinctive religiously grounded personality and piety. The social scientists and psychiatrists provided a description of Hutterite *Anfechtung* as an illness that began by the sudden onset of a spiritual crisis marked by (1) temptation by the Devil to blaspheme or renounce God; (2) awareness of overwhelming religious guilt for sin that seemed beyond forgiveness (obsessive ruminations over sin); and (3) alienation from an angry and now-distant God.[12] Kaplan and Plaut quote a definition offered by a minister. "When a person feels himself guilty, that he has committed some crime or sin and can't get rid of it. He is always thinking of it and it makes him uneasy and unhappy, until, if he keeps thinking of it, he becomes sicks. It always means that there is a guilty feeling in his conscience. He can't get rid of it unless he confesses. Often he can't overcome himself to confess it."[13]

Eaton and Weil provide several case studies to illustrate *Anfechtung*. A retired farm manager, aged 59, had suffered repeated episodes of religious depression since early adult life. He writes: "It came on very suddenly like a shock. When I was sitting down sometimes it just raised me up and whenever I saw a knife or a rope the devil said to me use it and end your troubles, there is no other way out. You are lost anyway. But I hurried away from such places and wept bitterly with streams of tears running out of my eyes and prayed to God."[14]

Another man languished for three years with *Anfechtung*. "He cried a lot and said his heart was heavy. He didn't want to eat much; he felt that he was a great sinner but couldn't explain why. Several times he said the devil was in him. He was a very hard worker in the colony but felt that his beliefs were too weak."[15]

Eaton and Weil attempt to explain the social and cultural factors that produced this distinctive depressive illness. They argue that childhood socialization encourages practices of will-breaking to mold the child into a good person, possessed of a strong conscience, and able to suppress impulsive desires in conformity with community standards. However, the researchers appear to undermine their main thesis by discounting cultural determinism and minimizing the influence of sociocultural forces as determinative of depressive illness. Because the majority of believers never succumb to *Anfechtung,* Eaton and Weil posit that psychological deficits peculiar to the stricken individuals, or genetic influences, provide a necessary and sufficient explanation of why some believers lapse into religious depression. Stricken believers merely use religious and cultural forms to express a mental illness produced by underlying somatic, genetic, or psychological causes.[16]

Kaplan and Plaut recast the meaning and explanation of *Anfechtung* as a variation of a functionalist sociology of conformity to group standards and deviance. Hutterite communal life constitutes a highly restrictive "narrow path," and depressive illness remains "beneath the surface of the apparently successful adjustment of Hutterites to a cultural pattern which seems to subordinate the individual to the group welfare in a rather extreme way."[17] They suggest that Hutterite culture encourages submission and overdependency of the individual to the collective. A "normal personality" has a weak ego with diminished capacities for autonomous action. The inability of the ego to negotiate the inner struggle between the repressive demands of religious belief and impulse, desire, and temptation produces intrapsychic conflict that is expressed in a religious vocabulary of abandonment by God. The experiences of shame, guilt, obsessions with sin and the demonic, and religious depression represent the externalization of the inner drama between the believer and God. *Anfechtung* reenacts the intrapsychic battle within the self, pitting the carnal and worldly desires of the heart against the normative demands of the church-community. Kaplan and Plaut view this struggle as a mechanism of social control in the social ritual where impulsive deviance overwhelms ideologically enforced *conformity*.[18]

The research teams did not succeed in developing a convincing explanation of how religious, cultural, or social factors account for the propensity of Hutterites to suffer religious depression. Eaton and Weil's cultural determinism thesis, which identified a distinctive depression-prone personality, overstated the evidence. They insisted on viewing the culturally distinctive syndrome of *Anfechtung* as an illustration of a more general anthropological theory of "culture and personality." Kaplan and Plaut puzzled over an anomaly that contradicted their impulse-deviance explanation. Paradoxically, those believers who succeeded in bridling their impulses and vanquishing their carnality in the intrapsychic warfare with the self, who led spotless outer lives of conformity to group standards, were the very people who became afflicted with religious depression. How could successful conformists suddenly succumb to deviance defined as *Anfechtung*? Kaplan remarks:

> The strange fact seems to be that the same individuals whom we earlier called saintly and healthy minded, for whom life seemed so non-problematic are the very people who become obsessed with the idea that they are sinners and are hopelessly damned. While the symptoms in this depression are both radically different from depression in our own society, they do have some distinctive elements . . . these symptoms are almost identical to those that were described by Martin Luther in an autobiographical account of his own depression.[19]

Kaplan and Plaut perceived Hutterite depression as an illustration of a functionalist theory of deviance and conformity. Neither team of researchers attempted to understand and explain *Anfechtung* on its own terms, as a culturally prescribed religious experience that was inextricably bound to Hutterite religious identity. Had Kaplan continued to investigate the surprising similarity between Luther's spiritual crisis and Hutterite *Anfechtungen*, he would have advanced the understanding of the affinity between Hutterian piety, religious personhood, and religious depression.

Hutterites have developed a literature of consolation for the troubled soul and a system of pastoral care in which the colony preacher, the family, and the community support the afflicted individual in his or her time of spiritual trial. Public confession of sin combined with edifying sermons provide a culturally specific modality of treatment that does not isolate or stigmatize the sufferer.[20] A traditional sermon dating from 1654, "Concerning the Struggle of the Soul," typifies the theme of tolerance of religious melancholy, combined with guidance and support for the disconsolate. This traditional ethnotherapy advises that most believers face trials and temptations from the Devil that must be resisted and overcome with renewed faith and spiritual maturity. In this manner *Anfechtung* cleanses, humbles, and teaches each child of God.

> Some suffer the most severe temptations at the beginning of their conversion, and some at the conclusion. Some are miserable all their life; some experience very minor temptation, according to the order of divine wisdom and justice.

Therefore we should not despair when we are being tempted, but implore God the Almighty all the more to show us mercy and to come to our aid in all our trials. For according to Paul's statements, He permits temptations in the degree that we can endure them. We are not going to be tempted beyond our endurance, thus we can persevere.[21]

Forty years after these studies, Hutterite society has experienced significant change and crisis as they seek to remain in dynamic tension and separation from the surrounding modern societies in the United States and Canada. Accommodations to modernity and controlled acculturation, as Hostetler maintains, are reflected in the movement toward a specialized, commercial monocrop farming economy, reduced fertility, new family patterns and gender relations, and interhof factionalism. Apostasy and defection of the young and decline of Hutterite religious fervor characterize contemporary Hutterite society. Karl A. Peter argues that few now recognize or embrace the Pietist struggle for *Gelassenheit*. Hutterite church-communities are less an ingathering of religiously qualified sectarians in separation from the world, and more an ethnic church or a series of ethicized tribal groups that dispense the certainty of institutionalized grace to members in good standing. "The individual's participation in the community of goods was now sufficient to obtain the certainty of salvation. Hutterites therefore were relieved of the internal turmoil characterized by the original *Wertrational* [value rational] orientation. . . . Salvation became spiritually effortless; what it demanded was behavioral participation in the community not spiritual struggle."[22] When religionists no longer emphasize Pietist themes of *Gelassenheit* and devotional fervor, the inner trials of *Anfechtungen* will become less common among the faithful.

The Bruderhof and other conservative Protestant groups figure prominently as a source of evangelical Pietist renewal in the crisis of contemporary Hutterite religiosity.[23] From the first contact with Eberhard Arnold in 1928 to Heini Arnold's reaffiliation in the 1970s and Johann Christoph Arnold's collaborative missionary community in Palmgrove, Nigeria, in the 1980s, the Arnoldleut, as the Western Hutterites term the Bruderhof, has always pursued Hutterite church affiliation as a process of absolute "uniting" and as part of an aggressive proselytizing campaign to instill evangelical Pietistic spirituality in their Western co-religionists. However, as Peter suggests, "The Hutterites looked upon evangelical Protestantism with dismay and even contempt, regarding its excessive fervor as debasing the sanctity of the deity."[24] The two groups separated in schism in the 1950s, reunited in 1972, and have again divided in controversy and acrimony in 1990–1995. As one astute Hutterite observed recently, "They saw us as a ready-made mission field and set about recruiting converts with missionary zeal and enthusiasm."[25]

Despite the Arnoldleut's differences in leadership from traditional Hutterites, centralized authority, theology, ritual, and lifestyle, the Bruderhof did win converts as they pursued intermarriage and unity among a faction of the Schmeideleut lead by Jacob Kleinsasser. Bruderhof evangelical Pietism, the appeal of a personal relationship with Jesus and a warm-hearted, Spirit-filled religious vocation reanimated Hutterite *Gelassenheit* and the attendant *Anfechtungen* of fervent religionists beset by Satan's temptation and religious melancholy.

The Mennonite Syndrome

Mennonites in the United States and Canada are an Anabaptist sect in separation from and in dynamic tension with the world. Mennonite congregations are made up of religiously qualified, regenerate believers who voluntarily enter into a church covenant following adult baptism. Core values include the priesthood of all believers, the central authority of the Bible, and *Gelassenheit*, or submission to the will of God and to the church's ethical code, or *Ordnung*. Mennonites strive to create holy communities to live in compliance with the ethical dictates of the Sermon on the Mount through *caritas*—acts of mutual aid, concern for the poor, and discipleship to Jesus. The idea of holy community refers to the mandate to keep the church-community pure and free from sin. Believers voluntarily submit to church discipline that includes the brotherly watch, fraternal admonition, and the ban or disfellowship for serious acts of unrepented sin. Finally, the holy community remains separate from the state; office holding, the swearing of oaths, and participation in war, military service, violence, or capital punishment are prohibited. Mennonites have a long tradition of pacifism and radical peace witness, marked by willingness to suffer persecution and even death in the imitation of Christ and in the fulfillment of their faith.[26]

Mennonites escaped religious persecution by migrating to North America during the eighteenth and nineteenth centuries, leaving the Netherlands in large numbers in 1659 and 1683, Switzerland in 1711, the Palatinate in the 1720s and Russia in the 1870s.[27] Traditionally, ethnic or "birthright" Mennonites share Germanic, Swiss, Moravian, Dutch, Prussian, and Russian ethnicity. With generations of intermarriage and sectarian separatism, Mennonite church-communities resembled ethicized tribes, or ethnic-religious enclaves.[28] During the twentieth century, Mennonite evangelism sent missions to the Caribbean, South America, Indonesia, and Africa creating a new majority of nonethnic, recently converted, or "convinced," Mennonites.

In addition to ethnic differentiation, Mennonites have a long and dolorous history of schism that has resulted in five major divisions: the Old Mennonite Church, General Conference Mennonite Church, Mennonite Brethren, Evangelical Mennonite Church, and Brethren in Christ Church. Within each branch exist scores of splinter congregations.

Mennonite church-communities impose upon themselves the seemingly impossible requirement of unanimity of belief and conduct. Every generation confronts vexing challenges that result in honest differences about how best to maintain religious fervor in the absence of external persecution, how to accommodate to the surrounding society, and how to interpret and implement Mennonite doctrine in light of changing circumstances. Invariably, opposing factions emerge. However, the church must operate with absolute unity of doctrine and practice. As Calvin Redekop explains, "Although deeply ironic, the attempt to retain unity of faith has almost constantly occasioned the possibility of disagreement and schism."[29]

No issue has produced greater dissension and schism over the past three centuries than the incremental incorporation of Pietist theology of conversion and evangelical-revivalistic methods of winning the faithful for the Church. The introduction of evangelical Pietist doctrine during the Great Awakening by George Whitefield (1739–40) and Count Zinzendorf (1741–43) transformed Mennonite doctrine and liturgy. Pietist thought offered a renewal of religious fervor, emphasizing inner-worldly, emotional, and contemplative portrayals of Christ's passion and inviting believers to experience *Anfechtung* as the spiritual struggle of the soul seeking repose in Jesus.

Evangelical Pietism in seasons of religious awakening introduced the model of the revivalist preacher speaking extemporaneously, with sermons intended to prick the hearts of slumbering sinners, to bring the congregation, en masse, into religious excitement and reaffirmation (reconversion) of their faith. Methodist revivalistic methods and New Light doctrines led to Mennonite schisms in the final third of the eighteenth century with the formation of Jacob Engle's River Brethren, Jacob Albright's Evangelical Association, and Phillip William Cotterbein and Martin Boehm's United Brethren in Christ.[30] "The new fellowships accommodated a piety and emotionalism that seemingly were experienced with some frequency, but which the established churches could not or would not absorb."[31]

Reverend Christian Newcomer, minister to the United Brethren in Christ, recounts his grandmother's conversion ordeal replete with seasons of religious melancholy. "She was very melancholy and sad, in great doubts about the salvation of her soul, and in distress of being lost. . . ."[32] Buelah Stauffer Hostetler explains,"Mennonites had difficulty dealing with just this type of religious personality, specifically with those who frequently found release in pietistic experiences. Martin Boehm, Christian Newcomer, and Jacob Albright all had experiences of melancholy, and all three had intense conversion experiences."[33]

The Second and Third Great Awakenings that swept through America in the nineteenth century, advanced evangelical Pietism into the mainstream of American Protestantism. Mennonite groups resisted, accommodated, and fragmented in schism over the issue of evangelical religion. The Oberholtzer schism of Franconia Mennonites in Pennsylvania in 1842 represents the largest and most dramatic schism sparked by the appropriation of evangelical values and practices. Mennonites divided over acceptance of Charles Grandison Finney's New School Presbyterian measures of protracted meetings, anxious benches, and praying for the unconverted by name. They divided over implementation of Methodist camp meetings and techniques of the Holiness revivals in the late nineteenth century.[34]

Sandra Cronk explains Mennonite resistance to what she terms "the Evangelical vision."

> The most basic problems lay in the individualistic and emotion-centered approach of the Evangelicals. The stress on conversion rather than yielding to the Ordnung struck at the expression of *Gelassenheit* through social rites. The Evangelicals were very optimistic about the possibility of God working through the reborn individual. For Amish and Mennonites the struggle to die to self was life-long. God's power was released only when the individual did not exercise his own will . . . membership in the community and participation in its rites was the means to salvation. God did not grant salvation because of inner experience. Salvation came only by actual participation in Christ, by suffering, yielding, dying to self as he did. They believed this was possible only in community and through the Ordnung.[35]

Mennonite church-communities traditionally emphasized salvation by the ethical stance of religious moralism, by yieldedness to the *Ordnung*. The Evangelical vision shifted emphasis away from the collective and ethical dimensions of salvation and articulated what William G. McLoughlin terms an Evangelical Arminianism.[36] For evangelicals, individuals once awakened to sin could repent and choose godliness and salvation. With the exception of Old Order Mennonites, most Progressive Mennonite churches incorporated evangelical Pietist theology of conversion and revival techniques, in varying degrees, by the 1920s.[37]

In the post–World War II era, American Mennonites have experienced a self-defined collective identity crisis. By 1989, 48 percent lived in urban centers, 27 percent worked as professionals or managers, and only 7 percent of Mennonites remained farmers.[38] No longer isolated in farming communities, in radical separation from the world as an ethnic and religious enclave, today Mennonites accept wider participation in American society through denominational accommodation. Urban, white-collar, and situated within bureaucratized life-orders, Mennonites embrace individuated religious and secular identities. Paul Peachey called attention to the identity crisis in the 1960s, during the renewed round of church schisms, and noted the psychological stresses for believers in such times of anomic disjuncture. He explains that "anyone acquainted with American Mennonite life today knows that many individuals undergo a great deal of stress with reference to their Mennonite legacy. Many, most directly affected by urbanization and related developments, find themselves unable to continue their affiliation with the community and its tradition."[39] Indeed, studies of Mennonite mental health have explained mental disorders as a function of religious disaffiliation and marginality associated with urbanization.

Despite the internal differentiations and collective identity crises, Mennonite society maintains "charter beliefs,"[40] or a Mennonite Ethos,[41] that incorporate evangelical Pietist doctrines of conversion. These charter beliefs of Mennonite doctrine and practice explain the propensity for Mennonites to succumb, with varying intensity, to times of spiritual despond or religious melancholy.

The publication of the Hutterite Mental Health Survey pointed to the fact that distinct ethnic and religious groups have unique epidemiologies of mental disorders. This study prompted several investigations of mental health among Mennonites. Writing in 1963 in *Mennonite Life*, Irmgard Thiessen shared her preliminary findings as a clinical psychologist treating Mennonite patients in Manitoba, Canada, which were confirmed by psychiatrists treating hospitalized Mennonites. She explains: "Experienced psychiatrists who have been treating Mennonites in mental hospitals talk about the 'Mennonite Psychosis.' They believe that the focal point of a mentally sick Mennonite is related to strong guilt feelings, hostility, ambivalence toward parental and religious values, a need to blame themselves for not being a good Christian in the sense of their church community."[42]

Thiessen continued her research by administering Thematic Apperception Tests and sentence completion projective tests to Mennonite college students and non-Mennonites in Manitoba. She found that Mennonites, especially youth from urban backgrounds, demonstrated a religiously grounded worldview and a personality dedicated to the realization of core Mennonite values of *Gelassenheit*, discipleship, devotional pietism, and conformity to a comprehensive ethical code. Religious responses by Mennonites to the incomplete sentence "What I feel most guilty about . . ." typically included the phrase ". . . is my lack of love for God." Respondents completed the sentence "My spiritual goal . . ." by stating ". . . is to be like Jesus." When provided with the stimulus "I lack . . ." Mennonite subjects responded with ". . . a real close walk with God."[43]

Mennonite respondents showed a propensity for sexual repression, self-blame, and a crushing burden of religious guilt stemming from their perceived sinful alienation from God and church-community. Psychiatrists, when confronted with these presenting symptoms, coined their own informal diagnostic category, the so-called "Mennonite psychosis."[44]

Thiessen, however, avoids answering the question that she posed: Is Mennonite belief, practice, and personality related to distinctive forms of mental health and disorder? She begs the question by concluding, "It is not the field of science to speculate on the merits or failures of a value system."[45] Thiessen does not attempt to understand and explain the unique religious meanings of the Mennonite psychosis; and she does not place this syndrome within the cultural context of the Canadian Mennonite Brethren. She might have asked: How does the Mennonite Ethos and morphology of conversion structure episodes of religious melancholy for many believers throughout the course of their spiritual pilgrimage?

Peter M. Hamm's *Continuity and Change among Canadian Mennonite Brethren* offers important insights about Mennonite conversion and piety that help explain the Mennonite psychosis. As a sect, or "Believer's Church," made up of the religiously qualified who join voluntarily as adults following conversion, baptism, and profession of the confession of faith, contemporary Mennonite Brethren embrace an evangelical Pietist practical theology.[46] Conversion requires a radical restructuring of self, a symbolic death of the natural man, and a regeneration or rebirth made possible by the ingrafting of the Holy Spirit as the infusion of grace. In Hamm's estimation, initial conversion requires experiential faith—the inner, subjective emotional encounter with Jesus, feeling the temptations of Satan, and the joyful submission to God's will. ". . . Canadian Mennonite Brethren have intense religious experiences, sensing keenly the presence of God and being saved by Christ, as well as the presence and activity of the devil. . . ."[47] First conversion commences a lifelong pilgrimage of spiritual maturation that includes progressive sanctification (obedience to God's ethical commands), daily devotional piety of private prayer, Bible reading, public worship, and periodic reconversion and rededication in community-wide revivals. As one Mennonite intellectual proclaimed in 1965, "Revivalism is the antidote for sin and lukewarmness in the life of the Christian, not for ignorance and simplicity."[48]

J. Howard Kauffman and Leland Harder's survey of five American Mennonite and Brethren in Christ denominations in 1975 found that American Mennonites have institutionalized evangelical Pietist models of making a Christian life. The authors conducted their survey during the height of the Fourth Great Awakening, at a time when one-third of all Americans declared themselves to be born again. When comparing Mennonite conversion and Pietistic devotionalism with Christian denominations in the wider society, the researchers found, "on those indicators for which comparable data on other denominations were available (definite conversion, experience of the presence of God, a feeling of being tempted by the devil, private prayer, family devotions, personal Bible study) Mennonite and Brethren in Christ rank higher than nearly all other religious groups."[49]

Believers confirm and strengthen their Mennonite ethnic and religious identity by embracing the core values of experiential faith and by appropriating the requirements of religiously grounded selfhood. They hope to cultivate a fervent, personal assurance of faith as a child of God. In addition, Mennonites strengthen their individual and collective religious identity through ethical conduct and religious activism. Mutual aid, charitable acts, community service, submission to the brotherly watch, fraternal correction, and church discipline constitute the ethical dimension of participation in the church-community.

For each religionist, the mix and balance of religious activism and Pietistic devotionalism creates the inner, psychological grounds for assurance of salvation. For those who succumb to the Mennonite psychosis (whatever other life-crisis or personal loss may be involved), doubt overwhelms faith. Absent the abiding assurance of grace, and absent the experiential enjoyment of the Holy Spirit, the believer succumbs to religious melancholy.

William Klassen, long associated with the Mennonite mental health movement, circulated an essay among Mennonite scholars and psychotherapists that he published in 1966. Based upon his own phenomenological research, Klassen identified "the Mennonite Syndrome" as a modal temperament marked by the inability to find diverse sources of gratification, a conflicted and neurotic sense of personal agency, and ahedonia—the failure to take pleasure in living. This personality type manifests a penchant for asceticism, submission to dogmatic authority, rigidity, and despondency.[50] He explains that "Mennonites have been more prone to be obsessive compulsive than to be psychopathic: we have had more trouble with the person who is obsessed with guilt than the one who has no apparent capacity to feel guilt."[51]

Mennonite culture, according to Klassen, does not permit the satisfactory expression of anger, aggression, or hostility. Mennonites learn from childhood to turn anger inward against the self, or to sublimate anger toward the other—who was frequently found to be a brother or sister in the faith. He explains: "We have made a gentle Jesus meek and mild, the hero of our cause and our anger is turned in upon ourselves so that depression is often the result. As we lived in our rural cloisters we sought to eradicate the world, the flesh and the devil and eventually the most vicious form the devil took was our fellow church member or the members of a sister Mennonite congregation."[52]

Al Dueck adds a final dimension to the portrait of Mennonite temperament and personality by citing the effects of evangelical child rearing in which parents break the will of the child in the interest of teaching submission to parental authority as a model for future yieldedness to God's will. Evangelical nurture values the creation of children who will develop into somber, rational adults who seek to maintain constant emotional equanimity. Dueck suggests that such adults are incapable of deep affect. "The vital springs of life are choked given the parental assumption that the self-will must be broken. Anger is not given expression but internalized. Centuries of authoritarian leadership and suffocating communal ties have carved a superego powerful enough to produce guilt and depression for generations to come."[53] Evangelical nurture and life within Mennonite communities tend to produce psyches that Dueck describes as wooden, guilt-ridden, and dependent.[54]

When we combine the insights of Thiessen, Klassen, and Dueck, the elements of religious melancholy fall into place. Mennonites develop a religiously grounded personality resting upon the tenets of an evangelical Pietism that values a warm-hearted relationship with God punctuated by times when believers feel overwhelmed by sinful alienation from God, temptation by Satan, and abandonment by God. Mennonite asceticism values productive work, and renounces the carnal pleasures of the flesh. For some this asceticism leads to ahedonia. Evangelical nurture offers scriptural validation for will-breaking as a means of engendering *Gelassenheit*, or yieldedness to God. However, the humble, *gelassen* adult children of God tend to direct anger and aggression inward. The ensemble of tendencies—times of abandonment by God, ahedonia, and self-punishment—promotes depressive illness. Mennonites who strive for the highest religious ideals of evangelical Pietist devotionalism, asceticism, evangelical nurture, and *Gelassenheit* will often suffer religious melancholy.

Contemporary Mennonite ethnic and religious identity has an affinity for religious melancholy. Not every believer and not every episode of religious despondency develops into a clinical case—a protracted and debilitating mental illness that requires pastoral care or psychotherapeutic-psychiatric intervention. Probably the preponderance of cases remain self-limiting, subclinical episodes of religious despair. As such, religious melancholy may foster an opportunity for spiritual quickening and maturation. Nevertheless, the conclusion stands: Mennonite collective identity fosters a religiously grounded self that is inextricably bound to the experience and expression of religious melancholy. As one astute Mennonite intellectual observes, "we have striven for personal and communal holiness and in that competition have caused disunity, schism, personal guilt, and an often censorious spirit."[55]

Affective Disorders among the Amish

The Amish church formed in a sectarian schism from Mennonite Swiss Brethren in 1692, under the leadership of Jacob Ammerman. Amish migrated to the United States from the Palatine in 1727–1770 and 1815–1860, developing prosperous farm settlements in Pennsylvania, Ohio, and the Midwest.[56] Amish charter beliefs include the *Gemeinde* (church-community) as a redemptive community of the ingathered faithful in radical separation from the world. The Amish imposed the brotherly watch to ensure that all baptized believers submit to the *Ordnung* or ethical code of church rules. The church operates by the principle of unanimity of belief and action. Elders impose the *meidung* or shunning of the unrepentant sinner who cannot or will not submit to the dictates of the *Ordnung*. Sectarian separatism involves plain dress, pacifism and nonresistance, refusal to swear oaths or hold elective office, and resistance to modern technology. Issues surrounding the rejection of worldliness in dress, behavior, or the use of technology have proved divisive, resulting in repeated schisms. John A. Hostetler, who has written a definitive study of Amish society, relates:

> The Amish, who work so hard to maintain unity and uniformity, nevertheless suffer the consequences of a fragmented social order. . . . Some have polarized over the shape or color of a garment; the style of a house, carriage or harness; the use of labor-saving farm machinery or the pace of singing. The list is mind-boggling. Beneath the surface are extended families, frequently fraught with envy or jealousy, that take opposing sides. . . . The Amish tend to suppress their feelings since no one wishes to be the cause of disunity or division. Typically, dissatisfied members migrate to a more compatible Old Order community or start a new settlement.[57]

Amish society is organized as a series of semi-autonomous, culturally and ethnically homogeneous church-communities that stand in religious rejection of the world and share a common religious worldview and praxis. The Amish live in integrated, traditional societies that minimize social differences and link believers together through similar beliefs, social roles, and participations. Amish social structure is characterized by a rudimentary occupational division of labor associated with a small-scale farm and craft economy. It allows for few differences in wealth and power and no formal education beyond eighth grade. Amish settlements thus constitute ethnic-religious enclaves made up of large, intact families; divorce is prohibited and marital endogamy perpetuates a complex web of kinship affinities.

Janice A. Egeland conducted ethnographic research from 1960 to 1966 among the Old Order Amish of Lancaster County, Pennsylvania. Her investigation focused upon folk medicine and folk healing through the practice of *Brauche* (pow wow), the cure of souls, and what today is termed ethnopsychiatry. Egeland found culturally distinct forms of depressive illness among Amish women, involving demonic attack or possession. One woman believed that she had engaged in sexual intercourse with Satan.[58] Egeland also found that certain types of illness and folk cures "runs in families along 'Freindschaft' lines," particularly in cases of affective disorder and suicide. She further investigated this insight as the principal investigator of the Amish Study, a comprehensive epidemiological study of mental disorders (1976–1980).

Egeland discovered that "despite its protective environment, Amish society, like the Hutterites, is not immune from psychiatric disturbances. . . ."[59] Egeland and her research team hoped to find a genetic marker and causation for affective disorder among the Amish, whom they viewed as a special social isolate marked by cultural and genetic homogeneity. After two decades of research, subsequent investigations have not supported the existence of an Amish gene for affective disorders. Social and cultural factors, rather, must explain affective disorders among this peculiar people.

The Amish Study researchers conducted a community-based epidemiological survey of active cases of mental illness that revealed 112 cases of mental illness among a population of 11,000. Of these clinical cases 71 percent received diagnoses of major affective disorder, equally divided between men and women. This rate represented 1 percent of the Amish population. The researchers concluded that "the rates for both mental illness and affective disorders specifically appear to be below average."[60]

Elvin B. Coblentz's epidemiological study (1991) of the largest Amish settlement in the world, the 20,800 Old Order Amish who reside in Holmes County, Ohio, discovered unusually high rates of social phobia among this Amish population, and psychosexual disorders among women.[61] However, "social phobia," the diagnostic category and testing instrument that identified this illness, may itself produce a false positive indication of clinical illness. The attributes of social phobia closely resemble the culturally prescribed ego-ideal or religiously grounded Amish personality yielded to God in *Gelassenheit*. Coblentz explains:

> The frequency of the diagnosis of social phobia is understandable to those versed in the practice and lifestyle of this unique population. The revered principle of being "quiet in the land" leads to the practice of submission, humility and unity, which leads to a placid, unassuming and tranquil lifestyle. Combining this personality style with the aforementioned practice of social isolation and withdrawal from the world, the individual could be described as shy, withdrawn, and socially apprehensive. Thus, the personality characteristics and reduction of social contacts may precipitate the appearance of social phobia symptomatology.[62]

C. B. MacDonald of the Oaklawn Psychiatric Center, a Mennonite-sponsored mental health clinic in Elkhart, Indiana, offers the following profile of Mennonite, Church of the Brethren, and Amish patients admitted for treatment in 1980. These groups "show a higher than average percentage of diagnoses in the following categories: depressive, obsessive, compulsive, adjustment reaction to adult life, passive aggressive, and marital maladjustment (listed in rank order of frequency)."[63]

The epidemiological profiles of the Amish do not offer a consistent or convincing representation of mental health and illness, especially affective disorders, within this subculture. These studies suffer from the attempt to apply an alien, secular psychiatric nosology to an ethnic-religious enclave that conceives of social identity, personality, health, and illness through a religious worldview and a traditional folk culture. Investigations of affective disorders among the Amish must recognize the relationship between religiously grounded personality, the unique lived experiences of believers, and depressive illness.

Amish communities provide a buffer from many of the social-psychological stresses of our modern society, in which individuals confront existential issues of lifestyle and value pluralism, alienation, social class, and ethnic and racial conflicts. While this community buffer protects believers from the predicaments associated with modernity, Amish life is itself marked by psychosocial stresses. As in other Anabaptist church-communities that place a premium upon immersion of self into high-demand group life, Amish society prevents the formation of individuated social or religious identity. Believers learn to stifle prideful self-expression (*Hochmut*) and cultivate selfless humility (*Demut*).[64] School children learn the acronym "JOY" to remind them that "*J* esus is first, *y* ou are last, and *o* thers are in between."[65] Believers live within a web of group affiliations, in compliance with the *Ordnung* and in submission to God's will. Like Hutterites, Bruderhof, and Mennonites, the Amish experience the intrapsychic burdens and costs of making a Christian life shaped by *Gelassenheit*. Hostetler explains:

> In Amish society the behavior patterns that indicate psychological problems are frequent visits to doctors, failure to find full satisfaction in a day's work, preoccupation with problems of religious orthodoxy, rigidity of attitude, and among males, the failure to marry. . . . Depression is a common symptom. Since there is no legitimate way of expressing frustration through aggression, turning sorrow inward and becoming depressed is a common mechanism."[66]

Amish social order rests, in large part, upon the theological foundation of the yielded self, self-denial through *Gelassenheit*.[67] *However,* self-denial and yieldedness to church authority and to divine will place believers under a considerable psychological burden. They dare not openly express anger, aggression, or antisocial impulses and thoughts. Each believer must stifle pride, self-interest, and ambition. Forms of depressive illness are among the psychological consequences for people who devote their lives to the realization of religious values and a *gelassen* religiously grounded self. Hostetler relates the cultural ideal of the believer who achieves a yieldedness to God. "The Amish stress the Anabaptist theme of *Gelassenheit* with its many meanings: resignation, calmness of mind, composure, staidness, conquest of selfishness, long-suffering, collectedness, silence of the soul, tranquility, inner surrender, yieldedness, equanimity, and detachment. 'We must reside quietly in Christ'."[68]

Probably the greatest burden of *Gelassenheit* befalls the man chosen by lot to fill a vacancy in the ministry. The Amish do not provide specialized training or ordination for the ministry and have not institutionalized a separate, professional clergy to minister to their church-communities.

Lay ministers respond to the call without soliciting this responsibility, which entails preaching, pastoral care, and leadership, coupled with the routine burdens of family and work. Egeland reports seeing the new minister and members of the congregation openly weeping at the ordination—grieving in this rite of passage for the lost simplicity of one's life. Ministers even receive sympathy cards from congregants at this time of symbolic death. As Egeland explains, minsters suffer disproportionately high rates of depression and suicide. "No other role seems to convey a greater risk for depression than that of the church leadership, and at no other time is it more necessary to tap the human resources and group values to maintain stability."[69] She reports the case of a young man, age 29, who could not bear the ministerial burden.

> On the Sunday prior to what was to have been his first sermon, the subject attended church in a different district where another newly ordained minister did his first preaching. After this service, the subject expressed that he didn't believe he could stand up that way on the following Sunday and had serious misgivings about his own abilities. He became quiet and seemed tired and remorseful. He refused to eat. Before going out to the barn, he said to his wife, "It all looks so very dark." He left a note, "I am going to the woods to end it all." A neighbor was summoned and arrived on horseback to precede the wife in a search. He found the subject in the cornfield where he had shot himself in the head with a shotgun. . . . Surgery was performed and the subject recovered and eventually assumed his ministerial duties."[70]

This young man would carry the burdens of *Gelassenheit*. Amish temperament supports a religiously grounded self that must stifle the expression of emotion and avoid externalizing feelings of fear, anger, hatred, and aggression. Through self-effacing *Gelassenheit,* believers strive for a humble life of self-denial. Not infrequently, believers succumb to despondency when confronted with the seemingly overwhelming demands of a yielded life.

CONCLUSION

The Tragic Sense of Life

> To endure life remains, when all is said, the first duty of
> all living beings. Illusion can have no value if it makes
> this more difficult for us.
> —Sigmund Freud, "Reflections Upon War and Death"

Late in his career, Sigmund Freud wrote two essays for general readers, *The Future of an Illusion* (1927) and *Civilization and Its Discontents* (1930). Modern civilization imposed harsh privations and instinctual renunciations upon men and women. He questioned how human happiness was possible when, according to Freud, "life, as we find it, is too hard for us; it brings us too many pains, disappointments and impossible tasks."[1] He identified palliative measures that assist us in enduring the rigors of modern life. Among these, the pursuit of art, science, meaningful work in a vocation, and loving social relationships create "substitutive satisfactions" that are guided by the principles of reason and necessity. According to Freud, these palliatives assist us in forming social and cultural illusions that make like worth living. Illusion here refers to cultural ideas and social arrangements that promote the fulfillment of human desires—wish fulfillment.[2]

Religion, however, was an illusion, not in the service of reason and necessity but born of infantile needs of the helpless child who searched for love and protection from the father. From a psychoanalytic perspective, religious institutions functioned as universal obsessional neuroses. Rituals practiced by individuals were "neurotic ceremonials" for the faithful,[3] providing them with answers to the tragic dimensions of human existence: the cruelty of fate, the inevitability of death, the problems of good and evil, and suffering. Freud openly questioned religion's ability to advance human happiness and to palliate the dissatisfactions of human existence. He doubted the value of an illusion if it makes life more difficult for us.

Freud's insights direct us to raise the question, How does Bruderhof religion make life more difficult for believers? It appears that religion offers the faithful satisfactions, not frustrations or renunciations. Bruderhof primitivist and evangelical Pietist "illusions" reflect the highest ideals of Protestantism—rebirth through discipleship in Christ, salvation, and the assurance of God's abiding love and protection. The Bruderhof offers the promise that rebirth, baptism, and surrender to the church-community will bring human happiness and transcendence of the tragic aspects of life. Benjamin Nelson describes these ideas, common in the history of Western civilization, as cosmic myths of utopia and ultimate transfiguration. He terms them redemptive futurism, "the fascination exerted over men's minds by these overpowering dreams of a final and perfect rebirth."[4] Bruderhof spirituality and life in community embrace these dreams, myths, and illusions, which exact considerable costs for the faithful, chief among them redemptive suffering and the appropriation of the tragic sense of life.[5]

The Bruderhof tragic sense of life differs from classical tragedy. Tragedy in Aristotle's *Poetics* and in Western thought portrays the downfall of a hero who has embraced a great ideal, and who proceeds toward an inevitable doom after angering the god Nemesis.[6] The tragic hero, a good but flawed person, is guilty of hubris and self-delusion.[7] We react with fear and pity to the hero's plight as an inescapable chain of events unfolds. The hero rages in jealousy, love, hatred, and madness before doom and death. "Tragedy offers 'salvation by knowledge,' an explanation of why catastrophe is built into human existence."[8]

The Christian idea of salvation by faith rejected the classical tragic sense that the Fates and the Furies will punish heroic men and women who pursue lofty ideals. Instead, Christianity promised transcendence, victory over human depravity, and the assurance that God's love abides, protecting believers who embrace the heroic demands of their religious commitment. Salvation is through faith, not knowledge.

Salvation does not, however, guarantee the end of suffering. Instead, the faithful must commit themselves to a life defined by redemptive suffering—a transformation of the tragic sense of life. As Louis A. Ruprecht, Jr., suggests, the Synoptic Gospels reveal Mark's tragic vision—the Christian mythos of Gethsemane.

> Salvation is **through** suffering, not **from** it. Suffering is not necessarily tragedy's last word, but it is decidedly the first. . . . And here is precisely where tragedies and gospels are speaking the same language: in the performance of human suffering, in the refusal to accept it blindly, in the will to understand something through it, and in the understanding, to see it transformed.[9]

Max Weber argues that the Apostolic Church intensified the experience of suffering for believers. "The principle that constituted the communal relations among the salvation prophecies was the suffering common to all believers. And this was the case whether the suffering actually existed or was a constant threat, whether it was external or internal."[10] Only though redemptive suffering would the faithful travel toward salvation and enjoy the experience of acosmic love, euphoria, ecstasy, and joy. Redemptive suffering and the Christian redefinition of the tragic sense of life, then, is the other side of joy.

Primitivist and Pietist church communities have embraced these intensified requirements for redemptive suffering. Bruderhof believers have suffered mightily in collective crises, purges, and reconstitutions of the Brotherhood. The faithful have quaked before the threat of the "enemies of faith" who, in the estimation of the Bruderhof, would destroy them for devoting their lives to Jesus. Many believers have suffered religious melancholy after losing the inner assurance that they were worthy of God's love or membership in the church-community. Those who would know joy must first traverse the spiritual itinerary of conversion, purgation of sin, and periodic reaffirmation of faith.

True believers whose religious character and personality were forged in the crucible of evangelical child rearing, *Gelassenheit,* and Pietist conversion have known the suffering of self-renunciation and submission to religious authoritarianism. As Benjamin Nelson understands, "the notion of the subordination of personality to the collective will is a vicious and destructive illusion. A community which knows only a single person, a Super-Person . . . is a living death."[11]

No one has been untouched by the suffering imposed by church discipline—shunning and internal exile, coerced confessions, and expulsion of individuals and families in times of crises and during mundane periods of Bruderhof history. Disrupted families, traumatic childhoods, and shattered lives are the costs of purity and the rituals of purification. Through religious doctrine, ritual praxis, and church polity, the Bruderhof has exacted great suffering from its members through the institutionalization of the tragic sense of life.

Eberhard Arnold proclaimed to the world that his brotherly community would be like a city upon a hill, a beacon for all to see the fuflfillment of primitivism. Arnoldism has promoted a soteriological community that promised believers joyful transcendence from the agonies of the "fall into modernity." By recreating a *Gemeinschaft,* members would flee from the collapse of traditional social structures and avoid the pitfalls of an urban, industrial, class-divided society. The rule of love, the ethic of absolute brotherliness, and the unanimity of church-fellowship would protect against the violence and coercion of the modern state or the formation of conflicts based upon inequalities of wealth, power, or status group. The modern "disintegration of moral language into a morass of emotive individualism; the sudden and shocking impossibility of religious belief; the nightmare of technology" could all be avoided.[12] The Bruderhof would produce new men and women of faith and purpose who would fulfill the highest ethical, religious, and social ideals of the Apostolic Church.

A sad irony concludes our study: high-minded men and women who would build the Kingdom of God through brotherhood and joy have not escaped the tragic sense of life, the intensification of redemptive suffering, and the other side of joy. Men and women committed to the utopian prospect of creating a heaven on earth instead have built purgatory. The travail of Pietist conversion and the rigors of living in a primitivist community of goods have made life unbearable for many apostates and believers.

Surely suffering will mark the Bruderhof's future as they travel the Pietist and Anabaptist journey toward individual and collective salvation through the making and remaking of their redemptive community. Religious melancholy will ever punctuate the childlike joy and travail of true believers in their heroic struggle to fulfill utopian ideals of the absolute ethic of brotherhood shared among the reborn in a redemptive church-community.

We allow Benjamin Nelson a last word. Like Freud, Nelson wished to free us from dreams, myths, and illusions that exacerbated human suffering and diminished our chances for happiness. Writing a sociology of the possible about community, he concludes: "Mankind must cease to dream of building a utopian society which will transcend the bonds of time, the taint of place, and the limits of political society. It must learn to accept the fact that there never has been and never will be an undivided, wholly consecrated community here below or anywhere else in this cosmos, where men are constituted as they are now and will, so far as one can tell, forever be."[13]

GLOSSARY

adiaphora things indifferent to or outside of the central doctrines of the church; peripheral matters.

Anfechtung (en) plural spiritual trials, cross-bearing, doubt about faith, loss of assurance of salvation. Originates in Martin Luther's Theology of the Cross. Important aspect of Lutheran spirituality and practical theology. Common among Hutterites; a form of religious melancholy.

automachia Pietist and early Protestant notion of the war against the carnal self; a process in making a godly life.

Ausschluss Bruderhof term for church discipline, admonishment, and fraternal correction of sin. Exclusion from the church community. The small exclusion is shunning, reassignment of work tasks, taking meals in private, and living in special quarters set aside for persons under church discipline. The larger exclusion is banishment from the community. Exclusion is motivated by love with the hope that the excluded sinner will repent and find a way back into the Brotherhood.

Bildung Nineteenth-century German concept of the making of self and identity through progressive self-cultivation by means of education and the attainment of artistic, spiritual, or ethical accomplishments.

Brauche Amish ceremony of folk healing derived from the Native American shamanistic ritual of pow wow.

Brüderlickkeitethik Max Weber's term for the ethic of brotherliness characteristic of the Apostolic Church.

Busskampf Pietist idea of the inner struggle of the soul against sin, pride, and the carnal self; *automachia*.

Demut Humility.

Erweckungsbswegung Nineteenth-century European revival movement, coinciding with the Third Great Awakening in America, circa 1875–1900.

Gefuhlskultur A form of aestheticism associated with European modernism in the early twentieth century that promoted a culture of feeling and artistic experience.

Geisteskrank Heini Arnold's concept of sickness of the spirit, the sick soul.

Gelassenheit Anabaptist concept that each believer must yield and surrender to God by godly living and by submission to religious authority exercised on behalf of God.

Gemeinde Bruderhof term for church-community based upon the model of the Apostolic Church. The ingathered faithful of baptized members bound together in complete unity will form the vessel to capture the Holy Spirit.

Gemeindestunde Bruderhof prayer circle or worship group restricted to baptized members or others (novices, guests) invited by the leadership.

Gesamthabitus Nineteenth-century concept of personality; the organization of life consistent with the pursuit of vocational or religious values.

Gesinnungsethik Max Weber's concept, "ethic of inwardness"; self-reflective and deliberate organization of life and conduct in pursuit of the attainment of inner, subjective states and outward goals. A type of social personality.

Hochmut Amish term for spiritual pride, self-concern.

Heilsgeschichte divine intercession into the world; collective redemption.

Innerlichkeit The cultivation of self-reflective, introspective experiences; the valuation of interiority, subjectivist culture in the early twentieth century.

Instmann Status-bound tenant or small landholder on large landed estates in Prussia; precapitalist agricultural workers in Germany.

Langweil Stage in the Pietist process of conversion; patiently waiting for the reception of the Holy Spirit—the experience of Grace.

Lebenscult Early twentieth-century European communal movement that championed free love.

Lebensführung Bureaucratic functionary; rational conduct of life of the trained specialist.

Meidung Amish system of church discipline, fraternal correction, and admonishment of sinners; exclusion.

Nachfolge Hutterite stage of conversion marked by unquestioning obedience to God, submission to God's will.

Ordnung Hutterite orders; codified ethical rules of conduct.

ordu salutis The spiritual itinerary of conversion; the succession of stages and experiences leading to salvation.

Sendbrief Hutterite circular letter distributed among colonies or hofs; news and announcements of important temporal or spiritual matters.

Seelengrund Extreme religious doubt and despair; forsaken by God.

Sophia Pietist stage of conversion; experience of grace through the reception of the Holy Spirit.

Tentatio Martin Luther's concept from Theology of the Cross; spiritual doubt, loss of assurance.

Volksgemeinschaft Concept of a racially based (Aryan) folk-community that would unite the German nation under the Nazi regime.

Vorsteher Hutterite leader, chief elder, or bishop of an association of communities. Interpreter of the Word and leader in spiritual and mundane affairs.

Werbung Bruderhof term for soliciting charitable donations of money or materials.

NOTES

Introduction

1. See Rosabeth Moss Kanter, *Commitment and Community* for a detailed discussion of these issues for American communes in the nineteenth century.

2. Mary Farrell Bednarowski, *New Religions and the Theological Imagination*, 3–5.

3. Barbara R. Thompson, "The Challenge of True Brotherhood," 24.

4. Julius H. Rubin, *Religious Melancholy and Protestant Experience in America*, 5.

5. John F. Schumaker, *Religion and Mental Health*, 3–4.

6. See Mark E. Crawford, Paul J. Handa, and Richard L. Weiner, "The Relationship Between Religion and Mental Health/Distress"; Robert A. Spilka and Bernard Bridges, "Religion and Mental Health of Women," 50–51; Bernard Spilka, "Functional and Dysfunctional Roles of Religion."

7. Richard N. Williams and James E. Faulconer, "Religion and Mental Health: a Hermeneutic Reconsideration," 335.

8. Samuel Pfeiffer, "Faith-Induced Neurosis: Myth or Reality?," 92.

9. *Diagnostic and Statistical Manual*, Fourth Edition, 685.

10. Antoine Vergote, *Guilt and Desire, Religious Attitudes and Their Pathological Derivatives*, 34–35. See also 25–27.

11. Bradley E. Starr, " 'The World's Most Perverse Habit': Ernst Troeltsch on Religion in the Conflict of Values," 234; Ernst Troeltsch, *The Social Teachings of the Christian Churches*, vol. 1, 222; Julius H. Rubin, *Religious Melancholy and Protestant Experience in America*, 2. See also Harvey Goldman, *Max Weber and Thomas Mann: Calling and the Shaping of the Self*.

12. Richard K. Fenn, *The Persistence of Purgatory*, 46.

13. Ibid., 7–14.

14. Ibid., 109.

15. I have used this terminology developed by Theodore Dwight Bozeman in *To Live Ancient Lives*, 14–20.

16. Franklin H. Littell, "The Power of the Restorationist Vision and Its Decline in Modern America," in Richard T. Hughes, ed., *The Primitive Church in the Modern World*, 62. Littell states, "Without strong eschatological notes, however, 'separation' from the world takes on a false face. The 'world' from which Christians are called to separate is not the created order (*Kosmos*) but this dying age (*Aeon*)."

17. Theodore Dwight Bozeman, *To Live Ancient Lives*, 11.

18. Ibid., 49.

19. Richard T. Hughes and C. Leonard Allen, *Illusions of Innocence*, 21. See also Richard T. Hughes, *The Primitive Church in the Modern World*, xi-xii.

20. Richard T. Hughes and C. Leonard Allen, *Illusions of Innocence*, 21-22.

21. Ibid., 78. The American tradition encompassing freedom of conscience and inalienable individual liberties of conscience codified in the Bill of Rights began with the tradition of religious dissent by the Baptist Roger Williams in Rhode Island, by the Quaker William Penn in Pennsylvania, and by many other dissenting Anabaptist groups. As Georg Jellinek states: "The idea of legally establishing inalienable, inherent, and sacred rights of the individual is not of political but religious origins. What has been held to be a work of the Revolution was in reality a fruit of the Reformation and its struggles. Its first apostle was not Lafayette but Roger Williams, who, driven by powerful and deep religious enthusiasm, went into the wilderness in order to found a government of religious liberty, and his name is uttered by Americans even today with the deepest respect." (p. 77)

22. Ibid., 22.

23. Ibid., 52. Theodore Dwight Bozeman, *To Live Ancient Lives*, 127.

24. Michael Walzer, *The Revolution of the Saints*, 47, 25-30.

25. Barry Alan Shain, *The Myth of American Individualism*, 201.

26. Ibid., 73.

27. See Roger Thompson, *Sex in Middlesex*. Puritan communities were bent on establishing pervasive and interlocking structures to maintain public order and to exert continual surveillance and social control over their inhabitants. The powerful institutional controls of town covenants, church covenants, "the brotherly watch over neighbors," the court system and legal code—all enforced strict public morality. Everywhere, citizens were called upon to exercise self-control and discipline, godliness, Sabbatarianism, a work ethic, and the ascetic control of lust in an ethic of sexual constraint. Thompson investigates how this institutional blueprint for a holy commonwealth fit the actual lives, experiences, and behaviors of the ordinary people of Middlesex County, Massachusetts, in the seventeenth century. See also Laurel Ulrich, *Good Wives*; John Demos, *A Little Commonwealth*; Philip J. Greven, *Four Generations*; and Kenneth A. Lockridge, *A New England Town*.

28. Barry Alan Shain, *The Myth of American Individualism*, 66-67.

29. See C. B. Macpherson, *The Political Theory of Possessive Individualism*, 3. Drawing upon the seventeenth-century political theories of Locke and Hobbes, Macpherson traces the roots of Liberal-Democratic theory to the problematic concept "possessive individualism." The individual was "essentially the proprietor of his own person or capacities, owing nothing to society for them. The individual was seen as neither a moral whole, nor as part of a larger social whole, but as an owner of himself. . . . The human essence is freedom from dependence on the wills of others and freedom is a function of possession. Society becomes a lot of free equal individuals related to each other as proprietors of their own capacities and of what they have acquired by their exercise."

30. Ibid., xvi.

31. Carol Weisbrod, *The Boundaries of Utopia*, 9.

32. Ibid., xii-xiii.

33. Ibid., xix.

34. Ibid., 35. See also the publications of the American Family Foundation and the work of anticult author Margaret Singer, *Cults in Our Midst*.

35. Carol Weisbrod, *The Boundaries of Utopia*, 209-10.

36. Barry Alan Shain, *The Myth of American Individualism*, 86.

37. See Nathanael Emmons, *Works*, vol. 3, 213-15; Samuel Hopkins, *The Works of President Edwards*, vol. I, 38-39.

38. Joseph A. Conforti, *Jonathan Edwards, Religious Tradition, and American Culture*, 98.

39. Catherine L. Albanese, *American Religions and Religion*, chapter 1.

40. Julius H. Rubin, Review of *Nature Religion in America*, 140.

41. See Laurence R. Moore, *Religious Outsiders and the Making of Americans*, 207–8.

42. Elmer T. Clark, *The Small Sects in America*, 218–31.

43. Several recent studies have explored these themes within the history of American religious pluralism. See Paul S. Boyer, *When Time Is No More*; Jon Butler, *Awash in a Sea of Faith*; Nathan O. Hatch, *The Democratization of American Christianity*; and Charles B. Strozier, *Apocalypse*.

44. Jon Butler, *Awash in a Sea of Faith*. See chapter 8, "Toward the Antebellum Spiritual Hothouse."

45. See Wendy E. Chmielewski, Louis J. Kern, and Marilyn Klee-Hartzell, eds., *Women in Spiritual and Communitarian Societies in the United States*.

46. Paul E. Johnson and Sean Wilentz, *The Kingdom of Matthias*, 6.

47. R. Laurence Moore, *Religious Outsiders and the Making of Americans*, 208.

48. Ibid, 208. James Hudnut-Beumler, *Looking for God in the Suburbs*, 31–84. See also Robert Wuthnow, *The Restructuring of American Religion*.

49. James Hudnut-Beumler, *Looking for God in the Suburbs*, 86.

50. Paul E. Johnson and Sean Wilentz argue that new religious prophets like Joseph Smith and Matthias came forward with an appeal to return a God-ordained traditional patriarchal family and social structure, as a conservative countertrend to the emerging companionate family and true womanhood in the nineteenth century Second Great Awakening, exemplified in the grand revivalism of Charles Grandison Finney. Paul E. Johnson and Sean Wilentz in *The Kingdom of Matthias*, 8–9, write: "In the wake of the great Finneyite revivals, businessmen whose fathers and grandfathers had assumed unquestioned control of their households began to pray with their wives and to give themselves over to a gentle, loving Jesus. Finneyite men worked honestly and hard, prayed for release from anger and passion, and used their money for Christian purposes, and willingly delegated day-to-day authority over child-rearing and other household affairs to their wives. Evangelical women, for their part, taught their children . . . how to pray, how to develop an instinctive knowledge of right and wrong, and how to nurture the moral discipline that would prepare them for conversion and lifelong Christian service. Reorganized in these ways, Finneyite households became models for what would eventually emerge as American Victorian domesticity." Neo-Fundamentalists like the contemporary Promise Keepers continue in this conservative trend and reject the increasing egalitarianism of the family and feminism with an appeal to return to patriarchal tradition. See Gustav Niebuhr, "Men Crowd Stadiums to Fulfill Their Souls."

51. Theodore Dwight Bozeman, *To Live Ancient Lives*, 9–10.

52. Eberhard Arnold, *Living Churches: The Essence of Their Life, Love to Christ and Love to the Brothers*, 1, 19–20.

53. Eberhard Arnold, *Why We Live in Community* (1995), 14

Chapter One

1. Ralph Waldo Emerson, *Selected Writings*, 154.

2. See Rosabeth Moss Kanter, *Commitment and Community*.

3. See Julius H. Rubin, *Religious Melancholy and Protestant Experience in America*, 10–12; John Owen King, *The Iron of Melancholy*.

4. Max Weber, "Religious Rejections of the World and Their Directions," 330.

5. See Emmy Arnold, *Eberhard Arnold's Life and Work*, and Emmy Arnold, *Torches Together*.

6. Emmy Arnold, *Eberhard Arnold's Life and Work*, 2.

7. Ibid., 3.

8. E.C.H. Arnold, "Eberhard Arnold, A Short Biography," 221.

9. The *Plough* has reprinted *Innerland* in a series of short books to make Arnold's work more accessible to readers and to use this work as a means to proselytize Arnold's teachings.

10. Harvey Goldman, *Max Weber and Thomas Mann*, 165.

11. Eberhard Arnold, *Innerland*, 35.

12. Ibid., 35.

13. Ibid., 505. See also 508, 60, 102, 175.

14. See Won Yong Ji, "Significance of Tentatio in Luther's Spirituality"; Warren C. Hovland, "*Anfechtung* in Luther's Biblical Exegesis"; and David P. Scaer, "The Concept of *Anfechtung* in Luther's Thought."

15. Eberhard Arnold, *Innerland*, 215.

16. Ibid., 215.

17. Ibid., 54.

18. Ibid., 217.

19. Emmy Arnold, *Torches Together*, 6.

20. Eberhard Arnold and Emmy Arnold, *Seeking for the Kingdom*, 24.

21. Ibid., 26.

22. Eberhard Arnold, *Innerland*, 16.

23. Ibid., 346.

24. F. Ernest Stoeffler, *German Pietism during the Eighteenth Century*, 265.

25. Eberhard Arnold, *Innerland*, 301–2.

26. F. Ernest Stoeffler, *German Pietism during the Eighteenth Century*, 12–16.

27. Ibid., 19.

28. Ibid., 179. See Stoeffler's discussion of the theology of Gottfried Arnold (1666–1714).

29. Eberhard Arnold and Emmy Arnold, *Seeking for the Kingdom*, 144, 56.

30. Ibid., 56.

31. Max Weber, *The Protestant Ethic and the Spirit of Capitalism*, 139.

32. Eberhard Arnold, *Innerland*, 144–45.

33. Robert Burton, *The Anatomy of Melancholy*, 946–47. See also Stanley W. Jackson, *Melancholia and Depression*, 325–44.

34. See Raymond H. Prince, "The Concept of Culture-Bound Syndrome."

35. Paul Tillich, *The Protestant Era*, 143.

36. Philip Greven, *The Protestant Temperament*, 144–45

37. Wolfgang Mommsen, *Max Weber and German Politics*, 19–20.

38. Ibid., 20.

39. Max Weber uses the musical metaphor of the virtuoso to distinguish the ways in which believers are differently qualified. He introduces the term "unmusical" in "The Social Psychology of the World Religions," stating, " 'Heroic' or 'virtuoso' religiosity is opposed to mass religiosity. By 'mass' we understand those who are religiously 'unmusical'; we do not, of course, mean those who occupy an inferior position in the secular status order."(287) Weber's later statement delivered in his address "Science as a Vocation," expanded his existentialist position regarding religious virtuosity. He writes: "The capacity for the accomplishment of religious virtuosos—the 'intellectual sacrifice'—is the decisive characteristic of the positively religious man." (154) Finally, Weber implies that for those moderns who cannot stand the unresolved tensions occasioned by the progressive rationalization, intellec-

tualization, and disenchantment of the world into modernity devoid of coherence and ultimate meaning, one could make the intellectual sacrifice and embrace a virtuoso religious vocation. Weber continues in "Science as a Vocation," "To the person who cannot bear the fate of the times like a man, one must say: may he rather return silently, without the usual publicity built-up of renegades, but simply and plainly. The arms of the old churches are open widely and compassionately for him." (155)

40. Rita Aldenhoff, "Max Weber and the Evangelical-Social Congress,"197.

41. Max Weber, "The National State and Economic Policy (Freiberg Address), 436.

42. Rita Aldenhoff, "Max Weber and the Evangelical-Social Congress," 199.

43. I am indebted to Benjamin Nelson's insight regarding Weber's historical ideal typology of *Herrschaft*, or imperative coordination. See Benjamin Nelson, *On the Roads to Modernity*.

44. Max Weber, "The National State and Economic Policy" (Freiburg Address), 447.

45. Lawrence A. Schaff, *Fleeing the Iron Cage*, 5.

46. Max Weber, "Religious Rejections of the World and Their Directions, 357.

47. Lawrence A. Schaff, *Fleeing the Iron Cage*, 93.

48. Ibid., 93.

49. Ibid., 81.

50. Max Weber, "Religious Rejections of the World and Their Directions," 329.

51. Ibid., 329.

52. Lawrence A. Schaff, *Fleeing the Iron Cage*, 94.

53. Max Weber, "Religious Rejections of the World and Their Directions," 330.

54. Ibid., 334.

55. See Martin Green, *The von Richthofen Sisters*.

56. Max Weber, "Religious Rejections of the World and Their Directions, 347.

57. Ibid., 342.

58. Mary Gluck, *Georg Lukács and His Generation 1900–1918*, 7.

59. Ibid., 115.

60. Lawrence A. Schaff, *Fleeing the Iron Cage*, 19.

61. Max Weber, "Religious Rejections of the World and Their Directions, 342.

62. Lawrence A. Schaff, *Fleeing the Iron Cage*, 97.

63. Max Weber, "Religious Rejections of the World and Their Directions," 357.

64. Fritz K. Ringer, *The Decline of the German Mandarins*, 163.

65. Harvey Goldman, *Politics, Death, and the Devil; Self and Power in Max Weber and Thomas Mann*, 11.

66. Ibid., 55, 71.

67. Ibid., 71.

68. Wolfgang Schluchter, "Value-Neutrality and the Ethic of Responsibility."

69. Max Weber, "Science as a Vocation," 155.

70. Max Weber, *Economy and Society*, vol. 2, 636–37.

71. Max Weber, "Religious Rejections of the World and Their Directions," 338.

72. Bryan S. Turner, *Max Weber: From History to Modernity*, 36–37.

73. Lawrence A. Schaff, 101.

Chapter Two

1. Emmy Arnold, *Torches Together*, 27.

2. Frank J. Gordon, "Protestantism and Socialism in the Weimar Republic," 438.

3. John Cort, *Christian Socialism*, 200.

4. Leonhard Ragaz, *Signs of the Kingdom*, 21.

5. John Cort, *Christian Socialism*, 205. See also Ragaz, *Signs of the Kingdom*, 28–31.

6. W. R. Ward, *Theology, Sociology, and Politics*, 139.

7. Herbert Hartwell, "Introduction," *The Theology of Karl Barth*, 12.

8. James Luther Adams, *An Examined Faith*, 146. Adams characterizes Barth's work as an emerging prophetic theology.

9. Otto Piper, *Recent Developments in German Protestantism*, 62.

10. James Luther Adams, *An Examined Faith*, 148.

11. Karl Barth, *The Word of God and the Word of Man*, 290.

12. Ibid., 320.

13. Ibid., 276. See also John Cort, *Christian Socialism*, 208–20.

14. Karl Barth, *The Word of God and the Word of Man*, 326.

15. Ibid., 327.

16. Eberhard Busch, *Karl Barth*, 110.

17. John Cort, *Christian Socialism*, 356.

18. Emmy Arnold, *Eberhard Arnold's Life and Work*, 3.

19. Peter D. Stachura, *The German Youth Movement 1900–1945*, 15.

20. Ibid., 16.

21. Ibid., 32–33.

22. Emmy Arnold, *Torches Together*, 23.

23. Otto Piper, *Recent Developments in German Protestantism*, 46.

24. See Detlev J. Peukert, *The Weimar Republic*.

25. Ibid., 6.

26. Peter D. Stachura, *The German Youth Movement, 1900–1945*, 46–47.

27. Detlev J. Peukert, *The Weimar Republic*, 90.

28. Emmy Arnold, *Torches Together*, 28.

29. Ibid., 29.

30. John Herman Sander, *The Development of Religious Socialism in Germany*, 126–27.

31. Ibid., 130.

32. Emmy Arnold, *Torches Together*, 35–36.

33. Ibid., 64.

34. Benjamin Zablocki, *The Joyful Community*, 63–73.

35. Emmy Arnold, *Torches Together*, 50–51.

36. Ibid., 69.

37. John McKelvie Whitworth, *God's Blueprints*, 170.

38. Emmy Arnold, *Torches Together*, 6. Arnold remembers with bitterness the New Work crisis and Sannerz defections of 1922. Writing in 1935, he states, "Groups of friends—some closer than others, but all friends who had been very dear to our hearts—turned away from us and became *enemies of the way*." (emphasis added) in Markus Baum, *Against the Wind*, 143.

39. Yaacov Oved, *Witness of the Brothers*, 39

40. Eberhard Arnold, *Why We Live in Community*, 1.

41. Ibid., 5.

42. Ibid., 1.

43. Ibid., 15.

44. Eberhard Arnold, *Salt and Light*, 187.

45. Ibid., 205.

46. See R. W. B. Lewis, *The American Adam*; Raymond Augustine Bauer, *The New Man in Soviet Psychology*; and Peter D. Stachura, *The German Youth Movement 1900–1945*, 50–70.

47. Raymond Augustine Bauer, *The New Man in Soviet Psychology*, 1.

48. Eberhard Arnold, *Why We Live in Community*, 15.

49. Eberhard Arnold, *A Testimony of Church-Community: From His Life and Writings*, 23.

50. Eberhard Arnold, *Salt and Light*, 47–48. See also Markus Baum, *Against the Wind*, 158–59. Regarding *Gemeinde*: "When it actually occurs, it is both a mystery and a gift."

51. Harry Liebersohn, *Fate and Utopia*, 27–30; Dagmar Barnouw, *Weimar Intellectuals and the Threat of Modernity*, 61.

52. Harry Liebersohn, *Fate and Utopia*, 24, 79–80. See also Katherine Roper, *German Encounters with Modernity*, 241.

53. Katherine Roper, *German Encounters with Modernity*, 4.

54. Ferdinand Toennies, *Community and Society*, 37.

55. Ferdinand Toennies, *On Sociology*, 69.

56. Harry Liebersohn, *Fate and Utopia*, 36.

57. Yaacov Oved, *Distant Brothers*, 8–9.

58. Martin Buber, *Paths in Utopia*, 48.

59. Eberhard Arnold, *Early Christians After the Death of the Apostles*, 21.

60. Wolfgang Schluchter, *Rationalism, Religion, and Domination*, 209–10.

61. Ibid., 210.

62. Wayne A. Meeks, *The First Urban Christians*, 90. See Meeks's analysis of early Church *pneumatikoi*.

63. Benjamin Nelson, *On the Roads to Modernity*, 92.

64. Wolfgang Schluchter, *Rationalism, Religion, and Domination*, 222–26.

65. Wayne A. Meeks, *The First Urban Christians*, 74.

66. Ibid., 85.

67. Ibid., 94.

68. Eberhard Arnold, *Salt and Light*, 205.

69. Eberhard Arnold, *When Time Was Fulfilled*, 124–25.

70. Ibid., 128.

71. Eberhard Arnold, *A Testimony of His Life and Work*, 18.

72. Emmy Arnold, *Torches Together*, 96–97.

73. Johann Blumhardt, *Thy Kingdom Come*, 86.

74. Ibid., 87.

75. R. Lejeune, *Christoph Blumhardt and His Message*, 49–50.

76. Ibid., 50.

77. Max Weber, *Economy and Society*, vol. 1, 241–43.

78. Ibid., 249.

79. Theodore Dwight Bozeman, *To Live Ancient Lives*, 57.

80. Thomas F. O'Dea, *The Sociology of Religion*, 90–98.

81. This was a phrase that Arnold repeated frequently in his journal and his letters home from North America published as *Brothers Unite*.

82. Emmy Arnold, *Torches Together*, 107.

83. Ibid., 108.

84. Ibid., 114.

85. Eberhard Arnold, *Brothers Unite*, x.

86. Bryan R. Wilson, *Religious Sects: A Sociological Study*, 102–5.

87. See John A. Hostetler, *Hutterite Society*, and Victor Peters, *All Things Common*.

88. Eberhard Arnold, *Brothers Unite*, 8.

89. Ibid., 285–86.

90. Ibid., 157.

91. Ibid., 10.

92. Yaacov Oved, *Witness of the Brothers*, 67.

93. Max Weber, "The Social Psychology of the World Religions," 294.

94. John A. Hostetler, *Hutterite Society*, 102; Victor Peters, *All Things Common*, 90.

95. John A. Hostetler, *Hutterite Society*, 142, 162.

96. Benjamin Zablocki, *The Joyful Community*, 204.

97. John A. Hostetler, *Hutterite Society*, 144.

98. Ibid., 144.

99. Benjamin Zablocki, *The Joyful Community*, 194.

100. Max Weber, *Economy and Society*, vol. 3, 1204.

101. Benjamin Zablocki, *The Joyful Community*, 217.

102. Ibid., 58.

103. Francis B. Hall, "Pitfalls of Intentional Community," 1000.

104. Ibid., 1002.

105. Ibid., 1002.

106. Yaacov Oved, *The Witness of the Brothers*, 29.

107. Wolfgang Schluchter, *Rationalism, Religion, and Domination*, 247.

108. Eberhard Arnold, *Innerland*, 271.

109. Benjamin Nelson, "The Future of Illusions," 976.

110. Ibid., 976.

111. Gordon Leff, *Heresy in the Later Middle Ages*, vol 2, 485.

112. Lester K. Little, *Liberty, Charity, and Fraternity*, 86.

113. Ibid., 58–59.

114. Nicholas Terpstra, *Lay Confraternities and Civil Religion in Renaissance Bologna*, 48.

115. Ronald F. E. Weissman, *Ritual Brotherhood in Renaissance Florence*, 95.

116. See also Andrew E. Barnes, *The Social Dimension of Piety*. Barnes investigates seventeenth-century lay confraternities in early modern Marseille and finds a similar erosion of democratic brotherhoods, the rise of internal cliques, and the eventual oligarchy and rule by notables in answer to the organizational problem of creating and securing sufficient income.

117. Ibid., 146–75.

118. Ronald F. E. Weissman, *Ritual Brotherhoods in Renaissance Florence*, 163.

119. T. J. Saxby, *The Quest for the New Jerusalem*, 3–19.

120. Ibid., 40.

121. Ibid., 165.

122. Ibid., 245–46.

123. Natalie Zemon Davis, *Women on the Margins*, 162.

124. Saxby, *The Quest for the New Jerusalem*, 248.

125. Ibid., 261.

126. Ibid., 248–49.

127. Ibid., 314.

128. Markus Baum, *Against the Wind*, 120.

Chapter Three

1. Hans Meier, "Hans Meier Tells His Story to a Friend," 7.

2. Donald F. Durnbaugh, "Relocation of the German Bruderhof to England, South America and North America," 67.

3. Ibid., 71.

4. Eberhard Arnold, *The Individual and World Need*, 31–32.

5. Donald F. Durnbaugh, "Relocation of the German Bruderhof to England, South America, and North America," 71.

6. Ben Macintyre, *Forgotten Fatherland*, 21–23.

7. Donald F. Durnbaugh, "Relocation of the German Bruderhof to England, South America, and North America," 75.

8. Joseph Winfield Fretz, *Pilgrims in Paraguay*, 54.

9. Ibid., 54.

10. Ibid., 57.

11. Bryan R. Wilson, *Religious Sects*, 118–21.

12. Martin Riesebrodt, *Pious Passion*, 17.

13. See Fritz Stern, *The Politics of Cultural Despair*, chapter 1, for a discussion of this cultural crisis in European civilization.

14. See Arlene S. Skolnick, *Embattled Paradise*, 38–46, for a discussion of the cultural malaise and public expression of alienation in the Cold War that she terms "the myth of suburbia." See also David Riesman, *The Lonely Crowd*, for a critique of the new white-collar social conformist, "the other-directed personality," and see William H. Whyte, *The Organization Man*.

15. Martin Riesebrodt, *Pious Passion*, 58.

16. The theological awakening that I term Arnoldism provided a reanimated model of spiritual conversion predicated upon the explicit avowal of a faith commitment emanating from a new set of canonical texts. Arnoldism encouraged profound devotionalism among adherents, directing them in the path toward salvation, combining the elements of ascetic discipline and a religiosity of feeling. Enthusiastic fervor underlay all action. As Bryan R. Wilson in *The Social Dimensions of Sectarianism*, 213, has identified, among new religious movements that persist and succeed, "fervour and discipline must go together, the one justifying the other. In persisting movements, a new balance of emotional control is struck at a far higher level of dedication—at least as far as the generality of the membership is concerned. . . ."

17. Merrill Mow, *Torches Rekindled*, 118.

18. Roger Allain, *The Community That Failed,* 120–21.

19. Ibid., 121.

20. Elizabeth Bohlken-Zumpe, *Torches Extinguished*, 55.

21. Ibid., 55.

22. Merrill Mow, *Torches Rekindled*, 119.

23. Ibid., 124.

24. Elizabeth Bohlken-Zumpe, *Torches Extinguished*, 66.

25. Roger Allain, *The Community That Failed*, 165–66.

26. Merrill Mow, *Torches Rekindled*, 122.

27. Ibid., 107.

28. Merrill Mow, *Torches Rekindled*, 121–22.

29. Bob and Shirley Wagoner, *Community in Paraguay*, 4.

30. Ibid., 5.

31. Ibid., 57.

32. Ibid., 72.

33. Ibid., 102.

34. Elizabeth Bohlken-Zumpe, *Torches Extinguished*, 121.

35. Ibid., 136.

36. Ibid., 137.

37. Roger Allain, *The Community That Failed*, 226.

38. Ibid., 197.

39. Ibid., 198

40. Ibid., 197.

41. Ibid., 36.

42. Ibid., 107.

43. Ibid., 109.

44. Ibid., 110.

45. Heini Arnold, *The Living Word in Men's Hearts*, 11.

46. Merrill Mow, *Torches Rekindled*, 52.

47. David Stanley Tillson, "A Pacifist Community in Peacetime," 113–14.

48. F. Ernest Stoeffler, *German Pietism during the Eighteenth Century*, 12–16.

49. Dietrich Bonhoeffer, *The Cost of Discipleship*, 100.

50. See Benjamin Nelson, "Self-Images and Systems of Spiritual Direction."

51. Merrill Mow, *Torches Rekindled*, 30.

52. Ibid., 28.

53. "The Forest River Affair," *KIT*, vol. VI, No. 1, 1994, 9.

54. Ibid., 8.

55. Dave and Neta Jackson, *Glimpses of Glory*, 51.

56. Ibid., 51.

57. Ibid., 118.

58. Ibid., 120.

59. Ibid., 121.

60. David and Shirley Eiler, "Impressions of the Woodcrest Bruderhof," 9–10.

61. Ibid., 9.

62. David Stanley Tillson, "A Pacifist Community in Peacetime," 231.

63. Ibid., 236.

64. Dave and Neta Jackson, *Living in a World Falling Apart*, 64.

65. Pitirim A. Sorokin, *The Ways and Power of Love*, 442.

66. Thomas F. O'Dea, "The Crisis of the Contemporary Religious Consciousness," 202.

67. Ibid., 184.

68. William G. McLoughlin, *Revivals, Awakenings, and Reform*, 2.

69. See Robert Wuthnow, *The Restructuring of American Religion*.

70. Roy A. Eckardt, "The New Look in American Piety," 411.

71. Ibid., 413.

72. Robert Wuthnow, *The Restructuring of American Religion*, 57.

73. Timothy P. Weber, "Fundamentalism Twice Removed," 266.

74. See Henry P. Van Dusen, "The Third Force's Lessons for Others."

75. William G. McLoughlin, "Is There a Third Force in Christendom?" 239.

76. Dean M. Kelley, *Why Strong Churches Are Growing*, 57.

77. Charles Lindholm, *Charisma*, 120.

78. Ibid., 121.

79. Joseph Veroff, Elizabeth Douvan, and Richard A. Kulka, *The Inner American*, 19.

80. David Chidester, *Salvation and Suicide*, 4.

81. David Eiler, "The Background and History of the Bruderhof," 15, quoted in David Stanley Tillson, "A Pacifist Community in Peacetime," 284.

82. Heini Arnold, *Freedom from Sinful Thoughts*, 4.

83. Mary Douglas, *Purity and Danger*, 4.

84. Elizabeth Bohlken-Zumpe, *Torches Extinguished*, 153.

85. Nadine Moonje Pleil, *Free from Bondage*, 193.

86. Benjamin Zablocki, *The Joyful Community*, 175.

87. Roger Allain, *The Community That Failed*, 313.

88. Eberhard Arnold, *Love and Marriage in the Spirit*, 21.

89. Ibid., 11.

90. Ibid., 87.

91. Mary Douglas, *Purity and Danger*, 96.

92. Johann Christoph Blumhardt and Christoph Friedrich Blumhardt, *Thoughts on Children*, 44–45.

93. Eberhard Arnold, *Children's Education in Community*, 7. Other accounts of "Bruderhof Orthodoxy" pertaining to children and education include: Francis Wardle, "Early Childhood Programs in Bruderhof Communities," *Child Welfare*, vol 53, no. 6, June 1974, pp. 360–65; Bob and Shirley Wagoner, *Community in Paraguay: A Visit to the Bruderhof*, Rifton, N.Y.: Plough Publishing House, 1991, pp. 198–219; Heini Arnold, "Young People and the Sermon on the Mount: Heini Arnold Meets with High School Groups in New Meadow Run, Deer Spring, and Woodcrest, September 5, 1976," Rifton, N.Y.: Plough Publishing House, 1977.

94. Eberhard Arnold, *Children's Education in Community*, 73.

95. Ibid., 4.

96. Ibid., 21.

97. Ibid., 4.

98. Ibid., 99. Sandy Zimmerman and Loretta Shirky speak to the experiences of these injured children. As Bruderhof women who cared for the youngest children at Woodcrest in the 1960s, they write: "We are painfully aware that in our human weakness we can lapse into a coldness of heart. And we see that as we do this we lead a child into inner turmoil which, if severe enough, can even develop into mental illness." (Ibid., 12.)

99. Roger Allain, *The Community That Failed*, 333–34.

100. Miriam Arnold Holmes, *Cast Out in the World*, 56.

101. Ibid., 58.

102. Ibid., 62.

103. Ibid., 270.

104. *KIT Annual*, 1991, 203.

105. Ibid., 204.

106. Roger Allain, *The Community That Failed*, 271.

107. Johann Christoph Arnold, *A Plea for Purity*, 110.

108. Andrei Codrescu, *Road Scholar*, 58.

109. *KIT Annual*, 1991, 7.

110. Ibid., 292.

111. Ibid., 97.

112. Ibid., 98.

113. Franklin H. Littell, "The Power of the Restorationist Vision and Its Decline in America," 58.

114. Nadine Moonje Pleil, *Free from Bondage*, 258.

115. Ibid., 222–23.

116. Heini Arnold, *In the Image of God: Marriage and Chastity in Christian Life*, 113–18.

117. Ibid., 69.

118. Ibid., 68–69.

119. Heini Arnold, *Man The Image of God and Modern Psychology*, 8–9.

120. Heini Arnold, *Jesus Calls Each One by Name*, 19.

121. Merrill Mow, *Torches Rekindled*, 150–51.

122. Elizabeth Bohlken-Zumpe, *Torches Extinguished*, 262–63.

122. Heini Arnold, *Freedom from Sinful Thoughts*, 15.

123. Merrill Mow, *Torches Rekindled*, 127.

124. Ramón Sender, "Heini Arnold and the Abuse of Charismatic Authority in the Early Bruderhof."

125. Ibid.

126. Merrill Mow, *Torches Rekindled*, 127.

127. Ibid., 127.

128. Benjamin Zablocki, *The Joyful Community*, 102.

129. Ibid., 102.

130. Ibid., 99.

131. Merrill Mow, *Torches Rekindled*, 150.

132. Benjamin Zablocki, *The Joyful Community*, 105.

133. Merrill Mow, *Torches Rekindled*, 163.

134. Ibid., 163.

135. Benjamin Zablocki, *The Joyful Community*, 108. Zablocki calls Heini Arnold "David" in this work.

136. Robert N. Peck, "An Ex-Member's View of the Bruderhof Communities from 1948–1961," 121.

137. Roger Allain, *The Community That Failed*, 329.

138. Ibid., 312.

139. Elizabeth Bohlken-Zumpe, *Torches Extinguished*, 202.

140. Ibid., 203.

141. Merrill Mow, *Torches Rekindled*, 175.

142. Benjamin Zablocki, *The Joyful Community*, 99.

143. Roger Allain, *The Community That Failed*, 332.

144. Louis Dumont, *Essays on Individualism*, 158.

145. Bob and Shirley Wagoner, *Community in Paraguay*, 260–61.

146. Merrill Mow, *Torches Rekindled*, 9–10. Heini Arnold's last will and testament, as reported by Yaacov Oved, expresses contempt for democracy. As Oved states, "In his [Heini's] view, majority rule is an open invitation to power struggles and factional organizations and he perceived this as one of the main reasons for the split [the Great Crisis] that had taken place in the sixties." Oved, *Witness of the Brothers*, 257.

147. Francis B. Hall, *Practical Spirituality*, 56.

Chapter Four

1. Heini Arnold, *In the Image of God, Marriage and Chastity in Christian Life*, 18–19.

2. Wayne E. Oates, *When Religion Gets Sick*, 20–21.

3. Heini Arnold, *Freedom from Sinful Thoughts*, viii.

4. Ibid., 75–76.

5. Ibid., 77.

6. Thomas Robbins, *Cults, Converts and Charisma*, 64.

7. Eberhard Arnold, *The Individual and World Need*, 34–35.

8. Won Young Ji, "Significance of Tentatio in Luther's Spirituality," 186.

9. Heini Arnold, *Man The Image of God and Modern Psychology*, 19.

10. Wayne E. Oates, *Anxiety in Christian Experience*, 119.

11. Julius H. Rubin, *Religious Melancholy and Protestant Experience in America*, 227–28. See also Ji, who contrasts the spiritual trials of *Anfechtungen* with contemporary Korean churches, which, like their American Fundamentalist and neo-evangelical counterparts, espouse a "theology of glory and triumphalism. Success and glory in life control the minds of Christians and motivate prospective Christians. They come to church in order to receive 'blessings,' in most instances, in a material sense, such as material prosperity, success in business and life, advantageous position in society, and healing and speaking in tongues." (186)

12. Wayne E. Oates, *Anxiety in Christian Experience*, 129.

13. Ibid., 148.

14. Elizabeth Bohlken-Zumpe, *Torches Extinguished*, 191.

15. KIT newsletter, vol V., no 11, November 1993, 9.

16. Merrill Mow, *Torches Rekindled*, 259.

17. See also Arthur S. Parsons, "Messianic Personalism: A Role Analysis of the Unification Church," and "The Secular Contribution to Religious Innovation."

18. Peter S. Gay, *Freud for Historians*, 25.

19. Janet Liebman Jacobs, *Divine Disenchantment*, 125.

20. James W. Jones, *Contemporary Psychoanalysis and Religion*, 65.

21. Ibid., 18–19.

22. See also Joachim Scharfenberg, *Sigmund Freud and His Critique of Religion*, 124.

23. Wayne Oates argues that many adolescents and young adults use religious affiliation and themes to mediate their quest for identity and autonomy. He writes in *When Religion Gets Sick*, Philadelphia: Westminster Press, 1970, 185, ". . . the religious factor (in mental illness) was a bondage to the idolatry of the small, restricted communal unity. . . . The religious loyalty of the family housed the parental domination and control of the child. Religion was used as a means of maintaining control of the child." In the Bruderhof, renunciation of individual autonomy was a spiritual exercise of evangelical humiliation, a measure of authentic faith-commitment and, simultaneously, a means of exerting control over members.

24. Elizabeth Bohlken-Zumpe, *Torches Extinguished*, 207.

25. Ibid., 211.

26. Janet Liebman Jacobs, *Divine Disenchantment*, 97.

27. Charles Derber has developed the term "attention deprivation," cited in David A. Anderson and Leon Snow, *Down on Their Luck*, 200.

28. Elizabeth Bohlken-Zumpe, *Torches Extinguished*, 211.

29. The presentation of Miriam Arnold Holmes is excerpted from her memoirs, *Cast Out in the World*.

30. Ibid., 175–76.

31. Ibid., 182.

32. Ibid., 185.

33. Ibid., 187.

34. Ibid., 193.

35. Ibid., 196.

36. Ibid., 197.

37. Ibid., 199.

38. Ibid., 264.

39. Susanna Kaysen, *Girl, Interrupted*, 5.

40. In Holmes's concluding chapter, "I Figure it Out!" she explains the role played by Heini Arnold: "I felt so relieved to be free of the family curse, caused by Heini's persecution of my brothers and me, as well as other immediate family members such as his brothers and sisters—not even sparing his mother. We all were used as pawns in his insatiable lust for power." Cast Out in the World, 296.

41. Miriam Arnold Holmes, *Cast Out in the World*, 273–74.

42. Ibid., 287

43. *KIT* newsletter, vol II, no. 8, September 1, 1990, 1.

44. Hans Küng, *Freud and the Problem of God*, 127.

45. David Lukoff, Francis Lu, and Robert Turner, "Toward a More Culturally Sensitive DSM-IV, Psychoreligious and Psychospiritual Problems," 675.

46. J. Heinrich Arnold, *Discipleship*, 125.

47. Ibid, 200.

48. Ibid., xiv.

49. Ibid., 203.

50. Ibid., 66.

51. Ibid., 153–54.

52. See Julius H. Rubin, *Religious Melancholy and Protestant Experience in America*, 82.

53. *KIT* newsletter, vol 3, no. 5, May 1991.

54. Ibid.

55. Julius H. Rubin, *Religious Melancholy and Protestant Experience in America*, 82–87, 176–88.

56. Ibid., 166–67.

57. *KIT* newsletter, vol. 4, no. 4, April 1993.

58. *KIT* newsletter, vol. 6, no. 5, May 1994.

59. Ibid.

60. Ibid.

61. *KIT* newsletter, vol 3, no. 3, March 1993, 4.

62. Sufferers from the Bruderhof Syndrome languished in spiritual desolation, unable to achieve self-denial and surrender to the cross as prescribed by the Pietist morphology of conversion. They provide repeated examples of the psychohistorical insights offered by Erik H. Erickson's *Young Man Luther*: the tyrannical regimen within patriarchal families, the annihilation of the autonomous will during early childhood and repeated in adolescence produces a religiously grounded temperament marked by ontological insecurity and shame. Bruderhof religiosity, derived from Luther's concept of *Anfechtung*, precipitates severe identity crises in adolescence and recurring episodes of adult religious melancholy. See my discussion of Erik Erickson and Luther in *Religious Melancholy and Protestant Experience in America*, 21–25. Erickson provides the central thesis of his study of the young Luther. "We will therefore concentrate on this process: how young Martin, at the end of a somber and harsh childhood, was precipitated into a severe identity crisis for which he sought delay and cure in the silence of the monastery; how being silent, he became 'possessed'; how being possessed, he gradually learned to speak a new language, *his* language; how being able to speak, he not only talked himself out of the monastery, and much of his country out of the Roman Church, but also formulated for himself and for all of mankind a new kind of ethical and psychological awareness: and how at the end, this awareness, too, was marred by a return of the demons, whoever they may have been." Erik H. Erikson, *Young Man Luther*, 47–48. Erikson argues that Luther intended "to free individual conscience from totalitarian dogma; he meant to give man credal wholeness, and alas, inadvertently helped to increase and to refine authoritarianism." Ibid., 252.

63. W. I. Thomas, *The Unadjusted Girl*, 72

64. Walter Klaassen, " 'Gelassenheit' and Creation," 23.

65. Ibid., 29.

66. Robert D. Cornwall, "The Way of the Cross," 36.

67. Ibid., 51–52.

68. Benjamin Zablocki, *The Joyful Community*, 184–92.

69. "Memories of Fred," 3.

70. Steven M. Tipton, *Getting Saved from the Sixties*, 2, 15.

71. Ibid., 18.

72. Ibid., 16.

73. David L. Harvey's study of a rural lower-class community discovers a common pattern among adolescent women during the 1960s and 1970s. These youth

rebelled against maternal authority and overdependence by using sexuality and romantic love to break away from maternal controls. Frequently, these young women began sexual activity in early adolescence, became pregnant by their teenage boyfriends at age sixteen, and rushed to marry. The bridal pregnancies, the economic and material needs, and the medical complications and uncertainties of teenage pregnancies soon brought these young women back into their mother's sphere of influence. The recently married, pregnant, and repentant daughter returns to the mother's influence as prodigal child with the gift of a child for the mother to raise. Potter explains that these young women did not become autonomous adults despite their marriage and first pregnancy markers for the passage to adulthood. Rather, they remained daughter/mothers in a symbiotic emotional trap with the mother/grandmother. The daughter did not make the full passage into adult status until her fourth decade when her own daughter became a teenage mother. See David L. Harvey, *Potter Addition, Poverty, Family, and Kinship in a Heartland Community*, New York: Aldine De Gruyter, 1993, pp. 135–56. Unlike the Potter Addition that identified mother–daughter emotional ties, the Bruderhof fostered these bonds between fathers and daughters.

74. E. M. Cioran wrote *On the Heights of Despair*, borrowing the title from the euphemism for suicide adopted by Rumanian newspapers after World War I.

75. Ibid., 55–56.

76. Benjamin Zablocki conducted six months of field work while living as a long-term guest on the Woodcrest Bruderhof during the late 1960s. He has written the most comprehensive study of this group, *The Joyful Community*. The Bruderhof rejected Zablocki's study, and as expression of their displeasure, they placed the book in a trash can located in the Servants' office. A decade following Zablocki's field work, a British sociologist, John McKelvie Whitworth, gained access to a hof under the pretense of being an ernest seeker and guest. In the 1980s, the Bruderhof renewed their relationship with the Israeli Kibbutz Movement and allowed Yaacov Oved of Yad Tabenkin to study the organization and economics of the contemporary Bruderhof. To date, Oved has published *Distant Brothers* and, in 1996, *Witness of the Brothers: A History of the Bruderhof*. The Bruderhof leadership had refused my repeated requests for information and denied permission to interview their members or conduct a systematic investigation of their American communities.

77. See Barry Schwartz, "The Social Context of Commemoration: A Study of Collective Memory"; Catherine Albanese, *Sons of the Fathers: The Civil Religion of the American Revolution*; Robert Bellah, *The Broken Covenant: American Civil Religion in Time of Trial*; and Eric Hobsbawm and Terence Ranger, *The Invention of Tradition*.

78. Eric Hobsbawm and Terence Ranger, *The Invention of Tradition*, 1.

79. Maurice Halbwachs, *On Collective Memory*, 188–89.

80. Ibid., 91.

81. Ibid., 94.

82. 84. See Francis X. Clines, "Sect's Tenet: Thou Shalt Not Traffic in Demon Gossip"; Joyce Hollyday, "The Stuff of Life: A Visit to the Bruderhof"; Connie Nash, "Bruderhof Women: A Testimony of Love"; and Judith Rice, "Hutterians."

83. See Elizabeth Royte, "Kindred Spirits," *Life*, December 1996; Evelyn Nieves, "Sometimes a Luxury Jet Serves God," the *New York Times*, October 13, 1996; and Timothy Appel, "Tiny Church's 'Christian Communism' Makes Money," the *Wall Street Journal*, July 5, 1996.

84. Michael S. Roth, *The Ironist's Cage*, 181.

85. Merrill Mow, *Torches Rekindled*, 124–25.

86. Ramón Sender, "The Peregrine Foundation Information Sheet."

87. The KIT Internet address is http://www.perefound.org. The Bruderhof address is http://www.Bruderhof.com.

88. Benjamin Zablocki, *The Joyful Community,* 285.

89. Susan Rothbaum, "Between Two Worlds: Issues of Separation and Identity After Leaving a Religious Community," 207.

90. Ibid., 208.

91. Benjamin Zablocki, *The Joyful Community,* 283.

92. Ibid., 253.

93. *KIT* newsletter, *Annual,* vol. 2, 1991, 195.

94. "A Graduate," *KIT* newsletter, vol 7, no. 6, June 1995, 4.

95. Peter L. Berger, *Invitation to Sociology,* 64.

96. Lawrence Foster, *Religion and Sexuality,* 51–54.

97. This term was introduced by Erving Goffman in *Asylums,* 152.

98. *KIT* newsletter, vol 4, no. 2, February 1992, 3.

99. Merrill Mow, *Torches Rekindled,* 265.

100. Ramón Sender, *KIT,* vol. 2, no. 2, February 1990.

101. Yaacov Oved, *Witness of the Brothers,* 282.

102. Ibid., 285.

103. "An Open Letter to the Bruderhof Communities," August 19, 1990, *KIT,* vol. 2, no. 8, September 1990.

104. Benjamin Zablocki, "Bill of Rights for Religious Communities and Their Members," *KIT,* vol. 3, no. 11, December 1991. See "Open Letter," September 1, 1991, in *KIT,* vol. 3, no. 9.

105. Yaacov Oved, *Witness of the Brothers,* 286.

106. The threat to Heini Arnold's life was published in the *Times Herald Record,* November 11, 1997 (Paul Brooks, "Bruderhof Head Finds Forgiveness Divine") and reprinted in *KIT,* 9, no. 12, December 1997, 1. See also Karen Bartomioli, "Extortion Case in New York Revives Issues Surrounding Life in Bruderhof Communities, the *Lakeville Journal,* November 11, 1997. David Maendel was convicted by the Ulster County Court on September 10, 1997 for trying to extort $15,000 from the Bruderhof. He addressed the court on November 8, 1997 during his sentencing hearing: "Maendel said he was deeply sorry for having broken the state law. 'I broke God's law too. . . . Since 1978 I have been barred from visiting the Bruderhof. I don't know if my mother is alive or dead,' he said. 'I ask Christoph Arnold if he had been barred from seeing his family, to what lengths would he go?' " Paul Brooks, the *Times Herald Record,* November 8, 1997.

107. Woodcrest Hutterian Brethren, March 23, 1992, *KIT,* vol. 4, no. 4, April 1992.

108. Woodcrest Hutterian Brethren, March 26, 1992, *KIT,* vol. 4, no. 4, April 1992.

109. Dick Domer, May 17, 1994, *KIT,* vol. 6, no. 6, June 1994.

110. Wayne and Betty Chesley, "Our Experiences with the Bruderhof Communities," http://www.personal.psu.edu/staff/w/x/wxc21.

111. 1995 Annual Report on the State of KIT, *KIT,* vol. 7, no. 7, 1995.

112. *KIT,* vol. 7, no. 7, July 1995.

113. Blaise Schweitzer, "For Hutterians, There's a Storm Before the Calm," *Kingston Daily Freeman,* July 27, 1995.

114. Wayne and Betty Chesley, "Our Experiences with the Bruderhof Communities," http://www.personal.psu.edu/staff/w/x/wxc21.

115. Blaise Schweitzer, "Differences Remain over Bruderhofs," *Kingston Daily Freeman,* July 28, 1995.

116. Peter Riedemann, *Account of Our Religion, Doctrine and Faith,* 114.

117. Transcript of an interview with Joseph Keiderling and Christian Domer, October 24, 1995, Yale University, New Haven, Connecticut.

118. Eberhard Arnold, *God's Revolution*, 201–2.

119. Walter Laqueur, *Fascism, Past, Present and Future*, 224–25.

120. J. Christoph Arnold, "A Meeting with Louis Farrakhan," the *Plough*, vol. 49, http://www.bruderhof.org.

Chapter Five

1. Lowell H. Zuck, "Spiritual Renewal in the Radical Reform Tradition," 24.

2. Prudence Yelinek, "Pilgrims in a Strange Land: Reflection on Spiritual Direction and the Church of the Brethren," 88; Carl F. Bowman, *Brethren Society*, 46–54.

3. Carl F. Bowman, *Brethren Society*, 50.

4. Prudence Yelinek, "Pilgrims in a Strange Land: Reflection on Spiritual Direction and the Church of the Brethren," 88–89.

5. Michael Holzbach, *The Forgotten People*, 163–64.

6. Ibid., 86.

7. Joseph W. Eaton and Robert J. Weil, *Culture and Mental Disorders*, 28.

8. Ibid., 45.

9. Joseph W. Eaton and Robert J. Weil, "Hutterite Mental Health Survey," 59.

10. Joseph W. Eaton and Robert J. Weil. *Culture and Mental Disorders*, 210.

11. John A. Hostetler, *Hutterite Society*, 262.

12. Joseph W. Eaton and Robert J. Weil, *Culture and Mental Disorders*, 101.

13. Thomas F. A. Plaut and Bert Kaplan, *Personality in a Communal Society*, 67.

14. Joseph W. Eaton and Robert J. Weil, *Culture and Mental Disorders*, 103.

15. Thomas F. A. Plaut and Bert Kaplan, *Personality in a Communal Society*, 68.

16. Joseph W. Eaton and Robert F. Weil, *Culture and Mental Disorders*, 106.

17. Thomas F. A. Plaut and Bert Kaplan, *Personality in a Communal Society*, viii.

18. Ibid., 74–75.

19. Bert Kaplan, "Hutterite Socialization and the Resolution of the Conformity-Deviance Conflict."

20. John A. Hostetler, *Hutterite Society*, 264.

21. *Albia Iulia Romanica, Cod. III*, 187.

22. Karl A. Peter, *The Dynamics of Hutterite Society*, 19.

23. Caroline M. Hartse, "The Emotional Acculturation of Hutterite Defectors," 70–71.

24. Karl A. Peter, *The Dynamics of Hutterite Society*, 48–49.

25. Rich Preheim, "Hutterites Break along East-West Lines," 6.

26. For a general introduction, see Calvin Redekop, *Mennonite Society*.

27. Ibid., 18.

28. Ibid., 30.

29. Ibid., 60.

30. Buelah Stauffer Hostetler, *American Mennonites and Protestant Movements*, 65.

31. Ibid., 66.

32. Christian Newcomer, *The Life and Journal of the Reverend Christian Newcomer*, 1.

33. Buelah Stauffer Hostetler, *American Mennonites and Protestant Movements*, 67. See also Richard K. MacMaster, *Land, Piety, and Peoplehood*, 220.

34. Buelah Stauffer Hostetler, *American Mennonites and Protestant Movements*, 150–55.

35. Sandra Cronk, "*Gelassenheit*: The Rites of the Redemptive Process in Old Order Amish and Old Order Mennonite Communities," 35.

36. William G. McLoughlin, *Revivals, Awakenings, and Reform*, 113–30.

37. John A. Hostetler, *The Sociology of Mennonite Evangelism*, 47–57.

38. Leo Driedger and Leland Harder, *Anabaptist-Mennonite Identities in Ferment*, 3.

39. Paul Peachey, "Identity Crises among American Mennonites," 245.

40. Buelah Stauffer Hostetler, *American Mennonites and Protestant Movements*, 92–96.

41. Calvin Redekop, *Mennonite Society*, 45.

42. Irmgard Thiessen, "Mental Health and the Mennonites," 114.

43. Irmgard Thiessen, "Values and Personality Characteristics of Mennonites in Manitoba," 52. See also Irmgard Thiessen et al., "A Comparison of Personality Characteristics of Mennonites and Non-Mennonites."

44. Irmgard Thiessen et al., " A Comparison of Personality Characteristics of Mennonites and Non-Mennonites," 130.

45. Irmgard Thiessen, "Values and Personality Characteristics of Mennonites in Manitoba," 60.

46. Peter M. Hamm, *Continuity and Change among Canadian Mennonite Brethren*, 96.

47. Ibid., 98.

48. John H. Redekop, "College Training—Where Are We heading?" 2.

49. J. Howard Kauffman and Leland Harder, *Anabaptists Four Centuries Later*, 100.

50. William Klassen, "The Mennonite Syndrome," 139–40.

51. Ibid., 140.

52. Ibid., 142.

53. Al Dueck, "Psychology and Mennonite Self-Understanding," 217.

54. Ibid., 220.

55. Walter Klaassen, "The Quest for Anabaptist Identity," 20.

56. John A. Hostetler, *Amish Society*, 33, 50.

57. Ibid., 284.

58. Janice Ann Egeland, "Belief and Behavior as Related to Illness: A Community Case Study of the Old Order Amish," 152.

59. Janice A. Egeland, "Cultural Factors and Social Stigma for Manic-Depression: The Amish Study," 281.

60. Janice A. Egeland and Abram M. Hostetter, "Amish Study," I, 59.

61. Elvin B. Coblentz, "Epidemiology of Mental Disorders and Help-Seeking Behavior among the Amish," 148.

62. Ibid., 205.

63. Bill W. Dick, "Psychology and Mennonite Studies," 151.

64. John A. Hostetler, *Amish Society*, 21–22.

65. Donald B. Kraybill, *The Riddle of Amish Culture*, 29–30.

66. John A. Hostetler, *Amish Society*, 332.

67. Donald B. Kraybill, *The Riddle of Amish Culture*, 24–33.

68. John A. Hostetler, *Amish Society*, 306.

69. Janice A. Egeland, "Cultural Factors and Social Stigma for Manic Depression: The Amish Study," 283.

70. Ibid., 283.

Conclusion

1. Sigmund Freud, *Civilization and Its Discontents*, 728.

2. Sigmund Freud, *The Future of an Illusion*, 703–4.

3. Sigmund Freud, "Obsessive Actions and Religious Practices," 435.

4. Benjamin Nelson, "Community—Dreams and Realities," 135.

5. Migel de Unamuno provides another voice from the interwar period. His 1921 masterpiece, *The Tragic Sense of Life*, is a philosophical response to the crises of modernity. Like Eberhard Arnold, Unamuno embraced the problems of faith, the need for salvation, the importance of love, and an ethic of brotherliness. Unlike Arnoldism, Unamuno affirms the primacy of the individual through his or her quest for salvation. The search plunges each searcher into the abyss of religious despair— the tragic sense of life. Unamuno explains, "I hope to gather everything together and to show that this religious despair which I have been talking about, and which is nothing other than the tragic sense of life itself, is though more or less hidden, the very foundation of the consciousness of civilized individuals and peoples to-day." (*The Tragic Sense of Life*, p. 125.)

6. Edmund Lab Cherbonnier, "Biblical Faith and the Idea of Tragedy," 29.

7. Ulrich Simon, *Pity and Terror, Christianity and Tragedy*, 2.

8. Edmund Lab Cherbonnier, "Biblical Faith and the Idea of Tragedy," 53.

9. Louis A. Ruprecht, Jr., *Tragic Posture and Tragic Vision*, 229.

10. Max Weber, "Religious Rejections of the World and Their Directions," 330.

11. Benjamin Nelson, "Community—Dreams and Realities," 147.

12. Louis A. Ruprecht, Jr., *Tragic Posture and Tragic Vision*, 13.

13. Benjamin Nelson, "Community—Dreams and Realities," 149–50.

BIBLIOGRAPHY

Abel, Theodore Fred. *Why Hitler Came into Power; An Answer Based on the Original Life Stories of Six Hundred of His Followers.* New York: Prentice-Hall, 1938.

Adams, James Luther. *An Examined Faith: Social Context and Religious Commitment.* Ed. George K. Beach. Boston: Beacon Press, 1991.

Adorno, T. W., Else Frenkel-Brunswik, Daniel J. Levinson, and Nevitt, R. Sanford. "The Authoritarian Personality." In *Studies in Prejudice*, ed. Max Horkheimer and Samuel H. Flowerman. New York: Harper & Brothers, 1950.

Aho, James A. *The Politics of Righteousness: Idaho Christian Patriotism.* Seattle: University of Washington Press, 1990.

Albanese, Catherine L. *Sons of the Fathers: The Civil Religion of the American Revolution.* Philadelphia: Temple University Press, 1976.

———. *Nature Religion in America: From the Algonkian Indians to the New Age.* Chicago: University of Chicago Press, 1990.

———. *America, Religions and Religion.* 2nd ed., Belmont, California: Wadsworth, 1992.

Aldenhoff, Rita. "Max Weber and the Evangelical-Social Congress." In *Max Weber and His Contemporaries*, ed. Wolfgang J. Mommsen and Jurgen Osterhammel. Boston: Allen and Unwin, 1987.

Alexander, Jeffrey C. *Twenty Lectures: Sociological Theory Since World War II.* New York: Columbia University Press, 1987.

Allain, Roger. *The Community That Failed: An Account of Twenty-Two Years in Bruderhof Communities in Europe and South America.* San Francisco: Carrier Pigeon Press: A Project of the Peregrine Foundation, 1992.

Anderson, Leon, and David A. Snow. *Down on Their Luck: A Study of Homeless Street People.* Berkeley: University of California Press, 1993.

Appel, Timothy. "Tiny Church's 'Christian Communism' Makes Money." the *Wall Street Journal*, July 5, 1996.

Apple, Michael W. *Cultural Politics and Education.* New York: Teachers College Press, 1996.

Arnold, Eberhard. *A Testimony of Church-Community: From His Life and Writings.* Rifton, N.Y.: Plough Publishing House, 1964b.

———. *Love and Marriage in the Spirit.* Rifton, N.Y.: Plough Publishing House, 1965a.

———. *When Time Was Fulfilled.* Rifton, N.Y.: Plough Publishing House, 1965b.

————. *Salt and Light: Talks and Writings on the Sermon on the Mount*. Rifton, N.Y.: Plough Publishing House, 1967.

————. *The Early Christians After the Death of the Apostles*. Rifton, N. Y.: Plough Publishing House, 1970a.

————. *Poems*. Rifton, N.Y.: Plough Publishing House, 1970b.

————. *Living Churches: The Essence of Their Life, Love to Christ and Love to the Brothers*, Rifton, N.Y.: Plough Publishing House, 1973.

————. *Seeking for the Kingdom*. Rifton, N.Y.: Plough Publishing House, 1974a.

————. *Children's Education in Community: The Basis of Bruderhof Education*. Rifton, N.Y.: Plough Publishing House, 1976a.

————. *Innerland: A Guide into the Heart and Soul of the Bible*. Rifton, N.Y.: Plough Publishing House, 1976b.

————. *Why We Live in Community*. Rifton, N.Y.: Plough Publishing House, 1976c.

————. *Why We Live in Community* (with two interpretive talks by Thomas Merton). Farmington, Pa.: Plough Publishing House, 1995.

————. *God's Revolution, The Witness of Eberhard Arnold*. Ed. John Howard Yoder. New York: Paulist Press, 1984.

————. *Brothers Unite: An Account of the Uniting of Eberhard Arnold and the Rhon Bruderhof with the Hutterian Church*. Translated by Hutterian Brethren. Edited by John A. Hostelter and Leonard Gross. Ulster Park, N.Y.: Plough Publishing House Hutterian Brethren, 1988.

————. *The Individual and World Need*. Farmington, Pa.: Plough Publishing House, 1993.

Arnold, Eberhard, and Emmy Arnold. *Seeking for the Kingdom: Origins of the Bruderhof Communities*. Ed. Heini Arnold and Annemarie Arnold. Rifton, N.Y.: Plough Publishing House, 1974b.

Arnold, E. C. H. "Eberhard Arnold, A Short Biography." *Mennonite Quarterly Review* 25, no. 3 (1951): 219–21.

Arnold, Emmy. *Eberhard Arnold's Life and Work*. Rifton, N.Y.: Plough Publishing Company, 1964a.

————. *Torches Together*. Rifton, N.Y.: Plough Publishing House, 1964c.

Arnold, Heini. *Freedom from Sinful Thoughts: Christ Alone Breaks the Curse*. Rifton, N.Y.: Plough Publishing House Hutterian Brethren, 1973.

————. *The Living Word in Men's Hearts*. Rifton, N.Y.: Plough Publishing House, 1975a.

————. *Man The Image of God and Modern Psychology*. Rifton, N.Y.: Plough Publishing House, 1975b.

————. *In the Image of God: Marriage and Chastity in Christian Life*. Rifton, N.Y.: Plough Publishing House, 1977a.

————. *Jesus Calls Each One by Name*. Rifton, N.Y.: Plough Publishing House, 1977b.

Arnold, Johann Christoph. *A Plea for Purity, Sex, Marriage and God*. Farmington, Pa.: Plough Publishing House, 1996.

Arnold, J Heinrich. *Discipleship*. Farmington, Pa.: Plough Publishing House, 1994.

Barayón, Ramón Sender. "Heini Arnold and the Early Woodcrest Community." *KIT* newsletter archives online, World Wide Web (www.perefound.org).

Barker, Eileen. *The Making of a Moonie: Choice or Brainwashing?* New York: Basil Blackwell, 1984.

————. *New Religious Movements: A Practical Introduction*. London: Her Majesty's Stationary Office, 1989.

Barnes, Andrew E. *The Social Dimension of Piety*. Studies in Contemporary Biblical and Theological Problems, series ed. C. S. P. Lawrence Boalt. New York: Paulist Press, 1994.

Barnouw, Dagmar. *Weimar Intellectuals and the Threat of Modernity*. Bloomington: Indiana University Press, 1988.

Barth, Karl. "The Christian's Place in Society" (address delivered at the Conference on Religion and Social Relations, Tambach, September, 1919). In *The Word of God and the Word of Man*, 272–327. Pilgrim Press, 1928a.

———. *The Word of God and the Word of Man*. Trans. by Douglas Horton. Boston: Pilgrim Press, 1928b.

———. *The Epistle to the Romans*. London: Epworth Press, 1955.

———. *The German Church Conflict*. Richmond: John Knox Press, 1956.

———. *The Theology of Karl Barth*. Edited and with an Introduction by Herbert Hartwell. London: Gerald Ducksworth & Company, 1964.

Baudouin, Charles. *Suggestion and Autosuggestion*. New York: Dodd, Meade and Company, 1922.

Bauer, Raymond Augustine. *The New Man in Soviet Psychology*. Cambridge, Massachusetts: Harvard University Press, 1952.

Baum, Markus. *Against the Wind: Eberhard Arnold and the Bruderhof*. Farmington, Pa: Plough Publishing House, 1998.

Bednarowski, Mary Farrell. *New Religions and the Theological Imagination*. Religion in North America, series ed. Catherine L. Albanese and Stephen J. Stein. Bloomington: Indiana University Press, 1989.

Beit-Hallahmi, Benjamin. *Despair and Deliverance: Private Salvation in Contemporary Israel*. State University of New York Press, 1992.

Bellah, Robert. *The Broken Covenant: American Civil Religion in Time of Trial*. New York: Seabury Press, 1976.

Bergen, Doris L. *Twisted Cross: The German Christian Movement in the Third Reich*. Chapel Hill: University of North Carolina Press, 1996.

Berger, Peter L. *Invitation to Sociology: A Humanistic Perspective*. Garden City, New York: Doubleday & Company, 1963.

Bessel, Richard. *Germany After the First World War*. Oxford: Clarendon Press, 1995.

Blumhardt, Johann. *Thy Kingdom Come*. Ed. Vernard Eller. Grand Rapids: William B. Eerdmans, 1980a.

Blumhardt, Johann Christoph, and Christoph Friedrich Blumhardt. *Thoughts About Children*. Rifton, N.Y.: Plough Publishing House, 1980b.

Bohlken-Zumpe, Elizabeth. *Torches Extinguished: Memories of a Communal Bruderhof Childhood in Paraguay, Europe and the USA*. San Francisco: Carrier Pigeon Press, 1993.

Bollas, Christopher. *Being a Character, Psychoanalysis and Self-Experience*. New York: Hill and Wang, 1992.

Bonhoeffer, Dietrich. *The Cost of Discipleship*. Revised and unabridged edition. New York: MacMillian Publishing Company, 1963.

———. *Life Together*. Trans. by John W. Doberstein. San Francisco: Harper Collins, 1994.

Bowman, Carl F. *Brethren Society: The Cultural Transformation of a "Peculiar People."* Baltimore: Johns Hopkins University Press, 1995.

Boyer, Paul S. *When Time Shall Be No More: Prophecy Belief in Modern American Culture*. Cambridge: Harvard University Press, 1992.

Bozeman, Theodore Dwight. *To Live Ancient Lives: The Primitivist Dimension in Puritanism*. Chapel Hill: University of North Carolina Press, 1988.

Bromley, David G., ed. *Falling from the Faith: Causes and Consequences of Religious Apostasy*. Beverly Hills: Sage Publications, 1988.

Bromley, David G., Jr., and Anson D. Shupe. Foreword by John Lofland. *"Moonies" in America: Cult, Church, and Crusade*. Sage Library of Social Research. Beverly Hills: Sage Publications, 1979.

Bryant, M. Darrol, and Herbert W. Richardson, eds. *A Time for Consideration: A Scholarly Appraisal of the Unification Church*. New York: The Edwin Mellon Press, 1978.

Buber, Martin. *Paths in Utopia*. Trans. R. F. C. Hull. London: Routledge and Kegan Paul, 1949.

Burton, Robert. *The Anatomy of Melancholy*. Ed. Floyd Dell and Paul Jordan-Smith. New York: Farrar and Rinehart, (1621) 1927.

Busch, Eberhard. *Karl Barth: His Life from letters and autobiographical texts*. Trans. John Bowden. Philadelphia: Fortress Press, 1976.

Butler, Jon. *Awash in a Sea of Faith: Christianizing the American People*. Cambridge: Harvard University Press, 1990.

Capps, Walter H. *The New Religious Right: Piety, Patriotism, and Politics*. Columbia: University of South Carolina Press, 1994.

Cherbonnier, Edmund Lab. "Biblical Faith and the Idea of Tragedy." In Nathan A. Scott, Jr., Ed., *The Tragic Vision and the Christian Faith*. New York: Association Press, 1957, 23–54.

Chidester, David. *Salvation and Suicide: An Interpretation of Jim Jones, the People's Temple, and Jonestown*. Bloomington, Indiana: Indiana University Press, 1988a.

———. "Stealing the Sacred Symbols: Biblical Interpretation in the People's Temple and the Unification Church." *Religion* 18 (June 1988b): 137–62.

Children in Community. Ed. The Hutterian Brethren. Rifton, N.Y.: Plough Publishing House, 1963.

Chmielewski, Wendy E., Louis J. Kern, and Marlyn Klee-Hartzell, eds. *Women in Spiritual and Communitarian Societies in the United States*. Syracuse, N.Y.: Syracuse University Press, 1993.

Chryssides, George D. *The Advent of Sun Myung Moon: The Origins, Beliefs and Practices of the Unification Church*. New York: St. Martin's Press, 1991.

Cioran, E. M. *On the Heights of Despair*. Trans. Ilinca Zarifopol-Johnston. Chicago: University of Chicago Press, 1992.

Clark, Elmer T. *The Small Sects in America*. Rev. ed. New York: Abingdon Press, 1949.

Clines, Francis X. "Sect's Tenet: Thou Shalt Not Traffic in Demon Gossip." *New York Times*, March 2, 1995, B1(N).

Coblentz, Elvin B. "Epidemiology of Mental Disorders and Help-Seeking Behavior among the Amish." Ph.D. dissertation, University of Akron, 1991.

Codrescu, Andrei. *Road Scholar: Coast to Coast Late in the Century*. New York: Hyperion, 1993.

Conforti, Joseph A. *Jonathan Edwards, Religious Tradition, and American Culture*. Chapel Hill: University of North Carolina Press, 1995.

Conkin, Paul K. *Two Paths to Utopia*. Lincoln: University of Nebraska Press, 1964.

Cornwall, Robert D. "The Way of the Cross: The Anabaptist Concept of *Gelassenheit*." *Studia Biblica et Theologica* 17, no. 1 (1989): 33–53.

Cort, John. *Christian Socialism: An Informal History*. Maryknoll, N.Y.: Orbis Books, 1988.

Craib, Ian. *Anthony Giddens*. New York: Routledge, 1992.

Crawford, Mark E., Paul J. Handal, and Richard L. Wiener. "The Relationship between Religion and Mental Health/Distress." *Review of Religious Research* 31 no. 1 (September 1989): 16–22.

Cronk, Sandra. "*Gelassenheit*: The Rites of the Redemptive Process in Old Order

Amish and Old Order Mennonite Communities." *Mennonite Quarterly Review* 55 (January 1981): 5–44.

Davis, Natalie Zemon. *Women on the Margins: Three Seventeenth-Century Lives*. Cambridge: Harvard University Press, 1995.

Dayton, Donald W. "Protestant Christian Missions to Korea as a Source of Unification Thought." In *Religion in the Pacific Era*, ed. Frank K. Flinn and Tyler Hendricks, 78–92. New York: Paragon House Publishers, 1985.

Deleuze, Gilles, and Felix Guattari. *Anti-Oedipus, Capitalism and Schizophrenia*. Trans. Robert Hurley, Mark Seem, and Helen R. Lane. New York: Viking Press, 1977.

DeMaria, Richard. "A Psycho-Social Analysis of Conversion." In *A Time for Consideration: A Scholarly Appraisal of the Unification Church*, ed. M. Darrol Bryant and Herbert W. Richardson. New York: Edwin Mellon Press, 1978.

Demos, John. *A Little Commonwealth: Family Life in Plymouth Colony*. New York: Oxford University Press, 1970.

Derber, Charles. *The Pursuit of Attention: Power and Individualism in Everyday Life*. New York: Oxford University Press, 1979.

Diagnostic and Statistical Manual. 4th ed. Washington, D.C.: American Psychiatric Association, 1994.

Dick, Bill W. "Psychology and Mennonite Studies." *Journal of Mennonite Studies* 1 (1983): 149–60.

Domer, Richard E., Winifred Hidel, and John Hinde. *May They All Be One*. Farmington, Pa: Plough Publishing House, 1992.

Douglas, Mary. *Purity And Danger: An Analysis of the Concepts of Pollution and Taboo*. New York: Routledge, 1988.

Dueck, Al. "Psychology and Mennonite Self-Understanding." In *Mennonite Identity: Historical and Contemporary Perspectives*, ed. Calvin Redekop and Stan Steiner, 203–24. Lanham, Md.: University Press of America, 1988.

———. "Story, Community and Ritual: Anabaptist Themes and Mental Health." *Mennonite Quarterly Review* 63, no. 1 (January 1989): 77–91.

Dumont, Louis. *Essays on Individualism: Modern Ideology in Anthropological Perspective*. Chicago: University of Chicago Press, 1992.

———. *The German Ideology: From France to Germany and Back*. Chicago: University of Chicago Press, 1994.

Durnbaugh, Donald F. *The Believers' Church, The History and Character of Radical Protestantism*. New York: Macmillian Company, 1968.

———. "Relocation of the German Bruderhof to England, South America, and North America." *Communal Studies* 11 (1991): 66–77.

Dusen, Henry P. Van. "The Third Force's Lessons for Others." *Life* (June 9, 1958): 122–23.

Eaton, Joseph W., Robert J. Weil, and Bert Kaplan. "Hutterite Mental Health Survey." *Mennonite Quarterly Review* 25, no. 1 (1951): 59–61.

Eaton, Joseph W., and Robert J. Weil. *Culture and Mental Disorders: A Comparative Study of the Hutterites and Other Populations*. Glencoe, Ill.: the Free Press, 1955.

Eckardt, A. Roy. "The New Look in American Piety." In *Religion, Society, and the Individual*, ed. J. Milton Yinger, 408–14. New York: Macmillan Company, 1957.

Egeland, Janice A. "Belief and Behavior as Related to Illness: A Community Case Study of the Old Order Amish." Ph. D. diss., Yale University, 1967.

———. "Bipolarity: The Iceberg of Affective Disorders?" *Comprehensive Psychiatry* 24, no. 4 (July/August 1983a): 337–44.

———. "Cultural Factors and Social Stigma for Manic-Depression: The Amish Study." *American Journal of Social Psychiatry* 6, no. 4 (Fall 1986): 279–86.

Egeland, Janice A., and Abram M. Hostetter. "Amish Study, I: Affective Disorders among the Amish, 1976–1980." *American Journal of Psychiatry* 140, no. 1 (January 1983b): 56–61.

Eiler, David, and Shirley Eiler. "Impressions of the Woodcrest Bruderhof Community, Rifton, New York." In *Bethany Theological Seminary Faculty Retreat in Oakbrook, Illinois*, 1957.

Emerson, Ralph Waldo. *The Selected Writings of Ralph Waldo Emerson*. New York: Modern Library, 1950.

Emmons, Nathanael. *The Works of Nathanael Emmons*. Boston: Congregational Board of Publication, 1860.

Erikson, Erik H. *Young Man Luther: A Study in Psychoanalysis and History*. New York: W. W. Norton & Company, 1958.

Evans, Rod L, and Irwin M. Berent. *Fundamentalism: Hazards and Heartbreaks*. LaSalle, Illinois: Open Court, 1989.

Fenn, Richard K. *The Persistence of Purgatory*. Cambridge: Cambridge University Press, 1995.

Foster, Lawrence. *Religion and Sexuality: The Shakers, the Mormons, and the Oneida Community*. Urbana: University of Illinois Press, 1984.

Fretz, Joseph Winfield. *Pilgrims in Paraguay: The Story of Mennonite Colonization in South America*. Scottdale, Pa.: Herald Press, 1953.

Freud, Sigmund. *The Future of an Illusion*. In Peter Gay, ed., *The Freud Reader* (1927). 685–722.

———. *Civilization and Its Discontents*. In Peter Gay, ed., *The Freud Reader* (1930). 722–72.

———. *Group Psychology and the Analysis of the Ego*. Standard ed., Trans. James Strachey. New York: W. W. Norton, 1959.

Gay, Peter. *Freud for Historians*. New York: Oxford University Press, 1985.

———. "Psychoanalysis in History." In *Psychology and Historical Interpretation*, ed. William McKinley Runyan, 107–20. New York: Oxford University Press, 1988.

———. *The Freud Reader*. New York: W. W. Norton, 1989.

Gerth, H. H., and C. Wright Mills, eds. *From Max Weber, Essays in Sociology*. New York: Oxford University Press, 1946.

Giddens, Anthony. *The Contemporary Critique of Historical Materialism*. vol. 2, *The Nation State and Violence*. Cambridge, England: Polity Press, 1985.

Gluck, Mary. *Georg Lukács and His Generation 1900–1918*. Cambridge, Mass.: Cambridge University Press, 1985.

Goffman, Erving. *Asylums: Essays on the Social Condtion of Mental Patients and Other Inmates*. Garden City: Anchor Doubleday, 1961.

Goldman, Harvey. *Max Weber and Thomas Mann: Calling and the Shaping of the Self*. Berkeley, California: University of California Press, 1988.

———. *Politics, Death, and the Devil: Self and Power in Max Weber and Thomas Mann*. Berkeley, California: University of California Press, 1992.

Gordon, Frank J. "Protestantism and Socialism in the Weimar Republic." *German Studies Review* 11 (October 1988): 423–43.

Green, Martin. *The von Richthofen Sisters; The Triumphant and the Tragic Modes of Love: Else and Frieda von Richthofen, Otto Gross, Max Weber, and D. H. Lawrence, in the Years 1870–1970*. New York: Basic Books, 1974.

Greenspahn, Robert N., and Frederick E. Bellah, eds. *Uncivil Religion: Interreligious Hostility in America*. New York: Crossroad, 1987.

Greven, Jr., Philip J. *Four Generations: Population, Land and Family in Colonial Andover, Massachusetts*. Ithaca: Cornell University Press, 1970.

———. *The Protestant Temperament: Patterns of Child-Rearing, Religious Experience, and the Self in Early America*. New York: New American Library, 1979.

Halbwachs, Maurice. *On Collective Memory*. Edited, translated, and with an Introduction by Lewis A. Coser. Chicago: University of Chicago Press, 1993.

Hall, Francis B. "Pitfalls of Intentional Community." *The Christian Century* (August 14, 1963): 1000–1003.

———. *Practical Spirituality, Selected Writings.*. Ed. Howard Alexander, Wilmer A. Cooper, and James Newby,. Dublin, Ind.: Prinit Press, 1984.

Hamm, Peter M. *Continuity and Change among Canadian Mennonite Brethren*. Vol. 3, *Religion and Identity: Social-Scientific Studies in Religion*, ed. Hans Mol. Waterloo, Ontario, Canada: Wilfrid Laurier University Press, 1987.

Harder, Leland, and Leo Driedger, eds. *Anabaptist-Mennonite Identities in Ferment*. Vol. 14. Occasional Papers. Elkhart, Indiana: Institute of Mennonite Studies, 1990.

Hartse, Caroline M. "The Emotional Acculturation of Hutterite Defectors." *Journal of Anthropological Research* 50, no. 1 (Spring 1994): 69–85.

Hartz, Gary W., and Henry C. Everett. "Fundamentalist Religion and Its Effect on Mental Health." *Journal of Religion and Health* 28, no. 3 (Fall 1989): 207–17.

Harvey, David L. *Potter Addition: Poverty, Family, and Kinship in a Heartland Community*. New York: Aldine De Gruyter, 1993.

Hatch, Nathan O. *The Democratization of American Christianity*. New Haven: Yale University Press, 1989.

Herberg, Will. *Protestant, Catholic, Jew: An Essay in American Religious Sociology*. New York: Doubleday and Company, 1955.

Hobsbawm, Eric, and Terence Ranger. *The Invention of Tradition*. Cambridge: Cambridge University Press, 1983.

Hodge, Dean R., Benton Johnson, and Donald A. Luidens. *Vanishing Boundaries: The Religion of Mainline Protestant Baby Boomers*. Louisville: Westminister J. Knox, 1994.

Hoffer, Eric. *The True Believer: Thoughts on the Nature of Mass Movements*. New York: Harper & Brothers, 1951.

Holl, Karl. *Gesammelte Aufsatze zur Kirchengeschichte*. Vol. 1. Tubingen: J. C. B. Mohr, 1928.

Hollyday, Joyce. "The Stuff of Life: A Visit to the Bruderhof." *Sojourners* 13, no. 5 (May 1984): 21–24.

Holmes, Miriam Arnold. *Cast Out in the World: From the Bruderhof Communities to a Life on Her Own*. San Francisco: Carrier Pigeon Press, 1997.

Holzbach, Michael. *The Forgotten People, A Year Among the Hutterites*. Trans. Stepah Lhotzky. Sioux Falls, S.D.: Ex Machina Publishing Company, 1993.

Hopkins, Samuel. *The Life of President Edwards*. London: James Black and Son, 1819.

Hostetler, Beulah Stauffer. *American Mennonites and Protestant Movements: A Community Paradigm*. Vol. 28, *Studies in Anabaptist and Mennonite History*, ed. Conrelius J. Dyck et. al. Scottdale, Pa.: Herald Press, 1987.

Hostetler, John A. *The Sociology of Mennonite Evangelism*. Scottdale, Pa.: Herald Press, 1954.

———. *Hutterite Society*. Baltimore: Johns Hopkins University Press, 1974.

———. "Aspects of Personality in Communal Society." In *Community, Self, and Identity*, ed. Bhabagrahi Misra and James Preston. The Hague: Mouton Publishers, 1978.

———. *Amish Society*. 4th ed. Baltimore: Johns Hopkins University Press, 1993.

Hovland, C. Warren. "*Anfechtung* in Luther's Biblical Exegesis." In *Reformation Studies: Essays in Honor of Roland H. Bainton*, ed. Franklin H. Littell, 47–60. Richmond: John Knox Press, 1962.

Hudnut-Beumler, James. *Looking for God in the Suburbs: The Religion of the American Dream and Its Critics, 1945–1965*. New Brunswick: Rutgers University Press, 1994.

Hughes, Richard T., ed. *The American Quest for the Primitive Church*. Urbana: University of Illinois Press, 1988a.

———. *The Primitive Church in the Modern World*. Urbana: University of Illinois Press, 1995.

Hughes, Richard T. and C. Leonard Allen. *Illusions of Innocence: Protestant Primitivism in America, 1630–1675*. Chicago: University of Chicago Press, 1988b.

Jackson, Dave and Neta Jackson. *Living in a World Falling Apart*. Carol Stream, Ill.: Creation House, 1974.

———. *Glimpses of Glory: Thirty Years of Community: The Story of Reba Place Fellowship*. Elgin, Ill.: Brethren Press, 1987.

Jackson, Stanley W. *Melancholia and Depression: From Hippocratic Times to Modern Times*. New Haven: Yale University Press, 1986.

Jacobs, Janet Liebman. *Divine Disenchantment: Deconverting from New Religions*. Bloomington: Indiana University Press, 1989.

Jantzen, Grace M. "Luther and the Mystics." *King's Theological Review* 8 (Autumn 1985): 43–50.

Jellinek, Georg. *The Declaration of the Rights of Man and of Citizens: a Contribution to Modern Constitutional History.*. Trans. Max Farrand. New York: Henry Holt and Company, 1901.

Ji, Won Yong. "Significance of Tentatio in Luther's Spirituality." *Concordia Journal* 15, no. 2 (1989): 181–89.

Johnson, Paul E., and Sean Wilentz. *The Kingdom of Matthias*. New York: Oxford University Press, 1994.

Jones, James W. *Contemporary Psychoanalysis and Religion: Transference and Transcendence*. New Haven: Yale University Press, 1991.

Kanter, Rosabeth Moss. *Commitment and Community; Communes and Utopias in Sociological Perspective*. Cambridge: Harvard University Press, 1972.

Kaplan, Bert L. "Hutterite Socialization and the Resolution of the Conformity-Deviance Conflict." In *Annual Meetings of the American Orthopsychiatry Association in Philadelphia, Pennsylvania*, 1958.

Kauffman, J. Howard, and Leland Harder. *Anabaptists Four Centuries Later, A Profile of Five Mennonite and Brethren in Christ Denominations*. Scottdale, Pa.: Herald Press, 1975.

Kaysen, Susanna. *Girl, Interrupted*. New York: Vintage Books, 1993.

Kelley, Dean M. *Why Conservative Churches Are Growing: A Study in the Sociology of Religion*. New York: Harper and Row, 1977.

Klaassen, Walter. " 'Gelassenheit' and Creation." *Conrad Grebel Review* 9 (Winter 1991): 23–36.

———. "The Quest for Anabaptist Identity." In *Anabaptist-Mennonite Identities in Ferment*, ed. Leo Driedger and Leland Harder. Elkhart, Ind.: Institute of Mennonite Studies, 1990.

Klassen, William. "The Mennonite Syndrome." *Mennonite Life* 21 (1966): 139–42.

———. "The Role of the Church in Community Psychiatry." *McCormick Quarterly* 21 (January 1967): 23–39.

Kraybill, Donald B. *The Riddle of Amish Culture*. Baltimore: Johns Hopkins University Press, 1989.

Kren, George M. "Psychohistorical Interpretations of National Socialism." *German Studies Review* 1, no. 3 (1978): 150–72.

Küng, Hans. *Freud and the Problem of God*. Enlarged Edition. Edited and translated by Edward Quinn. New Haven: Yale University Press, 1990.

Laqueur, Walter. *Fascism: Past, Present, Future*. New York: Oxford University Press, 1996.

Leff, Gordon. *Heresy in the Later Middle Ages: The Relation of Heterodoxy to Dissent c. 1250–1450*. New York: Barnes & Noble, 1967.

Lejeune, R. *Christoph Blumhardt and His Message*. Rifton, N.Y.: the Plough Publishing House, 1963.

Lewis, R. W. B. *The American Adam: Innocence, Tragedy, and Tradition in the Nineteenth Century*. Chicago: University of Chicago Press, 1955.

Lichti, James Irwin. "German Mennonites, Economics and the State." In *Anabaptist/ Mennonite Faith and Economics*, ed. Calvin Redekop, Victor A. Krahn, and Samuel J. Steiner, 82–110. New York: University Press of America, 1994.

Liebersohn, Harry. *Fate and Utopia in German Sociology, 1870–1923*. Cambridge: MIT Press, 1988.

Lifton, Robert Jay. *The Nazi Doctors: Medical Killing and the Psychology of Genocide*. New York: Basic Books, 1986.

Lindholm, Charles. *Charisma*. Cambridge: Blackwell, 1993.

Littell, Franklin H. "The Power of the Restorationist Vision and Its Decline in America." In *The Primitive Church in the Modern World*, ed. Richard T. Hughes. 49–73. Urbana: University of Illinois Press, 1995.

———, ed. *Reformation Studies: Essays in Honor of Roland H. Bainton*. Richmond: John Knox Press, 1962.

Little, Lester K. *Liberty, Charity, Fraternity: Lay Religious Confraternities at Bergamo in the Age of the Commune*. Bergamo: Pierluigi Lubrina Editore, 1988.

Lockridge, Kenneth A. *A New England Town: The First Hundred Years: Dedham, Massachusetts, 1636–1736*. New York: Norton, 1985.

Loewenberg, Peter. *Decoding the Past: The Psychohistorical Approach*. New York: Alfred A. Knopf, 1983.

———. *Fantasy and Reality in History*. New York: Oxford University Press, 1995.

Lukoff, David, Francis Lu, and Robert Turner. "Toward a More Culturally Sensitive DSM-IV, Psychoreligious and Psychospiritual Problems." *Journal of Nervous and Mental Disease* 180, no. 11 (November 1992): 673–82.

Macintyre, Ben. *Forgotten Fatherland: The Search for Elizabeth Nietzsche*. New York: Farrar Straus Giroux, 1992.

MacMaster, Richard K. *Land, Piety, Peoplehood: The Establishment of Mennonite Communities in America 1683–1790*. Vol. 1, *The Mennonite Experience in America*, ed. Robert S. Kreider. Scottdale, Pa.: Herald Press, 1985.

Macpherson, C. B. *The Political Theory of Possessive Individualism, Hobbes to Locke*. New York: Oxford University Press, 1962.

Madsen, Douglas and Peter S. Snow. *The Charismatic Bond: Political Behavior in Time of Crisis*. Cambridge: Harvard University Press, 1991.

Mason, Randall C. "The Psychology of the Self: Religion and Psychotherapy." In *Advances in Self-Psychology*, ed. Arnold Goldberg. New York: International Universities Press, 1980.

Mathisen, James A. "Thomas O'Dea's Dilemmas of Institutionalization: A Case Study and Re-evaluation after Twenty-five Years." *Sociological Analysis* 47, no. 4 (1987): 302–18.

McLoughlin, William G. "Pietism and the American Character." *American Quarterly* 17, no. 2 (Summer 1965): 163–86.

———. *Revivals, Awakenings, and Reform: An Essay on Religion and Social Change in America, 1607–1977*. Chicago: University of Chicago Press, 1978.

———. "Is There a Third Force in Christendom?" In *New and Intense Movements*, ed. Martin E. Marty, 11. New York: K. G. Saur, 1993 (1967).

Meeks, Wayne A. *The First Urban Christians: The Social World of the Apostle Paul*. New Haven: Yale University Press, 1983.

Meier, Hans. *Hans Meier Tells His Story to a Friend*. Rifton, N.Y.: Plough Publishing House, 1979.

Melton, J. Gordon. "Introduction: When Prophets Die: The Succession Crises in New Religions." In *When Prophets Die: The Postcharismatic Fate of New Religious Movements*, ed. Timothy Miller. State University of New York Press, 1991.

"Memories of Fred." (unpublished transcription of funeral rite and Love Meals in memoriam for Fred Goodwin, 1971.)

Mendes-Flohr, N., Nahum and Paul Glatzer, eds. *The Letters of Martin Buber, A Life of Dialogue*. New York: Schocken Books, 1991.

Merkl, Peter H. *Political Violence under the Swastika: 581 Early Nazis*. Princeton: Princeton University Press, 1975.

Milbank, John. *Theology and Social Theory: Beyond Secular Reason*. Oxford: Blackwell, 1990.

Miller, Alice. *Banished Knowledge, Facing Childhood Injuries*. New York: Anchor Books, 1990.

Miller, Timothy, ed. *When Prophets Die: The Postcharismatic Fate of New Religious Movements*. State University of New York Press, 1991.

Mitscherlich, Alexander. *Society without the Father: A Contribution to Social Psychology*. Trans. Eric Mosbacher. New York: Harcourt, Brace & World, 1963.

Mommsen, Wolfgang. *Max Weber and German Politics*. Chicago: University of Chicago Press, 1984.

Mommsen, Wolfgang J., and Jurgen Osterhammel, eds. *Max Weber and His Contemporaries*. Boston: Allen and Unwin, 1987.

Moore, R. Laurence. *Religious Outsiders and the Making of Americans*. New York: Oxford University Press, 1986.

Mow, Merrill. *Torches Rekindled: The Bruderhof's Struggle for Renewal*. Ulster Park, N.Y.: Plough Publishing House Hutterian Brethren, 1989.

Nash, Connie. "Bruderhof Women: A Testimony of Love." *Other Side* 22, no. 6 (August 1986): 12–15.

Nelson, Benjamin. "The Future of Illusions." In *Man in Contemporary Society*, 958–79, 2. New York: Columbia University Press, 1956.

———. "Community—Dreams and Realities." In *Community*. Nomos II, ed. Carl J. Friedrich, 135–151. New York: the Liberal Arts Press, 1959.

———. "Actors, Directors, Roles, Cues, Meanings, Identities: Further Thoughts on 'Anomie'." *Psychoanalytic Review* 52, no. 2 (1964): 135–60.

———. "Self-Images and Systems of Spiritual Direction in the History of European Civilization." In *The Quest for Self-Control: Classical Philosophies and Scientific Research*, ed. Samuel Z. Klausner. New York: the Free Press, 1965.

———. "The Omnipresence of the Grotesque." *The Psychoanalytic Review* 57, no. 3 (1970): 505–18.

———. *On the Roads to Modernity: Conscience, Science, and Civilizations; Selected Essays*, ed. Toby E. Huff. Totowa, N.J.: Rowman and Littlefield, 1981.

Newcomer, Christian. *The Life and Journal of the Reverend Christian Newcomer*. Hagerstown: F.G.W. Kapp, 1834.

Niebuhr, Gustav. "Men Crowd Stadiums to Fulfill Their Souls." *New York Times*, August 6, 1995, 1, 30.

Nieves, Evelyn. "Sometimes a Luxury Jet Serves God." *New York Times*, October 13, 1996.

O'Dea, Thomas F. "The Crisis of the Contemporary Religious Consciousness." In *Religion in America*, ed. William G. McLoughlin and Robert N. Bellah, 184–202. Boston: Beacon Press, 1966a.

————. *The Sociology of Religion*. Englewood Cliffs, N.J.: Prentice-Hall, 1966b.

————. *Alienation, Atheism and the Religious Crisis*. New York: Sheed and Ward, 1969.

Oates, Wayne E. *Anxiety in Christian Experience*. Philadelphia: Westminster Press, 1955a.

————. *Religious Factors in Mental Illness*. New York: Association Press, 1955b.

————. *When Religion Gets Sick*. Philadelphia: Westminster Press, 1970.

Oved, Yaacov. "Twenty Years in Primavera." In *Communal Studies Conference in Nouvoo, Illinois*, 1992.

————. *Distant Brothers: History of the Relations between the Bruderhof and the Kibbutz*. Trans. Hannah Lash and Yehuda Riemer. Ed. Yad Tabenkin. Farmington, Pa:. Plough Publishing House, 1993.

————. *The Witness of the Brothers: A History of the Bruderhof*. New Brunswick: Transaction Publishers, 1996.

Parsons, Arthur S. "Messianic Personalism: A Role Analysis of the Unification Church." *Journal for the Scientific Study of Religion* 25, no. 2 (1986): 141–61.

————. "The Secular Contribution to Religious Innovation: A Case Study of the Unification Church." *Sociological Analysis* 50, no. 3 (1989): 209–77.

Parsons, Talcott. *Talcott Parsons on National Socialism*. Edited and with an Introduction by Uta Gerhardt. New York: Aldine De Gruyter, 1993.

Payne, Stanley G. *A History of Fascism, 1914–1945*. Madison: University of Wisconsin Press, 1995.

Peachey, Paul. "Identity Crises among American Mennonites." *Mennonite Quarterly Review* 42, no. 4 (October 1968): 243–59.

Peck, Robert N. "An Ex-Member's View of the Bruderhof Communities from 1948–1961." In *Utopian Studies I*, ed. Kenneth Roemer Nicholas D. Smith and Gorman Beauchamp. Lanham, Md: University Press of America, 1987.

Peter, Karl A. *The Dynamics of Hutterite Society, An Analytic Approach*. Edmonton, Canada: University of Alberta Press, 1987.

Peters, Victor. *All Things Common: The Hutterian Way of Life*. New York: Harper and Row, 1965.

Peukert, Detlev J. *The Weimar Republic: The Crisis of Classical Modernity*. Trans. Richard Deveson. New York: Hill and Wang, 1992.

————. *Inside Nazi Germany: Conformity, Opposition, and Racism in Everyday Life*. Trans. Richard Deveson. New Haven: Yale University Press, 1987.

Pfiefer, Samuel. "Faith-Induced Neurosis: Myth or Reality." *Journal of Psychology and Theology* 22, no. 2 (1994): 87–96.

Piper, Otto. *Recent Developments in German Protestantism*. London: Student Christian Movement Press, 1934.

Plaut, Thomas F.A., and Bert Kaplan. *Personality in a Communal Society: An Analysis of the Mental Health of the Hutterites*. Social Science Studies, Lawrence, Kansas: University of Kansas Publications, 1956.

Pleil, Nadine Moonje. Free from Bondage: After Forty Years in Bruderhof Communities on Three Continents. *Women From Utopia*, Series ed. Gertrude Enders Huntington. San Francisco: Carrier Pigeon Press, 1994.

Preheim, Rich. "Hutterites Break Along East-West Lines." *Mennonite Weekly Review* (June 15, 1995), 1, 6.

Prince, Raymond H. "The Concept of Culture-Bound Syndrome: Anorexia Nervosa and Brain-Fag." *Social Science and Medicine* 21, no. 2 (1985): 197–203.

————. "Religious Experience and Psychopathology: Cross-Cultural Perpectives." In *Religion and Mental Health*, ed. John F. Schumaker. New York: Oxford University Press, 1992.

Ragaz, Leonhard. *Signs of the Kingdom.* Translated and edited by Paul Bock. Grand Rapids: William B. Eerdmans, 1984.

Redekop, Calvin. *Mennonite Society.* Baltimore: Johns Hopkins University Press, 1989.

Redekop, Calvin, and Samuel J. Steiner, eds. *Mennonite Identity, Historical and Contemporary Perspectives.* New York: University Press of America, 1988.

Redekop, Calvin, Victor A. Krahn, and Samuel J. Steiner, eds. *Anabaptist/Mennonite Faith and Economics.* New York: University Press of America, 1994.

Redekop, John H. "College Training—Where are we heading?" *Mennonite Brethren Herald* (February 19, 1965): 2.

Reich, Wilhelm. *The Mass Psychology of Fascism.* Trans. Vincent R. Carfagno. New York: Farrar, Straus & Giroux, 1970.

Rice, Judith. "Hutterians." *History Today* 44, no. 7 (1994): 8–11.

Richardson, James T., ed. *Conversion Careers: In and Out of the New Religions.* Sage Contemporary Social Science Issues. Beverly Hills: Sage Publications, 1978.

Riedemann, Peter. *Account of Our Religion, Doctrine and Faith.* Trans. Kathleen E. Hasenberg. London: Hodder and Stoughton, in conjuction with the Plough Publishing House, 1950.

Riesebrodt, Martin. *Pious Passion: The Emergence of Modern Fundamentalism in the United States and Iran.* Trans. Don Reneau. Comparative Studies in Religion and Society, series ed. Mark Juergensmeyer. Berkeley: University of California Press, 1993.

Riesman, David. *The Lonely Crowd: A Study of the Changing American Character.* New Haven: Yale University Press, 1950.

Ringer, Fritz K. *The Decline of the German Mandarins: The German Academic Community, 1880–1933.* Hanover, New Hampshire: University Press of New England, 1990.

Robbins, Thomas. *Cults, Converts and Charisma: The Sociology of New Religious Movements.* Beverly Hills: Sage Publications, 1988.

Roper, Katherine. *German Encounters with Modernity: Novels of Imperial Berlin.* New York: Humanities International Press, 1991.

Roth, Guenther, and Wolfgang Schluchter. *Max Weber's Vision of History: Ethics and Methods.* Berkeley: University of California Press, 1979.

Roth, Michael S. *Psycho-Analysis as History: Negation and Freedon in Freud.* Ithaca: Cornell University Press, 1987.

Roth, Michael S. *The Ironist's Cage: Memory, Trauma and the Construction of History.* New York: Columbia University Press, 1995.

Rothbaum, Susan. "Between Two Worlds, Issues of Separation and Identity After Leaving a Religious Community." In *Falling From Faith: Causes and Consequneces of Religious Apostasy,* ed. David G. Bromley, 205–41. Beverly Hills: Sage Publications, 1988.

Royte, Elizabeth. "Kindred Spirits." *Life* (December 1996): 88–94.

Rubenstein, Richard L. *After Auschwitz: History, Theology, and Contemporary Judaism.* 2nd ed., Baltimore: Johns Hopkins University Press, 1992.

Rubin, Julius H. "Review of *Nature Religion in America: From the Algonkian Indians to the New Age,*" by Catherine L. Albanese. *Sociological Analysis* 52, no. 1 (Spring 1991): 140–41.

———. *Religious Melancholy and Protestant Experience in America.* Religion in America, series ed. Harry S. Stout. New York: Oxford University Press, 1994.

Runyan, William McKinley, ed. *Psychology and Historical Interpetation.* New York: Oxford University Press, 1988.

Ruprecht, Jr., Louis A. *Tragic Posture and Tragic Vision: Against the Modern Failure of Nerve*. New York: Continuum Publishing Company, 1994.

Ruth, John L. *Maintaining the Right Fellowship: A Narrative Account of Life in the Oldest Mennonite Community in North America*. Vol. 26, *Studies in Anabaptist and Mennonite History*, ed. Cornelius J. Dyck et al. Scottdale, Pa.: Herald Press, 1984.

Sander, John Herman. "The Development of Religious Socialism in Germany." Ph.D. diss., Yale University, 1939.

Saxby, T. J. *The Quest for the New Jerusalem, Jean de Labadie and the Labadists, 1610–1744*. Dordrecht: Martinus Nijhoff Publishers, 1987.

Scaer, David P. "The Concept of *Anfechtung* in Luther's Thought." *Concordia Theological Quarterly* 47 (January 1983): 15–30.

Schaff, Lawrence A. *Fleeing the Iron Cage: Culture, Politics, and Modernity in the Thought of Max Weber*. Berkeley: University of California Press, 1989.

Schaeffer, Francis A. *A Christian Manifesto*. Westchester, Illinois: Crossway Books, 1982.

Scharfenberg, Joachim. *Sigmund Freud and His Critique of Religion*. Trans. O.C. Dean, Jr. Philadelphia: Fortress Press, 1988.

Schluchter, Wolfgang. "Value-Neutrality and the Ethic of Responsibility." In *Max Weber's Vision of History, Ethics and Methods*, ed. Guenther Roth and Wolfgang Schulchter. Berkeley: University of California Press, 1979.

———. *Rationalism, Religion, and Domination: A Weberian Perspective*. Trans. Neil Solomon. 1989.

Schumaker, John F., ed. *Religion and Mental Health*. New York: Oxford University Press, 1992.

Schupe, Anson. "Constructing Evil as a Social Process: The Unification Church and the Media." In *Uncivil Religion, Interreligious Hostility in America*, ed. Robert N. Bellah and Frederick E. Greenspahn. 205–18. New York: Crossroad, 1987.

Schwartz, Barry. "The Social Context of Commemoration: A Study in Collective Memory." *Social Forces* 61, no. 2 (1983): 374–402.

Scott, Nathan A., ed. *The Tragic Vision and the Christian Faith*. New York: Association Press, 1957.

Sender, Ramón. "The Peregrine Foundation Information Sheet." (P.O. Box 46041, San Francisco, CA 94146) 1993.

Shain, Barry Alan. *The Myth of American Individualism: The Protestant Origins of American Political Thought*. Princeton: Princeton University Press, 1994.

Shapiro, David. *Autonomy and Rigid Character*. New York: Basic Books, 1981.

Simin, Ulrich. *Pity and Terror, Christianity and Tragedy*. London: McMillian Press, 1989.

Singer, Margaret Thaler, with Janja Lalich. *Cults in Our Midst*. San Francisco: Jossey-Bass, 1995.

Skolnick, Arlene S. *Embattled Paradise: The American Family in an Age of Uncertainty*. New York: Basic Books, 1991.

Smucker, Donovan E. *The Sociology of Mennonites, Hutterites and Amish, A Bibliography with Annotations* Volume 2, 1977–1990. Waterloo, Ontario, Canada: Wilfrid Laurier University Press, 1991.

Sorokin, Pitirim A. *The Ways and Power of Love: Types, Factors, and Techniques of Moral Transformation*. Boston: The Beacon Press, 1954.

Spilka, Bernard. "Functional and Dysfunctional Roles of Religion: An Attributional Approach." *Journal of Psychology and Christianity* 8, no. 3 (1989): 5–15.

Spilka, Bernard, and Robert A. Bridges. "Religion and Mental Health of Women." In *Religion and Mental Health*, ed. John F. Schumaker, 43–53. New York: Oxford University Press, 1992.

Stachura, Peter D. *The German Youth Movement 1900–1945: An Interpretative and Documentary History*. New York: St. Martin's Press, 1981.

Starr, Bradley E. " 'The World's Most Perverse Habit': Ernst Troeltsch on Religion in the Conflict of Values." In *Anxiety, Guilt and Freedom: Religious Studies Perspectives, Essays in Honor of Donald Gard* Lanham: University Press of America, 1990.

Stern, Fritz. *The Politics of Cultural Despair: A Study in the Rise of the Germanic Ideology*. Berkeley: University of California Press, 1974.

Sternhell, Zeev. *Neither Right nor Left: Fascist Ideology in France*. Trans. David Maisel. Princeton: Princeton University Press, 1996.

Sternhell, Zeev, with Maria Sznajder and Maia Asheri. *The Birth of Fascist Ideology: From Cultural Rebellion to Political Revolution*. Trans. David Maisel. Princeton: Princeton University Press, 1994.

Stoeffler, F. Ernest. *German Pietism during the Eighteenth Century*. Philadelphia: Temple University Press, 1973.

Strozier, Charles B. *Apocalypse: On the Psychology of Fundamentalism in America*. Boston: Beacon Press, 1994.

Terpstra, Nicholas. *Lay Confraternities and Civic Religion in Renaissance Bologna*. Cambridge: Cambridge University Press, 1995.

Theweleit, Klaus. *Male Fantasies*. Trans. Stephen Conway, in collaboration with Erica Carter and Chris Turner. Minneapolis: University of Minneapolis Press, 1987.

Thiessen, Irmgard. "Mental Health and the Mennonites." *Mennonite Life* (July 1963): 114–15.

———. "Values and Personality Characteristics of Mennonites in Manitoba." *Mennonite Quarterly Review* 40, no. 1 (January 1966): 48–61.

Thiessen, Irmgard, Morgan W. Wright, and George C. Sisler. "A Comparison of Personality Characteristics of Mennonites with Non-Mennonites." *The Canadian Psychologist* 10, no. 2 (April 1969): 129–37.

Thomas, William I. *The Unadjusted Girl with Cases from the Standpoint for Behavior Analysis*. Researches in the Social, Cultural and Behavioral Sciences, series ed. Benjamin Nelson. New York: Harper & Row, 1967.

Thompson, Barbara R. "The Challenge of True Brotherhood." *Christianity Today* vol. 29, no. 5 (1985): 22–27.

Thompson, Roger. *Sex in Middlesex: Popular Mores in a Massachusetts County, 1649–1679*. Amherst: University of Massachusetts Press, 1986.

Tillich, Paul. *The Protestant Era*. Trans. James Luther Adams. Chicago: University of Chicago Press, 1948.

Tillson, David Stanley. "A Pacifist Community in Peacetime: An Introductory Description of the Woodcrest Bruderhof at Rifton, New York." D.S.S. diss., Syracuse University, 1958.

Tipton, Steven M. *Getting Saved from the Sixties: Moral Meaning in Conversion and Cultural Change*. Berkeley: University of California Press, 1982.

Toennies, Ferdinand. *Community and Society (Gemeinschaft und Gesellschaft)*. New York: Harper and Row, 1963.

———. *On Sociology: Pure, Applied, and Empirical Selected Writings*. Edited and with an Introduction by Werner J. Cahnman and Rudolf Heberle. Chicago: University of Chicago Press, 1971.

Troeltsch, Ernst. *Protestantism and Progress: A Historical Study of the Relation of Protestantism to the Modern World*. Trans. W. Montgomery. Boston: Beacon Press, 1958 (1912).

———. *The Social Teachings of the Christian Churches*. Vol. 2. Trans. Olive Wyon. Chicago: University of Chicago Press, 1981 (1911).

Turner, Bryan S. *Max Weber: From History to Modernity.* New York: Routledge, 1992.

Ulrich, Laurel. *Good Wives: Image and Reality in the Lives of Women in Northern New England, 1650–1750.* New York: Random House, 1982.

Unamuno, Miguel De. *The Tragic Sense of Life.* Trans. J. E. Crawford Flitch. New York: Dover Publications, 1954.

Vanauken, Sheldon. *A Severe Mercy.* New York: Harper Collins, 1987.

Van Dusen, Henry P. "The Third Force's Lessons for Others." *Life* (June 9, 1958) 113–21.

Vaughan, Richard P. *Mental Illness and the Religious Life.* Milwaukee: Bruce Publications, 1962.

Vergote, Antoine. *Guilt and Desire, Religious Attitudes and Their Pathological Derivatives.* Trans. M. H. Wood. New Haven: Yale University Press, 1988.

Veroff, Joseph, Elizabeth Douvan, and Richard A. Kulka. *The Inner American: A Self-Portrait from 1957 to 1976.* Basic Books, New York: 1981.

Wagoner, Bob, and Shirley Wagoner. *Community in Paraguay: A Visit to the Bruderhof.* Farmington, Pa.: Plough Publishing House, 1991.

Walzer, Michael. *The Revolution of the Saints: A Study in the Origins of Radical Politics.* Cambridge: Harvard University Press, 1965.

Ward, W. R. *Theology, Sociology and Politics: The German Protestant Social Conscience 1890–1933.* Berne: Switzerland: Peter Lang, 1979.

Weber, Max. "The Social Psychology of the World Religions." In *From Max Weber: Essays in Sociology,* ed. H. H. Gerth and C. Wright Mills. New York: Oxford University Press, 1946.

———. *The Protestant Ethic and the Spirit of Capitalism.* Translated by Talcott Parsons. New York: Charles Scribner's Sons, 1958.

———. *From Max Weber: Essays in Sociology.* Translated, edited, and with an Introduction by H. H. Gerth and C. Wright Mills. New York: Oxford University Press, 1967a.

———. "Politics as a Vocation." In *From Max Weber: Essays in Sociology,* ed. H. H. Gerth and C. Wright Mills, 77–128. New York: Oxford University Press, 1967b.

———. "Religious Rejections of the World and Their Directions." In *From Max Weber: Essays in Sociology,* ed. H. H. Gerth and C. Wright Mills. New York: Oxford University Press, 1967c.

———. "Science as a Vocation." In *From Max Weber: Essays in Sociology,* ed. H. H. Gerth and C. Wright Mills. 129–58. New York: Oxford University Press, 1967d.

———. *Economy and Society: An Outline of Interpretive Sociology.* vol. 3 volumes. Trans. Ephraim Fischoff. Ed. Guenther Roth and Claus Wittich. 1968.

———. "Developmental Tendencies in the Situation of East Elbian Rural Labourers." In *Max Weber and His Contemporaries,* Ed. Wolfgang and Osterhammel Mommsen Jurgen. 176–205. Boston: Allen and Unwin, 1987a.

———. "The National State and Ecomomic Policy" (Freiburg Address). In *Max Weber and His Contemporaries,* ed. Wolfgang and Osterhammel Mommsen Jurgen. 429–40. Boston: Allen and Unwin, 1987b.

Weber, Timothy P. "Fundamentalism Twice Removed: The Emergence and Shape of Progressive Evangelicalism." In *New Directions in American Religious History: Essays in Honor of Martin E. Marty,* ed. Jay P. Dolan and James P. Wind. 261–87. Grand Rapids, Michigan: William B. Eerdmans, 1993.

Weisbrod, Carol. *The Boundaries of Utopia.* New York: Pantheon Books, 1980.

Weissman, Ronald F. E. *Ritual Brotherhood in Renaissance Florence.* Population and Social Structure, Advances in Historical Demography, series ed. E. A. Hammel. New York: Academic Press, 1982.

Whitworth, John McKelvie. *God's Blueprints: A Sociological Study of Three Utopian Sects*. Boston, Massachusetts: Routledge & Kegan Paul, 1975.

Whyte, Willian Hollingsworth. *The Organization Man*. New York: Simon and Schuster, 1956.

Williams, Richard N., and James E. Faulconer. "Religion and Mental Health: A Hermeneutic Reconsideration." *Review of Religious Research* 35, no. 4 (June 1994): 335–49.

Wilson, Bryan R. *Religious Sects: A Sociological Study*. New York: McGraw-Hill, 1970.

———. *The Social Dimensions of Sectarianism: Sects and New Religious Movements in Contemporary Society*. Oxford: Oxford University Press, 1990.

———. *Religion in Sociological Perspective*. New York: Oxford University Press, 1982.

Witherington III, Ben. *Women in the Earliest Churches*. Cambridge, England: Cambridge University Press, 1988.

Wuthnow, Robert. *The Restructuring of American Religion: Society and Faith since World War II*. Princeton, New Jersey: Princeton University Press, 1988.

Yelinek, Prudence. "Pilgrims in a Strange Land: Reflections on Spiritual Direction and the Church of the Brethren." *Brethren Life and Thought* 34, no. 2 (Spring 1989): 85–90.

Zablocki, Benjamin. *The Joyful Community: An Account of the Bruderhof, A Communal Movement Now In Its Third Generation*. Baltimore, Maryland: Penguin Books, 1971.

Zuck, Lowell H. "Spiritual Renewal in the Radical Reform Tradition." *Brethren Life and Thought* 26 (Winter 1981): 18–30.

INDEX

evangelical nurture (*continued*)
  discipline of children and
    adolescents, 114
  Llewelyn Harries's discipline of
    children and adolescents, 113
  of problem children, 107, 114–15
  punishment for sexual impurity, 108–
    9
  Mennonite practices, 202–3
  "winning children for Jesus," 114
evangelical Pietist conversion, 28–29
  in Anabaptist sects, 191
  and anorexia nervosa, 150
  Arnoldism, 92
  and experience of ecstasy, 67
  in Fourth Great Awakening, 100–
    101
  in Hutterite theology, 65–66
  Mennonite opposition to, 199
  and tragic sense of life, 210–12
Evans, Gwynn, 122–23
Exclusion. *See Auschluss*
exorcism, 60, 112, 117
experiential eschatology, 103

faith-structure of consciousness, 58, 70–
    71
Farrakhan, Louis, 186
Faulconer, James E., 7
Faulkner, Daniel, 184
Fenn, Richard, K., 9–10
Finney, Charles Grandison, 29, 199
First Law of Sannerz, 54, 68–69, 189
Fischer, Karl, 48
Forest River Community, 111
Forest River House, 93
Foster, Lawrence, 176
Fourth Great Awakening, 16, 81, 101–
    2
Francke, August Hermann, 28
Francke, Sebastian, 22
Fretz, Joseph Winfield, 80–81
Freud, Sigmund, 209–10, 212

Gefuhlskultur, 38
Geisteskrank, 126
Gelassenheit
  and Amish life, 206–7
  in Anabaptist theology, 156–57, 159,
    191

Burdens of, 156–57
case histories of, 163–67
community-crisis and euphoria cycle,
    157–58
decline among Hutterites, 196
failure to achieve by apostates, 158–
    63, 173–74
Fred Goodwin, 158–63
Hannah Goodwin, 158–63
in Hutterite conversion, 66, 192
in Mennonite ethos, 200
and Mennonite evangelical nurture,
    203
and Saint John of the Cross, 173–74
and submission of women to
    patriarchal authority, 112, 166–
    67
Gemeinde
  Amish church-community, 203–4
  Amish religious identity, 205–6
  and Anabaptist redemptive
    community, 191
  and anthropology of the "New
    Man," 54
  and Apostolic Church, 36
  as authoritarian primitivism, 17, 189–
    90
  authoritarianism of Labadie's New
    Jerusalem, 74–75
  definition of, 54–55
  Eberhard Arnold's foundation for
    salvation community, 58–60
  Eberhard Arnold's models for, 55,
    59, 68–70, 90
  and ethic of brotherliness, 36–37
  as "illusion" in Judeo-Christian
    though, 70–71, 210–11
  Johann Blumhardt's model of, 60–61
  transition from democracy to
    authoritarianism, 67–68
Gemeninschaft
  emergence in Bruderhof, 68–69
  Toennies's organic community, 48,
    53, 70
George, Stefan, 38
German Pietist Movement, 28–29, 52–
    53, 92
German Youth Movement. *See*
    Wandervogel
Gesamthabitus, 25

introversionist sect, 81
invention of tradition, 168

Jackson, Dave, 95, 98
Jackson, Neta, 95, 98
Jacobs, Janet Liebman, 133–34, 135
James Valley Hutterian Brethren, 94
Jehovah's Witness, 101
"Jesus is Victor!", 60, 113, 117–24,
    128, 186
Ji, Wong Yong, 130
Johnson, Guy, 79
Johnson, Paul E., 15
Junkers, 34
Just-Us, 185

Kaplan, Bert, 192–94
Kauffman, J. Howard, 201
Kaysen, Susana, 143
Keiderling, Joseph, 183, 184
Kelley, Dean, 101–2
Kiefer, Ria, 178
King, Stephen, 116
Kingwood Community, 89
KIT (Keep In Touch)
    concern with Bruderhof mental
        health, 144
    death penalty hearings, 184–85
    founding of, 172
    newsletter and contested collective
        memory, 172–73, 176
    relations with Bruderhof, 178–81
    reunions and memorials, 173, 176–77
    types of persons associated with, 182–
        83
KITfolk, 172–73, 177, 182–83
Klaassen, Walter, 156–57
Klassen, William, 202–3
Kleinsasser, Fred, 93
Kleinsesser, Jacob, 197
Kohut, Heinz, 134–35
Koinonia, 95
Kurtz, Mark, 119, 133
Kurville, 55
Kutter, Hermann, 22

Labadie, Jean de, 73–77
Laudaner, Gustave, 21, 56–57
Laudesi, 71
Lebenscult Movement, 37

Lebensführung, 41
Lifton, Robert Jay, 176
Lindholm, Charles, 102
Littell, Franklin H., 114
love groups, 180–81
Lu, Francis, 145
Luckács, Georg, 38
Lukoff, David, 145
Luther, Martin
    Anfechtung, 26–27, 129–31, 195–96,
        230 n.62
    German Theology and Gelassenheit,
        156, 191
    Theology of the Cross, 26, 129–31,
        135, 136, 191

MacDonald, C. B., 205
Macedonia Cooperative Community,
    89
Maendel, Dan, 140
Maendel, Darius, 93
Maendel, David, 181
Maendel, Paul, 93
Marcuse, Herbert, 161
Mason, Arnold, 93
Matthias, 15, 219 n.50
McLoughlin, William G., 99, 101, 199
Meeks, Wayne, 58
Meidung, 203
Meier, Hans, 47, 77, 79, 93
Mennonite Central Committee, 79
Mennonite Church
    affinity with religious melancholy,
        203
    birthright Mennonites, 197
    convinced Mennonites, 197
    ethos, 200
    and evangelical nurture, 202–3
    history of, 96, 197–98
    identity crisis, 199–200
    major divisions and schisms, 197
    Mennonite psychosis, 200–1
    Mennonite Syndrome, 202–3
    mental health studies, 200–3
    Ordnung and core values, 197
    Pietistic conversion, 200–2
    religiously grounded personality, 203
    resistance to evangelical Pietism, 199
Mennonite Swiss Brethren, 203
Merton, Robert, 186

Miller, John, 95–96
Moody, Doug, 135–36, 178
Moore, R. Laurence, 14
Mother Teresa, 186
Mow, Anna, 192
Mow, Kathy, 133
Mow, Merrill
  account of exorcism of Miriam Way,
    93
  author of Bruderhof apologetic, 82,
    85, 170–71
  on burdens of leadership for Heini
    Arnold, 133, 177–78
  church discipline of Miriam Arnold
    Holmes, 141
  on Forest River Affair, 93
  and Great Crisis, 120–21
  and Woodcrest Spirit, 91–92
Muntzer, Thomas, 191

Nachfogle, 66
Nation of Islam, 186
National Commission on Capital
    Punishment (NCCP), 184–
    85
Nazi, 77–78
Nelson, Benjamin
  faith-structure of consciousness, 58,
    70
  sociology of the possible, 212
  subordination of individual to the
    collective, 211
  utopian illusions, 70–71, 210
Newcomer, Christian, 198
new evangelicalism, 101–2
New Jerusalem, 73–76
New Man
  in Arnoldism, 92
  and *automachia,* 53–54
  in Bruderhof and other utopian
    groups, 53
  in Bruderhof *Gemeinde,* 56
  Labadie's New Jerusalem, 75
  as New Adam, 26
New Work, 22–24, 43, 50–52, 68
Nouwen, Henri J. M., 170, 186

Oates, Wayne E., 127, 130–31
Oberholtzer schism, 199
Ockenga, Harold John, 100

O'Dea, Thomas, 62, 99
oikos, 58
Open Letter to the Bruderhof
    Communities, 179
ordo salutis, 26, 30
organic community, 52–55, 68
other side of joy
  as contradictions of religiously
    grounded personalty, 31
  and Eberhard Arnold on spiritual
    sickness, 31
  in exercise of church discipline, 67
  and Pietistic conversion, 18
  in tragic sense of life, 212
  utopian disillusionments, 71
Oved, Yaacov, 179

Peale, Norman Vincent, 99
Peck, Robert N., 120
Peter, Karl A., 196
Peukert, Detlev, 49
Pfeifer, Samuel, 8
Piper, Otto, 48
Plautt, Thomas F. A., 192–96
Pleil, Amadeus, 114–15
Pleil, Nadine Moonje, 105, 224, 135
Plough, 79, 90, 96, 98, 170, 185
Plough Publishing House, 91, 141
pneumatical exegesis of the Word, 91
Pope John Paul II, 186
popular religion, 16
  and cheap grace, 17
  critique of religion in America after
    World War II, 81
  possessive individualism, 12, 218
    n.29
Primavera, 70, 79–80, 85–87
primitivism
  within Anabaptist groups, 11
  and authoritarianism, 10–11, 19, 69,
    82, 189–90
  and Bruderhof, 8–11, 18, 57
  Labadie's New Jerusalem, 73–76
  and nineteenth-century utopian
    groups, 11, 13
  in Puritan thought, 9–10, 17–18
  and religious freedom, 19
  requirement of redemptive suffering,
    211
  in Second Great Awakening, 13

in ritual of purification during
community crisis, 111–13
repression of masturbation, 110–11,
149
Shain, Barry Alan, 10
Sheen, Fulton, 99
small sects, 14–15
Smith, Joseph, 15
spiritual sickness, 127
social phobia, 205
sociological study of Bruderhof, 4–5
Sophia, 28
Sorokin, Pitirim, 98
Spirit of Primavera
absence of Pietist conversion
experience, 84
and Arminian thought, 88
definition of, 85
and Elizabeth Bohlken-Zumpe
as found in Wheathill and
Primavera, 88
Stadler, Ulrich, 156
Stevenson, Alan, 93
Stoeffler, Ernest F., 28
strong churches, 101
struggle between two atmospheres, 85,
117, 136, 171
suicide, 145–46, 155, 165–76
Sumner, Bruce, 93
Sunday Circle, 38

Tambach Conference, 43, 45–47
Tauler, Johann, 156
tentatio, 129–30
theological imagination, 5
Thiessen, Irmgard, 200–201, 203
Third Force groups, 100–102
Thomas, W. I., 155–56
Thompson, Barbara, 5
Tillich, Paul, 16, 31
Tillson, David S., 97–98
Tipton, Steven J., 160–61
Toennies, Ferdinand, 48, 55–56, 70
Tolstoy, Leo, 39, 46
tragedy, 210
tragic sense of life, 210–12, 235 n.5
transmoral conscience, 31
Troeltsch, Ernest, 21
Turner, Robert, 145

unclean spirits, 59–60
United Brethren in Christ, 198
unpardonable sin, 144, 165
utopian contract, 13
utopian disillusionments, 71–72
utopian illusions, 69, 210–12

Vanauken, Sheldon, 3
Van Dusen, Henry, 101
Vergote, Antoine, 8
village community 10, 14, 17, 218
n.27
See also Gemeinschaft
Volksgemeinschaft, 49
von Hollander, Emmy, 23, 27
See also Emmy Arnold
Vorsteher, 65

Wagner, Richard, 38
Wagoner, Bob, 85–87, 123–24
Wagoner, Shirley, 85–87, 123–24
Waldner, David, 93
Waldner, Michael, 78
Walzer, Michael, 10
Wandervogel, 40, 48–49, 53
Way, Miriam, 117–19, 144
Weber, Max
on acosmic love, 23
Apostolic Church and suffering of
believers, 210–11
condition of East Elbian workers, 33–
35
development of early writings, 33
and Evangelical Social Congress, 33
existential condition of modernity,
35, 39
German Sociological School, 21, 39
on hierocracy, 66
individualist metaphysics, 39–41
on *Innerlichkeit,* 33, 36
iron cage and disenchantment, 35–
36, 41
on market economy, 40
rejection of religion of brotherliness,
39–40
religious personality and life order, 9,
25
religious rejection of the world, 36–
37